Growing Your Own Fruit & Veg

FOR DUMMIES®

by Geoff Stebbings

WILEY

A John Wiley and Sons, Ltd, Publication

Growing Your Own Fruit & Veg For Dummies®

Published by
John Wiley & Sons, Ltd
The Atrium
Southern Gate
Chichester
West Sussex
PO19 8SQ
England

E-mail (for orders and customer service enquires): cs-books@wiley.co.uk

Visit our Home Page on www.wiley.com

Copyright © 2009 John Wiley & Sons, Ltd, Chichester, West Sussex, England

Published by John Wiley & Sons, Ltd, Chichester, West Sussex

For general information on our other products and services, please contact our Customer Care Department within the U.S. at 800-762-2974, outside the U.S. at 317-572-3993, or fax 317-572-4002.

For technical support, please visit www.wiley.com/techsupport.

Wiley also publishes its books in a variety of electronic formats. Some content that appears in print may not be available in electronic books.

British Library Cataloguing in Publication Data: A catalogue record for this book is available from the British Library

ISBN: 978-0-470-69960-7

Printed and bound in Great Britain by Bell & Bain Ltd, Glasgow

10 9 8 7 6 5 4 3

WILEY

About the Author

Geoff Stebbings got hooked on gardening at the age of eight and soon knew that he wanted to make it his career. He had weekend gardening jobs while at school, as well as working for a greengrocer. He trained at the Royal Botanic Gardens, Kew, and has worked in garden centres and in a specialist nursery before becoming a Head Gardener, restoring a historic garden. It was while working here that Geoff became closely involved with the National Council for the Conservation of Plants and Gardens and he had responsibility for the National Collection of Award-Winning Iris.

In 1989, to try and get others interested in gardening, Geoff became a gardening writer and worked for *Garden News, Garden Answers, Practical Gardening* and *The Garden* – the journal of the Royal Horticultural Society. He then worked as a freelance writer for ten years and has written several books, including *The Gardener's Guide to Growing Irises, The Year-Round Garden* and *Spring Bulbs*.

Geoff also lectures widely and is a member of the Garden Roadshow, which travels around the country visiting major flower shows and answering people's problems. He is a keen gardener and grows a wide range of plants in his garden, greenhouses and on his allotments. His passions are iris and growing tasty food – especially tomatoes – but he says that he could never be a specialist because he loves growing anything and everything – except pampas grass!

Geoff is currently Editor of *Garden Answers* magazine.

Dedication

This book is dedicated to everyone who wants to discover the satisfaction of growing some of their own food. It's a voyage of discovery that never ends.

Publisher's Acknowledgements

We're proud of this book; please send us your comments through our Dummies online registration form located at www.dummies.com/register/.

Some of the people who helped bring this book to market include the following:

Acquisitions, Editorial, and Media Development

Development Editor: Steve Edwards

Content Editor: Jo Theedom

Commissioning Editor: Nicole Hermitage

Publishing Assistant: Jennifer Prytherch

Copy Editor: Andy Finch

Proofreader: David Price

Technical Editor: Sue Fisher

Executive Editor: Samantha Spickernell

Executive Project Editor: Daniel Mersey

Cover Photos: © blickwinkel/Alamy/(front); © Chuck Place/Alamy, © Organics Image Library/Alamy (back)

Cartoons: Ed McLachlan

Composition Services

Project Coordinator: Lynsey Stanford

Layout and Graphics: Christin Swinford

Proofreaders: Melissa Cossell

Indexer: Ty Koontz

Brand Reviewer: Jennifer Bingham, Zoë Wykes

Contents at a Glance

Table of Contents

Introduction

Gardening is an exciting journey. Every year is different: growing something new, experimenting with new varieties, and experiencing all that the British weather can throw at you (perfect weather one year and rotten weather the next!). No matter how many years you spend in the garden, you never get to know everything and you can always improve. But with every year you gain more experience, and the successes you have make your yearning for knowledge get even stronger.

Growing your own crops gets you outside in the open air and gives you plenty of exercise. More importantly, growing crops gets you back in touch with the seasons and with nature – something that modern living has moved us away from. You experience the near miracle of seeds germinating. You nurture your seedlings and young plants, do your best for them, battle against their enemies, enjoy the abundance of your plants, and finally feed your body with food that's fresh and richer in nutrients than anything you can buy.

Growing crops is fun and rewarding for all ages. Traditionally the domain of the retired, allotments are gaining more and more popularity with younger people. Children usually enjoy gardening where the results are quick and dramatic – fortunately many vegetables fit this description. Kids can also be proud to help provide food for the table. Gardening provides them with so much that they can't discover in the classroom.

Whether you've decided to grow your own crops because you want to know what you're eating, because you care about food miles, because you want to appreciate the differences in the seasons, or because you want to save money, you're bound to enjoy the experience. You'll never know everything, but after all, the journey and not the arriving is the real pleasure.

About This Book

Growing Your Own Fruit & Veg For Dummies enables you to get started in the adventure of growing your own food. I've packed each chapter with the information you need to get the best results and avoid common mistakes. I've written the book so that even if you've never grown anything before, you're able to get started, understand what you're doing, and know what to expect.

Gardening is a huge subject and the plants in this book are as varied as any in the flower garden, but getting to grips with the principles of growing fruit and veg stands you in good stead for growing anything. You can grow plants in as many different ways as there are gardeners and because most plants simply want to grow, sometimes very odd methods give good results. A book like this can't possibly deal with all the different ways to grow plants, so instead I concentrate on tried and trusted ways to sow, plant, grow and prune. As you become more experienced you may discover that you can cheat sometimes and still get good results, but follow the tips in this book and you're well on your way to success. Treat this book as an experienced friend guiding you as you enter the exciting world of growing your own food.

Conventions Used in This Book

To help you get the most from this book, I follow a few conventions:

- ✔ *Italic* emphasises and highlights new words or terms that I define.

- ✔ **Boldfaced** text indicates the action part of numbered steps.

- ✔ Monofont text displays web addresses.

- ✔ I give all measurements in metric (so that's centimetres and metres rather than inches and feet).

Foolish Assumptions

In writing this book, I made a few assumptions about who you are:

- ✔ You may be completely new to gardening, and don't know a propagator from a pumpkin! Or maybe you do, but just don't know where to start. Don't worry if you're a beginner. Everyone has to start somewhere and even gardeners who've been growing for decades are beginners with plants they've never grown before.

- ✔ You may have some experience of gardening, but of the flowers and shrubs kind, and want to get clued up about fruit and veg.

- ✔ You may have been growing your own food for years, but want to try something new.

➤ You don't have a garden the size of Wembley Stadium; you may not even have a garden at all.

➤ You have a stronger-than-usual fondness for mulberries and have noticed that I include them in this book!

As you can see, even seasoned gardeners can find what they need to know to grow unfamiliar crops within the lovely yellow and black covers of this book.

How This Book Is Organised

I've organised *Growing Your Own Fruit & Veg For Dummies* into five parts. Each part covers a range of subjects to get you growing your own food and is split into chapters to help you easily find the information you want.

Part 1: Getting Going with Growing

Before you even consider sowing a seed you need to know certain basics. This part helps you to understand why growing crops makes sense and to identify what tools you need to do it; it teaches you about the soil and the different places you can grow crops (including containers, raised beds and in the greenhouse); and it explains what to look for when buying plants and seeds and the best way to plan your plot for health and efficiency.

Part 11: Prepping Your Plot

Here I tackle the basic principles you need to understand to get the most out of gardening. Feeding and watering and pests and diseases are all here. I start by looking at soil: how to work out what type of soil you have, how to test and improve it and how to make compost. I go on to explain the various types of fertiliser, what they do and how to use them, and the secrets of watering and why your crops may need extra water. I put forward the case for organic gardening, looking at the advantages and disadvantages and considering whether going organic makes sense. Lastly, I look at what gardeners dread – all those pests and diseases that seem bent on destroying your crops – along with ways to keep the damage to a minimum.

Part III: Growing Tasty Veg

From the mundane and everyday to the exotic and unfamiliar, this part covers the delicious vegetables you can grow. I look at leafy vegetables that crop all year round, and which are packed with good things to make you healthy. You can also read about the root crops that people traditionally enjoy over winter, although you don't have to wait for the cold weather to arrive before you enjoy them. To add a dash of sunshine, this part goes on to look at summer crops that can make you believe you live in the Mediterranean. I then take a look at the useful and productive pods and grains that are the joys of the summer plot, many of which are easy to grow in the smallest garden, before exploring some of the more unfamiliar veg that you can grow on your plot.

Part IV: Growing Your Own Fruit Salad

With all the fruits that I guide you through in this part, you can soon find yourself throwing together the most varied and exotic fruit salad you've ever eaten! I start by helping the impatient gardener, who wants something tasty to eat in the shortest time, to avoid going hungry! You can then find advice about growing the soft fruits, currants and berries that really are the taste of summer, as well as the fruits that you can plant for the future – trees and shrubs that will feed you for many years to come and still be cropping for your children. Finally, I take a look at fruits that feel the cold and need the sunniest, most sheltered spot in your garden or a cosy indoor spot in a greenhouse or conservatory.

Part V: The Part of Tens

At the back of the book, I offer up a couple of fun chapters with some projects for you to try out and some tips for growing those herbs that some meals just can't do without!

Icons Used in This Book

Scattered throughout this book are icons to guide you along your way. Icons are a handy *For Dummies* way to draw your attention to special bits and pieces of information.

Keep your sights on the target for tips and suggestions from one who knows!

Remember these important points of information to stand a better chance of success on your plot.

Plenty of things can go wrong in the garden – from insects that are even more partial to your crops than you are, to weather conditions that can play havoc with your plans – and these icons help you to identify the potential spanners in your works.

You grow food because you want to eat it, right? This icon lets you know where I have some tasty ideas for using your crops in the kitchen: not recipes – just suggestions.

Fruit and veg are good for you: fact. This icon lets you know when I'm telling you just how good.

Maybe you became interested in growing your own fruit and veg because you're interested in the idea of organic gardening. If so, keep an eye open for this icon, which highlights places in the text where I have some info for you.

Where to Go from Here

I've organised this book so that you can just dip in and out of it as you like. You can read it from start to finish if you prefer, but you can also look up what you want to read about in the Table of Contents and jump straight in at that section. You can use this book in whatever way suits you best. If you're not sure where to start, you may want to turn to Part I. It gives you the basics for getting started from scratch, and points to places later in the book where you can go for more detailed information.

Good luck, and happy gardening!

Part I
Getting Going with Growing

'Small garden, giant vegetables,
just doesn't work, Ernest!'

In this part . . .

As with any new subject that you tackle, the first problem you're likely to come across is that you don't know where to start. You've decided that you want to grow some of your own food but want to get off on the right foot without making any silly mistakes. Well, gardening is all about discovering and although some firm rules need to be followed, others are more flexible.

You may have lots of reasons for wanting to grow your own fruit and veg, but whatever your reason, this part is all about the basics. This aspect includes having reasonable ambitions to start with and working out what you can reasonably grow in the area you have and what crops grow best where.

Just as importantly, you need your armoury of tools. You may be tempted to go out to a garden centre and spend a fortune, thinking that you need a wide range of tools to stand a chance of being successful. The truth is that you need surprisingly few tools, and that you end up rarely using half the tools you buy whereas the other half get worn away in no time!

Last but not least, you need to understand what you're growing and how some of the crops are grouped together – in this book and by gardeners – so you can find them in shops and catalogues. When you've grasped this information, you're ready to grow!

Chapter 1

Becoming a Grow-Your-Own Gardener

. . . .

In This Chapter

▶ Reaping the benefits of growing your own

▶ Gathering the tools you need

▶ Assessing your plot

▶ Deciding what crops to grow

. . . .

S o you've decided to grow your own fruit and vegetables. Congratulations! Few activities in life are more rewarding than producing your own food. You'll discover that nothing beats the satisfaction of picking a sun-ripened tomato and popping it straight in your mouth, or sitting down to lunch knowing that you grew all the veg yourself.

As you start down the road of growing your own, be prepared for a few twists and turns, and some highs and lows along the way. You may find some plants more challenging than others, and not everything will go to plan. But if you start with the simple things and follow the basic rules – which is where this book comes in – your successes are sure to outweigh any failures.

First of all, though, you need some real reasons to get growing – incentives to help you through the tough patches, a few tools, a plot of land, and an idea of what you want to grow. Let's go.

Recognising the Advantages of Growing Your Own

More and more people are becoming aware of the different benefits of growing your own fruit and veg. These vary from reducing your food costs and improving your health and diet to doing your bit for the planet through lower *food miles* – the distance food has to travel between where it grows and where it's eaten. People are acting upon this awareness, too; just look at the ever-growing waiting lists for allotment plots and the increasing sales of seeds of edible plants. Even people without access to a large plot are now discovering that their own gardens and patios can produce useful crops.

Saving money

Many people decide to grow their own fruit and veg because they think they're going to save money. Think carefully if you're one of these gardeners. Whether you actually save money depends on where you live and what access you currently have to fresh produce. For example, if you have a local market selling fresh produce you may already be able to buy cheap veg.

How you think about growing your own has a bearing on saving money, too. If you see it as a chore and cost in your labour, your fruit and veg may work out expensive. However, if you enjoy pottering, digging and generally being out in the open air, you can forget about including labour in with the costs.

For most people, and with careful planning, growing some types of crop yourself definitely can save you money. For example, you pay the same amount in a supermarket for a bag of salad leaves as you pay for a packet of seeds that produces dozens of bags of leaves. And because you can grow most vegetables from seed, doing so saves you more than if you buy them as plants.

With some crops, such as asparagus, you can choose between growing them from seed and buying a ready-grown plant. With other vegetables, however, such as Jerusalem artichokes or potatoes, you don't have a choice other than to buy them as ready-grown plants, roots or tubers.

Similarly, fruit trees won't save you time or money, at least until the tree is well established. For example, if you buy an apple tree to grow in a pot, the tree doesn't start turning a profit for many years because it can carry only small crops.

Eating fresh

Without a doubt, the fact that you can eat fruit and veg as fresh as nature intended is a huge benefit of growing your own. Picking and eating crops within minutes not only feels good, but it's also healthy for you.

Fruits that are fully ripe don't just taste great; they're packed with nutrients, too. Some crops, such as apples and pears, don't deteriorate much as they're transported and stored, but most do start to lose nutrients as soon as you pick them, especially leafy, green vegetables that contain a lot of vitamin C.

Some crops, such as chard, deteriorate so quickly that shops rarely sell them. Sweetcorn, too, loses its sweetness quickly after harvesting and growing your own is the only way to discover its raw sugary tenderness. Soft fruits such as currants, raspberries and strawberries also travel badly and are worth growing yourself. Similarly, the longer you store fruit and veg and the more they're processed, the more nutrients are lost.

You are what you eat, as the old saying goes, and so eating produce fresh from your own garden gives you the nutritional best from your crops, and your body is much better off as a result.

You'll also discover just how much tastier fruit and veg can be when *really* fresh. For example, did you know that when ripe, gooseberries aren't hard and acidic but soft and sweet? And have you ever eaten a peach fresh off the tree when the flesh is so juicy you need a napkin? Or have you eaten an apricot just as it's perfectly ripe, with flesh as sweet and juicy as a peach? All these treats, and many more, are yours to experience when you grow your own.

Growing food metres, not miles, from your doorstep

With concern about the welfare of the environment at an all-time high, you have a huge environmental advantage in growing your own fruit and veg. You can sidestep the issues of over-packaging, chemicals, fertilisers and *food miles* – where crops are flown and driven around the world – and reduce your own negative impact on the environment. You may not be able to grow all your needs but you can produce at least some crops within metres of your back door. Aside from keeping Mother Nature happy, just think of the convenience of being able to pop out and pick fresh tomatoes, salads or herbs.

Experiencing more variety

You rarely see certain crops, such as leaf beet, Swiss chard, purslane, mizuna and many more in the shops. They just don't travel well enough. If you're lucky enough to have a good farmers' market near where you live, you may be able to find some of these crops there when in season, but you can do without the risk by growing them at home. Many other crops, such as sprouting broccoli, rocket and asparagus peas cost a fortune if you do find them, and yet you can easily grow them yourself.

Strawberries, raspberries, blackberries and redcurrants are also expensive to buy, and are often damaged when you buy them. Because of this, soft fruit really is worth growing yourself, and you can grow different and often better varieties than you find in the shops. Did you know, for example, that goose-berries come in red and yellow as well as green? Commercial growers pick their varieties based on how consistent they are in size and shape, whether they have heavy crops, and whether they travel well. They often pick fruit unripe in order to transport it, and so you can never buy some fruits that are fully ripe. You can, on the other hand, choose varieties that have the best flavour, need fewer chemicals to produce (or none at all), are resistant to disease, or crop out of season, extending the time you can eat them.

Feasting without chemicals

In recent years consumers have become more concerned about additives and chemicals in food. Growing your own returns power to the consumer – you have the choice of what chemicals to put on your food or you can choose to grow crops entirely without using chemicals. You can grow some crops easily without having to spray them with chemicals, but others are more difficult. The cabbage family, for example, can be a challenge to grow well without resorting to some chemicals, but at least you choose what you apply to your crops and what you use. You can also select varieties that are resistant to disease so you have an easier time when growing organically.

Looking at the broader picture

Growing your own isn't just good for your finances and for the planet; growing your own is good for you, too! Gardening is a healthy activity, and helps to keep you fit. (An hour of digging can burn 500 calories, so just a little active gardening each week can boost your health in more ways than just providing vitamins!) You also get out in the sun (at least, when it comes out to play) and you're more in touch with the seasons and seasonal produce – qualities that are impossible to cost, but are really priceless.

Tooling Around: Kitting Yourself Out

Like any activity, gardening is more rewarding and a lot easier if you have the right tools and equipment. Choose wisely, and remember the old saying 'buy cheap, pay twice'. You may be able to pick up bargain tools, and some cheap tools can be good value, but well-made tools serve you better in the long run. Nothing is more annoying than setting aside time to hoe or dig and your tool breaking halfway through the task.

Always inspect tools before you buy. Check handles for balance and smoothness. Check the materials and the weight – you may find working with light tools easier. Buy tools that suit your size and build. Never be afraid of buying a smaller tool if you can't manage a large one – you work faster and more efficiently when you're comfortable.

Certain tools you need only once or twice a year, and so try not to get carried away filling your shed or garage with a huge armoury. Here's a rundown of the basic essential tools.

- **Spades and forks:** You can buy two basic sizes: the *digging* and *border* (or *ladies'*) sizes. The digging versions do as their name suggests. The border versions are great for general planting and soil cultivation, where their smaller size is an advantage.

    - **Spade:** You need a spade mainly for digging, but also for planting, harvesting some plants, and moving soil around. Prices vary hugely, as does design, but expect to pay around £20 for a decent stainless steel spade. Shaft length varies as well, so pick up and test the 'fit' of the spade before you buy. Some have treads on the blade, where you put your foot, to make digging easier, and the bottom edge of the blade should be sharp. Make sure that you see no rough splinters or protruding metal where the shaft fits into the *ferrule*, or tubular socket, on the blade because these may cut your hand. I recommend buying stainless steel spades – their highly polished blades don't just look the business, they're easy to clean and use, too, especially in heavy, clay soils.

    - **Fork:** You need a fork for digging, breaking up *clods* (lumps) of soil, loosening the soil surface in preparation for planting, and digging up plants and root crops such as carrots and potatoes. Forks are especially useful in soil that's very heavy (for example, clay soils) or full of stones, where getting a spade into the soil may be tricky. The fork to buy is the general digging fork that has four, evenly spaced *tines* (spikes). You can also buy a 'potato fork', which has broad, flat tines that are less likely to 'spear' the tubers as you lift them, but this is a luxury. A good fork costs about £20.

- **Rake:** A garden rake (not a grass or wire rake) is essential for levelling soil and removing stones and large lumps from the surface when preparing seedbeds and for evenly spreading fertiliser. You can purchase rakes as part of a multi-tool system. Prices start from as little as £10.

- **Measuring line:** You need a line of string for making sure your lines of seedlings are even and straight. You can buy a line or use two canes and some string. Nylon string is less likely to rot in use than natural twine.

- **Hoe:** You need at least one type of hoe to help you control weeds. The two basic, popular designs are the *Dutch* or *push hoe* and the *French* or *draw hoe*. If you buy only one hoe, and unless you're growing potatoes (which you can easily 'earth up' with a French hoe), the Dutch hoe, with a straight, sharp blade pointing away from you, is the most useful and versatile. When using, you keep the blade as horizontal as possible and push it just under the soil surface to chop the tops off weeds, which should then wilt and die. The French hoe has a curved 'neck' so the blade, tucked under the head of the tool, faces you and cuts through the soil as you pull the hoe towards you. With a French hoe, you can easily control the path of the blade and weed more accurately, with less risk of chopping off and damaging plants. Prices start from about £10.

✓ **Trowel:** You need a trowel for planting. A trowel is like a small spade with a pointed blade to make planting holes. Thin trowels are useful for weeding but most have the same basic shape. When choosing a trowel, make sure that the handle is comfortable and not sharp or rough. The only time you may be able to do without a trowel for planting is when you plant brassicas, because those plants prefer well-firmed soil, and a *dibber* (a solid, usually wooden shaft with an angled handle) is therefore better. You can pick up a good trowel from as little as £5.

✓ **Multi-headed tools:** Many systems offer a range of interchangeable handle lengths and tool heads. These enable you to have a variety of tools without buying lots of handles. Be aware, though, that you usually can't mix 'n' match tools and handles from different systems, so make sure that you choose the system offering the tools you need before you start to buy and commit yourself. Prices vary enormously but expect to pay £10 for a handle and about the same for most small tools.

✓ **Sprayer:** A good sprayer is useful; even if you intend to garden organically you're probably going to need to use some organic sprays to control common pests. *Trigger sprayers*, where each pull of the trigger releases a burst of spray, are cheap but hard work to use if you have to spray a lot of plants. *Pressure sprayers*, where you pump the handle to produce pressure in the container to produce a continuous burst of spray, cost more but are far easier to use.

Buying a sprayer means that you can buy and dilute concentrated chemicals. You don't have to buy ready-to-use chemicals, which, although convenient and handy when you start growing your own, are the most expensive way to buy chemicals. Ready-to-use chemicals also involve a lot of waste because you're buying diluted chemicals and a spray bottle with every purchase.

✓ **Propagator:** A propagator is useful for raising seedlings earlier than you can outside. A basic propagator consists of some sort of waterproof tray and a transparent lid. You can easily make your own but most gardeners buy one. Unheated, basic propagators, however, have limited use. Light is essential for seedlings so you need to place an unheated propagator in a greenhouse or on a windowsill, and without extra heat you're limited in what you can successfully grow. An electrically heated propagator without a thermostat is useful because it provides constant heat, but the temperature inside depends on the outside temperature, which is a problem when the weather's cold at night and too hot on a sunny windowsill. Heated propagators with a thermostat are considerably better, and can help to avoid overheating and damage to seedlings. Prices start from about £25 for a good thermostatically controlled propagator.

✔ **Pots:** The variety of pots and trays you need depends on what you intend to grow. You can sow many crops directly into the soil outside but you need to sow others, such as courgettes and other squashes, some brassicas, tomatoes and cucumbers, in pots and place them to start growing in warm conditions such as on a windowsill or in a propagator. For most purposes, 8-centimetre pots are ideal for sowing small quantities of seeds and for growing tomatoes and so on. Small seed trays are also useful for sowing seeds and growing micro-greens such as cress. Cell trays, divided into 6 or 12 individual cells, are also useful for sowing seeds individually and growing seedlings.

Use clean or new pots and trays for sowing seeds to reduce the risk of fungal diseases that harm seedlings.

✔ **Compost:** Potting compost comes in three basic types but don't confuse them with the compost from the heap at the bottom of your garden. Garden compost has its uses but is far too variable to use for sowing or growing in pots and best kept for mulching and use in the open garden.

Throughout the book, when I refer to compost in the context of raising plants, I mean one of these types of potting compost:

- **John Innes compost** is the traditional choice, available in four grades from seed sowing through Nos 1, 2, and 3 for plants as they get progressively bigger. John Innes composts are based on sterilised loam (soil) and contain some *peat* (partially decomposed organic matter with minimal plant nutrients). Their quality varies according to the loam and they aren't 100 per cent recommended for growing young plants. But No 3 is excellent for any plant you're growing in a pot for more than one year, such as fruit trees.

- **Multipurpose composts** were, until recently, based on peat, but with environmental concerns coming to the fore, most are now 'reduced-peat'. These composts are ideal for seed sowing and growing young plants but they contain enough nutrients for only a few weeks of growth, and so you then need to give them some supplementary feed.

- **Peat-free composts** are increasingly common and popular but they vary enormously, depending on their origins. Many are made of recycled products, and others are based on *coir* (coconut husk). You can achieve satisfactory results with most of them, but many contain less nitrogen, among other nutrients, and you may need to alter your watering and feeding regimes if you're used to peat-based composts. Peat-free composts are probably not ideal if you're just starting out with growing, especially for more difficult plants such as peppers and basil.

Buying cheap compost can be false economy. Buy from an outlet that stores compost under cover and never buy bags that have faded print or are soaking wet: use only fresh compost for seed sowing.

✔ **Clothing:** You can buy a range of clothing for gardening but in most cases old, stout clothing suffices. However, you do need gloves – especially when pruning thorny fruit such as raspberries and gooseberries – and stout footwear is essential when digging.

Be sure to use gloves and goggles when you're using a *line trimmer* (for trimming grass and vegetation), and when spraying always wear protective clothing as the product manufacturer recommends. Garden accidents are regrettably frequent but with some common sense you can avoid getting in harm's way.

Getting the Plot

Now you've decided to grow your own fruit and veg, you need to decide where to grow them. How much space you have doesn't matter, in fact, a big plot can sometimes be overwhelming. Whether you have a patio or a field you can make a start right away. All you have to do is make sure that what you want to grow and how you intend to do it suits your circumstances.

Back garden

People are sometimes put off growing their own fruit and veg because they think they need a lot of space or have to give over their attractive flowerbeds to vegetable plots. The fact that you don't need a dedicated vegetable garden to grow your own crops may come as a surprise. Having a dedicated plot does make things easier for you, and simplifies *crop rotation* (avoiding growing crops in the same soil every year), but isn't essential, and you can grow many crops among flowers. Nor do you need a large space – you just have to be more selective in what you choose to grow. Winter and spring crops usually occupy the ground for the longest periods so you may want to concentrate on fast-growing summer and autumn crops. What's more, you don't always have to sacrifice a good-looking garden when growing your own: fruit bushes and trees are often almost as attractive as ornamentals so you can easily incorporate them into your borders.

If you can give over an area of your garden to grow fruit and veg, a convenient way is to make raised beds. Chapter 2 tells you all you need to know about creating them.

Pots and containers

Maybe your garden is just too small to have flowerbeds or perhaps you've paved it over. Maybe you live in a tower block with just a windowsill available to you as a space for growing produce. No matter – pots and containers enable you to grow your own fruit and veg even when space is *really* limited. Growing in this way can save you time and even enable you to avoid some common problems.

Growing in pots and containers may seem a novel idea, but it's really not new at all. For centuries, miners in the north of England grew fruit in pots and developed *pot leeks* in their small backyards, though for showing rather than as food. You can do this, too. You don't need special containers; just find a container with drainage holes and if it doesn't have any drainage holes, drill to make some. Drainage holes are essential to ensure that the compost doesn't get waterlogged in wet weather. The size of the container is also important because small containers that hold a small volume of compost dry out quickly and aren't so easy to look after. But aside from these considerations, you may be surprised at what you can grow fruit and veg in: old compost bags, rubbish bins, wheelbarrows, old boots… Just use your imagination!

Chapter 2 is the place to go for more information about growing in containers.

Allotments

Allotments (and large plots) enable you to grow a wide range of crops and staple crops such as potatoes in large quantities. They come with their own advantages and problems, though. Previous growers have often cultivated allotments for many years so you may find that you have good, well-worked soil, or else stumble upon lots of pests and diseases already present on or near the plot. You may equally find that your allotment plot has been neglected and needs a lot of work to get into a usable state. But a good allotment plot is great to have, gives you more options when choosing what to grow and enables you to pick the brains of and have some laughs with other people gardening at the same allotments. Chapter 2 has the lowdown on acquiring and looking after an allotment.

Knowing What You're Growing

So you've decided that you want to grow your own. But do you know what fruit and vegetables actually are? From a botanical perspective, *vegetables* are the stems, roots and leaves of plants, whereas *fruits* are what results from a flower. So rhubarb is a vegetable and tomatoes, cucumbers, aubergines and chillies are fruits. But gardeners define things differently, and have a different perspective: to gardeners, *vegetables* are savoury and *fruits* are sweet!

Growing tasty veg

When you start to grow your own food you soon discover what a huge range is available. Your usual weekly shop will probably influence your choice of what veg to grow at first; looking through catalogues can open your eyes to many more crops. Take it steady, but don't be afraid to try something new.

Leaf crops

Leaf crops are important and healthy vegetables because of the nutritional value of their leaves. They are low in calories but high in other nutrients. The most important group are the *brassicas*, which include broccoli, cabbage, kale, cauliflower, oriental greens and sprouts. All brassicas prefer an alkaline soil (check out Chapter 4 for a full rundown of soil types), partly because they suffer from a soil-borne fungal disease called clubroot, which thrives in acid soil. The wealth of brassicas available means that you can harvest crops at any time of year. Many brassicas prefer heavy, clay soils but Oriental cabbages grow best in light soils rich in humus. Because other leaf crops, such as salad leaves, lettuce, chicory and leaf beet (chard), come from plants that are unrelated botanically, and tolerate a wide range of conditions, something is sure to thrive in your conditions. Salad crops are generally quick to grow and ideal for small gardens and for impatient gardeners.

Chapter 8 tells you all you need to know about growing leaf crops.

Root crops

Root crops – which include carrots, parsnips and swedes – count among their number some of the most important crops you can grow. Traditionally, root crops were important because they store well and provide food through the winter. Root crops are *biennial* plants, which means that they grow one year, flower the next, and then die. To help their flowering, early in the second year they store food in their roots – this store of sugars and starch is the bit that we eat, halfway through their lifecycle. Most root crops, onions and leeks included, grow best in light soils because heavy clay can impede the growth of the roots through the soil. Heavy manuring and stony soil can cause twisted, branched and misshapen roots.

I talk about how to raise your own root crops in Chapter 9.

Potatoes and other tubers

Potatoes are a staple crop and if you have a large plot you can easily grow large quantities to use throughout the winter. But you can also make use of even the smallest space to grow a few. Potatoes are grouped in various ways, such as by usage and skin colour, but usually by their time to maturity. So you can choose from *earlies*, *second earlies*, and *maincrop*. Of these varieties, earlies tend to have smaller tops (*haulms*) and because they mature before *blight*, the most destructive disease of potatoes, is widespread each summer, they are the easiest to grow. Earlies are also something of a treat, and so all in all they make the best use of space. Other tuber crops, such as Jerusalem and Chinese artichokes, are even easier to grow but less adaptable in the kitchen.

Head to Chapter 9 for the lowdown on growing your own spuds.

Greenhouse crops

Vegetables such as tomatoes, peppers, aubergines and cucumbers all need warmth to grow well. Each crop has varieties suitable for outdoor growing but they depend on good, warm weather and you need to provide them with shelter and careful positioning for them to thrive. Even so, they remain some of the most popular of all home-grown crops and are suitable for growing in containers. All greenhouse crops are far better in quality and taste if you grow them at home, and so make them top of your list of crops. Tomatoes, peppers and cape gooseberries make excellent choices for beginners.

I cover growing greenhouse crops in Chapter 10.

Pods

Peas and beans are worth growing, not just because they're better fresh than the ones you buy in shops but also because they add nitrogen, one of the main plant nutrients, to your soil. Runner beans are the most popular with home gardeners for a worthwhile crop, because the ones you buy in the shops are poor quality. French beans are equally popular, easier to grow, and you can get good crops. Broad beans take up a lot of space and are possibly not worthwhile in small gardens but are delicious if you pick them young. Peas are a luxury crop – they take up a lot of room, can be difficult to grow well because of the many problems that affect them, and frozen peas are, honestly, just as good as fresh peas if you cook them. But mangetout and sugarsnap peas are worth the effort if you have room to grow them.

Chapter 11 is the place to go for pod planting.

Herbs

You can grow a wealth of different herbs for adding flavour to your cooking and beauty to your garden. Herbs are a diverse group of plants that vary from fast-growing annuals to shrubs, and many flourish in gardens. They need a wide range of conditions and although some, such as basil, can be difficult to grow well, others like mint can become almost weed-like if they find cosy conditions in your garden. Start off growing herbs that you're likely to use, such as parsley, thyme, sage and mint and then try some of the more unusual herbs, as well as edible flowers such as nasturtiums.

Head to Chapter 17 for more info about herbs.

Planting luscious fruit

Fruits are generally divided into two categories: soft and top fruits. *Soft fruit* includes raspberries, strawberries, currants and gooseberries, which growers tend to harvest in midsummer, as well as blackberries, loganberries and blueberries. Most soft fruits are small plants and are well suited to growing in a limited space. Most are tough, frost-hardy, and not difficult to grow. Some, such as blueberries and strawberries, grow well in containers and so are worth considering if you don't have much space. Soft fruit plants are fairly quick to produce a crop, with most starting to crop in their second year onwards, so you don't get *too* hungry waiting to pick your own fruit! (Head to Chapters 13, 14, and 16 if you're looking to get started growing your own soft fruit.)

Fruits such as apples, pears, plums, cherries and peaches are all known as *top fruits*. They are large plants and most take two or three years before they start to crop. As well as needing more space than other fruits, they also come with other complications because most, apart from peaches and some special varieties, need another tree of a different variety to pollinate the flowers to get a crop. This means they need a fair amount of space but with careful training you can grow many varieties even in a small space. (Chapters 15 and 16 tell you all you need to know about growing top fruits.)

Fruits from seed

You can't grow many fruits from seed because they don't breed true to type, unlike vegetables, but those that you can at least give you a quick crop while you're waiting for your apple trees to start cropping. Cape gooseberries are a good fruit to grow from seed in a greenhouse or on the patio, giving you a tasty and worthwhile crop. The adventurous can try garden huckleberries, which need cooking to make them edible. You can grow other fruits such as strawberries and rhubarb from seed, but most are better bought as plants.

Buying plants

Most fruit plants crop for many years, and because you're investing a lot of time and space in them it pays to invest in good stock. Where possible, buy fruit from specialist nurseries that can supply you with detailed growing information as well as the latest varieties best suited to your needs. Most soft fruit sold by reputable nurseries and specialists is certified free of the yield-reducing viruses to which these fruits are prone, giving your plants the best possible start in life. Never accept old plants from other allotment holders in case they're infected with disease (the plants, not the gardeners!).

You can buy most fruit when dormant in winter but potted plants are available all year round. Potted plants generally cost a little more and you may not have such a wide choice of varieties.

Chapter 2

Assessing Your Territory

So you've decided to become a grow-your-own gardener. You've come to the right book! But before you get started with your crops you need to think about where to grow them because not all vegetables grow everywhere. Farmers grow specific crops in different parts of the country because different crops suit certain areas better than others. You don't need to worry about whether your vegetables meet farmers' exacting standards, but sensible preparation of your site, or matching the needs of a vegetable or fruit with your conditions, does make growing easier and more satisfying. Whether you decide to get an allotment or are restricted to your own back garden, you can choose from a wealth of crops to try and grow.

This chapter delves into preparing whatever site you have available for the fruit and veggies you want to grow.

Making the Most out of Your Back Garden

Not many people have a walled kitchen garden or a spare hectare or two to hand for growing crops. But you can produce worthwhile crops even in a small plot, so don't think you need vast tracts of land to grow your own food. You do need to be more discerning in what you grow and to use your ground intensively, but even if you have no soil, you can still be successful – just use your imagination.

Working with raised beds

Many beginners believe that you can only grow veg if you have raised beds; TV gardeners are never without them! But raised beds aren't essential. What they do provide, however, is a tidy, organised way to grow plants without the need to trample over the soil. Raised beds also enable you to increase the depth of fertile soil (useful when the natural soil in your garden is poor), to organise your space effectively, and even to grow crops on areas of hard surface without any natural soil (make sure you fill these to a minimum depth of 30 centimetres). Raised beds are easy to control and far less intimidating than a whole plot, and are ideal for children to look after. You can also easily cover them with protective fleece and the soil in them warms up more rapidly than soil at ground level, so raised beds are especially suitable for raising early crops. Planting in raised beds is usually intensive and you can plant right up to the edge and spill over the path.

You can make raised beds from wood, brick, railway sleepers, or with light-weight, off-the-shelf, raised bed kits. Although you can construct them to be waist high (useful for gardeners who find bending down to soil level difficult), most raised beds are 15–30 centimetres above soil level (most vegetables need a soil depth of at least 30 centimetres). 1-metre-square beds are practical, but any length or shape of bed no wider than 1.2 metres will enable you to reach across it without treading on the soil. Make paths between the beds about 45 centimetres wide.

You need to fill your beds with some sort of soil. One option is to take soil from somewhere else in the garden, but do make sure that it's good quality. Don't use infertile *subsoil* taken from deep in the ground, for example when digging a pond. Or you can buy good-quality *topsoil* from a garden centre, but make sure to specify that you need it weed free and always check a sample before ordering. Buying soil, however, is an expensive way to fill your beds.

Another possibility is to use recycled compost from your local waste-recycling centre, but this can be high in woody material and may be too free-draining and coarse for good growing. Therefore, recycled compost is best used to add to existing soil to lighten or enrich it rather than as the sole growing medium. Similarly, you can use reduced-peat or recycled multipurpose compost, but again as an additive to the soil rather than to fill beds, because it has low amounts of nutrients and decomposes in the beds, which shrink over a few years. When you've filled the beds they need regular topping up, with garden compost, well-rotted manure, leaf mould or used growing bags. Most gardeners don't dig the soil in their raised beds, but forking it over to incorporate organic matter is still worth doing.

When ready to use you can easily rotate your crops each season, growing root crops in one bed, brassicas in another, and so on (Chapter 3 has more on crop rotation). You don't need to plant in traditional rows but can sow or plant clumps or squares of crops.

Raised beds are naturally very well drained so you need to make sure that they have a source of water or your crops suffer in summer. If your raised bed sits of a hard surface you may need to be especially careful to irrigate them intensively in summer. You also need to maintain the state of your beds and keep any weeds that appear under control (jump ahead to the 'Perennial weeds' and 'Annual weeds' sections for more info).

Gardening in containers: Pot training

You can grow most fruit and vegetables, for a while at least, in containers. Fast-growing salads are the obvious choice, and potatoes are just perfect for containers. A group of pots in a corner of the garden can be productive and attractive and is the sensible option if you don't have much time or space. You do need to buy compost to fill them with, making the crop relatively expensive, but although not the cheapest way to grow crops you can be assured of their freshness, so the cost is worthwhile. Some plants benefit from all the attention you lavish on them in their pots and, because they're likely to be in the warmest area of your garden, perhaps on the patio, tender plants such as basil and peppers tend to thrive. Having your pots near the house saves you having to wander about in the dark for that last-minute bunch of herbs too!

Not all vegetables are very productive, though, and so may not be the best choice for growing in containers. For example, a globe artichoke plant, which needs a container at least 45 centimetres deep and wide and which produces a maximum of only five or six artichokes, isn't a sensible proposition unless you're desperate for garden-fresh artichokes! And the fact that you need to water your crop constantly, and probably feed it too, means that growing in containers isn't always as labour-saving as it first seems.

Because you can fill pots with special compost, you can grow fruit, such as blueberries and cranberries, which need the acid soil rarely found in gardens. The fact that the soil surface is well above the ground is also a benefit when you grow carrots. Their most serious pest is carrot root fly but the adults, seemingly scared of heights, rarely fly more than 45 centimetres above the ground, and so your pots of carrots may well escape damage without any extra effort.

Although many fruit bushes and trees can become large and take up space for a long period, you can use a few tricks to squeeze them into a small space. For example, you can grow red- and white currants and gooseberries in pots and as *standard plants* on a tall, single stem, and grow other plants around the base. You can buy peaches, pears, apricots and apples as dwarf varieties and grow them in pots, too, and against walls and fences. Strawberries, though not without their problems, grow almost anywhere, including hanging baskets and growing bags. So wherever you garden and no matter how small your plot, you still have plenty of options open to you.

Types of container

When growing short-term crops such as salads, carrots and most other vegetables, it really doesn't matter what shape or size of container you use. Recycled containers such as plastic barrels, buckets and tubs are all suitable and though they may not look attractive they are perfectly good enough for your plants. You can even use compost bags. When you turn them inside out, with the black inside showing, the tops rolled down, and with some holes in the base for drainage, they make great containers for growing – especially potatoes! You can even use bags of compost in the same way as growing bags, cutting out on the container altogether if you make sure that you cut slits near the underside to prevent waterlogging.

Terracotta and other ceramic pots look good and their sides offer insulation to roots, but if they are unglazed the sides lose water and the plants need extra irrigation. Make sure that you buy frost-proof pots, which don't break in cold weather: frost-resistant pots aren't frost-proof. Odd-shaped pots with curved sides or incurved tops split after frosty weather if the wet compost expands as it freezes.

Plastic pots are light, which can be useful when moving them around, but is a disadvantage if they contain tall, shrubby plants that may blow over. Their sides are usually thin and so give the roots no protection from frost or summer heat. Modern designs, in many colours, are often indistinguishable from stone or terracotta, and look attractive.

The ideal container for most crops is at least 30 centimetres wide and deep. Whatever container you use, make sure that it has holes in the base for drainage. Although plants need water, none of them flourish if the container fills with water and the roots drown. You can place the pot on a saucer, to help with watering in dry spells, but the pot must have holes to allow excess water to flow away.

Small pots and containers that are less than 15 centimetres in depth dry out infuriatingly quickly, and so are best reserved for baby leaf salads. When you grow permanent plants such as fruit trees, fruit bushes and perennial or shrubby herbs such as bay, which may need to be moved to a bigger pot after a year or two, use containers that have straight sides and are wider at the top than the base or you'll have problems re-potting them. When planting any shrub in a pot, move it in stages from its original pot to its final pot. Small plants often struggle to cope when surrounded by a mass of new compost. For example, if a gooseberry is in a 20-centimetre-wide pot, plant it in a 30-centimetre pot for the first year or two, move it into a 40-centimetre pot, and then into a final, larger pot. Apples and other tree fruit eventually need half barrels or other large containers.

Types of compost

For most vegetables you can use a basic multipurpose compost. However, paying for a good-quality compost rather than the cheapest is always worth the expense. Most composts are based on peat or, increasingly, contain a proportion of recycled materials or are wholly composed of recycled materials. All these composts gradually decompose in the pot but are suitable for several crops, over a period of about a year.

 After filling, you can grow an early crop of salad leaves and, after you pull them up, grow a crop of maincrop carrots for harvesting in autumn. The following year you need to replace the top layer of compost but after that remember to replace all of the compost. You can use the discarded compost as a mulch or planting compost in the garden so you put it to good use. These composts contain enough nutrients for about four weeks of growth, unless otherwise stated on the bag, so you'll need to feed your plants after that period (see Chapter 5 for more about keeping your plants well fed and watered).

 Plant anything that will be in a container for more than a year, such as all fruit bushes, trees and shrubby herbs, in a soil-based compost such as John Innes compost. These loam-based composts don't decompose over time or lose their structure, so keep the roots healthy, and their heaviness gives the tall plants stability. Loam-based composts also retain nutrients better, so regular feeding, though beneficial, is not so vital.

Growing in bags

Growing bags were originally developed for commercial growers of tomatoes, and are now very popular with home gardeners. They vary greatly in price and quality, with the cheapest bags containing poor compost – and not much of it! Growing bags are suitable for tomatoes and peppers but the small volume of compost means the plants can dry out fast in summer so water them with extreme care. Unless you buy premium-quality bags, the plants will also need feeding three weeks after planting because they contain few nutrients. Remember also that you need to provide the right growing conditions for your plants so you can put the bags outside for tough crops or in the greenhouse if your plants need more warmth. The other thing to remember is to limit the number of plants (no more than three tomatoes or two courgettes per bag, for example) so they have enough room for roots and tops to grow.

Nurturing vertical gardens

If space is really at a premium, don't forget that you can use vertical spaces for lots of crops. Hanging baskets and window boxes are perfect for this but you can also, with some ingenuity, hang up growing bags, cutting holes in the sides for plants. You can even use large catering tins, banging holes in the base for drainage, attached to trellis or fence posts. A sunny wall or fence is best for most crops but remember that the reflected heat from a wall dries out pots and baskets quickly so you need to pay particular attention to watering. A west-facing wall may be more successful than one that gets sun all day. Small baskets and other hanging containers, with small volumes of compost, dry out more rapidly than large containers.

Small, short-term plants are the best choices for hanging baskets and window boxes and any multipurpose compost suffices for these plants. You can buy special container compost that usually contains both controlled-release fertiliser and water-retaining gel to help prevent the compost drying out so quickly. You can buy both these products and add them to ordinary compost if you prefer. Unless you're able to water frequently, investing in an automatic watering system run from an outside tap is worth consideration. These systems, controlled by a battery-powered, computerised timer, aren't expensive and are useful for your containers too, taking the worry out of watering.

Ideal crops for hanging baskets and window boxes include:

- ✔ Bush and trailing tomatoes
- ✔ Most herbs, especially thyme, parsley, sage, basil and chives

✔ Leafy salads, including lettuce, rocket and baby leaf endive and chicory

✔ Strawberries

Growing under Cover

One factor you can't rely on when gardening is the weather. A greenhouse or polytunnel allows you to control growing conditions a little, which means that you can produce plants and grow crops that are unreliable outside. The other benefit is that you can get gardening early in the season and when the weather is too cold or wet to do much outside.

Growing in a greenhouse

Growing under cover expands the range of plants you can grow and extends the growing season. Even in an unheated greenhouse you can grow tomatoes, peppers, aubergines, cucumbers and other summer crops with greater reliability, and the possibility of fresh grapes, peaches and nectarines becomes a reality. You can also raise your own plants more easily and reliably, which gives you control over what varieties you grow.

Size matters

Always buy the biggest greenhouse you can afford or can fit into your plot. First, you're sure to fill your greenhouse quickly, with crops or ornamentals, especially if you heat it in winter, and second, maintaining good growing conditions is far easier in a large greenhouse than a small one. Small greenhouses get very hot in summer and excessively high temperatures can damage plants.

Siting your greenhouse

Ideally, choose an open, sunny spot for your greenhouse. Although you may want to hide it for aesthetic reasons, placing your greenhouse under trees or beside a hedge limits light and thus plant growth; in addition, you run the risk of falling branches damaging the structure. If you want to heat the greenhouse with electricity you need to place it near your main dwelling.

If the axis of the structure runs north/south, both sides get equal light; if it runs east/west, the south side is sunnier and the whole house is generally hotter in summer.

If your greenhouse is made of glass, be aware that stray balls and children may pose a risk to safety.

Cold frames

Cold frames are mini-greenhouses that make a useful addition to a greenhouse. You can use cold frames to acclimatise your plants to outside conditions in late spring and also for growing early and late crops of salads. Cold frames vary in price and materials – look out for wooden sides or 'twin-skinned' polycarbonate glazing, which retain heat better than aluminium and glass or thin plastic.

Other things you need

Most greenhouses include only minimal roof vents. You need to buy extra to make sure that you can keep the greenhouse cool in summer. Adding louvre vents at the base in a few places aids air circulation. Adding automatic vent openers (which need no power supply) also makes life easier because they ventilate your plants even when you're not there. You also need staging, at least in some places, so that your young plants are easier to tend. A supply of water is essential, and a heater of some kind and a propagator enable you to raise your own plants, saving money and gaining satisfaction. Finally, you also need pots and trays.

Growing in a polytunnel

If you take the plunge and decide on a *polytunnel* (a hooped, temporary structure clad in flexible polythene), you won't regret your decision. Some plants grow better under plastic than in a greenhouse and even on a cold, windy spring day you can feel as if you're in a different country in your polytunnel, protected from the wind. Polytunnels can be cold in winter because they aren't insulated and are not airtight, so heating them isn't practical, but they warm up quickly in spring.

Planning for your polytunnel

When choosing your tunnel, consider the following:

- **Buy the biggest polytunnel you can afford.** They come in various widths and a tunnel measuring 3 metres or more in width is most sensible. Smaller polytunnels are available but the minimum practical size is about 2.4 x 2.4 metres. You need a path down the middle and this size leaves sensibly wide beds both sides. Some polytunnels have more vertical sides than others and these allow more growing room.

✔ **Choose a tunnel of strong construction.** Allotment sites can be windy. The polythene 'skin' of polytunnels generally needs to be replaced after three to five years. You can choose from various grades and qualities of polythene and, because re-skinning is a chore, the less often you have to do it, the happier you'll be. Cheap models may be a poor investment, so choose the best quality.

The polythene is usually held in place in a trench around the outside, weighted down with soil. Make sure that you leave an area around the tunnel so you can replace it. Some polytunnels are fixed with wooden battens and these are slightly less work to fit and replace.

✔ **Avoid siting the tunnel near regular bonfires because falling hot ash can damage the cover.**

✔ **Ensure that the door is wide enough to get a barrow through.**

✔ **Make sure that the tunnel has a door at both ends, for ventilation in summer.**

✔ **Site your tunnel near to a source of water, because you need to irrigate your crops, especially in summer.**

Advantages of a polytunnel

You can find yourself enjoying these benefits after investing in a polytunnel:

✔ Polytunnels are generally much cheaper, size for size, than a greenhouse and, as temporary structures, they are allowed on sites where permanent buildings aren't permitted.

✔ Polytunnels provide less trouble with watering because you're planting in the soil rather than in pots.

✔ Polytunnels can be used as a greenhouse to raise tender plants and to dry off and ripen onions, garlic, drying beans and other crops.

✔ Polytunnels are useful for giving some frost protection to stored root crops in winter.

✔ Polytunnels are perfect for growing peaches and nectarines. Growing under cover, peaches and nectarines are much less likely to suffer from the common peach leaf curl disease and are more likely to be healthy and productive.

✔ Polytunnels allow you to grow a wide range of crops – many that can be grown outside and all those you'd normally grow in a greenhouse.

✔ Polytunnels are warm in spring, hot in summer, and their humid atmosphere suits a range of crops that struggle to thrive outside in the average summer, including:

- Aubergines

- Chillies

- Cucumbers (if shaded)

- Peppers

- Tomatoes (that need to be free from blight, which often affects plants outside).

You can also try more exotic crops:

- Cape gooseberries (physalis)

- Grapes and kiwi fruit (actinidia) that are more likely to produce a worthwhile crop (if you've room for permanent plants)

- Melons and pepinos

- Sweet potatoes

- Tomatillos (for salsa)

- Yard long beans.

✔ Polytunnels enable the soil to warm more quickly and stay warm longer, as well as providing protection from the wind and rain, which helps you to extend your growing season at both ends (see Chapter 3 for more about the planting calendar).

Growing indoors

Although greenhouses make growing crops and raising young plants much easier, if you don't have one you can grow seedlings inside your home instead. Indoors, you need to make sure your seedlings get as much light as possible, so delay sowing until March at the earliest, when the sun is getting stronger, and use a heated propagator to provide a stable temperature for seedlings. The process of *hardening off*, or getting the plants used to outside conditions, is very important because indoor-grown plants are very soft and tender and need special care.

Lack of light can be the biggest problem with growing plants indoors – even a bright windowsill doesn't give young seedlings as much light as they need – and seedlings can grow spindly, especially if you're tempted to sow too early.

Getting your Share of Allotment Gardening

Many gardeners aspire to renting an *allotment* – a plot of land that you rent for growing your crops. Dreaming of the camaraderie, cups of tea, chit-chat and large areas of soil to cultivate is a wonderful idea. But vacant plots aren't always the fertile oases you may expect. Although you can try to keep the workload down to a minimum, an allotment can quickly become a tie and a chore so be prepared for some hard work. However, the rewards are considerable and an allotment enables you to grow crops that just aren't sensible on a small plot or in an average garden, such as cardoons and the related globe artichokes, Jerusalem artichokes, asparagus, rhubarb, and large quantities of soft and tree fruit. With a large area of land to cultivate you can grow some crops in large quantities, enabling you to stock the freezer and turn your garage into a winter larder. And who knows, you may even be able to live *The Good Life* and become self-sufficient in most of your fruit and veg needs!

Acquiring your plot

You can get an allotment in various ways – your local or parish council office, library or residents' association are good places to start. Alternatively, you can just wander down to your local allotments and enquire there.

Most people rent a plot for a year, but unless you neglect your plot or cause a nuisance rental is automatically extended. Rents vary from as little as £20 a year to over £100, often depending on the facilities at the site. Waiting lists are common, but if you're lucky enough to get a plot immediately, get in now!

Choosing your plot

When you get your allotment plot you may have no option but to take the only vacant one. If you're lucky enough to have a choice of plots, however, consider the following and choose wisely – it may make life much easier for you:

✔ **Look out for pernicious, perennial weeds if you get to look over potential plots in summer.** Avoid, if possible, land with severe infestations of bindweed, ground elder, creeping thistle and, in particular, mare's tail. These weeds make growing conditions difficult for your crops. (See the sections 'Perennial weeds' and 'Annual weeds' later in this chapter for more about weeds.)

✔ **Put a spade into the soil and assess the soil.** Clay soils are harder to dig and not as good for root crops, though they do suit some crops well, such as cabbages and cauliflowers. If you dig up lots of old metalwork you may have a plot that hasn't been cultivated for ages and it will take longer to get into a workable, fertile state.

✔ **Choose a plot near to a tap, if available.** The location saves you a lot of legwork in summer.

✔ **Avoid plots situated next to obviously unkempt plots.** Weed seeds and roots are more likely to invade your site.

✔ **Avoid plots that are overhung by trees or close to hedges.** Competition from tree roots and the lack of light reduces the productivity of your site.

A shed, greenhouse or polytunnel, even in a poor state, is a useful addition to your plot. Because these structures are temporary you should have no problem putting one up, but do check the rules on your site.

Divvying up your plot: Deep beds or raised beds

You need to decide how to divide up your plot. You may choose to divide it with grass paths or cultivate the whole area. For the purposes of crop rotation (see Chapter 3) dividing the plot into three or four equal areas is the easiest, but not necessarily the most practical, way forward. Most people cultivate the soil regularly and find digging is good for their crops and good exercise for them, but some believe that making deep beds or raised beds is more rewarding.

Deep beds are beds that have lots of organic matter added to them and are then heavily mulched so that worms do the work of turning the soil, and the paths between the growing areas are permanent, often covered with old carpet or straw. This approach works well with some crops but worms are intrinsically lazy and, apart from in cold or dry weather, don't burrow deep into the soil, and so they're not as effective at getting organic matter into the depths of the soil as you and your spade. Deep beds usually don't have permanent, defined sides like raised beds (see the 'Working with raised beds' section earlier in this chapter). Because of this they're more messy and so are more suitable for allotments than your own garden – unless you have lots of room.

Avoiding common allotment pitfalls

Many people who've tried their hand at allotment growing – myself included – have got things wrong occasionally. In this section I list some of the more common mistakes so that you can be wise to them before you get going.

Taking on too much land

You're probably filled with enthusiasm when you first take on your allotment, but you may discover that it takes up more time than you can afford. If the plot is wild and unkempt, focus your efforts on one manageable area. Cover the rest of the plot with carpet or weed control membrane, or spray with weedkiller, for the first season so that the ground is ready to use the next season (see the 'Clearing Old Plots' section later in this chapter). Starting with a small plot, and wanting more room, is better than your plot becoming a burden.

Planting too quickly

Making sure that you clear your planting area well before putting in your first crops is especially important with perennials such as asparagus, or fruit such as raspberries and strawberries. Clearing away and killing weeds is much easier if the ground is free of crops than trying to hand weed or dig out weed roots among your plants. Clear a small area carefully so you can grow some crops early in the first season, but then concentrate on getting the rest of the area completely free of perennial weeds for the remainder of the first season.

Growing what you don't eat

You may find that you get carried away when you're looking through catalogues or trying to fill out a planting plan and end up growing lots of crops just for the sake of it, instead of growing food you actually enjoy eating. Having your plot filled with crops all year round is good use of your land, but is of little use if you're not going to use them. If you're not going to use an area for a few months, sow it with *green manure* (plants or mixtures of plants that you sow on bare pieces of land and dig into the soil before they flower) to improve the soil. Avoiding famines and gluts of crops isn't easy, but being strict about how you treat all those spare seedlings and trying to sow little and often helps you avoid having to give away armfuls of cauliflowers and courgettes to friends who really never want to see one again!

Inheriting pests and diseases

In the garden, where a wide range of plants grows and where you may not have grown vegetables before, you're unlikely to inherit a large pest and disease population. But on an allotment, where crops have grown for decades, reservoirs of problems may be present – on neighbouring plots if not on your own. Some pests, such as brassica whitefly, and diseases such as downy mildew and leek rust that spread rapidly when conditions suit them, are inevitable on your plants if they are present on adjacent plots.

You'll quickly discover your local problems and need to be ready to spray or, where possible, choose resistant varieties. (See Chapter 7 for more info about pests and diseases.)

Inheriting fruit bushes

You may think that inheriting some fruit bushes and plants on your new plot is quite a bonus, but they may not be as good as they first look. Most soft fruit bushes have a limited life, especially raspberries and strawberries, and blackcurrants may also be infected with virus. Take the first year to examine these bushes and plants carefully and assess their health. You may be better off removing them and starting again, but don't put new plants of the same type in the same position on the plot for at least a couple of years. Of course, you can plant other – different – fruits or veg immediately.

Here are the things to look for on fruit bushes and plants that you inherit:

- **Blackcurrants** suffer from *reversion virus*, which causes the leaf shape to alter from five-lobed to three-lobed and reduces crop yields with shorter clusters of fruit. Reversion virus is spread by a mite that overwinters in the round, enlarged growth buds. Affected plants can't be cured.

- **Plums** must never be pruned in winter or airborne spores of *silver leaf disease* may infect their cut surfaces. You can identify this disease, which reduces yield, by the silvery sheen to the foliage. No cure exists.

- **Raspberries** suffer from a wide range of problems. The most serious is *virus infection*, which is spread by aphids and causes yellow mottling of the leaves and stunted growth with low yields. This condition is different from chlorosis, which is yellowing of the leaves but with green veins. Chlorosis is caused by the soil being too alkaline (in other words, the soil contains too much lime) and can be countered by adding organic matter or sulphur to the soil. Raspberries also suffer from cane blight, which causes dark marks on the stems and then dieback. No cure exists.

- **Strawberries** suffer from a virus (for which no cure exists) that causes mottled foliage and reduced crops. Strawberry beds also get crowded because of young plants on runners (known as *creeping stems*) and crowded plants don't crop well. As a general rule, you need to replant strawberries every three years.

Dealing with attack

You aren't the only one waiting for your first tasty currants, sweetcorn and cabbages. In addition to insect pests that quickly descend on your young plants, bigger critters appreciate your efforts, too. Especially susceptible crops include peas (which pigeons eat as soon as they emerge – if rats and mice haven't eaten the seeds first), brassicas in winter (which pigeons devastate), and most fruit, especially strawberries, currants and blueberries, which blackbirds devour as they ripen. You also need to keep rabbits out of your plot and rats may attack crops, such as sweetcorn, especially in late summer. I offer you my tips for protecting your crops against particular pests with each veg and fruit entry in this book and give more detailed advice in Chapter 7.

Clearing Old Plots

If you're one of the lucky ones, you may rent a clean plot that has only just been vacated. But you're more likely to take on a plot containing a mass of weeds that makes your heart sink. The biggest mistake you can make is to dot your plants around in small cleared areas, thinking that weeds that have grown for years will give up and die just because you've arrived on their patch.

All weeds are a nuisance but they can be grouped into two types – perennial and annual – according to how long they live. You're likely to have both types of weed on your allotment and understanding the two types gives you a better chance of beating them.

Perennial weeds

Perennial weeds live for more than one year and have underground roots or stems that enable them to live from one year to another. They can survive neglect and compete with grass, and so are the weeds that greet you on neglected plots. Their underground stems give them the potential to grow again even if you chop off the tops or spray them with a contact weedkiller.

You can simply dig up some perennial weeds but others grow back from small parts of plants left under the soil. However, because they can't withstand persistent cultivation of the soil, these weeds gradually decline after you've cleared the plot and have it under control.

Veg that becomes a weed

Some vegetables, especially the more unusual types, can become weeds. Years ago I planted giant spinach and left it to seed. For years afterwards it appeared all over the garden. Bloody dock can be a similar problem and even leaf beet can seed everywhere if you leave bolted plants to mature. You may also find that lamb's lettuce and land cress turns up in unexpected places, so beware – you may find that you have more of a particular vegetable to eat than you first expected!

Perennial weeds to get rid of include:

- ✔ **Mare's tail** is possibly the worst weed of all and often a sign of light, sandy soils. Growth is narrow and leafless, looking like slender Christmas trees. Weedkillers aren't especially effective on mare's tail's waterproofed cover, and the exceptionally deep roots mean that it's impossible to dig out. Elimination of this weed is unlikely but you can manage it by spraying, pulling out and hoeing as often as you can. The slender leaves mean that mare's tail isn't the most harmful of weeds – just the most persistent.

- ✔ **Ground elder** is a destructive weed that spreads quickly, and the brittle white underground stems break as you dig them up. Even small pieces make new plants that form a dense carpet of bright green leaves that smother other small plants and airy clusters of small, white flowers. Knowing that ground elder was originally introduced as a vegetable itself is of no comfort when you're struggling against this weed!

- ✔ **Couch grass (twitch)** often invades plots from grass paths, and has sharp-pointed underground stems that spear carrots and potatoes. Removing couch grass by digging makes for hard but effective work.

- ✔ **Creeping thistle** is the most common thistle and has small, mauve flowers and very spiky leaves. Creeping thistle is tall, sends out white, underground stems to colonise new areas while growing and flowering, and smothers most crops.

- ✔ **Bindweed**, both white-flowered bindweed (or *bellbine*) and the smaller pink-flowered field bindweed, have brittle, white underground stems that snap as you dig them up and grow into new plants. The twining stems grow up around and strangle taller plants. Bindweed is almost impossible to dig up completely.

- ✔ **Stinging nettles** are usually considered a sign of good, rich soil. They spread by horizontal stems to cover large areas but are easy to dig out, if you wear gloves. Stinging nettles are a useful food plant for many butterfly caterpillars so you may want to leave a clump in place.

- ✔ **Bramble** is a woody weed that spreads by bird-dropped seeds and by arching stems that root as they touch the soil. Weedkillers are effective but leave behind a tangle of dead, brittle stems, and so manual clearance is essential.

- ✔ **Japanese knotweed** is a vigorous, large weed with tall, cane-like stems that colonise any soil and shade out all other plants. Its woody root-stock is difficult to dig out. You can have a go if you're feeling strong but be aware that you must never dump the roots on wasteland or they'll just re-grow! Japanese knotweed does succumb to repeated use of systemic weedkiller, so can be beaten.

Impeding perennial weeds

You have several options available to help you clear your weeds and keep them under control.

Mulching

A *mulch* is a layer that forms a barrier between the soil and the air. You can use mulches to retain soil moisture and to suppress and control perennial weeds by depriving them of light, weakening and eventually killing them. To do this you need a fabric mulch that is impenetrable to shoots. You can buy black landscaping fabric and hold it down on the soil around the edges with soil or with old tyres or bricks. You can also use old carpet. (Ideally avoid using foam-backed carpets because the foam deteriorates and may mix into the soil.) Loose mulches such as composted bark or lawn mowings (see Figure 2-l) are good around crops because they retain moisture, but perennial weeds do grow through them. If applying mulches in summer you need to chop down the growth first.

When you apply a mulch to suppress weeds, ideally leave it in place for a full year to ensure that all the tough perennial weeds have been well and truly killed.

Figure 2-1: Laying grass cuttings on top of newspaper makes a good mulch around crops.

These mulches retain some soil moisture but may also encourage slugs.

Digging

If you're feeling active you can attempt to dig up your perennial weeds. This method is necessary and effective for brambles and nettles but for weeds with a network of underground stems, such as ground elder and bindweed, you're unlikely to remove all the pieces of root. The problem is worse in clay soils where the soil remains in clods and is difficult to break up. In some cases, when the soil is parched and the roots are more flexible and less prone to breaking, you may be able to fork out the roots, but in these conditions clay soils are almost impossible to dig.

Don't put perennial weed roots into the compost heap unless you lay them in the sun to wither until dead or place them in a bucket of water so they rot first. If you don't do this, you'll be seeing them again pretty soon.

Weedkillers

Although most weedkillers don't affect the soil or your plants, the two basic types available aren't selective so it's a good idea to keep them off your crops' foliage.

The two basic types of weedkiller are:

- ✓ **Contact weedkillers** may be based on natural fatty acids and are suitable for organic growers. They act by dissolving the waxy coating of leaves and allowing the plant to dehydrate. They only affect the parts directly sprayed and don't have any direct effect on the roots of the weed. They are most effective against annual weeds.

- ✓ **Systemic weedkillers** are sprayed on the weeds, absorbed by the foliage, and move within the plant to affect the roots. In many cases they kill the plants completely. Systemic weedkillers are also effective against all annual weeds. Because of their mode of control, these weedkillers generally work slowly as the chemical is moved throughout the plant, but you can also buy combination weedkillers that combine the activity of several chemicals to give a quick and more lasting effect. Be careful, though, because these combination weedkillers, and all weedkillers except lawn weedkillers, aren't selective and kill any plant they come into contact with. However, most aren't absorbed through bark so you can spray them around dormant shrubs including fruit bushes and trees as long as you're careful not to spray the leaves of the plant.

I don't recommend that you ever use path weedkillers on land that you're using to grow crops because they aren't selective and they prevent the germination of all seeds, including vegetables and flowers. Most weedkillers, though, have no or little effect on the soil and in many cases you can plant or sow crops immediately, or within days, of spraying.

Be careful when using weedkillers. Remember to read the warning in the weedkiller section of 'Impeding annual weeds' later in this chapter.

Annual weeds

Annual weeds grow quickly but, because they need bare soil to grow, can't compete with a dense cover of perennial weeds. They tend to be more common on cultivated soil. When you remove the cover of perennials you find that seeds, which have been dormant for years in the soil, start to grow. The constant turning of cultivated soil and the lack of permanent plant cover suit annual weeds perfectly.

Removing or killing annual weeds before they set seed is vital or the problem increases each year. Not all annuals take a full year to develop and set seed; some can reach maturity and seed within a few months. Annual weed seeds most commonly germinate in spring, as the weather warms, and in late summer when the soil is warm but increasing moisture at the soil surface enables them to grow. Some may be killed by frost but the majority survive, as small seedlings, to grow quickly in spring.

You'd do well to banish annual weeds from your plot because all the time they remain they'll compete with your plants for light, water and nutrients. Here are some of the most annoying annual weeds:

- ✔ **Groundsel** is a quick grower with small, yellow flowers. If the weather is cool and wet, groundsel has the ability to set seeds even when hoed off.

- ✔ **Chickweed's** tiny, delicate seedlings rapidly spread to form dense carpets of pale green with small white flowers. This weed seeds profusely and the brittle stems snap when pulled up, allowing the roots to sprout again. Cucumber mosaic virus, which affects courgettes, overwinters on this weed. Chickweed is quite tasty as a salad.

- ✔ **Goosegrass (cleavers)** has small seedlings that rapidly turn into tall, branching plants that clamber over other plants. Natural 'Velcro' makes the leaves and large, round seeds stick to clothing. Goosegrass rapidly swamps your crops.

- ✔ **Annual meadowgrass** is a small grass that germinates in autumn and forms lawns that seed in spring. The plants then die off in summer. This weed can be a real problem in seedbeds.

- ✔ **Bittercress** is a weed that grows, flowers and seeds in a few months. The seeds are ejected from the seedpods following the small white flowers. Bittercress can easily get out of control and cover the ground, and it also grows and seeds in the poorest soil.

- ✔ **Purple deadnettle** is a pretty weed with attractive, mauve flowers but can quickly form large colonies that smother early crops, particularly when at its worst in spring. You may want to leave purple deadnettle in wild areas because it's a nectar source for bumblebees in spring.

- ✔ **Annual nettle** has the same sting as its perennial cousin but is smaller and seeds prolifically, forming carpets of stinging leaves.

✔ **Galinsoga (gallant soldier)** is a large, rangy weed that has hairy leaves and yellow and white daisy-like flowers; it thrives in drier soils, mostly in the south of England.

Impeding annual weeds

You can choose from a number of methods to control the annual weeds that sprout up on your plot.

Mulching

You can control annuals with a thick mulch of organic material. This method prevents seed germination or forms a dense barrier that weeds can't push through as they grow. Ideally, you need to make this mulch 8 centimetres deep. Such a thick layer isn't practical around all crops but is suitable for fruit trees, bushes and many long-lived vegetables such as asparagus and Brussels sprouts. Well-made garden compost, bark and mushroom compost are all suitable. You can also use grass clippings from the lawn, on their own or laid over newspaper as an efficient and free mulch.

Stale seedbed

A *stale seedbed* is an effective method of controlling annual weeds and giving your vegetable seedlings a fighting chance against annual weeds. Prepare the area for sowing as usual and cover it in clear plastic sheet or *horticultural fleece* (a thin cloth available in garden centres). Peg down the plastic sheet or fleece and leave the area for several weeks, during which annual weeds grow in great numbers. When you remove the cover, lightly hoe off the weeds or spray them with a contact weedkiller. In this way you remove many of the viable weed seeds in the surface of the soil and reduce germination when you sow your vegetables in the area, as long as you don't disturb the soil surface too much.

Hoeing

Although it only has limited use against perennial weeds, hoeing is the traditional, fast method of killing annual weeds (refer to Chapter 1 for a description of the different types of hoe). Pushing or pulling the blade of the hoe through the soil, just below the surface, cuts the tops off the roots, which are then unable to make new growth. In addition to killing weeds, hoeing can actually prevent seeds from germinating. Regular hoeing keeps the surface of the soil dry and dusty, which acts as a mulch; the lower levels of the soil are therefore kept moist and seeds prevented from growing in the dusty surface. Hoeing is most effective when the soil is dry and on a hot, dry or windy day because the weeds wilt and stand no chance of rooting again. Although hoeing is not very effective against perennial weeds, it does have some effect – if you constantly remove the tops from a plant it eventually weakens and dies.

Hoe off weeds before they flower and set seeds. If the weeds are small you can leave them on the soil surface to dry out and die, but if they're larger, raking them off and adding them to the compost heap is better and neater.

Hoe with care around your crops. You can hoe along rows and hand weed among the plants. Short-handled hoes help in these cases, enabling you to see exactly what you're chopping off.

Hand weeding

Pulling up weeds by hand is laborious but sometimes the only way to remove them, and usually the only way to kill weeds along rows of crops. You can use a hand fork or trowel to help lift the roots of stubborn weeds and to remove any perennials you find along the rows. The job is easier on a dry day and when the weeds themselves are dry. You can add the weeds to the compost heap unless they're setting seed.

Weedkillers

Although you can use systemic weedkillers (where the chemical kills the weed gradually from within) they aren't necessary for annual weeds. Instead, you can effectively use contact weedkillers (where the chemical begins to kill the weed on contact), including organic products based on natural plant fatty acids. Many work quickly but aren't selective and must be kept off the foliage of valuable plants. Their continued use may result in compacted soil and accentuate moss growth, so they aren't a complete substitute for hoeing or other methods of cultivating the soil.

Always wear protective clothing such as gloves, goggles and a simple face mask when handling any chemicals and use weedkillers only on still days, avoiding windy conditions when spray may drift onto valuable plants or neighbouring plots. Like all garden chemicals nowadays, weedkillers are extensively tested and, providing you remember these rules and follow the instructions, they pose little or no hazard to you or to bird or animal life.

Manufacturers are also making weedkillers easier to use every year. In addition to concentrates that you need to dilute, you can buy ready-to-use sprays that save you time. Ready-to-use sprays have been formulated to have a long shelf life, but if you dilute concentrates you must use the spray immediately. Try not to mix up more spray than you need but if you do, pour or spray the excess on a spare piece of ground. Never make the spray stronger than recommended, adding a bit for luck.

Don't ever risk making up and using your own home-made chemical weedkillers. Not only are they unlikely to be effective, they are also strictly illegal.

Digging

Because annual weeds don't have the capacity to grow from the roots, you can clear the soil of them by digging them into the soil. Doing this actually adds humus and nutrients to the soil and is really a form of green manure. You can also use a rotary cultivator to incorporate them into the soil, but be sure to catch them before they set seed or you're simply burying the problem for another year.

Fire

Although it may seem extreme, you can use fire to kill weeds with a gas-powered weeder. These run on cans of gas and are easy and safe to use but you must be careful in hot, dry conditions that you don't set light to dry materials. You don't need to burn the weeds to a crisp; in fact this makes the job slow and expensive. All you need to do is lightly scorch the weeds so the cells are damaged and they collapse. Using fire in this way is most effective on small weeds.

Weeding paths

Many site's plots are divided with grass paths, which as well as needing occasional mowing can also be a source of weeds such as couch grass and mare's tail. So, in addition to keeping paths in good order, leave a strip alongside them that you can periodically spray with weedkiller to prevent weed encroaching on your plot. You may also want to make paths through your plot; old carpet (without foam underlay) is ideal for this or you may want to use straw that you can dig in at a later date. Straw may encourage slugs but is a good soil conditioner and a cheap path material if you can obtain it locally.

Chapter 3

Deciding What, When, Where and How To Grow

Starting to grow your own fruit and veg is exciting stuff, and you're probably raring to grow. You could just pop along to the garden centre, grab some seeds and get sowing – but wait! Rather than just growing the first thing that pops into your head you need to think about planning – after all, the rest of your family may not like eating what you want to grow, and you may not have ideal conditions for it anyway. Doing a bit of planning first means that you get far better results in the end and a lot more satisfaction.

In this chapter I look at the things you need to consider before jumping in with both feet and deciding that you want to grow a particular crop. Remember that the key to a happy life of gardening is having lots of success early on, and you're most likely to achieve this by stopping and thinking for a moment before putting those first, fragile seeds in your ground. Read on . . .

Deciding What to Grow: Where and When

Without wanting to state the obvious, before you can get started you need to consider what you want to grow. First and foremost, base your choices most on what you actually want to eat. Never grow crops just for the sake of it or because you think you ought to grow them.

When you grow your own fruit and veg, you eat seasonally. Most crops have a season and producing them out of season can be difficult or impossible, so work with nature and not against it. You soon find a greater pleasure in eating seasonal food instead of the imported produce that you buy in the shops all year round. As well as being fresher, fruit and vegetables are more of a pleasure when you know that they have a limited season, and so you really look forward to the first runner beans or cauliflowers. I look at the times to harvest your crops in Parts III and IV.

Making a planting calendar

To make sure that you remember when to plant and sow, draw up a *planting calendar*. You can do this in one of two main ways:

- ✔ The simplest method is simply to get an empty book and mark each page with the weeks of the year, so you need at least 52 pages! Look at the instructions with your seed packets and plants and write down what to sow on each week's page. This method is most useful for plants such as salads that you need to sow at intervals through the summer – forgetting is just too easy!

  You can also use your book as a diary, making notes of your successes and failures – it'll be a good reference in future years.

- ✔ The more complex method is to draw your veg plot on a piece of graph paper. Mark the months along the top in twelve columns. Then fill in the boxes for each crop, to show how long they're going to be in the ground. For example, in one row you may sow broad beans in March, extending from March to the end of July when you harvest them and replace with sprouts or a winter cabbage. Or you may have an early potato, lifted in July and replaced with a sowing of turnips in early August that remains in the soil until November. Figure 3-1 shows an example of this kind of planting calendar.

Of course, planning things so precisely is all well and good, but plants don't always do what you expect, sometimes failing entirely, and seasons vary: these things happen. Don't take setbacks personally – just put them down to experience, and remember for next time. Just be prepared to be flexible and make changes to your planting plans as you go through the year. The 'Catch cropping' section later in this chapter gives you a few tips on how to fill any gaps that appear in your calendar and on your plot.

Figure 3-1: A sample planting calendar.

BED 1	Jan	Feb	Mar	Apr	May	Jun	Jul	Aug	Sep	Oct	Nov	Dec
Row 1: Broad beans and spring cabbage			Broad beans	Broad beans	Broad beans	Broad beans	Broad beans	Cabbage	Cabbage	Cabbage	Cabbage	Cabbage
Row 2: Broad beans and pak choi			Broad beans	Broad beans	Broad beans	Broad beans	Broad beans	Pak choi	Pak choi	Pak choi		
Row 3: Leeks and French beans	Leeks	Leeks	Leeks		French beans	French beans	French beans	French beans	French beans			
Row 4: Leeks and French beans	Leeks	Leeks	Leeks		French beans	French beans	French beans	French beans	French beans			
Row 5: Jerusalem artichokes and runner beans	Jerusalem artichokes	Jerusalem artichokes			Runner beans	Runner beans	Runner beans	Runner beans	Runner beans	Runner beans		
Row 6: Peas and garlic			Peas	Peas	Peas	Peas	Peas		Garlic	Garlic	Garlic	Garlic

BED 2	Jan	Feb	Mar	Apr	May	Jun	Jul	Aug	Sep	Oct	Nov	Dec
Row 1: Early potatoes and endive			Early potatoes	Early potatoes	Early potatoes	Early potatoes	Early potatoes	Endive	Endive	Endive	Endive	
Row 2: Early potatoes and turnip			Early potatoes	Early potatoes	Early potatoes	Early potatoes	Early potatoes	Turnips	Turnips	Turnips	Turnips	
Row 3: Beetroot			Beetroot	Beetroot	Beetroot	Beetroot	Beetroot	Beetroot	Beetroot			
Row 4: Leaf beet and tomatoes	Leaf beet	Leaf beet	Leaf beet	Leaf beet	Tomatoes	Tomatoes	Tomatoes	Tomatoes	Tomatoes			
Row 5: Onions and land cress			Onions	Onions	Onions	Onions	Onions	Onions	Land cress	Land cress	Land cress	Land cress
Row 6: Courgettes					Courgettes	Courgettes	Courgettes	Courgettes	Courgettes	Courgettes		

Extending the growing season

Polytunnels enable gardeners to tweak their gardening calendars. The nature of the polytunnel environment means that the soil there warms more quickly than outside and stays warm longer into autumn, enabling you to extend the growing season at both ends. In spring you can get sowing with root crops and salads at least a month earlier than outside and be enjoying your own radish and salads in time for Easter. You can also plant early potatoes and get an extra-early crop. Dwarf French beans are another worthwhile crop and by sowing them early you can interplant them with tomatoes and they'll have cropped by the time the tomatoes shade them.

At the other end of the season the lack of wind and rain is a bonus when plants outside suffer from grey mould and can rot. You can sow salads including Oriental cabbage, endives and chicories and harvest them well into autumn. Others, such as lamb's lettuce and land cress, which are hardy but stop growing in winter, are much more productive and keep in better condition in a tunnel. You can even grow autumn-fruiting raspberries in a tunnel if you have room. These often fail to ripen their late fruits in cold areas where the first frosts strike early but with protection they start growing and fruiting earlier and longer.

Plotting for success

You'll find that your plot isn't ideal for all crops. In general, though, potatoes are best in soils that are slightly acidic or neutral (a low pH), and brassicas are best on neutral or slightly alkaline (higher pH), heavier soils. Root crops are best in light soils that aren't too stony and most vegetables are best in sunny spots – spinach and some salads are the exception. Even so, some crops can be difficult and swede is trickier than most. In the fruit world, strawberries and raspberries tend to prefer acid soils and blueberries need very acid soil, but the good news is that in general most other fruits aren't so bothered.

The key thing is to check that the crop you want to grow will like the conditions on your plot. I describe the conditions that each crop requires under their entries in Parts III and IV, and Chapter 4 tells you more about the wonderful world of soil.

If you have trouble growing a particular crop, try several times before you admit defeat. If you're growing on an allotment, ask fellow plot holders for tips. Their experience of gardening in that allotment may be an invaluable source of information for you.

Choosing Your Fruit and Veg

You have the luxury of being able to choose from dozens of different fruits and vegetables you could grow and hundreds of varieties. That is part of the joy of growing your own. But just where do you start when it comes to making a choice? Here of course!

Going for yield or flavour

As a grow-your-own gardener, you have different priorities from commercial growers. Your crops don't need to be ready on a particular day and you don't need huge yields. A reasonable return for your efforts is always nice, but as a grow-your-own gardener you have the luxury of being able to select varieties for reasons other than yield.

Because you allow your fruit and veg to mature or ripen on the plant and eat it when really fresh, just about any vegetable or fruit that you grow yourself has more flavour than any you can buy in the shops. Better still, you can select varieties that are specially bred or selected for their flavour. For example, those in the know regard pale 'Lebanese' type courgettes as having the best flavour whereas you may not expect courgettes to have much flavour at all. Also, yellow courgettes have a finer texture and different flavour to green ones and yet green courgettes are all you can buy in the shops. You'll notice the huge difference when you eat your first home-grown cucumber – it actually tastes of something!

Take the opportunity to experiment and grow a range of varieties. You soon discover which tomatoes you prefer for flavour, texture and colour as well as size. As a grow-your-own gardener, you're no longer restricted by what fits neatly into a plastic carton on the shelves. The world is your pumpkin!

Picking modern or heritage varieties

Many gardeners ignore the huge strides that plant breeders have made in developing new varieties of fruit and veg, and instead are drawn to the warm glow they get when growing something that fed their ancestors. Old fruit and vegetable varieties, often called *heritage* or *heirloom* varieties, can definitely be worth growing, primarily because they were selected over many generations to suit certain needs and often, principally, for flavour. However, they can be more difficult to grow than many modern varieties, and are sometimes more susceptible to diseases. Many of these varieties are now endangered because legislation in many countries forbids their sale, often because these varieties don't breed completely true to type and are difficult to keep 'pure'. However, gardeners can grow and exchange them and even sell them as plants, though not as seeds. Strange but true!

Large research companies have bred most modern varieties of fruit and veg for farmers who supply produce for the supermarkets. Although flavour and diversity aren't always the most important considerations, these companies have made big steps in countering disease problems and have often made the plants easier to grow. In some cases modern varieties have extended the diversity of our vegetables and fruit. Modern cauliflowers come in purple, orange, green and white and you can find purple, red and yellow carrots. Yellow beet is no longer a rarity and red onions, purple radishes and exotic-sounding squashes are widely available.

Breeders are introducing new types of vegetable and fruit and extending growing seasons. For example, purple sprouting broccoli was once a crop that you could harvest only in spring, but new varieties crop in summer as well, just a few months after sowing, so you can enjoy this healthy vegetable for many more months. Also, you can harvest modern Brussels sprouts as early as August instead of October, as used to be the case. Experts are also breeding some veg to be smaller. This means you can fit more of them in your plot and that growing them in pots on the patio is easier. Look for small cabbages with fewer large, outer leaves and compact courgettes.

Breeders have also improved the resistance to disease in many crops as consumers have become keener on organic, chemical-free produce. Modern varieties of cabbage and cauliflower are resistant to clubroot and carrots have partial resistance to carrot root fly. These improvements are all advantages over the heritage varieties.

Heritage vegetable varieties do have their advantages. As you become experienced at growing, you may want to try growing some for their distinctiveness and their link with the past as well as for their flavour; but ignore at your peril the developments that have made so many crops easier to grow.

And this year's winner is ...

The Royal Horticultural Society regularly trials flowers and vegetables at its gardens throughout the UK and bestows the RHS Award of Garden Merit (AGM) on any types that are markedly superior in these trials. You can be sure that a plant you see with an AGM is exceptionally good. If a plant doesn't have one, though, don't think the variety isn't worth growing – it may have wonderful flavour but just not crop heavily or it may need extra effort to grow.

Crossing

Although a few vegetables and fruits, such as land cress and medlars, are very similar to the wild plant, most others have been developed over time by gardeners, so have become very different. Gardeners have done this partly by a process known as *hybridising* or *crossing* – selecting plants with desirable traits, such as orange roots in carrots, and then combining two or more different traits from two parent plants in their offspring. In this way, the marvellous 'improved' and diverse varieties we grow today have been produced.

Looking at hybrid varieties

Most fruits and vegetables you grow are *hybrids* – the results of crossing different parents of the same sort of plant. Some of these hybrids may be *F1 hybrids,* which are special because two parents are selected that breed perfectly true to type. The plants have to be crossed (see the sidebar 'Crossing') every time seed is needed because their offspring don't breed true, unlike most other vegetables (you can't save the seeds from them and get the same plant the following year). Therefore, the seed is more expensive to produce, but F1 hybrids are usually worth the extra money because of the special features they may have, such as improved yield, vigour or uniformity of taste. F1 hybrids may even be all-female, as is the case with many cucumbers. The plants rarely make male flowers and can't produce seeds naturally, meaning that they crop better and are easier to grow.

Selecting Seeds or Plants

Whether you start with seeds or plants depends on several factors. Most fruits are only available as plants, so you don't always have a choice. Most vegetables are grown from seed, but if you prefer you can buy young plants, saving you precious time and effort but costing you more. The choice is up to you, and can depend on the facilities you have at home and on your plot. If you plan to buy plants, do be aware that although some seed companies offer modern and novelty varieties as plants, the choice that garden centres offer is often quite meagre and only of standard varieties.

Growing from seed

To grow fruit and vegetable seeds successfully you need to supply three things – without one of these factors the seeds don't grow:

✔ Right temperature (usually 20 degrees Celsius for fruit and veg)

✔ Moisture

✔ Air

Most seeds should start to *germinate* (grow) between one and three weeks after you sow them but a few, particularly parsley and parsnips, can take longer.

You can grow most vegetables from seed. If you're aiming for an early crop, you need to sow the seeds before conditions outside are suitable for growing, so you're best off sowing those vegetables under cover in trays or pots rather than direct where they're to grow. A greenhouse with some heat is ideal, but any well-lit spot under cover, such as a conservatory, porch or a sunny windowsill, works well. You also need to do this if the plants you're growing need a long growing season; sown outside, they don't have long enough growing periods to produce reasonable crops. Some seeds are expensive, too, especially F1 hybrids, so you want every one of them to grow. In these cases, the protected conditions in a greenhouse may be more suitable than leaving them to fend for themselves outside.

Not everything is suitable for sowing in containers. Root crops such as long-rooted carrots, parsnips and beetroot dislike being transplanted from the seed tray to the garden and you have to sow them in such large numbers that starting them in seed trays and then moving them isn't cost-effective. After all, one tomato seed produces one plant that produces dozens of fruits – a carrot seed produces just one carrot!

Even with very careful sowing, if you've sown your seeds in containers or in seedbeds, you soon need to thin out and transplant your seedlings. Plants that are crowded compete for light, nutrients and water, often causing them to run to seed (bolt) prematurely.

In this section I take you through the general steps you need to know about sowing, thinning and transplanting. Any important detailed stuff about individual plants, and about raising the plants from here on and harvesting them, is contained under the plant headings in Chapters 8–16.

Sowing in containers

To sow your seeds in containers you need the following:

✔ **Compost.** You can raise most seeds in multipurpose compost, whether peat-free, peat-based or reduced peat. Whichever you go for, be sure to buy fresh, good-quality compost.

REMEMBER

Always buy compost as you need it and don't store it for more than six months, because nutrients in the compost can deteriorate over time. Opened bags may fill with water and acquire weed seeds and fungal diseases. Never buy bags of compost that shops have stored for long periods outside (you can usually spot these bags because they are wet and heavy and the print may be faded).

✔ **Pots and trays.** Always use clean pots and trays. Wash used ones in hot water first because debris can harbour pests and diseases.

✔ **Sieve.** A garden sieve; that is not the one from your kitchen!

✔ **Watering can.** You need one with a *rose* (sprinkler) on the end of the spout.

✔ **Perlite or vermiculite.** These items are volcanic rocks. You heat them so that they expand and you add them to compost to improve the drainage and structure without adding any nutrients. Perlite and vermiculite are sterile when packed so are ideal for seed sowing and seed composts.

✔ **Propagator of some kind.** A propagator is a tray – heated or unheated – with a transparent top for rooting cuttings and germinating seeds. Having one isn't essential, but is useful because it enables you to ensure that the conditions are just right for germination. Controlling soil moisture and temperature is much harder outside.

Rooting out some vegetable seed suppliers

Here's a list of good stockists who can help with all your vegetable seed requirements!

✔ **D T Brown & Co** Tel 0845 166 2275
www.dtbrownseeds.co.uk

✔ **Dobies** Tel 0844 701 7623
www.dobies.co.uk

✔ **Edwin Tucker & Sons Ltd**
Tel 01364 652 233
www.edwintucker.com

✔ **Mr Fothergills seeds** Tel 01638 751 161
www.mr-fothergills.co.uk

✔ **Marshalls seeds** Tel 01480 443 390
www.marshalls-seeds.co.uk

✔ **The Organic gardening catalogue**
Tel 0845 130 1304
www.organiccatalog.com/catalog

✔ **Seeds of Italy** Tel 020 8427 5020
www.seedsofitaly.com

✔ **Simply vegetables** Tel 0870 460 9445
www.plantsofdistinction.co.uk

✔ **Suffolk herbs** Tel 01376 572 456
www.suffolkherbs.com

✔ **Suttons** Tel 0870 220 2899
www.suttons-seeds.co.uk

✔ **Thompson & Morgan** Tel 01473 688 821
www.thompson-morgan.com

In their early stages, seedlings are vulnerable to many dangers such as drying out, overwatering and fungal diseases. For this reason, to reduce the likelihood of failure, be sure to use clean, or new, pots and labels and fresh compost.

So you've now got all the kit you need to begin sowing your seeds. Ideally prepare the trays a few hours before sowing (but don't worry too much if you can't). Here's how to do it:

1. **Ideally working on a bench, open the compost bag and tip some out.** Loosen it to break up any lumps.

2. **Loosely fill your pots or trays and tap them on your work surface to firm the compost.** Don't be tempted to firm compost too much because this squeezes the air out, increasing the chance of the compost getting too wet and leading to *damping off* (take a look at Chapter 7 to read more about damping off).

   Sow large seeds such as beans, marrows and courgettes in individual pots or cell trays (trays comprising 6–12 compartments). You need more room in the propagator for these but the benefit is that you can plant them out later with no disturbance to the roots. Sweetcorn prefers narrow deep pots such as Rootrainers – deep, narrow, grooved containers that encourage good root growth.

3. **Level the compost with your hand.** If you want you can then sieve some compost on top to get an even surface – useful for fine seeds such as celeriac.

4. **Water the tray or pot with fresh, clean water (not from a water butt) using a can with a fine rose so the compost is soaked.** This also settles and firms the compost.

   You're now ready to sow. Before you begin, think about how many plants you want. Quantities of seed in packets vary enormously and most F1 hybrid seed, which is expensive, comes in small packets. Regular cabbage seed comes in packs containing hundreds of seeds and you don't need all those in one go.

5. **Tip some seeds into your hand and sow from there, or sow direct from the pack.** Sow about twice the number of plants you think you're going to need, allowing for some not growing and some wastage.

6. **Sow the seeds thinly on the surface.** If you plant seeds too close together, the seedlings are difficult to transplant without damaging them, and damping off disease (see Chapter 7) spreads rapidly through the tray.

7. **Cover the seeds with a few millimetres of compost, perlite or vermiculite.** You don't need to sieve the compost on top – just sprinkle it between your fingers. (See Figure 3-2.)

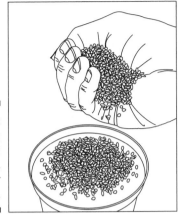

Figure 3-2:
Covering
seed with
compost,
perlite, or
vermiculite.

8. **Give the seeds a warm place to grow.** A propagator is ideal. A temperature of about 21°C is perfect for most fruit and veg seeds. A slightly lower temperature is suitable for hardy veg, such as cabbages, and slightly higher temperatures are better for warm-climate crops, such as aubergines and peppers.

9. **Give the seeds another good watering if the surface appears to be drying out.** Be careful, though, because *misting* (squirting water frequently on the soil surface) too often encourages damping off (see Chapter 7 for more about damping off). You may find that you don't need to water your trays again until the seeds *germinate* or sprout but do check them daily. If the seeds dry out as they start to grow, they'll die.

Some gardeners prefer to water their seeds by placing the tray in a container of water (about 1 centimetre deep) for about 10 minutes to dampen the compost. Doing this prevents the base of the seedlings getting wet and reduces fungal diseases.

The time that seeds take to germinate varies according to the variety and how warm they are. Cabbage starts to appear within a week, tomatoes in about two, but chillies and peppers may take three weeks or more and need watering during that time. Most seeds should show signs of growth within a month.

When your seeds appear as small seedlings remember to give them good light, and perhaps reduce the temperature a little, to prevent them becoming thin and spindly. Spindly seedlings are difficult to *prick out* (transplant).

Thinning and transplanting in containers

When your seedlings' leaves are fully expanded and the first 'true' leaf starts to appear in the centre, you need to move the seedlings into bigger trays, cell trays or pots. At this stage the seedlings are large enough to handle but the roots have not yet branched and had a chance to get tangled. Seedlings are very delicate, and although they can survive if you damage or break a seed leaf, be careful not to crush the stems or the plant will die. You can use various tools to transplant your seedlings, such as a pencil, a dibber or an old kitchen fork.

Here's the next stage:

1. **Have your new pots or cell trays ready first and make sure that the seedlings are moist before you start.** Fill the pots or trays just as you did for seed sowing, lightly firming the compost by tapping the pot and roughly levelling it. Don't water your seedlings at this stage.

2. **Lift the seedlings out of their tray in clumps.** Push a kitchen fork or dibber under the seedlings, lift them in a clump, and put them to one side. You may well find that they fall apart naturally but if they need help, gently pull them away from each other by holding only their seed leaves. You can divide very small seedlings such as celery or parsley at root level with a couple of pencils or labels, but take care not to damage the stems.

3. **Use a dibber or pencil to make a hole in the compost of the new pot. Hold the seedling by a leaf and lower it into the hole until it's at the same level it was in the seed tray.** If your seedlings are slightly spindly you can put them a little deeper. Figure 3-3 shows how to do this.

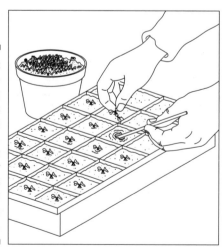

Figure 3-3: Transplanting seedlings is a delicate operation. Hold them by their leaves to avoid crushing the stems.

4. **Fill a number of pots, or a tray, or all the cells in the tray in this way and then give them a good watering (see Figure 3-4).** The seedlings may flop over but as they establish they pick themselves up.

Figure 3-4:
Thoroughly
water
transplanted
seedlings.

5. **Ideally, put them in a shady place for a few days to get over the transplanting shock and then move them to brighter light to enable them to grow.**

6. **After about two weeks, as the seedlings start to grow, begin liquid feeding them with a general-purpose fertiliser.** Most multipurpose composts only have enough fertiliser in them for a short period of growth. As the seedlings get bigger, feeding them becomes more important because young plants starved of nutrients don't grow well when you plant them out into their final positions.

Sowing in seedbeds

Traditionally, growers sow some vegetables such as leeks and brassicas (cabbage, broccoli, and so on) in seedbeds outside. The advantage of this method is that seedbeds are easier to manage than pots in a greenhouse or cold frame, needing less frequent watering than when in containers, but the disadvantage is that seedlings here take more of a shock when they're transplanted.

Follow these steps for sowing in seedbeds:

1. **Fork over your soil, breaking up any large lumps and removing any stones.** Rake the soil level so that the surface soil has a fine texture to it.

2. **Place a *line* (a string between two canes) on the soil to mark a straight row and take out a *drill* (shallow trench) with a hoe or trowel.** The drill needs to be only 1 centimetre deep for most seeds. You can set out rows in seedbeds as close as 15 centimetres because you're transplanting seedlings from them at a young age. If the weather is hot and dry, wet the drill with water from a can (without a rose) before you start sowing.

3. **Sow the seeds thinly along the drill and lightly cover the seeds with soil.**

4. **Give the covered drill a good watering with a fine rose or spray so you don't wash the seeds away.** Don't allow the seeds to dry out as they germinate.

Covering the sown area with horticultural fleece helps speed up germination, or you can put a *cloche* (a glass or plastic cover) over the area to help prevent evaporation.

Thinning and transplanting in seedbeds

You need to thin out and transplant your seedlings as soon as they have one or two true leaves. Here's what to do:

1. **Thin out your seedlings so they're about 3–5 centimetres apart**. If you can, do this on a dull day when the soil is moist so that any root damage you may cause to the remaining seedlings doesn't cause wilting. If possible avoid dry, hot, windy weather, which can cause wilting. If you can't avoid these conditions, water the row of seedlings the night before you intend to thin them and again immediately afterwards.

2. **Put a fork under the row of seedlings to lift them.** Try to cause as little damage to the roots as possible.

3. **Take clumps of seedlings to the area where they are to be replanted and divide them immediately before planting.**

4. **Make sure that the soil is ready to receive the young transplants.** Use a trowel to make transplanting holes and ease the roots into the holes. Most seedlings benefit if you plant them slightly deeper than they were in the seedbed.

5. **Firm the seedlings in well with your hands and water them immediately.**

Sowing where plants are to grow

You can sow most vegetables, including all root crops, where they're to mature. Here's how to go about doing it:

Before you do start sowing, in early spring or in autumn you can cover the soil with fleece or plastic to warm the soil.

1. **Fork and dig the whole area over well before you start sowing.** Sowing is only possible when you've broken the soil surface down into a fine *tilth* (a fine texture with no big lumps), so you may need to fork the surface, hoe, and rake it to get it level and to remove stones and large clumps of earth.

   In some cases (such as when your soil is poor and sandy or heavy clay) you may want to add organic matter to improve the soil as well as add nutrients. Most root crops don't need recently manured soil though, so if you're growing a variety of crops on a piece of land you may be better off adding fertiliser afterwards as a *top dressing* along rows of crops that benefit from additional feeding.

2. **Mark out a straight row in the soil and using a hoe take out a *drill* (shallow trench) about 1 centimetre deep (see Figure 3-5).** The distance to leave between them depends on what you're growing but 20–25 centimetres is fine for salads and carrots. Water it first if the soil is dry.

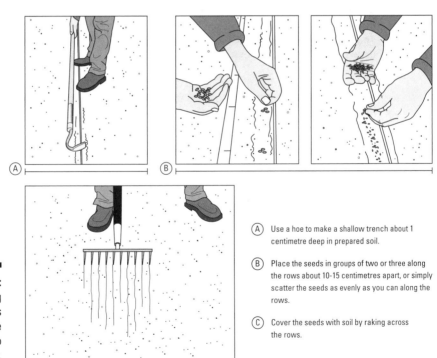

Figure 3-5: Sowing seeds where the plants are to grow.

(A) Use a hoe to make a shallow trench about 1 centimetre deep in prepared soil.

(B) Place the seeds in groups of two or three along the rows about 10-15 centimetres apart, or simply scatter the seeds as evenly as you can along the rows.

(C) Cover the seeds with soil by raking across the rows.

3. **Sow the seeds and cover them lightly with soil (see Figure 3-5).** Sowing seeds thinly in the rows to avoid the seedlings being too close together is best. If you do sow them too close together, you'll waste seed by having to thin out the seedlings later to give them room to grow. You can also damage the remaining seedlings unless you're very careful.

In some cases, such as when the weather isn't as warm as you may have hoped, or when you need to protect the plants from insects such as brassica whitefly or carrot root fly, cover the area with horticultural fleece.

Choosing successful plants

Some fruit and vegetables, particularly rhubarb, globe artichokes and asparagus, are best bought as plants. Growing them from seed has disadvantages. For example, the many varieties of strawberries all have attractive features but you can buy only a few seed-raised varieties, which often don't breed completely true to type and aren't as good as most types that you buy as plants. You're better off buying plants of a good variety. The same is true of globe artichokes, where many seedlings produce spiky heads that aren't as attractive to eat, unless you get a good seed strain. You can grow good asparagus from seed but you'll be one year behind compared with buying *crowns* (young plants), where the first year of growth from seed has been done for you.

Looking for vegetable plants in garden centres and shops can be a hit and miss affair. If you're buying plants that are frost-tender, including courgettes and marrows, tomatoes, cucumbers, aubergines, peppers and herbs such as basil, the garden centre should have put them in a frost-free place with good light. If not, don't buy them. Seed catalogues are a safer bet, and most now sell a wide range of vegetable plants. These catalogues are good value, especially if you only need a small number of plants, and you can be sure that they are good varieties, delivered at the right time, and are well grown.

Most plants should be a good green colour and look sprightly. If they look straggly, or are yellow, tangled together or floppy, they may be chilled, overwatered or just past their best. Look to see if the soil is moist. Never buy plants that are standing in water – it can rot the roots – or that are wilting. Very dry plants may not recover and they may even bolt some time after.

When buying fruit plants and trees, again try a specialist who delivers at the best time of year. Mail order nurseries send out *bare-root* plants between autumn and spring, and these usually grow much better than potted plants in the long term. You need to unpack bare-root plants immediately on arrival and check that the roots are moist (they should be packed in peat or wet straw). If the roots are dry, soak them in a bucket of water immediately for a few hours. If you're not ready to plant them, you need to cover the roots with compost to keep them moist until you're ready to go.

At the same time of time of year, garden centres and shops may stock dormant plants *root-wrapped.* These are plants without leaves that growers have dug up and wrapped their roots in a plastic bag or black polythene with some peat to keep the roots moist. When stored in cool conditions, root-wrapped plants can remain in good condition for many months. But when kept in a warm shop the shoots start to grow and the roots dry out. So be wary of these plants: look at the stems to make sure that they are alive and feel the weight of the package – if it's light as a feather, the plant has probably dried out and died. Shop plants that are alive but with slender white shoots in late winter will be damaged by frost when you plant them out and so aren't a good buy.

You can buy fruit in pots all year round from garden centres – for planting in summer as well as winter. However, although this is convenient, the range is usually limited. Also, planting in summer isn't easy because you need to water your plants well all through the hot weather to keep them alive and it requires more commitment than autumn or winter planting.

Fruit trees and bushes are a long-term investment of time and money and may not start cropping for several years. So don't settle for a common variety offered at a poor garden centre, and never buy a plant labelled just 'blackcurrant' or 'red apple'. You can buy dozens of varieties of gooseberry, hundreds of apples, and even a dozen or so types of blackcurrant from specialists, and you owe it to yourself to get the best variety for your needs.

When buying potted plants, make sure that the plants haven't been in the pot for too long: weeds in the top and roots growing from the base are a sure sign of this problem, and these pot-bound plants are unlikely to do well.

Plucking the right fruit plant suppliers

When buying fruit plants, you need to be sure that you're buying quality stock. Here are a few of the best outlets:

Blackmoor Nurseries Tel 01420 473576
www.blackmoor.co.uk

Deacon's Nursery Tel 01983 840750
www.deaconsnurseryfruits.co.uk

Keepers nursery Tel 01622 726465
www.keepers-nursery.co.uk

Ken Muir Ltd Tel 0870 7479111
www.kenmuir.co.uk

Reads Nursery Tel 01508 548395
www.readsnursery.co.uk

J Tweedie fruit trees Tel 01387 720880

Buying plants to save time

If you're too busy or you just forgot to prepare your plot or sow your seeds on time, you can just go out and buy plants! You can buy lots of vegetable plants but the most useful are leeks and winter brassicas, which you usually sow in May, a time of year when forgetting to sow more seeds is all too easy because you have so much else to do in the garden.

Planning Your Plot

Some gardeners spend a lot of time planning their vegetable plot as though it were a military campaign. Doing so can be difficult in your first year when you don't have much experience of how long plants take to grow, but do have a go because you're sure to discover a lot in the process.

Most seed packets have details of when to sow and when to harvest, which is good basic information to help you plan.

Planning the layout

The most important aspect of planning any plot is to consider what garden-ers call *crop rotation*: dividing your plot into three or four roughly equal-sized parts and making sure that you don't grow the same crop, or group of plants, on each plot in succeeding years. If the plot has three parts, any one crop is grown on that plot every three years. The reason for crop rota-tion is that growing the crop on each piece of land only every three or four years reduces the chance of any pest or soil-borne disease specific to a crop increasing in population and becoming a nuisance. Most pests, including carrot root fly, brassica whitefly and caterpillars, aren't completely stopped by this method, but it does prevent the soil becoming 'sick' of a certain crop and empty of important nutrients. Check out Chapter 7 for more info about crop rotation.

Catch cropping

Lots of plants are in the ground for many months before you harvest them. Even with careful planning, you may find that a patch of your soil isn't planted with anything between one main crop and another. In this situation, and also where you have limited space, *catch crops* are useful. Catch crops are plants that grow very quickly and occupy the soil briefly between other crops that stay in the soil for a much longer time, and you can harvest them while they're immature.

The classic catch crop choice is radish, but you can eat only so many radishes and so fast-growing salad leaves are another good option. For this reason, keeping a few packets of easy-to-grow crops is always a good idea. Fast-growing salads, some French beans for summer sowing (you can sow them up to July), some courgette seeds (they grow fast and cover the soil), leaf beet, and some annual herbs such as parsley, coriander and summer savoury are excellent for popping in to fill any gaps. Remember that although growers usually plant in rows of one crop, you can always fill any gaps in the rows with a different crop, as long as it's likely to mature in about the same time.

You may even want to sow a row or patch of hardy annual flowers to fill any gaps in your plot. Tall varieties such as larkspur, nigella and even sunflowers are good for cutting and small annuals such as limnanthes and alyssum just add some colour. But most importantly, many of these varieties have simple flowers that attract butterflies, bees and hoverflies. You need bees to pollinate crops such as beans and tomatoes and the larvae of hoverflies are even more aggressive eaters of aphids (green- and blackfly) than ladybirds. So why not have a splash of colour on your plot? It does your veg and your soul a lot of good!

Intercropping

Another way to make the most of your space is by *intercropping*, where you sow fast-growing crops between existing rows of other large, slower-growing crops that take longer to mature, before they cover the ground completely. Crops that grow slowly include some of the brassicas, such as Brussels sprouts and sprouting broccoli, parsnips and leeks, and between these rows you can sow lettuce, salad crops, kohl rabi and of course radish. If you sow them at the same time that you plant the brassicas, you can harvest them and clear the ground by the time the brassicas start to shade the ground.

Part II
Prepping Your Plot

'Edmund's very green-minded – he's obsessed
with feeding the soil whilst protecting our
birdlife.'

In this part . . .

*B*efore you can grow anything, you need somewhere to plant. Some lucky people inherit a perfect plot with ideal soil and no weeds, but the chances are you can't get started straight away because you have a tangled web of weeds to do battle with first. Weeds need not be as daunting as they first appear and in this part I tell you how to tackle the most troublesome – the good news is that you can tame even the weediest plot and make it productive.

Getting an allotment makes your life as a gardener easier because it gives you lots of space. Polytunnels and greenhouses are a great help, too. However, too many people start with great enthusiasm and simply get overwhelmed, so this part gives you ways to avoid some of the most common pitfalls.

Even if you don't have a huge plot to grow on, don't despair; even a small plot – or a patio – can produce worthwhile crops. You can grow many in containers and you can find all the encouragement you need in this part of the book.

One bonus of growing your own crops is that you can be certain what chemicals you've used or you can grow them organically and not use chemicals at all. In this part I explain how to do this and look at the advantages of choosing this option.

So whatever the size of your plot, or your aspirations, this part is just what you need.

Chapter 4

Getting Down and Dirty with Your Soil

*W*hatever hobby or activity you enjoy, you need to know and understand your raw materials, and when growing your own fruit and veg, nothing is more important or fundamental than understanding your soil.

Your soil is a valuable asset – looking after it keeps your plants happy and makes your life a lot easier. So get to know your soil, look after it, treat it with respect, and it'll reward you for the care you lavish upon it.

Delving into the Make-up of Soil

Soil is a complex combination of living and dead materials, and without it gardeners would struggle to grow much. The nirvana of soils is well-drained, rich *loam*. Loam isn't a single soil type but a mix of various types of soil particles. Soil is much more than particles, however; healthy soil also contains live and dead organic matter, water, air, creepy crawlies, bacteria and fungi.

Mineral particles

Mineral particles in the average soil vary from stones, which are the largest particles, through gravel of increasingly smaller sizes, to sands, silt and finally clay – the smallest particle of all. Although the mineral particles in soil add some nutrients to the soil, most of them aren't soluble in water and so don't supply much in the way of plant food.

Clay particles are the only variety of mineral that encourages nutrients, because they have electrical charges that attract and retain nutrients in the soil. Clay particles form *lattices* or layers in the soil that are bound by water. When a lot of water is present, the lattices slide across each other, but when dry, they stick together in a solid mass, which explains why clay soils can be slippery when saturated but can dry to a solid lump.

Organic matter

Healthy soil is full of humus. No, put the breadstick down; *humus* is a general term for organic matter, not a chickpea dip. Humus is basically dead plant remains – a brown, sticky, treacle-like material that absorbs and retains nutrients and sticks soil particles together in crumbs to make the soil easier to work. Humus improves the fertility of your soil and also has other benefits for your soil and plants, depending on the stage of decomposition. Organic matter in a raw state, such as dead leaves or bark chips, has little value apart from opening up the soil, improving water and air penetration. But as bacteria decompose the organic matter in the soil, it gradually becomes humus.

Water

All plants need water in the soil for absorbing nutrients and moving them around the plant. Plants need water throughout their lives and some are especially needy at certain times in their lifespan – usually when the crop is developing. Plants that go short of water show their distress in various ways. Their immediate response appears as wilting or limp leaves, but the effects also show up in the longer term, such as in reduced crops. They may shed small fruits if they lack water. For example, when tomatoes lack water, the fruits develop blossom end rot. In other crops, such as onions, shortage of water makes the plants try to bloom, resulting in no crop at all. So apply water regularly and evenly to your plants.

I give you the tips you need on keeping your plants watered in Chapter 5.

Air

Plant roots need to breathe and if the soil is compacted or completely saturated with water they become deprived of air and can't grow. Some plants are able to penetrate dense, compacted soils but few thrive in these conditions and rootcrops can't survive in them at all. You can increase the air in soil by digging, incorporating organic matter or coarse particles (grit or sand), and by making raised beds; you can find out how to do the latter in Chapter 2.

Soil insects, bacteria and fungi

Most decomposition of organic matter, such as dead leaves and roots, in the soil is done initially by *fungi* (which live in the soil and are often microscopic) and then by bacteria. Soil insects including millipedes and woodlice are also beneficial because they eat and digest woody material. Worms pull leaves into the soil at night and without woodlice we'd be up to our ankles in dead leaves and twigs! Digging good quality organic matter into your soil can help give this process a boost and improves your soil in so many ways.

Assessing Your Soil

In the same way that you need to know the essentials about how your car works before driving it, you need to know about your soil before trying to grow plants in it. Soil may seem mysterious and you may not know much about it at the moment, but in just a few minutes you can discover what your soil is like, and thereby avoid lots of problems when it comes to growing fruit and vegetables.

Analysing your soil

Before you start growing your own fruit and veg, take the time to work out what type of soil you have. Doing this type of test helps you to assess what crops are likely to thrive, and enables you to avoid simple mistakes and look after your soil. I recommend testing your soil in two main ways – by physical analysis and chemical analysis.

Physical analysis

Knowing the basic structure of your soil helps you to look after it. Although all soils have many constituent parts, few are a perfect balance of them all and simple tests – getting your hands dirty – can reveal what soil you have. Here's what to do:

1. **Take some soil in your hand, wet it and rub it between your fingers and thumb.** If it feels gritty, your soil is sandy, probably drains fast in summer, and may be low in nutrients. A smooth feel suggests silt or clay, which usually means good fertility. Also be aware of stones, gravel and organic matter, which may influence your opinion.

2. **Take some more soil, squeeze it gently in your hand so it forms a lump, and open your hand. Push the soil lump with your finger and see how easily it crumbles.** If it doesn't stay as a lump at all your soil is probably high in sand, grit or stones. If it crumbles and breaks up quite

easily as you poke it, the soil has a good mix of all particles and, probably, organic matter. If it doesn't break up at all and you have to pull it apart, the soil is predominantly clay. To check, roll some soil into a sausage in your hands (you may need to wet it to do this) and try to form it into a doughnut shape. If the soil easily forms this shape, it's predominantly clay.

Chemical analysis

Knowing the pH value of your soil is important. The *pH* is a measure of acidity or alkalinity that you can use to assess your soil. Acid soils are often deficient in calcium, which all plants need in order to thrive. Very alkaline soils can cause certain minerals, such as iron and magnesium, to be less available to some plants. The good news is that the vast majority of plants aren't too fussy about soil pH and grow in a wide range of soils.

You can buy kits for one soil test that come with full instructions, cost less than a packet of seeds, and tell you your soil pH. More elaborate soil test kits enable you to test for the main plant nutrients (nitrogen, phosphorus and potassium) and give information on what to add and how much to apply to correct any deficiency. However, if you apply organic matter regularly to your soil, apply balanced fertilisers, and grow a range of crops, an imbalance or deficiency of major plant nutrients is unlikely.

I recommend doing several tests over a large plot because of anomalies in your soil profile and natural differences across the plot. Take several small samples from just under the soil surface, and avoid areas next to compost bins or where you've recently applied any lime, manure or fertiliser.

The pH scale runs from 0 to 14. A pH of 7 is neutral – neither acid nor alkaline. A rating of less than 7 is increasingly acid and a rating higher than 7 is increasingly alkaline (limey). Most soils have a pH between 6 and 8.5, and most plants grow well in the range from 6.5 to 7.5. A soil pH of 6.5 to 7 is ideal for the widest range. Few vegetables or fruit are particularly sensitive to pH above 7 (potatoes, blueberries and raspberries are the exceptions) and some, such as brassicas, prefer a high soil pH. Acid soils may be deficient in calcium, an important plant nutrient needed in the formation of plant cells, which is why gardeners traditionally add lime to their soil.

Looking at soil types

Although gardeners often refer to soils simply as heavy or light, rich or hungry, and moist, wet or dry, soil is classified in many different ways.

Different types of soil, such as sandy or clay, can be acid, neutral or alkaline.

Increasing the depth of topsoil

Because plants grow best in fertile topsoil, they grow better if this layer is nice and thick. You can increase the depth of your topsoil in two ways – by adding organic matter to the top or to the bottom! Lots of mulching adds organic matter for worms to take down into the soil, but not as far as the subsoil. The other option, which is harder work, is to *double dig*. This involves taking out a trench, forking organic matter into the subsoil, without bringing it to the surface, and replacing the topsoil.

Topsoil and subsoil

Whatever your soil type, the upper layer, called *topsoil*, is a darker colour than the soil lower down, known as *subsoil*. The topsoil is usually at least 20 centimetres deep and is where most roots grow. It should be fertile and rich in organic matter, including worms and other creatures. If you have thin topsoil on your plot, concentrate on increasing its depth (see the sidebar 'Increasing the depth of topsoil' for more). If you're making raised beds and buying topsoil, always check it first to ensure that the topsoil is of good quality and not full of weed roots.

You often find a distinct change where the subsoil starts. This lower layer is the natural, basic soil and may be a sticky clay or flinty gravel. Worms don't live or carry organic material into the subsoil except in times of drought, so the subsoil contains little organic matter, air or life, and few plant roots penetrate this layer. If you bring this layer to the soil surface through digging, plants don't grow well in it.

Heavy soils

Heavy soils usually contain a lot of clay, are wet in winter, are difficult to dig, and resemble concrete as they dry out. Because they retain so much moisture, especially in winter, they warm up slowly in spring and so can still be cold. Before growing fruit and veg in heavy soils, you need to 'lighten' them and improve drainage by adding as much organic matter as you can. Do this every year, because the organic matter decomposes as it forms humus, especially if you have alkaline soil above a chalk foundation. You can also add fine gravel or sand to the soil – hard work, but the effort produces a longer-term effect.

Make use of the action of frost in winter to break up heavy soil. Get your digging done before the end of the year and leave the soil in large clumps so that frost and thaw breaks up the clay as the water freezes and expands.

As a general rule, stay off soils – especially clay soils – when they are soaking wet because tramping up and down compacts them, squeezing out the air, and undoing all the good work you did while winter digging. Lay down boards to walk on when soils are wet.

Clay soils aren't all bad. They are rich in nutrients and retain moisture in dry spells. If you tame them, clay soils are among the best for growing your own fruit and veg.

Light soils

Light soils are those that contain lots of sand, gravel and stones. They drain freely, can be very dry in summer, and don't retain soil nutrients well because water and nutrients run through them rapidly. However, light soils are easy to dig (use a fork if the soil has lots of stones) and they warm up quickly in spring, making them good for early sowings and most root crops (although too many stones in the soil causes the roots to bend and fork). You can improve light soils by adding organic matter to help retain nutrients and moisture.

Peaty soils

Some areas have soils that are peaty and high in organic matter. These soils are light to work, grow most plants well, and are rich in nutrients. However, peaty soils are often thin and lie over rock or clay, so you need to dig in organic matter to keep them in good condition and help them to retain nutrients.

Chalky soils

Chalky soils are often thin and – because of the subsoil or underlying rock – alkaline. The alkalinity encourages bacteria in the soil to convert any organic matter quickly into humus, which makes chalky soils difficult to improve. You shouldn't have trouble growing a wide range of crops in chalky soils, except those that dislike alkaline soils, but you must keep liberally adding organic matter every year.

Loamy soils

Loam is a happy medium of all soil types and is easy to work, dark in colour, and rich in nutrients. All gardeners dream about having light loam in their gardens, but even this needs maintaining with organic matter.

Urban soils

Soils in small gardens in towns and cities are often exhausted! They've frequently been cultivated for decades and, because of the effort it takes to get organic matter to the site, they may not contain a great deal of humus. Nearby hedges take water and nutrients out of the soil, and their spreading roots make some soil improvement essential. Because large settlements are often built in lowland areas, many urban soils are also silty and light to work, but you may also have clay or sand. To improve urban soils, adding lots of organic matter – and fast – is essential.

Using weeds as indicators of soil type

Gardeners usually think of weeds as a nuisance but they can be useful indicators of the type of soil they're growing in. Most annual weeds grow anywhere if the soil is disturbed, but many perennials do prefer distinct soil types.

Here are a few weeds that you can look to to tell you what kind of soil you've got. You can also flip back to Chapter 2 for more about weeds.

Acid Soils	*Alkaline Soils*	*Light, Dry Soils*	*Poorly Drained Soils*
Cinquefoil	Black meddick	Annual nettles	Buttercup
Daisy	Cowslip	Bramble	Comfrey
Foxglove	Knapweed	Dock	Dock
Heather	Oxeye daisy	Groundsel	Meadowsweet
Periwinkle	Salad burnet	Poppy	Purple loosestrife
	Valerian	Red dead-nettle	Mint
	Yarrow	Speedwell	Primrose

 If the whole garden is paved over, you can construct raised beds or grow in containers, but you then need to import soil or compost to fill them. (Refer to Chapter 2 for more info about raised beds and containers.)

Improving Your Soil

By looking after your soil you enable all your plants to grow more healthily. The easiest way to do this is to add organic matter, which improves drainage while increasing the amount of water the soil retains. As a bonus, organic matter even adds valuable plant nutrients to the soil. The key is to add it regularly – as often as possible – because the task of looking after your soil is an ongoing one.

Adding organic matter

You can improve all soils simply by regularly adding organic matter. This routine helps to add and retain moisture, nutrients and air, as well as improving water drainage and increasing the activity of soil micro-organisms. Organic matter also lightens heavy soils and increases the fertility of light, sandy soils; it's one product you can't get enough of.

You can add a number of different types of organic matter to improve the quality of your soil and get it in tip-top condition for growing fruit and veg. Here are some of the things you can add to your soil:

- **Composted bark** is used as a mulch around ornamental plants, has no nutrients and can rob the soil of nitrogen. You can use bark as a moisture-retaining mulch around permanent fruit bushes or dig it in to lighten heavy soils, but it's not of great value in the vegetable garden.

- **Garden compost** varies enormously in quality and nutrients, but is free and available from the bottom of your own garden. However, you're unlikely ever to make enough for your needs and will almost certainly need to use one of the other products listed here as well. See the section 'Making compost' later in this chapter for tips on how to go about making your own garden compost.

- **Green manures** are plants or mixtures of plants that you sow on bare pieces of land and dig into the soil before they flower, and are a cheap and valuable way to add both organic matter and nutrients to soils. You can sow green manures at any time of the year if you have spare soil that isn't carrying a crop, but the best time to sow is in late summer. Sow rye, phacelia or mustard – or field beans, alfalfa or clover to add nitrogen to the soil – and leave them to grow over winter. Ideally, dig them in, while still growing, in spring. You're adding lots of bulk to the soil and the green manure plants help to prevent loss of nitrogen from the soil over the winter. If the plants have become too tall to easily dig in, you can just cut them off and add them to the compost heap. Be aware, however, that green manures may increase the slug population on your plot.

- **Manure** comes in many varieties, but horse manure is generally the best, especially for heavy soils. The manure itself is fairly rich in nutrients but the bedding used by the horses and mixed into it is key to the quality of the manure. Straw is best because it decomposes rapidly but many horses are bedded on sawdust or woodchips, which take longer to break down and need nitrogen to do so. If the sawdust and woodchips have been added to the manure in a raw state, they may temporarily take nitrogen from the soil to the detriment of your plants.

Horse manure is especially useful to add to the compost heap to help make great compost.

I recommend using well-rotted manure that has been stacked and left – under cover so the nutrients haven't been washed away – for at least six months, but this is sometimes hard to find. If you can only get fresh manure, pile it into your compost bin to let it age. You can use fairly fresh strawy manure around 'hungry' plants, such as marrows, courgettes and other squashes in summer, as a mulch with great results.

Cow manure is sometimes available but is best composted by mixing it with straw and putting it in the compost heap for a few months. Poultry manure is rich in nutrients but don't add it in a raw state close to plants – be sure to add it to the compost heap first.

✔ **Mushroom compost** is one of the best products – clean, free from weeds and seeds, and with some nutrients. However, because the compost has already carried a crop of mushrooms most of the nutrients have been used, although you may get a bonus crop of mushrooms! This compost is lightweight and pleasant to handle, but quite expensive, so you're best off buying it by the lorry load if you can, or at least in large quantities, rather than in bags. You may have a bit left over, so why not share it with your neighbours! Mushroom compost is perfect for digging in, for raised beds, and for mulching, but it contains lime and so isn't ideal for crops such as raspberries and potatoes that dislike lime.

✔ **Planting compost** is sold at most garden centres, and may or may not contain peat. Peat is a valuable commodity and shouldn't be used as a soil conditioner because it's a limited resource and is not renewable. Choose a reduced-peat or peat-free compost, which although generally too expensive to use in large volumes in the soil, are useful for filling or adding to raised beds and pots.

✔ **Recycled compost**, made from recycled domestic garden waste, is often available at your local waste-recycling centre. Recycled compost inevitably includes a lot of woody waste that gardeners can't deal with at home, and which remains in the soil for a significant time before decomposing. Therefore, it tends to be very free draining. This type of compost usually has a low nutrient value, but is a good way to get air into heavy soils. Each batch varies in quality, but is generally good value and useful.

✔ **Sawdust and wood shavings** conserve moisture when you use them as a mulch, but they both deplete the soil of nitrogen, so don't use them in a raw state on the soil. If you have access to large amounts of sawdust and shavings, the best idea is to add them to the compost heap or mix with manure, particularly poultry manure.

✔ **Spent hops** are clean, light and easy to use for digging into soil or for use as a mulch. You need to live near a brewery to have access to spent hops, which have very low levels of nutrients but in large quantities are a good source of organic matter. Don't buy small, expensive bags in garden centres if you can find other, cheaper sources of organic matter.

✔ **Straw** has limited value on its own, but does add humus to the soil. Straw can be very cheap if you can buy bales, but the downsides of using straw are that it can encourage slugs and that it may blow away in windy weather. Also, avoid putting straw that may have been sprayed with herbicide around tomatoes, which are extremely sensitive to hormone weedkillers.

To use straw, spread it over the soil in autumn and dig it in when you can over the winter to lighten heavy soils or use it for paths or as a mulch in summer. Mix it into your compost heap to keep it open and to balance large amounts of wet material.

Making compost

Making your own compost is one of the most positive things you can do in your garden. In one fell swoop you're recycling, saving on your carbon footprint, improving your soil for future generations, and making your plants grow better. There – I bet you feel better already! Instead of being one of those gardeners who drive off in their cars to take their garden waste to the tip, you can just chop it up and add it to the compost heap, saving fuel, time and money.

A compost heap is a community of living things and is so good for wildlife. After you've spread the compost as a mulch around the garden, blackbirds will have a great time tossing it around looking for lunch. Compost is great for your plants too, being a good source of organic matter to improve and feed the soil with, adding in valuable – and free – nutrients.

Many gardeners have a compost bin and recognise the importance of making compost, but so often the results don't quite match the expectations. The reason for the disappointing result is that you actually have to *make* compost, instead of just putting a load of debris in a bin and expecting wonderful, fertile compost to come out of the bottom. Think of it as making a cake – compost needs a recipe and the ingredients have to be in the right proportions for you to get a good result. You need a combination of woody, carbon-rich material to form the majority of the finished compost, and soft, moist, nitrogen-rich material, which decomposes quickly to provide food for the beneficial bacteria and keeps the heap moist.

Using compost bins and getting good compost

You can buy many different types of compost bins in garden centres. Compost bins keep things tidy and speed up the process by insulating the contents, keeping out excess rain, and keeping the edges of the heap moist. By placing a bin on soil it'll be 'inoculated' with worms and other creatures more quickly but where you put it doesn't matter too much – just position it somewhere handy so that you make use of it.

Bear these tips in mind when making compost:

- ✔ Avoid thick layers of one material. If you're producing a large amount of one product at one time – by pulling up lots of bedding plants or weeds, or raking up leaves – try to mix them with other materials. In particular, never compost grass cuttings on their own, but instead mix them with other materials such as:

  - Annual weeds, clippings, and kitchen waste (veg peelings)

  - Soft, wet material

  - Straw, cardboard, paper, dried leaves and dead herbaceous stems

  - Woody material, including shredded branches and twigs

Avoid adding the following:

- Any cooked food
- Any meat or dairy products
- Human, cat or dog faeces
- Live perennial roots.

✔ Turn the compost at least once in the six months it takes to be ready. The best way is to have two bins, one to store the materials and one for the actual decomposition. Fill one heap and then turn the contents into the second, to make the compost. Then fill the first bin again.

✔ Get a large bin if you can. To decompose garden waste effectively, bacteria need to build up heat. Small bins don't heat up enough to kill all weed seeds; wooden bins or those with thick, double-skinned or insulated sides are best at helping the bacteria do this. Large bins, ideally 1 metre in diameter, produce better compost than small ones, which are unlikely to get warm enough to kill weed roots, weed seeds or diseased material.

✔ Cover the heap in winter, to prevent it getting too wet and nutrients being washed away by rain, but make sure that the heap is moist in summer so it doesn't dry out.

✔ Avoid putting material affected by a soil-borne disease onto your heap, because it may then spread to other areas of your garden.

✔ Cut up or shred woody material so that it decomposes rapidly, because material in small pieces has a larger surface area for fungi and bacteria to work on.

You can add an *activator* – a source of nitrogen or bacteria – to boost the speed of decomposition in your compost heap. You can buy specialist compost activators or add nitrogen in an organic form such as dried blood, hoof and horn, or urine, all of which you can find in garden centres. To add bacteria, you can buy shop-bought activators, but just adding some garden soil or old compost to the heap also does the trick.

Many gardeners have a patch of comfrey growing in their gardens. Comfrey is vigorous and leafy and has deep roots that pull up nutrients from the soil. You can cut off the leaves at ground level several times throughout spring and summer and add them to the compost bin, where they boost decomposition and add vital nutrients to the mix.

Compost the leaves that fall in autumn on their own; they make a fantastic soil conditioner. Leaves do take longer to compost than most other items, though, unless you mix them with some softer, wet material such as grass cuttings.

Dealing with compost problems

Even when following the preceding tips, getting compost right isn't always easy. Table 4-1 troubleshoots some of the most common problems.

Table 4-1	Fixing the Most Common Composting Problems	
Problem	*Cause*	*Remedy*
Wet, smelly compost	Too much soft material in the compost and not enough woody stuff.	Tip out the compost, mix with straw, shredded paper or cardboard, and restack. Keep the compost covered to prevent it getting too wet.
Ants and other insects	Usually the result of too much dry material in the compost or the heap being too dry so it doesn't decompose and heat up.	Add more water and activator.
Nothing much happens	Almost always the result of the heap being too dry.	Add more water and activator.
Lots of tiny flies (fungus gnats) appear every time you open the lid of your compost bin	The heap is too wet.	You need to dry the heap out. Mix dry material with the contents and keep the heap covered.
Overly large numbers of soil animals such as millipedes and woodlice	A sign that the heap is cool and not ideal for bacterial decomposition.	Add more water or activator to the heap.

Chapter 5

Feeding and Watering Your Plants

In This Chapter

▶ Understanding plant needs

▶ Applying fertilisers

▶ Keeping your crops watered

'*W*hat goes around, comes around', as the saying goes, and this adage certainly applies to those of us who grow our own fruit and veg. Before you can eat the crops that you've grown, you first need to keep your crops well fed while they develop. You can't just put your plants in the soil and expect them to thrive.

How you look after your plants makes the difference between getting a just-so crop and a really good crop. They often need feeding and certainly need watering, if only as they get established or in extreme drought. If you grow your plants in containers, they totally rely on you for their food and water. If you grow your plants in the soil, feeding is a bit of a luxury for them because most of the nutrients they need are already there, but doing so can pay dividends. After all, you can't expect a fruit tree or bush to keep on producing heavy crops year after year if you don't put something back into the soil.

In this chapter I share some top tips on making sure that your plants never go thirsty, and examine how to provide the essential 'foods' that most crops need to survive and thrive. You can also take a look at Chapter 4 for the lowdown on how to improve your soil with organic matter and compost.

Watering Your Crops

All plants need water – your crops included. Some plants don't need much whereas others suffer if they're dry at any time. Just to complicate things, other plants mustn't be short of water at specific times or they may not develop properly.

The water you give should not just be enough to prevent them from wilting but enough to make them grow vigorously. If potatoes are short of water as the tubers develop, those tubers can be misshapen and may have hollow areas inside. If tomatoes are short of water as the fruits grow, they develop black, sunken areas. If carrots become dry, their roots split.

Knowing when to water

All plants need to be watered at certain critical times – generally as the seeds are germinating and when you've transplanted or planted them out.

The first few weeks after sowing are a critical time for seeds and seedlings, especially if they're small seeds sown near the surface. Larger seeds planted deeply, such as most beans, some squashes and peas, are less likely to dry out as they start to germinate. Seeds die if they dry out while starting to germinate and they won't appear above the soil surface. In long dry spells this requirement may mean that you need to water every day until the seedlings appear, their roots penetrate the soil and they can fend for themselves.

When transplanting or planting, choose a dull day with not too much wind (wind dries out soil and plants) and make sure that you water the plants well before planting. Not only does this approach make them moist, but it also ensures that the roots are in contact with the soil, enabling them to grow and find their own water.

Apart from new additions to your plot that need frequent watering, the best general advice is to give a thorough soak every week or two so that you soak the whole soil profile. Giving a little water frequently moistens only the upper surface of the soil and causes the roots to stay in the upper parts, making them even more vulnerable to drought. If you can, direct the water to the base of each plant rather than to the whole of the soil surface. Wetting the whole soil surface wastes water, which evaporates, causes weed seeds to germinate, and *caps* the soil (in other words, it destroys the friable, loose surface caused by hoeing that actually helps to prevent water loss).

The best time to water is in the evening or early in the morning when the soil is cool, so that more water penetrates the soil and less of it evaporates and gets wasted. Try to avoid sprinkling water over the foliage of plants where it will evaporate and do no good at all.

Fruit and vegetables growing in containers need constant watering. Their water needs change through the season – they need more in hot weather, and as the plants increase in size. Always give them a thorough soak when you water so that the whole of the compost, from top to bottom, is wetted.

If you have to leave your pots for more than a day you can take several steps to ensure they don't go dry:

- Make sure you give the pots a really good soak the night before you leave and again just before you go.
- Ask a neighbour or friend to water them. Make sure that you place the pots close together and leave buckets and cans of water ready so the job is as easy and quick as possible – and so they don't miss any pots.
- Place the pots in a shady area so that the plants need less water.
- Stand the pots in saucers and hanging baskets on buckets of water.
- Rig up an automatic watering system so you don't have to worry at all, but do this a week before you're due to leave so you can check that you've set it up correctly and that you've programmed it to deliver enough water.

Making water go further

Many people use water without thinking twice, but water is a valuable resource. Bear these few tips in mind to help reduce the amount of water that you use:

- Never apply water at the middle of the day, which is when it evaporates the fastest.
- Try to water early in the morning or, ideally, in the evening.
- Reduce your watering needs by using mulches (see Chapter 2) around your crops wherever possible.

Grey water

Grey water is water that has already been used and includes water from the washing up bowl, washing machine and the bath. To help you collect grey water, you can buy diverter kits that fill covered butts from downpipes and also products to reduce the unpleasant smells if you store water for more than very short periods.

Using grey water on most crops is perfectly safe, but not for extended periods on container plants and not for sensitive plants such as blueberries.

Rainwater

Rainwater should be pure and is ideal for all crops. Make sure that you store the rainwater in a covered butt to prevent accidents, the growth of algae (green water), and breeding mosquitoes. You can link several butts together to store significant quantities over winter for use in summer.

Don't use rainwater for delicate seedlings in the greenhouse in case it contains disease organisms.

Reducing water needs

You can reduce the water needs of your plants in several clever ways:

- ✔ **Avoid growing crops that need a lot of additional watering**, such as celery and runner beans, if your soil is naturally free draining.

- ✔ **Mulch permanent plants and slow-growing crops.** Mulching isn't practical for all crops – mulching seedlings without killing them is difficult – but it can be useful.

  A *mulch* is a loose layer on the soil surface that slows the evaporation of water from the soil into the atmosphere. You can use straw, bark or garden compost, and even cardboard, plastic sheets and weed-suppressing fabric, but these aren't easy to use around all crops. If you have large amounts of grass cuttings from your lawn you can use these very effectively around plants if you lay down newspaper or cardboard first and then cover this with grass clippings. Dig in the rotted paper and grass at the end of the growing season to counteract any possible problems as they decompose.

  Some other mulches, such as straw, garden compost, and shredded twigs also keep down annual weeds. You can rake them up and compost them at the end of the season.

- ✔ **Shelter your plants from hot sun and wind.** Although most crops grow best in full sun, sheltering them reduces the amount of water they need.

- ✔ **Improve the water-holding capacity of your soil.** You can do this by adding lots of organic matter (see Chapter 4). In small areas you can add water-retaining gel – a polymer that absorbs many times its own volume of water, releasing it when the soil dries out, and repeats this action for many years. This gel is expensive, however, for anything other than small areas.

- ✔ **Work with the weather.** Try to plant and sow in cool, wet weather to reduce the amount of watering the plants need.

- ✔ **Hoe often.** By keeping weeds down you reduce the amount of water that they take from the soil. Hoeing also reduces evaporation from the soil because, although the surface appears dusty, this dry layer acts as a mulch.

- ✔ **Sow plants where they're to grow, where possible.** Newly planted crops always need a lot of water to get established. Those that have been sown where they are to grow generally have deeper roots for the size of plant and often grow more quickly. So although plants may be slightly behind in development at first, because they're sown outside rather than in a greenhouse, sweetcorn, squashes and beans may need less watering if you sow them where they're to grow.

A real time-saver

If you're short of time you can automate your watering to look after your plants – at least to some extent. The simplest way to do this, and one of the most effective ways to water, is to lay or bury just under the soil a hose with perforations along lines of crops. You can then attach the hose to mains water or a water butt and leave it to slowly ooze water.

Technologically inclined people can attach a simple, battery-powered watering computer to a tap, setting up a simple micro-irrigation system comprising mini-sprinklers and drippers to water your plants at night, when watering is most effective. These systems are especially useful for containers where regular watering is essential and time-consuming.

Eating Well: How Plants Feed

Plants make much of their own food by harnessing the power of sunlight and combining carbon dioxide and water to make simple carbohydrates, such as sugar. Plants can then convert these sugars into starches, fats and other forms of carbohydrate such as wood to thicken stems, enabling the plants to grow. But plants need many other nutrients that they can get only from the soil and which they use to make a host of other chemicals such as pigments and proteins.

Plants feed on a range of chemicals in varying amounts from the soil. In relatively large amounts, plants need nitrogen, phosphorus and potassium (also known as potash). These chemicals are usually readily available in most soils, but not usually in sufficient quantity, so adding extra chemicals can boost your plants' growth and give you much better crops. Using general-purpose compound fertilisers means that you don't always need to think too hard about these different chemicals – they do all the hard work for you and treat your plants to a balanced diet!

In very poor soils it may be that your plants suffer from a nutrient deficiency. These deficiencies are rarely severe enough to stop plants growing, though they may prevent your plants from doing their absolute best. The most common are deficiencies of iron and magnesium – which occur when plants that like acid soils (such as raspberries) are grown on alkaline soils and show as yellow leaves with green veins – and nitrogen deficiency in leafy crops like cabbage, which grow poorly, especially in spring.

Take special care to feed any plants that you have growing in containers; their roots are confined and they rely on you to supply all the nutrients they need.

Nitrogen (chemical symbol N)

Nitrogen is an important nutrient that all plants need because it:

- ✔ Encourages good growth of leaves.
- ✔ Boosts development of branches and stems.

Nitrogen occurs naturally in the soil, coming from decomposing plant remains, animal urine and faeces, lightning (which combines atmospheric nitrogen, the most abundant gas, with water), and soil-dwelling bacteria living on the roots of plants such as peas and beans, which also capture gaseous nitrogen and trap it as nitrates that plants can absorb. If a plant lacks nitrogen, the growing tip remains green but the older leaves turn yellow as the plant moves the nitrogen to the actively growing area.

You can buy nitrogen in fertilisers that contain ammonia and nitrates, though some plants are sensitive to ammonia, so use these with caution. Common nitrogen fertilisers include sulphate of ammonia, dried blood, and hoof and horn, and gardeners most often use these on brassicas or leafy, salad crops in spring to give a boost of growth. High levels of nitrogen lead to soft, vigorous, lush leafy growth, so the best time of year to use these fertilisers is spring, when plants are actively growing, rather than in late summer when the soft growth produced is more liable to be damaged by cold weather. Nitrogen is very soluble and gets leached through the soil and so an application in spring can be useful after winter rains on bare soil.

Sowing green manures on bare areas in autumn helps to prevent nitrogen leaching through the soil in winter. Digging them into the soil in spring releases the nutrients for later crops. See Chapter 4 for more details.

Phosphorus (chemical symbol P)

Phosphorus is an essential nutrient for all plant growth, especially because it:

- ✔ Promotes healthy roots.
- ✔ Enables seed germination.

Growers most commonly add phosphorus at planting time, as bone meal or superphosphate, but few soils are deficient in phosphorus and you rarely need to add it specifically. Most *compound fertilisers* (which I discuss later in this chapter) contain sufficient phosphorus for all the plants you're likely to grow. Plants that do lack phosphorus are likely to be less productive than you'd expect and suffer from stunted growth.

Potassium (chemical symbol K)

Plants need potassium because it:

- ✔ Tends to 'toughen' growth, making plants woodier and so better able to withstand cold, winter weather.
- ✔ Slows leafy growth, acting as a balance to nitrogen.
- ✔ Promotes the production of the flowers and fruit that are essential for plants such as tomatoes, peppers, and beans.

Gardeners usually apply potassium in late summer, especially on fruit bushes and trees, to encourage growth of the flower buds that will open the following year. You find potassium in all compound fertilisers, in sulphate of potash and in wood ash, but this latter potassium is soluble so don't leave the ash outside until you need it!

Plants lacking potassium tend to produce low yields and have a lower resistance to disease than plants that get enough potassium.

Trace elements

The elements that plants need only in small amounts are called *trace elements*, which include magnesium, iron, copper, sulphur, calcium, manganese, boron and molybdenum. Plants need trace elements because they:

- ✔ Promote the production of compounds such as proteins, pigments and vitamins.
- ✔ Ensure growth and fruitfulness.

Trace elements are almost always present in the soil but a few plants are sensitive to deficiencies; a high pH (alkalinity) in the soil may reduce the availability of some elements, especially iron and magnesium. Balanced fertilisers and all organic fertilisers contain trace elements – just look for them on the label.

Using Fertilisers

We may talk about feeding plants, but you don't see many plants with teeth – they can really only drink. You need to dissolve in water any fertiliser before you add it to the soil or compost so the roots can absorb it. Plants are able to absorb only very simple molecules and if you add an organic fertiliser that provides nitrogen, for example, in the form of proteins, the micro-organisms in the soil have to break this down into nitrates before the plant gets any benefit from it.

What do those numbers mean?

Look on any fertiliser pack and you can see a code-like series of letters and numbers such as N7P7K7. This code is a legal requirement and tells you the proportions of the three main plant nutrients – nitrogen (N), phosphorus (P) and potassium (K). N7P7K7 is the analysis of *Growmore*, a standard, general-purpose fertiliser that supplies equal amounts of the three main plant foods. If the analysis is 'weighted' towards nitrogen, the 'code' may look something like N14P7K7, and the fertiliser is better for leafy crops. If the fertiliser is weighted towards potassium, as in N7P7K14, it's better for fruiting plants, such as tomatoes.

Fertilisers come in various forms. All retailers stock row upon row of different types, with some varieties claiming to be ideal for all plants whereas others are aimed at feeding specific plants or plant groups. Some fertilisers may have complicated names such as 'sulphate of ammonia' that leave you puzzled. If you're uncertain of what to buy, stick with a name you know such as Phostrogen or Tomorite and buy a general fertiliser – it isn't going to harm anything. But knowing a bit more can help you to give your plants exactly what they need, so you end up with healthier plants. That's where this section comes in.

Improving your soil with organic matter helps it to retain nutrients and is the first thing to get right for your plants' benefit. Keeping your soil in good condition keeps your plants healthy. If your soil isn't that great to start with, though, or if you discover that it has a nutrient deficiency, feeding your plants by applying fertiliser to them or to the soil they grow in can help to give their growth a boost. (Chapter 4 tells you how to keep your soil in tip-top condition.)

Spring and summer are the ideal times of year to apply fertiliser to your crops. Applying fertiliser in autumn or winter, when plants aren't actively growing, is pointless because the nutrients leach out of the soil and are wasted. Nutrients are also wasted if you apply lime to the soil at the same time as fertilisers. Lime is alkaline and most fertilisers are acid. If they mix, they react with each other and their effect is useless.

Lime

Although most soils contain calcium – a vital trace element for plants – gardeners sometimes add garden lime to the soil to raise the pH and make it more alkaline (refer to Chapter 4 to read about pH levels in soil). The dreaded clubroot disease – which can prevent the healthy growth of brassicas – is less likely to make unwelcome appearances in soil with a high pH.

The best way to apply lime is to add it little and often, at up to 250 grams per square metre every year, until you get the soil up to the pH level your plants need.

Always apply fertiliser little and often and don't be too heavy handed. An overly strong chemical concentration in the soil can damage and suck water out of the roots, and prevent the plant from absorbing beneficial nutrients.

Solid fertilisers

Growers of fruit and veg most often use solid fertilisers in the open garden to feed crops. The range available can be bewildering, with some varieties manufactured and others based on naturally occurring organic materials (see the section 'Organic fertilisers' later in this chapter).

You can apply solid or granular fertiliser before planting or sowing, or apply it to the soil's surface (a process known as *top dressing*) around established plants. Check the pack first to see what amount you need (you scatter at most about 100 grams per square metre) and apply by raking or lightly forking it into the soil surface, or around established plants.

Compound fertilisers

Compound fertilisers contain balanced amounts of the three main plant nutrients – nitrogen, phosphorus and potassium – and often trace elements, too. They may be manufactured for specific crops such as onions or potatoes but most of them are general-purpose and you can safely use them around all plants. If you're worried about which fertilisers to use, compound fertilisers are the ones for you – they may not be perfect but they certainly won't do any harm!

Look at the analysis on the label to check that the proportions of nitrogen and potassium are suited to your crop – high nitrogen for leafy crops and high potassium for fruiting crops.

'Straight' fertilisers

'Straight' fertilisers are simple chemicals that provide just one major plant nutrient – for example, sulphate of ammonia which provides just nitrogen. They may be useful when you've carried out a soil test and know that your soil lacks a particular nutrient. Be careful though, because applying large amounts of just one nutrient can cause a nutritional imbalance, and so you need to get it right. However, adding a nitrogenous fertiliser is useful for leafy crops in spring, and adding potassium in late summer encourages flowering the following year, and is useful for encouraging crops of fruit such as plums and apples.

Controlled-release fertilisers

Controlled-release fertilisers were developed so that you don't have to worry about the fertiliser running out and leaving it too long before reapplying it to your plants. Each granule of controlled-release fertiliser is coated with a special resin that only allows the nutrients to be released when soil conditions are right for plant growth – when moist and warm. The granules generally provide nutrients evenly over a period of four to six months.

These fertilisers are available in various mixes of nutrients but are pricey and expensive for wide use in the open garden. However, they're perfect for crops in containers because they feed your plants evenly over the whole growing season. You can also add them to the compost before planting and to old compost to revitalise it.

Liquid fertilisers

Applying liquid fertiliser is the quickest way to feed your plants. You can buy liquid fertilisers as soluble powders and liquid; you can also buy some ready diluted, but these are more pricey.

Liquid fertilisers are quick-acting – plants can make use of them almost immediately – but they have only a short-term effect. You need to apply them regularly to container plants, which rely on you for all their nutrients and water (Chapter 2 contains more information on growing in containers). In the open garden consider liquid fertiliser as an extra boost of food – you shouldn't normally need to apply it to plants in the open ground.

I recommend feeding your plants once a week while they're actively growing – refer to the guidelines on the pack for the amount. If you prefer you can apply fertiliser more frequently at half-strength but be sure not to apply fertiliser on dry compost or at higher strengths than the pack states because this may scorch the roots.

Generally, only apply liquid fertilisers to moist soil. If the soil is dry, especially when you have plants in containers, water them a few hours prior to feeding so the liquid fertiliser can spread throughout the compost. You can mix the fertilisers with water at half-strength and apply them more often than once a week, but be careful not to make up the solution stronger than the label recommends.

Avoiding animal products

If you want to avoid fertilisers that contain animal products, you can stick to chemical fertilisers. If you prefer to remain organic, seaweed is a good option but it isn't that rich in major plant nutrients. Making your own garden compost and leaf mould adds some extra nutrients to the soil, and rock dust (crushed basalt) – a recent addition to the veg grower's world – is reputed to re-mineralise old, tired soils.

The most useful liquid fertiliser is tomato fertiliser, which is high in potassium and you can use on all fruiting plants. Added calcium in the fertiliser is a bonus, because tomatoes need this to prevent blossom end rot.

Foliar feeding

Foliar feeding is the application of liquid fertilisers, usually at half-strength, to the leaves of plants. Your crops can absorb some nutrients through their leaves, although some, such as most brassicas, have leaves that repel water and so the effect on these is minimal. However, foliar feeding is a useful way to boost most fruit and vegetables – especially any that have damaged root systems or are 'poorly' in some other way. Although this shouldn't apply to most of your crops, foliar feeding may give a helping hand to raspberries that have suffered from waterlogging in winter and are suffering some root damage, or to fast-growing plants such as tomatoes and cucumbers.

Plant tonics

Most plant tonics are based on seaweed or humic acid. Some plant tonic products for sale may not supply a great deal of major nutrients. However, they may benefit your plants by providing trace elements or vitamins, *auxins* (plant hormones), or other compounds that stimulate growth. Although tonics aren't essential and most gardeners don't use them, some tonics do strengthen plants and help them to grow. Tonics are most likely to make a difference on plants in containers such as tomatoes, peppers, aubergines and courgettes.

Organic fertilisers

Your plants aren't fussy whether the nutrients you give them are organic or not, but your plants will thank you for the treat of receiving organic fertilisers. Because most organic fertilisers are made up of dead plants or animals, they contain a wide range of chemicals – not just the main one you're hoping to supply – and are the equivalent of a hearty feast for your plants. Soil organisms have to decompose organic fertilisers before the plants can use them and this process increases the soil flora and fauna that indirectly benefit your plants.

Because they contain lots of other substances, such as proteins and carbohydrates, as well as the plant nutrients you need, organic fertilisers are generally not as concentrated as other fertilisers. As a result, you're less likely to add too much unless you go on a feeding frenzy! And because they have to be decomposed before they release their nutrients your plants don't suddenly get a burst of food and then a slump like a sugar rush – think of them like low-GI fertilisers!

The downside of organic fertilisers is that they can be expensive compared to manufactured varieties, and slightly unpleasant to handle. They also encourage foraging badgers, foxes and dogs into your fruit and veg garden.

Dried blood

Dried blood is available to everyone – not just vampires – at garden centres, and is a fast-acting source of nitrogen. Adding dried blood to the soil before planting your crops and sprinkling or adding it when watering around them in spring, boosts leafy growth of spring cabbage, for example.

Hoof and horn

Hoof and horn is a generally slow-acting source of nitrogen. Depending how finely it's been ground, it should start to release nitrogen within weeks and last for several months. You can dig in hoof and horn before planting or sprinkle it around long-term, leafy crops like cabbages and Brussels sprouts.

Hoof and horn also comes in handy as a good compost activator. (Get down and dirty with compost in Chapter 4.)

Fish, blood, and bone

This mix contains all three materials and supplies nitrogen, phosphorus and potassium. Fish, blood and bone releases its nutrients slowly and so makes a good, general purpose fertiliser for crops that stay in the soil for more than a few months.

Bonemeal

Bonemeal is made from ground-up bones, and provides phosphorus for plant roots and some calcium for your crops. However, bonemeal has limited application in your vegetable and fruit garden because your soil has enough phosphorus anyway and most general fertilisers, such as fish, blood and bone, have enough for your plants and also contain other useful nutrients.

Chicken manure

The new kid on the organic fertiliser block, chicken manure is a useful fertiliser, relatively high in nitrogen, cleaner to handle than you may think, but with a pungent smell. You can use chicken manure liberally around all plants to give them a balanced meal.

Seaweed meal

Seaweed isn't rich in major plant nutrients but does contain *alginates*, which can boost some plant growth and may improve soil, as well as many trace elements. Use seaweed meal in conjunction with other fertilisers as a tonic.

Chapter 6

Becoming a Greener Gardener: Growing Organic

*G*rowing your crops organically can be an appealing prospect and growing food without resorting to artificial chemicals is a sound idea. After all, in the modern world more and more people want to know exactly what they're eating. In fact, organic gardening has never been more popular.

Gardeners who adopt organic methods today often do so out of concern for their health or the environment, but a big part of the reason for the growth of organic gardening is that in some ways gardeners don't have much choice. Legislation has made it financially unviable for manufacturers to produce some chemicals for home gardeners, and this situation is unlikely to change much in the near future. This means that the chemical arsenal available for fighting pests and diseases will only get smaller.

Organic gardening isn't a new idea and neither is it quirky. Instead, organic gardening is based on sound principles, such as growing plants that best suit your conditions and avoiding cultivating large areas of a single crop – a practice that decreases biodiversity and encourages population explosions of one pest or disease without encouraging natural ways of controlling them. Indeed, most principles of organic gardening were used by our grandfathers decades ago, and until widely available chemicals arrived on the agricultural scene, everybody grew their food organically.

Organic gardeners avoid the use of manufactured fertilisers, pesticides and fungicides that may not kill pests alone but beneficial organisms too and, by encouraging a natural balance, the idea is that no pest or disease ever reaches serious proportions. Organic gardening involves a degree of compromise – you're unlikely to escape some attack from pests and diseases – but organic growers argue that food grown without artificial chemicals is better for you. That's a heated debate, but what isn't in question is that many organic principles are grounded in common sense.

Put simply, people who grow their fruit and veg organically look at the whole picture on their plots, tending to all their plants' needs rather than applying a cure to one or two symptoms. You can think of organic gardening a bit like holistic medicine, in that you don't just treat the symptom, you look after the whole body.

Deciding How Organic You Want to Be: Horses for Courses

Yes – you do have a choice! Commercial organic growers need to follow strict rules about what they can and can't do. You, on the other hand, can be as organic as you want. Purists may argue that you can no more be partly organic than partly vegetarian, but by not labelling yourself you can plough your own furrow! After all, gardening is rewarding and fun, and the point of growing your own crops is that you get something to eat. So weigh up what is most important to you and pick and choose from the main principles.

Going organic means that your options are more limited when you come to feed your plants, maintain your beds and control pests, so life isn't so easy for the organic gardener. But you can find solutions to every problem even if you have to think a bit harder about what to do instead of reaching for the nearest bottle of chemicals! Being armed with information is the best way to make choices and to help you wade through the many practical, ethical and environmental considerations of going organic. But at the end of the day, even if you don't want to go down the organic route, you can borrow many good principles from organic gardening while counting yourself as a 'normal' gardener.

Going organic throws up some difficult problems, requires extra work on your part and takes up more of your time. Whether the benefits are worthwhile is your decision, but you can cheat a little at first and go more and more organic as you gain experience.

Every year in the garden is different and results vary. With every dig of the spade you gain experience and strive for better results. So even if at first you fail with organic crops, do keep trying!

Understanding the Ins and Outs of Organic Gardening

Organic gardening isn't complicated, but to count yourself as a grower of organic fruit and vegetables, you need to know what organic gardening actually involves. That's where this section comes in.

Knowing your priorities: The soil comes first

In organic gardening, the answer really does lie in the soil. Soil is a complex, living mixture of minerals and organic matter, constantly changing but always full of the things plants need, and getting it in good condition is essential.

The soil is a huge reservoir of nutrients and you need to keep it fully stocked. As we harvest our crops we take many nutrients away from our plots, and we need to put as much back as possible. So build an extra compost heap, get a delivery of mushroom compost, and pester your local stable or farmer for manure to add more nutrients to the soil! That way your soil will improve every year, your crops will grow better, and you will leave your soil in improved condition for the next generation of gardeners. (Chapter 4 contains lots more tips on how to get your soil into great shape.)

Stocking your soil with the nutrients that come from organic matter is the key to getting and keeping your soil in tip-top condition. If you only use inorganic fertilisers and never add any organic matter, the bacteria and fungi in the soil continue to break down the existing organic matter so that eventually only mineral particles remain. These particles, except for clay particles, don't bind the soil together and aren't good at retaining nutrients. Eventually the bacteria and fungi decrease because of the lack of organic matter and the possible increase in soil acidity through the use of fertilisers, and the soil will slowly 'die'. The nutrients that you add will leach through the soil so you have to add more to keep the plants growing. Contrast this with what happens when you add organic matter – improving the holding of nutrients in the soil, reducing leaching, increasing the moisture-holding capacity of the soil, increasing the life and aeration of the soil, and improving the ability of plants to look after themselves – and you soon see the right way to go.

If you take over an abandoned allotment you're likely to find only a few chemical residues, and the natural growth and death of weeds will have added at least some organic matter to the soil. But if you start in a small, urban garden or a new home where the builders have spread just a thin layer of soil over a base of rubble, you may well have a tougher job on your hands to get the soil in good shape.

Adapting to your environment

Plants are at their best in shrugging off pests and diseases when they're growing healthily. It makes sense. If you're in good shape you're less prone to diseases, too. So if you do all that you can to get your site right for your plants, they should grow well. This idea is fundamental to organic growing and is rather like a holistic approach to gardening – rather than treating the symptoms, look at the bigger picture, and prevent rather than treat.

When you travel around the country you can see that farmers grow one or two crops in one region while in another region the crops are totally different. Growers follow this practice because plants vary in their requirements. So it follows that your own style of gardening, the direction in which your garden faces, your soil, and your local climate work better for growing some crops than others. Gardeners, however, don't want to grow just one or two crops but instead want to try and grow as many things as they like to eat. This means you may find yourself growing fruit or veg that doesn't suit your conditions. These plants might struggle, making them more prone to pests or diseases. Organic gardeners accept these limitations if they're so severe that plants can only grow with chemical intervention.

When gardening organically, you need to assess and adapt to your environment by choosing plants best suited to your conditions to ensure that they naturally grow better, are less stressed, and less likely to fall foul of pests and disease. For example, if your garden is subject to late frosts in spring, avoid fruits such as plums that flower in early spring, and don't plant or sow too early. Don't hang around waiting for raspberries to grow on chalk, and avoid planting root crops in heavy soil. If your soil is dry and the site sunny, give plants that prefer rich, moist soils such as celery a wide berth and concentrate instead on herbs, artichokes, tomatoes, peppers and beans. If you have clay soil, you probably also have lots of slugs. Slugs are a potential problem to potatoes but the simple answer is to lift the potatoes as soon as possible and not leave them in the soil for the slugs to feast on.

This approach isn't always practical, but you can also adapt your conditions to suit the crop. For example, if your garden is on an exposed site and prone to destructive strong winds, you can plant a windbreak of tough shrubs or resistant, tall crops such as Jerusalem artichokes so the wind doesn't prevent flying insects from pollinating your fruit trees or rip the leaves off delicate plants like runner beans. Or, if your plot is in the shade of trees, you may have success by growing in containers or raised beds (but make sure you separate them from the underlying soil with a weed fabric or the tree roots will grow upwards into the fertile soil above).

Not every problem has an organic solution, and so you must try to anticipate and avoid problems before they happen. By adapting to your conditions, you're doing just that.

Choosing the right varieties

Choosing the right plant to grow is one thing; choosing the right variety of that plant is another way to increase your chances of raising a successful organic crop. Plant breeders work hard to produce varieties that resist a wide range of growing problems, and some older varieties also have desirable attributes that may suit your conditions. If you look around you'll find lots of varieties of fruits and vegetables that help you grow organically and an increasing range of crops that are resistant, though not immune, to many common and important problems.

Don't just accept the first variety you see up for sale. Instead, assess your soil, environment and needs before looking so that you can seek out varieties that suit your conditions.

When choosing the varieties you want to grow, look out for resistance to disease. You can find:

- ✔ Brassicas that are resistant to clubroot
- ✔ Carrots resistant to carrot fly
- ✔ Courgettes resistant to cucumber mosaic virus and mildew
- ✔ Cucumbers resistant to mildew and other fungal diseases
- ✔ Leeks resistant to rust
- ✔ Lettuce resistant to root aphids
- ✔ Spinach and swede resistant to mildew

. . . and many more. You can even grow fruits that are less prone than other varieties to common pests and diseases such as mildew-resistant strawberries, a peach that resists peach leaf curl, and gooseberries that don't get mildew. Choosing these varieties are small changes to make, but they can affect your plot's yield and keep the number of worry lines on your face to a minimum! I highlight these varieties for you in Parts III and IV.

Choosing organic seeds

Before they go off for sale, seeds are often treated with chemicals to enhance germination and prevent seedling diseases. However, the range of organic seeds available, produced without the use of chemicals, is increasing. Most seed catalogues and ranges in garden centres now include a selection of organically produced seeds. However, whether organically produced seed makes a great difference to the finished crop in terms of yield, taste or general growth is open to debate, but you may want to try them to make up your own mind.

Although the number of seeds produced in this way is growing, that number is still small. Buying only organic seeds limits the range of plants you can grow.

Timing your crops carefully

Attempting to grow plants out of season is fraught with problems; for example, soil fungi can strike if you sow seeds too early and leaf fungi can hit plants growing too late in the season. Taking care to plant crops at the right time can protect them from damage from the weather, from pests and from other problems. (I give you planting times for individual plants in Chapters 8–16.)

Some plants are time-sensitive. Most Oriental vegetables, for example, are sensitive to day length and, even though new varieties are less prone to bolting if you sow them too early, sowing them after the longest day makes sense if you want them to grow to maturity.

Other plants are prone to bolting if they suffer from cold temperatures after they begin to grow. Onions are a typical example. So avoid planting too early. Seeds need warmth to grow and some types, such as French beans, rot rather than sprout if the soil is cold and wet, so delay sowing until the soil is warm.

Potatoes are another crop for which you need to get your timing just right. Blight is the most serious problem for potatoes but usually only strikes in hot, stormy weather after July. So if you live in an area where blight is common, try to avoid growing maincrop potatoes and choose early potatoes instead to harvest before then. Timing can also protect carrots from carrot root fly. By sowing early, under cloches or fleece, or late, in early July, you can miss the main generation of the pest and your carrots then stand a better chance of surviving!

Gardening without chemicals

Mention organic gardening and most people immediately accept that it means avoiding the use of chemicals. The theory at least is that if plants are growing as well as they possibly could be, they won't need constant spraying as they struggle against poor growing conditions. So whereas non-organic gardeners use chemicals in pesticides, fungicides, weedkillers and fertilisers, organic gardeners try to avoid them through prevention rather than cure. However, even organic gardeners have to contend with problems and do resort to using a few chemicals (see the 'Mother Nature's chemistry lab' sidebar).

 Some chemicals that gardeners used in the past are now banned substances. Some have been withdrawn from sale because of the threat they posed to gardeners' health but most because they became uneconomic to manufacture. Therefore, fewer chemicals are now available to gardeners, leaving organic methods as your only option for dealing with certain problems. For example, no soil insecticides are available for home gardeners to use on vegetables and the only way to control cabbage root fly is to outwit the insects and install collars around the base of the plants. Similarly, covering your plants with fleece is the only practical way to prevent carrot root fly affecting most varieties.

Many organic gardeners make their own pesticides or fungicides, often derived from rotting in water plants such as rhubarb leaves, nettles and comfrey, or they use washing-up liquid. However, unlike proprietary chemicals that are extensively tested and can only be sold after they are proved to be safe and effective, you can't test 'home brews' for safety or effectiveness in the same way, and you can't be sure if they work or if they'll damage your plants. Also, the chance of replicating any effective usage is very low. But a more serious reason not to make your own insecticides is that it is against the law!

Gardening without using chemical insecticides enables you to strike a balance in your garden between controlling pests and encouraging beneficial wildlife, without completely eliminating the pests that they come there to eat. For example, using insecticide to wipe out all the slugs and snails in your garden would lead to fewer hedgehogs and thrushes – not because they'd been poisoned but because you've comprehensively removed their food from your garden. In the same way, by eliminating all the aphids in your garden with insecticides, you leave the ladybirds with nothing to eat, but by avoiding insecticides – even organic insecticides – altogether, you give the beneficial insects a better chance to control the pests naturally. Very often aphids appear in early spring and breed rapidly, looking as though they'll kill everything, but then the predators move in and slowly the eat the pests.

Mother Nature's chemistry lab

You may think that going organic means that chemicals are completely out of bounds. Not so! Organic gardening does allow the use of some chemicals. For example, as a fungicide gardenerscan use liquid or powdered sulphur and for controlling pests they're able to use pyrethrum – both natural substances that aren't organic at all. Most organic gardeners also use liquid copper sulphate as a fungicide and fatty acids for insecticide. Mother Nature herself wields an armoury of noxious chemicals: all plants contain chemicals to some extent, some of which are pretty nasty.

Keeping pests away

Without resorting to chemicals, some pests are difficult to control, but alternative methods of control can be just as effective. Your aim is to have a healthy, well-balanced garden home for natural predators that reduce pest numbers – although they rarely wipe out the pests, simply because doing so would mean starvation. For the pests that remain, you have a range of options to prevent them getting to your plants, as follows:

✔ **Erecting physical barriers.** This is the only solution for some pests, especially the larger ones.

• **Growing plants under horticultural fleece or fine netting.** These items act as a barrier to prevent pests from getting to your prized carrots or succulent strawberries. Suspend netting well above the foliage and make sure that snow doesn't weigh it down or pigeons will land on it and peck your plants through the net. Fine (1-centimetre) netting is also effective for protecting brassicas against cabbage white butterflies but, again, make sure it stays well above the leaves or the butterflies will land on the net and lay their eggs through it.

If you're serious about growing redcurrants and raspberries you may want to invest in a fruit cage. This is a walk-in structure covered in fine net to prevent birds stealing your ripe fruit.

Chapter 2 tells you more about using horticultural fleece.

• **Using collars of cardboard or plastic fitted around stems at planting time.** This tactic takes advantage of the fact that carrot root fly never fly more than 45cm above the soil, and is good for keeping brassicas pest-free.

The collar should be at least 15 centimetres in diameter (it can be square). Fit it by cutting a slit from the edge to the centre and after slipping it around the base of the stem, tuck the edges into the soil. As the fly crawls down the stem to lay eggs on the roots, the barrier stops it and the fly gives up – to fly on to your neighbours!

- **Erecting a fence.** Rabbits can quickly ruin your crops and most plants are up for grabs – squashes, tomatoes and potatoes among them. Fence your crops in and the rabbits out by putting up chicken wire with a 2.5 centimetre-mesh around your plot. The wire should be 1 metre high and about 20 centimetres at the base; pull it out and bury it 10 centimetres deep on the outside of your plot to prevent the rabbits burrowing under the fence. If you have troubles with badgers you need something much more stout!

- **Putting other barriers in place.** Some pests slither and slide and the most troublesome of all are slugs and snails. Garderners variously use dried, crushed eggshells, coarse, sharp grit, and copper rings to protect their plants from these pests.

✔ **Setting traps.** Knowing your enemy can help you protect your plants. You can trap slugs by putting beer in shallow containers placed in your border, or with orange and grapefruit skins. Similarly, you can trap earwigs with straw or shredded paper in inverted pots on canes set among your plants. But with traps, make sure that you empty them regularly or you simply provide homes or food for the pests.

✔ **Picking pests off by hand.** This approach isn't as tricky as it sounds; aphids are easily crushed and caterpillars are usually visible when you get used to looking for them and know where they hide (which is usually under the leaves during the day).

✔ **Encouraging wildlife into your garden.** You may find this especially important in your first year if your garden has been heavily sprayed with pesticides in the past, because few predators remain to control pests (check out 'Encouraging beneficial wildlife', later in this chapter).

✔ **Buying a range of biological controls, usually predatory or parasitic insects or *nematodes* (small, worm-like creatures).** However, most of these creatures are only effective in enclosed environments such as greenhouses because they fly away outside.

The most popular biological controls are parasitic wasps that kill greenhouse whitefly. Each wasp (*encarsia*) lays an egg in the developing whitefly and kills it – the wasp hatches out of the dead carcass. You can also buy predators for red spider mite and mealy bug for use in greenhouses, as well as native predators such as ladybirds, but they're expensive. The biological controls for both vine weevil and slugs (not snails) are efficient and their success depends on your soil conditions and ambient temperature. You buy them in *suspended animation*, add them to water and then to the soil in the open garden or in containers, and they then give control throughout summer.

✔ **Using organic pesticide sprays.** These sprays kill insects by blocking their breathing holes or dissolving their waxy coats to dehydrate them. Sprays can keep brassica whitefly, cabbage white butterflies and mealy aphids under control but remember that these sprays kill most insects – not just pests – so use them with caution and ideally at dawn or dusk when bees aren't active.

✔ **Spraying water.** Using a strong jet of water to knock pests off the plants is another effective method of control. Power washers work well against woolly aphids on apple trees in winter, for example, but make sure the water jet isn't so strong that you knock the leaves off the plant or you do more harm than good.

Discouraging disease

Diseases are rather more difficult to deal with organically because you can't remove an infection when it's established in a plant, although you may be able to prevent further infection. You can, however, take several steps to reduce the risk of disease affecting your plants:

✔ **Try to avoid the atmosphere getting too moist wherever possible (for example, when growing in a greenhouse).** Most fungal diseases thrive in a moist atmosphere. In the greenhouse, try to avoid getting leaves wet, especially in cool weather. Unfortunately you can't do much about this outside, so expect to remove a few leaves on affected plants to try and improve air movement so that the leaves dry off.

✔ **Ensure that your plants aren't too crowded together.** Crowding plants together also prevents air movement around them and means the leaves stay damp because of poor air circulation.

✔ **Apply nitrogen fertiliser sensibly when plants are growing.** Too much fertiliser produces easily infected soft, sappy growth. Applying fertilisers high in potassium tends to make growth tougher and more likely to resist infection.

Brassicas are the biggest challenge of all to grow disease-free because lots of potential problems can affect them. However, you can thwart the soil-borne fungus *clubroot* by growing resistant varieties (see Chapter 8), adding lime to the soil, or growing plants until they are quite large, in 12-centimetre pots, before planting out.

Wiping out weeds

Annual weeds are no more difficult to deal with if you're an organic gardener than if you use chemicals, because hoeing is the best way to keep them under control, but perennial weeds are a different matter. Tackling an overgrown plot with just hand weeding, digging and mulching as methods to get your plot clear organically can be tough but rewarding work (although you may think differently and never want to garden again!). I give you the lowdown on dealing with weeds organically in Chapter 2.

If you want to go completely organic, close your eyes now! Many gardeners who are otherwise organic choose initially to use a weedkiller that contains glyphosate. This chemical doesn't leave a residue in the soil and kills the roots of perennials such as bindweed and couch (twitch) grass, which are almost impossible to kill through digging alone. If you choose to use glyphosate, do so when the weeds are actively growing and have a large leaf area. Be warned though – glyphosate kills any plant that you spray it on, breaks down on contact with soil, and isn't absorbed through bark. The effects of glyphosate don't show for a few weeks and you may need to apply more than once on re-growth of strong weeds.

Reducing, reusing, recycling

Most people – and not just organic gardeners – are aware of the need to make the most of resources and the importance of reducing our use of materials, reusing things and recycling. Although even gardeners who want to be organic have to use non-renewable materials such as fleece or plastics, lots *can* be reused. As a bonus, some of these ideas can save you money too, such as using plastic bottles as propagator tops instead of buying them.

To be a truly organic gardener, you may wish to avoid the plastics and other materials (such as woven membranes and fleeces) that many gardeners use to suppress weeds, keep out pests and aid growing. Wood products are an alternative but although wood is a renewable source, it decays and so has a finite life. Some manufacturers are making biodegradable pots from bamboo, but you may decide that reusing yoghurt pots is actually kinder to the earth. Taken to its logical extreme, consuming any bought material is using a resource, so organic gardeners have to take a middle-of-the-road line here or be very restricted in their options.

Many 'organic' products, including peat alternatives, have a large carbon footprint when imported from abroad. This means that fossil fuels are used to transport them, adding carbon dioxide to the environment. Using locally produced products, which have to be transported shorter distances, where possible is a better alternative.

The best approach is to buy and consume as little as you can, compost all your waste, recycle water, reuse materials and reduce your carbon footprint as much as possible.

Cultivating comfrey

Many organic gardeners can't manage without a patch of comfrey, which grows almost anywhere and has deep roots that bring up valuable nutrients. The leaves are rich in many minerals, particularly phosphates, and you can cut them off and add them to the compost heap, make them into a (smelly) organic liquid fertiliser, or use them as a mulch around plants. Established comfrey plants grow to 1 metre high and wide and the flowers are attractive to bumble bees, although you need to remove the leaves before the flowers appear. Simply cut off the foliage near ground level. You should be able to harvest the leaves two or three times a year.

Choose your comfrey wisely! Buying *thongs* or roots of Bocking 24 is the way to go, because they don't set seed or spread across your plot.

To make comfrey fertiliser, just follow these easy steps:

1. **Fill a bucket, with a hole in the base, with tightly packed comfrey leaves.** Top up with more leaves as necessary.

2. **Place a brick or other weight on the leaves to compress them.**

3. **Stand the bucket in a bowl to collect the smelly brown liquid that results and dilute this in water to the colour of tea and use on your plants.**

You can use nettles in a similar way, but be warned – the results are even smellier!

Comfrey has bristly leaves that can cause skin irritation.

Living with imperfection

Organic gardening is often a case of working with nature rather than against it, and of accepting some damage to your crops. This is something that we've come to find unacceptable in the supermarket crops many of us are accustomed to – produce that has to be graded to meet regulations imposed to meet targets and achieve price points. But when you grow your own and discover that carrots come ready-coated in dirt and that cabbages often have caterpillars that you need to pick off, you come to accept small deficiencies in appearance for the advantage in taste and freshness. In most cases it doesn't matter if a few holes are present in your crops or if you need to pick off a few leaves with mildew. These kinds of imperfections don't affect the eating quality of the crops, so don't panic. Although experts have bred modern varieties to produce uniform-sized produce, this just isn't an important consideration for many people.

Supermarkets are just beginning to realise that not everyone wants perfect, blemish-free fruits and vegetables. If you decide to grow organically, your produce may well have its share of marks and nibbles – which doesn't matter at all – but you can head off the worst of the problems by following the advice I give you in earlier sections of this chapter. You can, however, accept only a certain amount of damage from pests such as rabbits, slugs and caterpillars.

Gardening with nature

Even when sticking to your organic principles, as soon as you take up a spade, remove any weeds and plant some tomatoes, you're altering nature, because you're changing the environment. But the most basic principles of gardening – those that you adopt when going organic – tend to go along with the way nature wants you to do your gardening. We plant at the right time, grow plants that suit our garden, and where they're most likely to thrive.

Encouraging beneficial wildlife

Wildlife is wonderful in the garden but even I sometimes curse the blackbirds who bring up their young on my blueberries and redcurrants. Some wildlife is even more destructive, but one of the best things you can do to help your garden is to encourage beneficial wildlife to your plot, particularly birds, to even up the balance of pest and predator. Thrushes wolf down snails, and tits, lacewings, hoverflies and ladybirds all just love the taste of aphids. Even sparrows eat insects and help to keep your plants free from pests.

Here are a few more tips on how to entice the birds and the bees to your plot:

- ✓ **Do without the chemicals.** Refer to the 'Gardening without chemicals' section earlier in the chapter for more info.

- ✓ Sow flowers, such as poached egg flower (limnanthes), marigolds, phacelia and fennel, to encourage beneficial insects. Not all insects count as unwelcome pests; for example, although hoverflies look like wasps, they're harmless and mostly eat pollen, and their larvae devour vast quantities of aphids. Do your bit to encourage them to your garden and you'll have fewer pests to contend with. Bees, who move on to pollinate your crops, are beneficial too.

- ✓ **Leave a small area of long grass to encourage ground beetles, which love to tuck into slugs.**

- ✓ **Dig a small pond to bring a lot more wildlife to your plot, including frogs and toads, which eat slugs and woodlice, among other creatures.** A shady area works fine if you don't want to give up valuable growing space in the sun.

- ✓ **Have some weed species such as dead nettles and stinging nettles near your plot because they're good for wildlife.** Nettles are food for butterflies (apart from the cabbage white butterflies who don't eat them and which you can do without anyway!) and aphids, which in turn ensure that you have a healthy ladybird population. Dead nettles flower early in spring and provide vital nectar for bumble-bees. You don't need to let these weeds run wild – just have a clump or two. The young shoots of nettles are actually edible if lightly and quickly boiled and are a useful green veg in early spring!

✔ **Grow a hedge of native plants (such as elder and sloe) or those that berry (such as hawthorn and viburnum) to screen your plot from winds.** This protection not only gives your crops a boost, but also encourages birds that eat pests to nest. Even the much-maligned conifer provides good nesting sites and a perfect place for ladybirds to overwinter in.

✔ **Offer your wildlife some accommodation.**

- Put up nesting boxes to encourage the tits and sparrows that eat aphids and the bees that pollinate your plants.

- Allow some ivy to cover walls and fences to provide shelter for wrens, which search for insects to eat. Ivy also provides a home for hibernating butterflies that will grace your garden in summer and lacewings, which devour aphids for you.

- Plant some dense conifers – perfect places for aphid-eating ladybirds to hibernate in winter.

- Don't be too tidy! Leave some old, dead plant stems in the garden for insects to shelter in over winter, especially if the stems are hollow.

- Leave an area of long grass or nettles in a corner of the garden. Nettles are great wildlife plants. Caterpillars of many butterflies eat them, and aphids colonise them in spring, which encourages tits to your garden and provides food for the first generation of ladybirds.

- Make a log pile to provide shelter for frogs, which eat pests, and install a hedgehog house. It needn't be elaborate – just find some logs and stack them, leaving a range of different-sized gaps between the pieces. Ideally, put your hedgehog house on soil so that toads can burrow under the timber and hibernate. As the bark rots, woodlice will move in and live and form a ready food supply for the toads. As fungi start to grow, these also provide food for lots of insects. If you can't find logs, ordinary untreated timber works fine as long as you leave lots of gaps.

- If you feel really kind you can buy all manner of homes for beneficial insects such as lacewings and ladybirds. These homes are often attractive and fascinating for children. You can find these in good garden centres or buy them via mail order.

Getting pally with companion planting

In *companion planting* you choose neighbouring plants carefully so they encourage or hinder the growth of other plants. This area is a tricky part of gardening and for each gardener who swears that companion planting works, you meet another who's less convinced.

They're a-comin' ta getcha...

Here are just a few common garden pests and the beneficial creatures that keep them at bay:

✔ Ants – a favourite meal for toads and birds

✔ Aphids – favoured by ladybirds, hoverflies and lacewings

✔ Cockchafers – the larvae make a tasty dish for starlings and other birds

✔ Earwigs – birds, frogs and toads just love their taste

✔ Leafminers – are preyed on by parasitic wasps

✔ Pea and bean weevils – birds and some other beetles eat these

✔ Sawflies – are a favourite of birds and spiders

✔ Wireworms – birds keep these pests at bay

✔ Woodlice – frogs, toads, birds, shrews and spiders all attack and keep these pests under control

Some companion planting ideas are based on common sense. For example, some gardeners grow garlic and onions to help reduce fungal diseases on other plants, and nasturtiums to discourage woolly aphids on apple trees. Others grow tomatoes and basil to boost each other's growth, and clover in the lawn to benefit grass growth because clover produces nitrogen from its roots that feeds the lawn. Likewise, sweetcorn and brassicas grow well with peas and beans because the latter have nodules in their roots with bacteria that add nitrogen to the soil, a nutrient that brassicas and sweetcorn need. Other ideas are less obvious, such as nasturtiums under apple trees deterring woolly aphids. The negative effect that some plants have on others may simply be down to one plant growing more vigorously than another and stealing the most water, nutrients and light.

Here are a few combinations of plants that grow well together:

✔ Asparagus, tomatoes and parsley

✔ Aubergine and peppers

✔ Beetroot, beans, brassicas and onions

✔ Broad beans, brassicas, carrots, potatoes and summer savory

✔ Cabbage and celery

✔ Carrots, leeks, onions, peas and chives

✔ Celery and leeks

- ✔ Courgettes, sunflowers, beans, peas and dill
- ✔ French beans and sweetcorn
- ✔ Lettuce, carrots, courgettes, radishes and strawberries
- ✔ Potatoes, beans, brassicas, sweetcorn and turnips

Just as important is to make sure that you don't grow large areas of any one plant, because this allows pests to spread quickly through a crop. Interspersing your plants with different crops or sowing rows of flowers between them encourages a wide range of insects, some of which are beneficial.

Offering up crops for sacrifice

Sometimes you just can't avoid getting some pests and diseases on your plot. However, to stay on top of the problem you can make use of a variation on the companion plant idea, based not on some altruism on the part of the plants but on the fact that some plants are so desirable to pests that they leave others alone.

You can effectively sacrifice certain plants to pests and diseases to keep them away from the crops that really matter. For example, nasturtiums are a difficult plant to grow well because blackfly and cabbage white caterpillars find it irresistible. You can use nasturtiums among brassicas and broad beans to attract the pests away from your crops.

Sacrificial crops are even worthwhile when you're cultivating a pest-resistant variety. For example, the new carrots that are resistant to carrot root fly have variable success because the flies still lay their eggs on them when no other carrots are around. These varieties are more successful with a sacrificial row of ordinary carrots growing among the resistant varieties to lure the pests away.

Slugs and snails are indiscriminate browsers of a wide range of plants but they have a big appetite for succulent lettuce. If you sow some lettuce among other crops you may find that the lettuces protect the other plants.

Getting biodynamic

Biodynamic gardening aims to harness the life forces of plants and the earth so that gardeners only compost young plants, full of life force, rather than old ones. This practice is gaining popularity and is an extension of organic gardening in that gardeners consider not just the chemical needs of plants but also their life forces and energies from the earth.

Mooning around in the garden

Planting by the lunar calendar is an ancient idea that connects what you do in the garden with the patterns and rhythms of the moon, the idea being that you sow leaf, flower and root crops at the most suitable time in the lunar cycle. Having been around for so long, this practice is more than just a fad and many gardeners swear that it's effective. Other gardeners, though, think of lunar gardening as nothing more than hocus pocus. A good place to find out more information is the Lunar Organics website at www.lunarorganics.com. If you're interested, you can take a look and make up your own mind about it.

Assessing the Pros and Cons

Whether or not to go organic is a tough call. Although the basics of organic gardening are sensible and rooted in common sense, getting started in organic gardening can be tough and I suggest that you be flexible and take advantage of all the help you can get when starting out – deciding not to use any chemicals at all is making life more difficult for yourself (see the 'Deciding How Organic You Want to Be: Horses for Courses' section earlier in this chapter). While many people say you can't be partly organic, I disagree. I adopt a middle-of-the-road approach, but the decision is yours!

Whenever you make a decision, you have pros and cons to think of. Here is a rundown of things to consider when deciding whether to take the plunge and go organic:

✔ **Health:** Organic gardeners may claim that organic produce is actually more nutritious than conventionally grown food, although little evidence exists that this is so. However, food grown naturally, in season and without excess chemicals and water, is more nutritious than a lot of what you can buy in the shops. Leafy crops and root crops especially, which often have the biggest pesticide residues, may be worth growing organically.

Eating as much fruit and veg as possible, whether organic or not, benefits your health.

✔ **Cost:** Being organic doesn't necessarily have substantial cost implications, although it can do. Some organic products have a price premium and organic fertilisers usually cost more than their chemical alternatives, but if you don't buy them, and reuse and recycle as much as possible instead, you can save money.

✔ **Quality:** People look at quality in different ways. Organic crops may not always be as picture-postcard perfect as the ones you see in the shops, which can put some people off, but if you're not bothered by a few imperfections you can have the satisfaction of enjoying produce that you've grown in closer connection with Mother Nature.

✔ **Environment:** Most people nowadays are keen to leave our inheritors a healthy, fertile planet rather than a dust bowl. We all need to look after our small pieces of the planet and caring for the soil with organic principles and allowing wildlife to survive helps you to do your bit in protecting the earth for future generations.

Additionally, if you're an organic consumer rather than an organic recycler, you could end up buying lots of 'green' products you don't need, adding to your carbon footprint rather than reducing it. So if you want to be organic and green, think carefully about what you really need before you buy it.

✔ **Taste:** The issue of taste is a tricky one. Many gardeners swear that organic food tastes better. Certainly, naturally grown crops that aren't pumped full of water and fertiliser are likely to have more taste, but whether this is entirely due to them being organic is debatable. What is certain is that fresh, home-grown food is best for you.

✔ **Practicality:** In most cases, organic principles are common sense and should result in good crops. The trouble comes when something goes wrong and you want to reach for a spray to help. Although some sprays that organic gardeners approve of are natural, they're no less harmful to beneficial insects than chemicals are. So rather than letting the pest or disease run wild, you have other options such as picking off pests or sacrificing a crop for the greater good, though this takes more time and effort than the non-organic choices. I suppose whether or not you do this depends on how hungry you are!

Chapter 7

Spotting Signs of Trouble

· ·

In This Chapter

▶ Forestalling problems on your plot

▶ Forecasting problems with the weather

▶ Dealing with common pests and diseases

· ·

*Y*ou're a lucky gardener indeed if you manage to have a full season without being affected by pest or disease problems. In fact, I'd say its more or less impossible, unfortunately. Some problems affect just specific crops, whereas others are ready to pounce on almost anything growing, but although these problems are almost inevitable, the good news is that they're not worth losing sleep over. By knowing what to expect and how to deal with a pest or a disease when it strikes, you can be ready to take action, and that's what this chapter is all about.

Keeping Problems at Bay

You can reduce or avoid many potential problems, including nutrient deficiencies, pests and diseases, through sensible planning. Not all crops are going to grow well in your area and if you avoid planting a huge plantation of any one crop you're less likely to suffer from a pest or disease or its effect.

Selecting suitable crops

Choosing crops that are best suited to your soil and climate can help you to avoid many common problems that grow-your-own gardeners often face. Choosing varieties that have some resistance to particular troubles can boost your chances of successful crop cultivation still further. Modern breeding has produced new varieties that have at least some resistance to many fungal diseases, although resistance to insects is less common. I tell you about the conditions that different crops like best, and give you plenty of varieties to choose from, in the chapters of Parts III and IV.

When selecting crops, some gardeners adopt the practice of *companion planting* – using plants to repel pests and disease or to benefit a crop in some way such as attracting pollinators or beneficial insects such as hoverflies. Chapter 6 tells you more about companion planting.

Looking at crop rotation

Crop rotation means avoiding growing the same crop on a given piece of land for three or four years. If you grow a crop in the same place, in the same soil, for many years, not only do pests and diseases particular to those crops build up in the soil and surrounding vegetation, but also the soil gets depleted of any nutrients associated with that crop. For this reason gardeners use crop rotation to help keep their plots in good shape and divide their crops into the following four groups, which have generally common likes and dislikes:

- ✔ **Legumes** – all peas and beans
- ✔ **Onion family** – onions, garlic, leeks and shallots
- ✔ **Carrot and tomato family** – carrots, parsnips, celery, potatoes, tomatoes and peppers
- ✔ **Brassicas** – cabbages, cauliflower, radishes, swede and turnips

The vegetables in this list don't generally suffer from serious, soil-based problems and come from varied plant families. So, for practical purposes, if you don't intend growing a lot of vegetables from the second group, for example, you can fit your courgettes, marrows, leaf beet or beetroot into that group. You don't have to be too strict about crop rotation; the key thing is to try and avoid growing the same crop in the same soil for two years running.

Not all these crops like the same conditions, so the order in which you plant them can be important. For example, brassicas benefit from lime being added to the soil but potatoes develop scab in limy soil. Peas and beans add nitrogen to the soil but root crops, in general, don't respond well to heavy feeding. Follow this order on your beds and you can't go far wrong:

1. **Ideally, divide your plot into four, roughly equal sections. Call them plots A–D.**

2. **In the first year, plant legumes in plot A, the onion family in plot B, the carrot and tomato family in plot C, and brassicas in plot D.**

3. **In the second year, plant the onion family in plot A, the carrot and tomato family in plot B, brassicas in plot C, and legumes in plot D.**

4. **In the third year, plant the carrot and tomato family in plot A, brassicas in plot B, legumes in plot C, and the onion family in plot D.**

5. **In the fourth year, plant brassicas in plot A, legumes in plot B, the onion family in plot C, and the carrot and tomato family in plot D.**

6. **In the fifth year, plant as in the first year: legumes in plot A, the onion family in plot B, the carrot and tomato family in plot C, and brassicas in plot D, and so on.**

In this way, all the plants benefit from what has grown there before and you grow only a particular plant group in a plot once every four years, apart from any miscellaneous vegetables you also grow that don't fit into the main plant groups.

Add lime to the brassica crop plot in the autumn before planting, to counter the possibility of clubroot. In this rotation system, the effect of lime benefits the brassica crop but has less effect for the following legume crop, which also likes lime. It has less effect still for the onions, which aren't too fussy and least of all for the potato crop, which dislikes lime. You can then add lime (a white powder) in the autumn of that year, ready for the brassicas again. In general, a good amount is to add about 100–200 grams of lime per square metre.

Green manures are useful for revitalising soil. If sown in early autumn, perhaps after a potato crop is lifted, they add organic matter to the soil and if it includes legumes, add nitrogen to the soil too, which brassicas appreciate in the following year. (I talk at more length about green manures in Chapter 4.)

Of course, crop rotation may not always be possible and you're bound to plant some fruit trees and bushes and permanent crops. Also, depending on the setup in your garden, dividing your plot into four areas may not always be practical. You may only have one or two raised beds. But I suggest that you still follow the basic principle of crop rotation – that is to avoid planting the same crop, or any members of the plant group, in the same soil year after year – to prevent the accumulation of pest and disease problems.

A few exceptions exist to the rule of moving crops around the garden. For example, you may have a neighbour, friend or fellow plot holder who digs out a bean trench in autumn in the same place year after year to incorporate his old veg plants and kitchen waste that add organic matter and nutrients to enrich the soil. Many people make a marrow bed and fill this with manure every winter. Both methods probably get great results because the crops are enriching the soil and making conditions perfect. But the constant danger is that a specific problem is accumulating in the soil and that one year the crop may fail. The better move is always to avoid cropping the land with the same crop for many years.

Because most fruit plants occupy the soil for many years, crop rotation doesn't really apply to fruit. But you need to replace strawberries after two or three years and raspberries usually after about ten to fifteen years. You can't include them in a normal crop rotation but, when you come to replant them, make sure you plant them in soil that hasn't hosted the same plant for at least several years beforehand.

Identifying the Most Common Problems

Some problems are likely to affect your crops, whatever you plant and wherever you grow. You have to be prepared for certain problems every season, although others are less frequent.

Considering climatic problems

Every gardener's favourite subject – the British weather! In general, even despite recent changes in the weather, the UK has a fairly moderate climate. Winters aren't too severe or summers too hot for most crops. Even when more extreme weather does arrive the home gardener can stay contented by growing a wide range of crops: for example, an unusually hot, dry spell in summer may not suit everything, but a few plants just love those conditions (although spelling disaster for celery, this weather leads to a bumper crop of peppers and tomatoes). Gardeners can do little about the weather, but understanding how it affects crops enables you to look after your plants and protect them against the elements when more extreme weather hits.

Wind

Wind has several, more subtle effects apart from blowing down rows of runner beans and sweetcorn! As wind speed increases, more water evaporates from the soil and from plant leaves, and so their need for water increases. Even in cool weather, wind can dehydrate plant leaves.

Large-leaved, big plants such as courgettes, marrows and other squashes are most prone to wind damage. Wind can also ruin runner beans and so dwarf varieties make a good choice on windy sites. Most brassicas withstand wind well, though you may need to support overwintered crops such as Brussels sprouts and broccoli by staking them.

Fruit, especially tree fruit, which flowers early in the year, isn't well suited to exposed, windy sites – wind is the usual culprit when a fruit plant or tree performs poorly. Bees, though hardworking, aren't as likely to fly and pollinate trees that are growing in exposed sites.

Wind is especially damaging to young plants that you've grown in the greenhouse, under a cold frame (a low, mini-greenhouse) or indoors. Their growth is soft and unused to any wind at all, and so when planted out they get scorched by the sun and dehydrated by wind. Make sure that you *harden off* your plants – that is, acclimatise them to outside conditions before planting them out. Do this by putting them outside on mild, cloudy days, but protecting them from night frost, for a week or so before planting out.

Cold, spring winds make producing early crops very difficult and, although they help dry the soil, aren't good news for the veg gardener. Consider growing early crops under cloches or fleece but make sure that you fix them securely or you may lose your equipment as well as your veg! Polytunnels are useful too, but make sure that you buy one with strong, steel hoops and that you securely fix the cover.

Shelter from strong and persistent wind aids all crops. On windy sites plant a hedge or some screening shrubs, or erect a windbreak (something that doesn't cause too much shade) to reduce wind speed. You can also consider planting some fast-growing willows, a few hazels or even bamboo, not only to reduce wind but also to provide supports to stake and prop up plants. Jerusalem artichokes also make a good windbreak as well as a tasty crop!

Frost

Believe it or not, winter frosts are generally a good thing for gardeners. They help to reduce pest numbers and, if you've got your digging done early, frost helps to break up large clods of clay soils. On a freezing January day you may dream of warmer climes, but frost doesn't damage most plants and actually benefits the majority. The damaging and dangerous frosts are late frosts, which usually arrive in April and into May when plants have started growing or flowering.

Spring frosts rarely damage hardy, well-established vegetables, but don't plant out tender veg plants such as tomatoes until all risk of spring frost has passed. Late frosts are frequently damaging to blackcurrants and strawberries and frost often ruins the blossom of plums, peaches and apricots at flowering time.

The benefits of cold

Many of our crops would grow better if we had warmer weather, especially in summer, but lots of fruit actually needs cold in winter for it to flower and then produce fruit. This is because apples, pears and many others have the ability to 'count' how many cold days they've had and only when enough cold days have passed do they 'know' that winter is over and produce flower buds. In frost-free climates apples will not crop.

Temperatures can vary substantially on hills. Cold air tends to roll down hills at night and accumulate in frost pockets in lowland areas. Dense hedges and especially fences and walls set halfway down the slope can trap this cold air and damage blossom. You can't do much about this, but be aware that if you live at the bottom of a hill you can get more late frosts than someone living halfway up the same hill! You may need to adjust your planting accordingly by avoiding fruit that flowers early or avoiding early sowings.

Cold snaps

Weather can be unpredictable, with warm spells following cold weather. These variations don't harm most plants but some vegetables may respond oddly because they think that summer is over and winter has arrived. When the weather warms up again they think spring has sprung and try to flower. So apple trees may open some flower buds in late summer, which usually causes no harm. Cold snaps can have a worse effect on onions, carrots, beetroot, and sometimes even Brussels sprouts and leeks, encouraging them to produce flower stems, which means you don't get a crop.

Rather than gardening strictly by the calendar, watch the weather instead and bear in mind where you live – a huge difference in season exists between the mild south-west and the colder north-east. Be flexible. Seasons vary enormously, as do instructions on seed packets. The average seed packet advises that you sow carrots between March and May. The weather in March can be warm and ideal for seed germination or it can be freezing cold and wet. Seeds sown in cold, wet weather rot instead of germinating and you have to sow again a month or more later. Never be in a hurry to sow too early – later sowings always catch up!

Drought

Although most plants survive short periods of dry weather, you want your vegetable and fruit plants to do more than just survive – you want them to thrive and to produce crops. Plants kept short of water suffer in various ways (see the sidebar 'The effects of drought'). Any plants in pots are particularly prone to drying out, so make sure that you water them regularly.

The danger of late spring frosts

Although winter cold doesn't damage hardy blackcurrants and other soft fruits, late frosts can have a devastating effect on the plants and their crops. This is because, in our topsy-turvy climate when a cold snap can follow a warm spell, some plants are tricked into producing tender new growth too early. This growth, often accompanied by flowers, is what a late frost is most likely to harm rather than the main plant itself.

The effects of drought

Drought affects crops in a variety of ways. Here are some examples:

- Potatoes deprived of adequate water as the tubers are swelling may become hollow or stop growing and restart when the soil becomes moist again, leading to unusual and awkward shapes.

- The roots of carrots, parsnips, radish and other root crops deprived of water stop growing and then grow again as the soil is moistened. Frequently, the roots split lengthways making them useless. If this doesn't happen the plants are stressed and instead of producing edible roots they send up a flower stem (bolt) and don't produce a crop.

- If stressed by water shortage, spinach and other leafy crops such as lettuce and pak choi stop producing leaves and start to flower and no more leaves can be harvested from them.

- Tomatoes are tough plants and gardeners generally go by the rule that if they're grown 'hard' and have to struggle a little for water, the fruits taste better than if the plants have all their water requirements provided in excess, leading to 'flabby' tasteless fruits. However, don't take this idea too far. Allowing plants to dry out between watering – easy to do if plants are growing in containers or growing bags – often causes the skins to toughen and when they are watered again the plants take up water and the skins split. More seriously, this watering regime also leads to blossom end rot: a black, sunken area in the base of the fruits. (See Chapter 7 for more on plant disease.)

- Onions kept short of water while they grow are more likely to bolt and produce a flower stem. Once set in motion, the bulbs don't develop and the crop is lost.

- If strawberries are short of water as the fruits start to swell soon after the petals of the flowers drop, they don't grow into soft and delicious summer fruits but become malformed and less pleasant.

- Other fruits are affected by drought in different ways. Apples, pears, plums, among others, shed their small, developing fruits if they're short of water in early summer. This effect is sometimes called *June drop* and is often natural – the tree seems to know whether it can carry its crop to maturity and, if the initial fruit set is heavy, it sheds some of its fruits. But June drop is more serious if the soil is dry. With other fruits, such as cherries and plums, a period of drought followed by watering or rain causes the skins of the fruits to split as the trees take up water rapidly.

 Newly sown and germinating seedlings are very vulnerable to drying out before they've emerged from the soil and this problem is a common cause of failure. In dry weather, always water the seed row before sowing so the seeds have instant contact with moisture. (I give you more tips on watering your plants in Chapter 5.)

Wet, dull weather

Just as lack of water can cause problems, so can too much. Rain usually comes with dull skies and lack of sun, meaning that fruits don't ripen well, pods rot off and courgettes go mouldy on the plant. Unfortunately, you can't do a great deal to prevent too much rain, though I offer a few suggestions in the 'Waterlogging' section later in this chapter.

Sorting out soil problems

Nutritional problems that are down to a lack of nutrients in the soil sometimes occur, but they are uncommon. You can avoid them by adding in organic matter and using organic fertilisers to naturally supply trace elements, which sometimes cause problems if they're in short supply. (Refer to Chapter 4 for tips on keeping your soil in good shape.)

Most worries that gardeners have with soil are down to a lack of water or a deluge of it.

Waterlogging

Waterlogged soil deprives plant roots of air, which they can't live without. So although adequate moisture is essential, standing water on the soil surface, or a zone of wet soil near the surface, prevents plants from growing well. Also, because waterlogged soil takes longer than average to warm up in spring, it delays successful sowing. Seeds don't germinate in wet, cold soils.

Many different factors can lead to waterlogging of the soil, including clay particles preventing a natural lack of water flow through the soil, repeated walking on the soil causing compaction, or a layer in the soil, perhaps below the soil surface, that stops water draining away. Of course, heavy rain can also cause waterlogging. The problem is most likely in winter and on clay soils.

Installing drainage is expensive and may not always sort the problem, so the easiest way to deal with waterlogging is probably to plant your plants in raised beds or on ridges to raise the crops above the wet soil, which can be especially useful with onions and garlic. Digging the soil to relieve soil compaction, and digging in organic matter and grit, also helps to reduce surface waterlogging. Soils are most likely to be waterlogged in winter and it may be best to avoid sowing crops that occupy soils at that time.

Drought

Light, sandy soils cause a different problem because they dry out rapidly. In drought conditions, fruits are shed, crops are poor, and seedlings die. You can make things better for your plants by adding as much organic matter as you can to your soil (a good amount would be a barrowful per square metre) and by mulching crops, at least 3 centimetres deep, as well as watering them regularly.

Dealing with common pests

Some pests go crazy for certain crops, and I discuss these in the 'Controlling Plant-Specific Problems' section later on, but many creatures aren't so fussy and attack a wide range of fruit and vegetable crops. Some are serious whereas others are only a nuisance. Read this wanted list and be ready for the garden invaders.

Aphids

Sometimes called *plant lice*, aphids are abundant pests that come in various colours and forms and though some are specific to certain plants, aphids can attack almost every plant in your garden. They are small with soft bodies that a wide range of other creatures such as ladybirds and birds devour. But, to make up for this weakness, aphids reproduce at an alarming rate, and a few aphids can turn into a colony in just a few days.

Fortunately, aphids, which include all those creatures we call greenfly and blackfly (even though they may also be pink or brown!), are easy to kill with most types of insecticides (including organic types) and are also easy to squash if you want to be really organic and thrifty. You can also cover plants with fleece to prevent aphid attacks.

What aphids do is to suck the sap out of plants, and they can cause distortion of young plant growths. More seriously, they can spread viral infections from one plant to another. These infections cause a wide range of diseases, from *cucumber mosaic virus* that weakens, stunts and eventually kills courgettes, marrows and squashes to *reversion virus* in blackcurrants. Viral infections also cause a general lack of vigour and yellowing of leaves in strawberries.

No cure exists for virus diseases. Because they generally lead to a lack of vigour and cropping, you need to make sure that all fruit plants, which you can expect to last for many years, are free from virus diseases. This should be clearly stated when you buy them. When viruses attack vegetables, however, you can generally do little but remove and dispose of affected plants to prevent the spread of the disease.

Cutworms

Cutworms are brownish caterpillars that live in the soil and feed on plant roots and stems, especially brassicas and lettuce. They slice through the stems and 'fell' young plants. No chemical treatment exists for dealing with the menace of cutworms, but digging often exposes them, allowing you to then kill them by squashing them, chopping them in half, or throwing them to birds.

Scale

Scale insects are small, brown, oval creatures protected by a waxy shell. They are most common on shoots and stems and beside the main veins on the underside of leaves and tend to be pests of evergreen shrubs such as bay and citrus. They hardly look like an insect at all and rarely move when they've found a place to feed where they just suck the sap from plants. As they suck, they secrete a sticky substance called *honeydew*. This honeydew falls onto the lower leaves and becomes colonised with a black fungus called *sooty mould*, which is more obvious than the scale insect and may be the first sign of trouble. You can scrape scales off or you can spray with a systemic insecticide. Eventually the sooty mould washes off.

Rabbits

In rural areas rabbits can be destructive pests, devouring most crops, although they usually avoid potatoes, tomatoes, artichokes and all the squashes including courgettes and marrows. They eat all fruit bushes and even strip the bark from trees in winter.

Spiral, plastic tree guards protect trees and some spray-on repellants have an effect but the most effective method of preventing damage by rabbits is to erect some sort of barrier to keep them away from your crops. Chicken wire netting that's 1-metre wide, with the bottom 20 centimetres bent away from your plot along the soil surface and then buried, stops the scrabbling rabbits burrowing under and getting to your prized veg.

Rodents

Rodents can be a real nuisance and I find that rats, in particular, love cape gooseberries. The other crop that's always attacked is sweetcorn, but you may find that strawberries also attract rats and other rodents. Rats are difficult to control and you must use rat bait with care because it may affect hedgehogs as well as birds. If you do use it, make sure that your bait traps that aren't accessible to other wildlife.

Birds

Although we're all keen to encourage birds into our gardens – and some, such as tits and sparrows, eat lots of caterpillars, aphids and other pests, especially when feeding their young, some birds are pests. The most serious are blackbirds and pigeons, especially the big woodpigeons that are becoming increasingly common in urban areas as well as in the countryside.

Blackbirds eat most fruits as soon as they ripen and help themselves to your blueberries, raspberries, strawberries, redcurrants and many more fruits besides. The only effective way to control them is with netting, either draped over the plants or by growing the plants in a *fruit cage* (a permanent structure draped in netting). Pigeons are more of a problem with vegetables and are at their worst when pecking and eating the shoots of peas as they emerge in spring and in winter when pecking at and eating the foliage of brassicas such as cabbages, especially in cold weather. Again, netting is the best solution to the problem.

Slugs and snails

Slugs and snails are the most common and destructive of garden pests. They are most abundant and most active at night, in wet seasons, and in gardens with heavy clay or humus-rich soils because of the moisture they need to live. Slugs are less active in dry weather but snails can retreat into their waterproof homes and are better able to survive drought. Snails can also climb walls, trees and canes to get at plants.

Although they attack plants at all stages of growth, slugs and snails do most damage when plants are young. Tender growth is most appealing to these pests, and just a few bites can reduce a young plant to a bare stem. Although slugs and snails both usually eat leaves, they eat almost all plant matter including pods, fruits and underground tubers – nothing is safe from them!

Fortunately, you can try many different methods, with varying degrees of efficiency, for controlling slugs and snails:

✔ **Barrier methods.** Using barriers includes placing small pieces of rock that absorb water around the stem of a plant, so forming an unpleasant surface for the creatures to pass. You can also use sharp grit, baked eggshells, coarse hair and copper rings. However, although barriers may be effective, they are rarely practical for large numbers of small seedlings and are best for use around isolated, vulnerable plants such as newly planted courgettes.

✔ **Natural methods.** Encouraging wildlife, such as birds, hedgehogs, toads and other predators into your garden is good practice. They help to maintain a natural balance between pests and predators, and certainly keep pest populations in check, but you can't rely on them to protect all your plants all the time; don't expect a couple of passing hedgehogs to protect all your newly planted runner beans or lettuce seedlings.

✔ **Trapping.** Employing something more desirable to pests than your plants as bait to entice them into a trap has some effect. Beer traps (shallow saucers filled with beer placed among your plants) are popular but they may trap and kill other, useful creatures as well as drowning slugs. A better option is to lay out upturned grapefruit or orange skins, a handful of lettuce leaves or potato peelings in the evening, and make sure that you pick them up, with the slugs, in the morning. If you just leave them for days you're simply feeding the slugs! After you catch your slugs and snails you can deal with them as you see fit, perhaps releasing them somewhere else (not over the neighbour's hedge, though!) if you're a kindly soul!

✔ **Pellets.** Using pellets is the most effective way to control slugs and snails. Despite commonly held beliefs, they don't pose any threat to pets, children or wildlife, though, of course, eliminating all the slugs from your garden starves their predators. Modern slug pellets contain *metaldehyde*, which isn't a poison but dries out the slugs and snails. They also contain *bitrex*, which makes them unpalatable to most animals and children.

Pellets are most effective in dry weather because the slugs and snails, which are dried out by the metaldhyde, are less likely to recover then than in wet weather. Sprinkle them regularly but sparingly and they decompose in the soil to water vapour and carbon dioxide as they get wet. Try to avoid putting rings of pellets around plants because this uses far more than you need, and the possibility exists that a creature could then ingest enough to make it ill, which would be unlikely if you scattered them 10 centimetres apart, as manufacturers usually recommend.

In addition to copper rings and other barriers, you can now buy pellets based on a wide variety of naturally occurring products including wool waste.

✔ **Biological controls.** Employing this method is effective against soildwelling slugs that aren't affected by pellets on the surface, but not against snails. Biological controls use a natural predator called a *nematode*. You buy nematodes in a refrigerated pack, tip the contents into water, stir, and water the solution, containing millions of nematodes, onto the soil. They then seek out and kill the slugs underground so you don't see any dead bodies. Biological controls are less effective in dry and heavy clay soils and work best between late spring and late summer.

Wireworm

Wireworms aren't worms at all but the larvae of click beetles. The beetles don't cause much damage but the larvae, which are thin and shaded brown and cream with legs at the front end, eat plant roots and burrow into potato tubers, causing extensive damage. They live in this destructive stage for many years. Wireworms are usually more serious on newer plots because they are common in lawns and have a fondness for grass roots – when you dig over unused land or a lawn to make a veg patch, lots of wireworms are in the soil. When you start growing crops, the larvae, which live in the larval stage for many years before maturing, have nothing else to eat and so turn their attentions to your potatoes.

Wireworms generally become less troublesome the more you dig. Digging exposes the grubs to insect-eating birds such as robins and starlings and reduces their numbers, but no chemical method of controlling wireworm exists. If the problem is severe, sow a green manure crop of mustard – this speeds up their life cycle and the grubs mature quickly, become beetles, and fly off. You can also trap wireworms by putting half a potato tuber in the ground for a day or two and then digging it up.

Flea beetles

The flea beetle is a tiny beetle that you may never see (they jump fast when they see you – hence the name) but you'll certainly spot the damage they do. They eat small, round holes in the leaves of even the tiniest seedlings and, if there are lots of them, the seedlings may never get a chance to grow and will disappear. If they get through the first few weeks of their life the seedlings usually recover and grow to maturity.

Flea beetles only affect brassicas, so watch for them on cabbages, radish, cauliflowers, turnips and rocket. Sprinkling plants with dust (dry soil) can deter flea beetles or you can drag a yellow sticky whitefly trap (the kind you buy for greenhouses) along the rows quickly – they jump up in a panic and get stuck on the trap!

Fighting off common diseases

Some plant diseases can affect almost anything in your garden. Fungi such as mildew cause most of them, They're spread by spores carried in the wind and they land on suitable leaves where they germinate and invade the plant tissue; or are sometimes present on infected plant material. They then generally cause discoloration of the leaf before releasing spores themselves, making the infection more obvious, with white spores (in mildew) or orange spores (in rusts). In a few cases the fungi remain in the soil, sometimes for many years, even though the host plant isn't growing there.

A few diseases are caused by viruses. These microscopic organisms invade plant cells and, when present, are impossible for the home gardener to cure. If a seed-raised plant, such as courgettes, is infected you simply have to cull it. The problem is worse with long-lived plants such as fruit, where the virus weakens the plant, reducing crops, and you have to discard the plant. But while fungi are usually present in the air and spread on the wind, viruses are spread in the sap, either by aphids or by other insects that suck the sap and cross-infect plants, or by gardeners who bruise plants and pass on the sap.

In a similar way to insect attacks, diseases are generally more likely to strike and be most severe when the plants are stressed by poor growing conditions, drought or bad cultivation. However, some fungal diseases also strike if plants are grown too *soft*. This term means that the plants have been fed with too much nitrogen and watered to such an extent – pampered, if you like – that they can't fight off any disease. However, some plants almost inevitably get fungal infections but unless you're growing for showing you don't need to spray with fungicides – it depends on how perfect you need your crops to be (you don't want mildew on gooseberries at the local flower show!) and whether the disease is just cosmetic or likely to really damage the plant (such as chocolate spot on broad beans).

Testing of gardening chemicals is now more extensive than ever before and new generations of chemicals are ever more specific in the pests and diseases they target and less of a threat to non-target organisms. So, if you want to use chemicals you can be pretty sure that, if you follow the instructions on the label, at the times specified, and you don't exceed the correct doses, they pose little or no threat to your health. In fact, the chemicals you buy today are probably safer than at any time gardeners have been using them.

Don't be tempted to have a go at making your own pesticides, even from seemingly innocuous substances – it's illegal. Also, because home-made pesticides are untested they may damage the health of both you and your plants.

If you prefer to try an organic fungicide, you can use sprays based on copper and sulphur.

Increasing the amount of potassium in the fertilisers you use may help to make plants more resistant to disease. You can also choose to grow plants that are resistant, but remember that this is all they are – they're not disease-proof!

Mildew

Mildews are fungal diseases that affect many fruit and vegetable plants. They come in two basic types: powdery and downy. Although people usually associate mildew with dampness, drought is the most common contributory factor. When plants are short of water at the roots, or stressed, they are more susceptible to getting mildew.

Mildew spores are carried in the air. They land on the plant and, if the surface is moist and the plant right for them, the spore germinates, just like a seed, and infects the leaf. The spore then grows and, in time, turns the leaf white as it produces more spores. In some cases the mildew is largely cosmetic and looks unsightly but it weakens the plant as it reduces the efficiency of the leaf. In some cases mildew can kill all or part of the leaf, weakening the plant even more.

Powdery mildew is the most common of the two types and is the slightly easier type to control. It affects apples, courgettes and other squashes, spinach, leaf beet and cucumbers, weakening the plants, reducing yields, and shortening their lives. Dry compost encourages powdery mildew, so keep your plants moist to prevent this. Downy mildews, with fluffy fungal growth, are less common and usually affect the leaves of lettuce and onions.

Good growing conditions are the first and most important line of prevention against mildew. For extra protection against mildew on your plants, use a good fungicide. Although applied fungicides prevent infection, they can't remove or eliminate existing fungal infections. So, if you want to use fungicides, apply them as a preventative measure or at the first sign of infection.

Not all fungicides treat all fungal diseases and not all are suitable for fruit and veg, so check labels carefully. For example, no fungicide is effective against white rot on onions or grey mould (botrytis), a common disease.

Rust

Rusts are fungal diseases that are most common in wet weather and usually show up towards the end of the growing season as yellow spots on the upper surface of leaves, and later as brown or orange spore clusters, often on the underside of the leaf. Sometimes the leaves drop off the plants prematurely, weakening them (as in the case of raspberries) or they may cause large areas of the leaf to die (as happens with garlic). Rusts are difficult to control but often cause only minimal damage to the harvestable part of the plant, even though they look alarming.

Rusts are less common than mildew on most crops and are usually specific to particular crops. Leeks and garlic are the vegetables most commonly affected. Rust doesn't usually affect the edible part of leeks or garlic but may reduce the yield in garlic because it can damage the foliage so much that it dies down prematurely. Rusts do also affect fruits such as pears and plums but only the leaves and not the edible part.

Spray fungicide onto plants that are likely to be infected to prevent rust attack, checking that the spray is suitable for vegetables and fruits. Make sure that you spray *before* the coloured clusters begin to appear on the plant, otherwise rust has taken hold and you're too late. Avoiding excess nitrogen fertiliser and applying potash, especially in mid- to late summer while the crops are growing, and choosing rust-resistant varieties are also helpful.

Viruses

Viruses are gradual diseases that are often unnoticed but that eventually reduce crops even if they don't immediately destroy the plants. They are microscopic organisms that affect most plants and are usually spread in the sap by aphids moving from plant to plant, and by gardeners, who unknowingly spread them when pinching out or cutting plants. Virus symptoms vary but are usually loss of vigour, smaller crops, distortion of the leaves, and yellowing in spots, patches, or between the veins.

Virus diseases affect most soft fruits, which is why obtaining certified, virus-free stock is essential when buying new plants. The other group of plants that suffer from viruses are cucumbers, squashes and their relatives, the effect of which is to rapidly reduce the vigour of the plants.

Virus diseases can't be cured and you need to dig up and burn any affected plants to prevent infection spreading to other, healthy plants.

Damping off disease

Fungi cause this soil-borne disease which attacks seedlings. As damping-off disease travels through the soil, it attacks the base of the seedling and causes the base to wither so that the seedling falls over and dies. No cure exists for damping-off disease and even seedlings that don't appear affected usually die when you transplant them from the infected pot. A traditional way to halt the disease is to water your seedlings with *Cheshunt compound* but it's not always successful. The best way to avoid the problem is simply by adopting good growing practices.

Controlling Plant-Specific Problems

Not all pests and diseases attack every plant. Some are rather more choosy, and have a particular taste for just one or two of your crops. Here, I identify the worst offenders, and arm you with effective ways in which to tackle them.

Keeping your vegetables happy

Vegetables may have one or a whole range of pests and diseases that are specific to them. This fact doesn't mean that you're inevitably going to come across them all, but some are quite likely and it certainly pays to be aware that they're about. A few pests and diseases are serious and difficult to combat and can limit what you're able to grow.

Brassicas

Although the brassica group of plants includes some of our most important crops (such as Brussels sprouts, cabbage, broccoli and kale), an alarming number of pests and diseases are waiting in the wings to eat or destroy your plants:

- ✔ **Clubroot** is the most serious of the diseases affecting brassicas. It's caused by a fungus in the soil and can be spread by walking from an infected plot, carrying the disease on your shoes, or when planting seedlings that were grown in infected soil. When clubroot infects plants, it causes the roots to swell and become misshapen and the plant grows poorly and may die.

  The fungus thrives in acid soils and so adding lime to your soil is your first line of defence. You can also reduce the effect of clubroot by growing your plants in pots till they are semi-mature, at least by potting them into 10-centimetre pots before planting them out. They then stand a chance of maturing before the disease affects them severely. You can also choose the clubroot-resistant varieties of cabbage and cauliflower that have been introduced in recent years.

  Never accept brassica plants that have been grown in the open ground – they may have been in infected soil.

- ✔ **White blister** is a disease that can spread from the hedge garlic weed or from other infected plants and causes large white, raised, powdery areas on plant leaves. It often occurs when plants are crowded together, restricting the air flow around the leaves. Spacing plants well and controlling weeds helps to reduce this problem. No cure exists except to remove infected leaves, but white blister is rarely so serious that it reduces the yield of your plants.

✔ **Cabbage root fly** is a pest that can kill plants rapidly. The flies land on the plants and crawl down the stems to lay eggs in the soil at the base of the stem. The eggs hatch into maggots that then eat the roots, leading the plants to turn purple-yellow and pink and to die.

You can prevent the fly from laying eggs by putting a 'collar' around the base of each plant. You can buy these collars from garden centres or make them with cardboard or plastic. They should be 15–20 centimetres in diameter with a slit from one edge to the centre so they fit tightly around the stem of the plant.

✔ **Brassica whitefly** is a common pest that looks like greenhouse whitefly but is able to survive winters outside. In severe infestations, great clouds of insects fly up when you disturb the infected plants. Brassica whitefly secrete a sticky substance called *honeydew*, which drops onto lower leaves where a fungus called *sooty mould* uses it as a food source and turns the leaves sticky and black. Use an organic or chemical pesticide spray to control them from an early stage to prevent large colonies developing.

✔ **Mealy cabbage aphids** can be hard pests to spot because they are grey, the same colour as cabbage leaves. They also get into the buttons of sprouts and the tips of broccoli. They often infect young plants and cause distortion of the young foliage and growing tip. Mealy cabbage aphids are difficult to control without using organic or chemical pesticide sprays, but you can rub them off the leaves of young plants.

✔ **Cabbage white butterflies** are the most serious pest affecting brassicas and come in two species that, though similar as adults, have different caterpillars. The large cabbage white has yellow and black speckled caterpillars and the small cabbage white has green caterpillars. The adults of both types flutter over plants and lay eggs on the under surface of the leaves. The caterpillars eat the leaves and can reduce them to lace, while their faeces drop into the centre of the plant and make it inedible.

You can pick off caterpillars by hand or use an organic or chemical pesticide spray. Placing netting over your plants (refer to Chapter 6 for more on this) is also practical and effective.

✔ **Pigeons** can devastate crops, especially in winter when little other green food is around for them to eat. They sit on broccoli and sprouts, reducing the leaves to tatters and leave their calling card just to add insult to injury. To keep them away from your brassicas, try bird scarers such as CDs hung on strings, or net the crop.

Carrots

The most serious pest affecting carrots is carrot root fly. This small fly lays eggs in the soil beside the plants, and the eggs hatch into grubs that burrow into the roots and make shallow tunnels and wounds. The adults find the carrots by smell and the most dangerous time is when you're thinning the rows to give the carrots room to develop. When doing this, you break the roots and foliage and release the aroma of carrots. So by sowing thinly at the outset, you have less thinning to do and you stand a better chance of maggot-free roots!

No chemical treatment is available for dealing with carrot root fly, but planting alternate rows of carrots and onions, or another strong smelling crop, may disguise the carrot smell and reduce the problem. Sprays that mask the carrot smell, such as garlic spray, are also helpful. You can also choose to grow varieties of carrots, such as Sytan and Flyaway, which aren't as attractive to the insects. However, carrot root fly will attack even these if no other carrots are around. You can make them more effective by sowing a patch of ordinary carrots nearby as a sacrificial crop to lure the pest away from the ones you intend to eat.

Carrot root fly are slightly odd creatures because they don't fly far off the ground and rarely stray more than 45 centimetres above ground level. Because of this you can protect your plants by growing them in pots to raise the soil level, or erect a screen around the plants. Alternatively you can cover the whole row or rows with fleece after sowing to protect them and leave it on all the time the crop is growing.

Timing sowings may also help your carrots to avoid attack. Early sowings, perhaps under plastic cloches or fleece, and late sowings, in early summer, are sometimes less likely to be attacked, but don't rely on this as your only preventative measure.

Courgettes, squashes and marrows

Courgettes, squashes and marrows are generally easy to grow but you may encounter a few common problems:

- ✔ **Mildew** is the most common disease and is caused by a moist atmosphere and dryness at the roots. It usually affects these plants at some time during the season. If mildew appears at the end of summer the crop isn't affected too much, but if it strikes earlier in the year it can weaken the plants. Silvery blotches are natural on courgettes and marrows but if the plants appear to be showered with talcum powder, they're affected by powdery mildew.

  To boost your chances of avoiding mildew, you can choose to grow one of the many varieties that are resistant, though not immune, to the disease. Although difficult to control, liberal watering, which the plants need anyway, also helps to reduce the problem. If your plants do get mildew, you can remove the worst affected leaves, but living with the problem is generally best because spraying is rarely effective after the disease gets a hold and although the plants will lose vigour, it doesn't affect the fruit – so you can carry on picking!

✔ **Viruses** are more serious and *cucumber mosaic virus* is the most common sort. Spread by aphids, it can overwinter in chickweed and when the aphids move to your crop of cucumbers, courgettes or other squashes, they infect the plants with the disease. Infected plants have small, distorted leaves mottled with yellow and the fruits are also malformed and mottled. Plants don't recover and lose vigour. If you don't pull up and destroy the plants, the virus spreads to others.

The common weed chickweed harbours the cucumber mosaic virus. Make sure that you keep this weed under control to avoid your squashes becoming infected. You can also help to prevent the virus by choosing to grow resistant varieties that are slower to succumb to the disease.

Cucumbers

Cucumbers are productive and easy to grow but many things can go wrong with them including aphids, which are generally easy to deal with, and red spider mite and whitefly, which are not (see the later sections on 'Grapes' and 'Tomatoes' respectively). Cucumbers are also affected by cucumber mosaic virus (see the preceding 'Courgettes, squashes and marrows section').

Most problems affecting cucumbers are fungal. *Stem rot* is the most serious problem, usually caused by overwatering plants and their being too cold. It attacks near ground level and plants start to wilt in warm weather, often recovering temporarily by dawn the next day. You can sometimes save plants by piling up soil around the base of the stem to enable them to form new roots.

Cucumbers can also be affected by a wide range of garden chemicals, so I recommend using a biological control – encarsia – for whitefly, the most common pest. *Encarsia* is a parasitic wasp that you can order by mail order. Introduce it in late spring, before the pest gets completely out of control.

Onions, leeks and garlic

Because they're closely related, onions, leeks and garlic crops suffer from similar problems, as follows:

✔ **Bolting** is a common cause of failure with onions, especially those grown from *sets* (immature, small onions that you buy and plant to grow a crop) rather than seed. Usually caused by a check to growth due to drought, late frost or a cold period after growth has started, bolting can often be caused by sowing or planting at the wrong time. Bolting is difficult to avoid in some seasons. When it happens, rather than forming a large bulb, plants send up a flowering stem. Even if you lift them early as immature onions, they aren't much use because the flower stem is woody and inedible. Some plants are more prone to bolting than others – red onions are especially prone to the problem. You can plant *heat-treated sets* (that the suppliers have subjected to warmth to prevent flowering) to reduce the likelihood of bolting.

✔ **Onion fly** is an uncommon but serious pest, which causes plants that start well to droop and their leaves to turn yellow, ruining the crop. Flies lay eggs at the base of plants and these hatch into maggots that burrow into the base of the bulb. Sets are less often affected than plants grown from seed. No chemical control exists for dealing with onion fly, so your only option is to destroy affected plants.

✔ **White rot** is a devastating soil-borne fungal disease. Affected onions fail to mature or don't store well, with white mould at their base. No chemical cure exists for dealing with white rot. In addition, the fungus remains dormant in the soil for many years, even without growing onions, and so your only option is to avoid growing onions or related plants (including shallots and chives) in the soil for many years.

✔ **Downy mildew** never used to be a common problem but as more people grow overwintered (Japanese-type) onions for an early summer crop, it's being seen more often and can be serious in wet seasons. The onion leaves shrivel from the tip and the bulbs don't grow or store well. To minimise the chances of downy mildew putting in an appearance, try to avoid close planting and overwatering your onions. Fungicides can be effective if you apply them early, before symptoms appear.

✔ **Rust** mostly affects leeks and garlic, but can affect other veg as well. See the earlier section in this chapter 'Fighting off common diseases.'

✔ **Leek moth** is a growing problem that is most troublesome in late summer and autumn and can cause severe loss of crops. The moth lays its eggs on plants and the grubs tunnel inside the leaves and into the stems. Growing plants under fleece where practical is a good way of keeping the moths at bay. Remember to remove and burn any badly infected plants.

Parsnips

Parsnips are generally free from problems, although old seed doesn't germinate well and seed sown too early may rot in the wet soil. The only other problem that affects parsnips is *canker*, a disease largely caused by poor or dry soil and weak growth, which shows as black, cracked marks at the top of the root. To avoid canker, don't sow too early, water in dry weather to keep plants growing well, and sow resistant varieties.

Peas and beans

Runner beans are generally free from problems, apart from difficulties with the plants actually producing a crop of pods (which can be caused by many factors including drought and hot weather) and slugs and snails eating the young plants. The other serious problem is *anthracnose*, a disease that causes brown, sunken areas on the pods, which later turn pink. Leaves and stems may also have brown patches and may die. In severe cases the whole plant can die. Pull out and burn affected plants and don't collect your own seeds from infected plants.

Chocolate spot is the only serious disease that affects broad beans. Affected plants become covered in chocolate brown patches and can be killed by the disease. Adding lime to the soil and making sure that the plants aren't too crowded may reduce the disease. You can spray with carbendazim fungicide to prevent severe infection.

The blackfly aphid affects a wide range of plants, including all beans, but broad beans are especially prone. In theory, you can reduce the severity of attacks by getting your sowing done early and pinching out the shoot tips above the top flower. But in practice broad beans almost always get attacked. Ladybirds and hoverfly larvae naturally control light infestations but in severe attacks spraying with a chemical or organic insecticide may be necessary; avoid spraying when plants are in full flower.

Several pests find themselves irresistibly drawn to the tastiness of peas:

- **Pea moth** is the most serious pest affecting peas. The tiny moths lay eggs on the pods. The eggs eventually hatch into grubs that eat the seeds, meaning that you get a nasty surprise when you harvest your crop because the pods are filled with maggots. You can spray with a bifenthrin insecticide immediately after flowering but sowing early or later than usual, with a fast-maturing variety (an early type), often avoids the problem.

- **Pea and bean weevil** is a rarely seen small insect whose calling card is small notches around the edges of the leaves. Although the damage doesn't harm mature plants, it can weaken or kill seedlings. To control the pest, spray plants with insecticide containing bifenthrin.

- **Pigeons** are a particular pest of peas and can strip the leaves from and kill emerging seedlings. Netting, or growing peas in a fruit cage or under cloches at the early stage, is the only practical control.

Potatoes

As one of the most important of all crops, it stands to reason that potatoes have their share of problems!

- **Potato blight,** a fungus, is the most serious potato disease. For the air-carried spores to infect a leaf, the foliage must be damp for 24 hours, and blight affects plants most seriously in stormy, wet weather from midsummer onwards. Plants go black and collapse rapidly and the spores drop onto the soil and get washed onto the tubers, causing them to rot in the soil, ruining crops. When you comes to harvest them you find that the potatoes are either completely rotten and stinky or they'll rot later when in storage.

   Potato blight doesn't persist from one year to the next on your plot unless you leave semi-rotted, infected tubers in the soil to sprout the following year and provide a new source of infection. Spraying with a fungicide containing copper or mancozeb protects plants but its efficiency depends on the weather – the spray is less effective in persistently wet weather. Early potato varieties (in other words, those that you harvest before midsummer) usually escape infection, and some maincrop varieties also have some resistance. (I describe these varieties in Chapter 9.)

Potato blight also affects tomatoes growing outside.

✔ **Keel slugs** are a particular pest to potatoes (most slugs attack a wide range of crops). The small black keel slugs burrow into tubers and make them less attractive in the kitchen. They are difficult to control and are more of a problem in wet summers and on heavy clay soils. Pellets are of limited use against keel slugs because they're most effective on slugs on the soil surface. Biological controls, in the form of parasitic nematodes that you water onto the soil, are your best option.

✔ **Wireworms** are a common potato pest because gardeners often use potatoes as the first crop in a new plot where the digging required for the crop helps to clear the land. I tell you how to deal with wireworms in the 'Dealing with common pests' section earlier in this chapter.

✔ **Scab** is a purely cosmetic problem that causes rough patches on the skins of tubers. No effective ways of dealing with scab exist, other than buying resistant varieties, but fortunately scab is only skin deep and doesn't affect the eating quality of the potatoes. Scab is most common on sandy or dry soils or if the soil has been recently limed.

✔ **Potato cyst eelworm** is a potentially serious pest but is fortunately uncommon in most gardens. The eelworms are microscopic creatures that invade the plant and produce tiny lumps on the roots (not to be confused with the nodules on pea and bean roots). The lower leaves turn brown and wilt, and growth is stunted and plants die prematurely. No cure is available, but thankfully you're unlikely ever to see this problem if you buy and grow fresh, certified seed potatoes every spring.

Always buy certified seed potatoes and never plant tubers you bought for eating so that you avoid the possibility of contaminating your plot.

Sweetcorn

Most corn grown in the UK is sweetcorn, which growers harvest when immature. Sweetcorn loves moisture, warmth and sun but doesn't like excessively wet soil. Remember these facts and your sweetcorn shouldn't have any problems at all. One fungal disease that affects sweetcorn, called *smut*, causes the cobs to become misshapen and black, and has no cure or prevention. The only other problem with sweetcorn is rodents, which love to eat the maturing cobs. The answer here is to use humane traps or put down poison stations, but be careful here – use rat poison with extreme care to prevent hedgehogs and other mammals eating it.

Tomatoes

Tomatoes are the most popular of all home-grown crops and are generally easy to grow. Breeders have overcome some traditional problems such as soil fungi by creating resistant varieties, but a few problems are likely to crop up:

- **Tomato blight** is the same disease as potato blight and shows the same symptoms. It can attack the plants only when the leaves are damp and so is not usually a problem on plants growing under cover. However, in humid weather blight can affect indoor plants if the leaves remain wet for long periods, so avoid wetting the foliage in late afternoon or the evening when the leaves may stay wet for many hours. A few varieties, such as Legend, have some resistance.

- **Blossom end rot** isn't a disease, although it looks like one. Most common on plants in growing bags and in pots, blossom end rot is a problem caused by cultivation, and specifically by a lack of calcium. All cells need calcium transported to them in water. If plants aren't watered regularly or often enough, calcium doesn't reach the parts of the plants farthest from the roots – the tip of the fruits. The cells here die and a black, sunken area develops at the base of both green and ripe fruits.

  To combat blossom end rot ensure that in summer, when the plants are fully grown, you give them a lot of water. If the plants dry out and wilt, the young fruits may get damaged and blossom end rot may appear.

  Plants in soil are less likely to dry out completely to the stage where they wilt. Keep plants evenly moist or grow them in greenhouse beds or soil and you may never experience blossom end rot. Good tomato feed has added calcium to try to alleviate the problem.

- **Greenhouse whitefly** is different to brassica whitefly and is usually confined to greenhouses and polytunnels, though it may survive outside in warm summers. The tiny, white, moth-like adults suck sap and drip *honeydew*, which is later colonised by sooty mould, making the lower leaves black. As well as weakening plants, whitefly can also spread virus diseases. They breed quickly in warm weather and their scale-like larvae also suck sap before they hatch as adults. This young stage is resistant to most insecticides except systemic insecticides (which I discuss in Chapter 2).

  To combat whitefly, you can use a biological control and introduce a predatory, tiny wasp called encarsia before infestations become too serious. You can order this wasp by post (most gardening magazines carry suppliers' adverts) and introduce it to the greenhouse before the whitefly population reaches epidemic levels. The adults then lay their eggs inside the young whitefly. As the eggs hatch, the new wasps eat the whitefly from the inside before emerging to start the cycle again.

  Alternatively, repeated spraying with insecticide can also be effective – but don't use this if you already have the biological control in the greenhouse or it'll kill the wasps too.

For a more simple control you can use a vacuum cleaner to suck up the whitefly adults on a regular basis or use yellow sticky traps. Hang these above the plants and when you disturb the whitefly by brushing the plants the whitefly are attracted to the yellow strips of sticky plastic and get stuck there.

- **Cracking** occurs when plants are dry, especially in hot weather, and the tomatoes stop growing and the skins toughen up. Then, when it rains, especially if conditions are cool, the plants absorb lots of water, the tomatoes swell, and because the skins are tough, they split. Some varieties are much more prone to this than others but trying to keep plants evenly moist reduces the problem. Take a look at Chapter 10 to see which varieties are best for avoiding cracking.

- **Greenback** is a problem associated with some varieties and is basically 'sunburn', often a result of gardeners stripping the leaves off plants in an effort to ripen the fruits. The tops (or *shoulders*) of fruits affected by greenback stay green, even when the fruit is ripe. The fruits also stay crunchy and, though edible, aren't pleasant. The best thing you can do to avoid greenback is to shade plants and refrain from stripping off green leaves.

Warmth and no direct sunlight actually makes fruits turn red, so stripping leaves off tomato plants does nothing to ripen them anyway!

- **A lack of flowers,** especially on young plants, is often a problem. Plants seem to grow forever without making their first flower cluster or *truss*, which would mean growing tall without ever producing any fruits. To avoid this problem don't put plants into their final pots or in the ground until they've produced the first truss in their small pots. You don't need to wait until the flowers open but just until you see them form. The 'stress' of being in the small pots causes the plants to form flowers and then when you plant them out they are in 'flowering mode' and continue to form trusses.

- **A poor fruit set** is when the plant produces flowers that drop off and no fruits develop. It can be caused by a lack of water, extreme high temperatures, or cold, and in some varieties is a natural occurrence. For example, some beefsteak and heirloom varieties don't set well and only a few flowers on each truss form fruits. In the case of beefsteaks, the plants can't physically carry more than two or three fruits per truss anyway because they're so large. Gently tapping the flowers with your hand or misting them with water in the summer, when temperatures should be suitable for fruit setting, usually overcomes the problem.

- **Leaf problems** are as often imagined as real. For example, gardeners call some tomatoes *potato-leaved* because their leaves are more like a potato than a tomato. Some tomatoes have very fern-like leaves, which is all quite natural. Curling of the leaves in the growing tip can also be worrying but is also entirely natural. When plants are growing vigorously the leaves often curl outwards and downwards. Leaves curling inwards may show that problems exist, such as cold temperatures at night, which you can't do much about after the symptoms appear, but otherwise don't worry.

In some cases, however, the leaves may become distorted and fern-like, with unusually narrow leaf segments, because of contact with hormone weedkiller, as used on lawns. Tomatoes are very sensitive to hormone weedkillers and even the fumes can cause distortion from which plants rarely recover. In some cases fruits form, but they're usually tainted and inedible.

Fending off fruit pests and diseases

Unfortunately, a number of pests and diseases often attack the fruits that gardeners grow most commonly, and you can count yourself lucky if you never have to deal with any of them! Some are more serious than others. Those that attack foliage generally weaken the plants, whereas those that attack the fruits may not cause harm to the plant but do spoil your crop. Of course, birds are always a threat to your fruits, and currants, blackberries, blueberries, strawberries and raspberries are best grown in a fruit cage to prevent our feathered friends stealing the lion's share of your crop.

Apples

A bewildering array of problems can attack apples. You can plant resistant varieties to avoid many fungal problems, such as scab and mildew, but most insect pests are less discerning and aren't dissuaded from attacking your trees by good cultivation. The following list of potential problems starts with the most common and destructive – the codling moth!

✔ **Codling moths** lay their eggs on the tiny fruit in early summer. Nothing is more disappointing, or unpleasant, than biting into an apple and finding a grub inside – except finding half a grub! You can usually tell if codling moths have affected a fruit because you can see a small, black hole where the grub may have crawled out of the fruit.

You can deal with codling moths by using insecticide spray, although timing when to use the spray can be difficult. A good method is to use *pheromone traps* (plastic tents that you hang in the trees in late spring) as a control or to time your spraying accurately. In the base of the tents is a sticky pad containing female pheromones (sex hormones) to attract the male moths to a sticky end. If the tree is too large to spray, or you don't want to spray, these traps catch many male moths, which are then unable to fertilise the females. Alternatively, when you start to catch the males you know the time has come to spray the tree with an insecticide.

✔ **Woolly aphids** infest both young and old apple shoots, feeding in large colonies and causing the plant's bark to swell around them, which looks unsightly and also protects the insects from attack by birds. Their woolly coating protects them from birds and other predators, and gardeners sometimes mistake them for some sort of fungus. To deal with woolly aphids, cut away any badly affected shoots, and remove colonies when the tree is dormant with a fierce jet of water. You can also brush them off where possible or spray the tree with an insecticide.

- **Sawfly** is a pest that leaves a ribbon-like scar on the apple skin where the adult laid eggs. These eggs hatch into grubs that feed in the centre of the fruit before leaving and dropping to the ground in midsummer. Sawfly is a lesser problem in most gardens, but spraying with insecticide when the flowers have dropped their petals reduces damage.

- **Scab** is a fungal disease that affects pears as well as apples and can also affect the leaves and twigs. Showing as corky, split areas on the fruit surface, the damage is only skin deep. Scab is worse in wet seasons and you can prevent it with fungicide sprays.

Don't confuse scab with natural russeting – a dull brown area on many varieties.

- **Mildew** is a fungal disease that gardeners often associate with dryness at the roots. It can weaken young trees but only affects the leaves, covering them in a white powder and usually twisting and killing them. To deal with mildew, cut away the affected ends of young shoots in mid- to late summer (this summer pruning helps fruit bud production too) or spray in early summer with a fungicide to prevent the disease. Maintain the vigour of the tree by making sure that you feed and water it well. If a tree is growing in a grassy area, keep an area of at least 1 metre in diameter free of grass around the trunk to reduce competition from grass roots.

- **Bitter pit** isn't a disease but a condition caused by cultivation conditions and is most common on Bramley apples, especially young trees and the largest fruits. Bitter pit is associated with calcium (discussed in relation to blossom end rot in the 'Tomatoes' section earlier in this chapter) and may cause fruits to have smelly, sunken brown spots on the skins and the peeled flesh to be dotted with small brown areas. Affected apples are still edible, but try to avoid bitter pit by keeping young trees watered in dry spells and adding lime to the soil in autumn to ensure that they don't run short of calcium.

- **Brown rot** is one of the most common troubles of apples and also affects pears, peaches, cherries and plums. At its worst in cool, wet summers, the fungus may first attack the fruit through a hole in the skin made by an insect or bird. A small brown area rapidly grows and creates concentric rings of buff-coloured spots that release spores.

If a diseased fruit is touching other apples or other fruit, the disease spreads quickly from one to another. No chemical cure exists and you need to pick off all affected fruits immediately and put them in the bin. Diseased fruits don't fall in autumn but shrivel up and become 'mummified'. If you leave them on the tree they provide new infection for the following year but, more importantly, they cause *dieback* (where the twigs and branches literally die back).

Blackberries

Blackberries and other hybrid berries sometimes suffer from uneven ripening, where the individual sections of the fruits don't all go black and some remain red. Mites are the cause of this problem, for which no chemical control exists. You can reduce or eliminate the problem by cutting the whole plant down to the ground and burning (or disposing of) the whole part of the plant above ground. New shoots grow vigorously the following year and should be free from the pest. Such harsh treatment doesn't damage the plants, although you don't get a crop for the following year.

Citrus

Oranges, limes and especially lemons are now very popular pot plants. These citrus fruits are easy to grow, look beautiful, have delightfully fragrant flowers and provide an interesting crop too. But they do attract a few problems:

- ✔ **Tortrix moths** are small, triangular, brown moths that you rarely notice, but their caterpillars are a nuisance on citrus fruits. The moths lay eggs on leaves and the caterpillars avoid detection by stitching the leaves together with silk so they can feed on the leaves unseen. They may occasionally eat into fruits too. Pick off or crush any suspect leaves to eliminate the caterpillars.

- ✔ **Scale insect** is the most serious pest that affects citrus, but does affect other plants as well. Refer back to the 'Dealing with common pests' section earlier in the chapter for the lowdown on scale.

Currants

Blackcurrants are prone to suffer from mildew, although breeders are creating more-resistant modern varieties (see the section on 'Fighting off common diseases' earlier on for more about mildew). Far more serious, though, is the combined problem of *big bud mite* and the *reversion* virus disease it carries and spreads. Big bud mite is a tiny creature that generally sets up home in the growth buds of blackcurrants. Infected buds become swollen and round rather than narrow, and infected plants produce much shorter clusters of flowers and therefore much lighter crops of fruit. These plants typically have leaves that, instead of having five distinct lobes, have only three.

No effective treatment for big bud mite and reversion virus exists other than to pick off the buds or prune out badly affected branches. Although affected plants live and crop for many years, it's best to dig them up and burn them to avoid the problem spreading.

Some recent varieties have a resistance to big bud mite, but if you plan to grow any new bushes, clear and burn any old, infected plants first.

Red- and white currants are basically the same and attract the usual problem of birds eating the fruits – particularly redcurrants – as they ripen (jump back to the section on birds earlier in the chapter for some tips on dealing with them). The only serious problem with these fruits, however, is *currant blister aphid*. This aphid lives at the tips of new shoots and feeds on the underside of the leaves, causing the leaves to develop raised blisters that frequently turn red and look like a disease has struck. You can control this aphid with a contact insecticide, directed up under the foliage, or with a systemic insecticide. This rarely causes the plant harm but if you prefer not to use chemicals, simply cutting off the shoot tips is the best organic option.

Gooseberries

Gooseberries are generally an easy crop to cultivate but can become affected by two main problems:

- ✔ **Gooseberry sawfly** is the most serious pest with a taste for gooseberry. The adults lay eggs on the foliage in the centre of the plant and these hatch into small caterpillars that start to feed as a cluster. As they strip the foliage they move to the outer branches and eventually a plant can be devoid of all foliage. Natural predators, such as birds, are rarely effective, especially because gardeners often grow the fruit in a cage to protect the fruits themselves from birds! Spraying with an insecticide for caterpillars is usually necessary because, although plants recover from attacks, repeated defoliation over the years weakens the bushes.

- ✔ **American gooseberry mildew** is the most serious disease that affects gooseberry plants, covering the leaves, stems and often the fruits with a white powdery coating that causes distortion. You can cut back any badly affected shoot tips but once the leaves are white, it's too late to spray with a fungicide.

Berries affected with American gooseberry mildew aren't attractive but are still edible.

Grapes

People may associate grapes with warmer climes, but they're actually hardy and easy to grow, and new varieties crop more reliably than older kinds in the UK's unpredictable summers. Grapes suffer from some of the usual problems, such as aphids and whitefly as well as scale, but also have a few other more specific problems, many of which are cultural rather than caused by disease:

✔ **Red spider mite** is a minute pest that affects most fruit growing in greenhouses and sometimes outside too in hot summers. Hot, dry conditions suit red spider mites. They feed on the leaves, sucking the sap from cells and forming a fine webbing over the leaves – much finer than a spider's web. An early sign of red spider mite infestation is a yellow mottling of the foliage, especially the young leaves at the shoot tips and at the top of the greenhouse where conditions are hottest and driest. The leaves may become bronzed, brown and crispy around the edges and fall prematurely.

Few insecticides are effective against red spider mite and maintaining good ventilation to reduce temperature, regular misting to increase humidity, and wetting the foliage all limit red spider mite numbers and damage.

In greenhouses you can introduce a biological control (a parasitic mite that eats red spider mite) at the start of the season, which is effective.

✔ **Vine mildew** is similar to mildew on other plants. You first see vine mildew on the leaves, which develop a white, powdery coating that spreads to the fruits, which often split and get infected with grey mould. To keep this disease under control, pick up fallen leaves in autumn and try to increase ventilation in summer. Pinching off excess growth throughout the summer, to improve air movement around the plant, also helps.

✔ **Shanking** is a cultivation-related problem that can arise from allowing too many bunches to develop on the plant, from waterlogging of the soil, or from drought. The individual fruit stalks shrivel, and the fruits shrivel too and taste unpleasant.

Peaches

Apart from general pests, diseases and calcium deficiency (see the later section on 'Plums and cherries'), only one problem makes life difficult for anyone growing peaches (and nectarines, which are simply hairless peaches) – *peach leaf curl*.

Peach leaf curl is a fungal disease that causes the foliage to curl and turn bright red. After a while the foliage drops prematurely. If this happens repeatedly over many years, the tree becomes severely weakened. The fungus remains on the tree in the bark and on the buds and re-infects the tree in spring. Protecting the tree with a waterproof cover such as a clear plastic sheet, or growing the plants in a polytunnel or greenhouse, prevents the leaves being infected each spring. Otherwise spray the tree with a fungicide in early spring, just as the buds are starting to grow and again after flowering. Peach leaf curl disease is a constant threat each year so you need to be vigilant every season.

Pears

Pears have two main, common problems – pear leaf blister mite and pear midge – and a less common one, pear rust:

- **Pear leaf blister mite** affects free-standing trees as well as wall-trained trees. The tiny mites cause small, yellow pimples that change to black blisters later in the season. Affected leaves fall early, which can weaken the tree a little. No chemical treatment exists for dealing with the problem, so be sure to pick off any affected leaves as soon as you see them.

- **Pear midge** is more destructive and you notice its presence when the small fruits turn black and fall off. The midge lays eggs in the tiny fruitlets and these develop into maggots and feed in a cavity within the pear. When the maggots are ready to *pupate* (in other words, change from maggots to adults), the pears drop to the ground and the maggots crawl out and remain in the soil under the tree until the following spring when they emerge as adults. Chemicals have a limited effect on pear midges, though you can spray with an insecticide as soon as the petals have dropped from the flowers. This kills some of the eggs and tiny maggots but you have to get the timing perfect for spraying to be effective and this is difficult to predict. A better, and more organic, tactic is to pick off or pick up all the fallen, black fruits and fork over the soil under the tree frequently so that birds can feed on the grubs.

- **Pear rust** is a less common problem that causes rusty orange lumps to grow on the underside of leaves. Often these lumps are spiky and look different from most other rusts. Fortunately, pear rust is mainly a cosmetic problem and doesn't do much harm. Where possible, the best course of action is simply to pick off the affected leaves.

Plums and cherries

Both plum and cherry trees have several pests and diseases that can affect your crop. They are prone to bacterial diseases that can cause branches to die back, often associated with a sticky gummy ooze called *gummosis*. Trees usually survive for many years with bacterial infections, especially if they're otherwise healthy, but they eventually have so much dieback that you need to remove them.

- **Calcium deficiency**, a situation where the trees don't absorb enough calcium because of drought, causes the stone in the centre of plums, peaches and cherries to form wrongly and the young fruits to fall prematurely or be misshapen. All *stone fruits* – those that have a large stone (seed) in the centre – as well as most tree fruit need calcium (lime) to produce fruit and so tend to prefer alkaline soils. Although most plants may suffer from a lack of calcium, a deficiency is especially noticeable in stone fruits (see *bitter pit* in the earlier section on 'Apples' too). You can at least reduce the effects of calcium deficiency by applying a fertiliser rich in calcium, such as bonemeal or fish, blood and bone, and trying to make sure the plants don't go short of water.

✔ **Silver leaf** is the most serious fungal disease that affects these fruits. It produces tiny purple bracket fungi on the bark of infected trees that release spores into the air in winter. Affected trees produce leaves that have a silvery sheen; branches die back and crops are reduced.

No cure for silver leaf exists, but you can prevent infection by removing affected branches. When cut, affected branches have a brown stain in the centre, so prune back to where no internal staining is visible. Only prune in summer when the trees are in leaf. If you prune the trees in winter, the airborne spores can infect the wounds.

False silver leaf is a common disorder on Victoria plums and is the result of poor cultivation. You can diagnose this condition because the branches have no internal staining.

✔ **Shot hole** is a disease most common on both ornamental and edible cherries. On affected plants, small yellow spots first appear on leaves: these turn brown and then drop out of the leaf, making the tree look as if it has been at the angry end of a shot gun! No cure exists but trees usually survive if you feed and water them well.

✔ **Plum moth** is a serious problem, the equivalent of codling moth in apples. Plum moths lay eggs on the tiny plums and after hatching, the maggots burrow into the fruits and feed on the flesh, close to the stone. You can't tell they're there until you eat the plum and discover the white or pink maggots, along with their droppings.

The simplest way to control plum moth is to hang traps in your trees in spring. Plum moth traps work by releasing *pheromones* (sex hormones) that attract male moths to a sticky pad where they get trapped and die, preventing fertilisation of the females and the laying of fertile eggs to some extent.

Raspberries

Raspberries can attract a host of potential pests and diseases but thankfully very few of them are common. Here are the ones to watch out for:

✔ **Spur blight** is a fungus, more common on summer-fruiting varieties than on those that fruit in autumn. The canes that grow the first year start to develop purple patches around the dormant buds at the ends of the shoots in autumn. These patches spread, turn silvery as the fungus invades the stem, and kill the upper part of it. Wet weather makes the problem worse. All you can do to control spur blight is to cut out the affected stems.

✔ **Raspberry beetle** is the most serious of all raspberry problems, and can also affect hybrid berries (such as loganberries and tayberries) and blackberries. The small, adult beetles feed on the flowers and lay eggs, which hatch out and feed as grubs in the fruit. Insecticides are effective but timing the spraying correctly (the correct time to spray is just as the fruits are turning pink) is vital.

Autumn-fruiting raspberries often escape attack.

✔ **Virus** diseases, spread by aphids, are serious. *Mosaic virus* is the main virus that affects raspberries, causing the leaves to develop irregular yellowish patches and plants to become stunted and less productive. If infected plants are present on allotment sites, your plants are almost certain to get this virus eventually. No cure exists for virus diseases and the way to deal with them is to dig out and burn the infected plants.

✔ **Grey mould** is a common problem that affects raspberries, strawberries and other fruits, especially autumn-fruiting varieties and in cool, wet summers. It shows as a grey 'fluff' on the fruits and spreads rapidly if fruits touch. Chemical controls aren't very effective against grey mould, so pick off and dispose of infected fruits and try to improve air circulation around the fruits by removing some leaves.

Strawberries

Strawberries suffer from similar problems to raspberries. The most serious are viruses that cause leaf yellowing and reduced vigour, grey mould, and slugs and snails attacking the ripening fruits.

Strawberries also suffer from *vine weevil*. The adult insects are about 1 centimetre long and crawl around plants and soil throughout summer laying eggs. These hatch into grubs that are again about a centimetre long, creamy white with a brown head, and which live and feed underground. These grubs are most serious for container plants where the strawberry roots are contained. In many cases the grubs eat all the roots and the plants wilt and die. The best treatment against vine weevil on edible crops is to water parasitic nematodes onto the soil or compost from late spring to autumn. (See Chapter 6 for more about nematodes.)

Part III
Growing Tasty Veg

'If I could speak a foreign language then
I would know how this exotic vegetable I bought
will eventually turn out.'

In this part . . .

Making the decision to grow your own veg is your first step, but you need to know what to put in the ground to start. You also need to consider your soil and your location, and what you can do to make sure that your plants have the best possible chance of growing.

It may be that some plants just can't grow on your plot. This part helps you to recognise when this is the case and when to accept that nature knows best.

One problem that I help you with is deciding where to begin; with so many tasty and healthy vegetables to choose from, this can be tricky. A good method is to decide which ones you like eating best, and then to look them up in this section and try growing these. Another option is to plump for leafy crops such as salads, baby leaves, spinach and leaf beet – crops that are either difficult to find in shops, expensive to buy, or that deteriorate and lose their vitamins as soon as you pick them. This isn't a problem, though, when you grow your own and can eat them straight from the garden.

Most people start with summer veg, with tomatoes the most popular of all summer crops – reliable and easy to grow, even if you have just a small patio or balcony, and much tastier than any you can buy in the shops.

The miracle of harvesting your first crops, grown from seed, and nurtured by you throughout their lives, is an experience you'll never forget. This part enables you to achieve that aim.

Chapter 8

Looking After Leafy Crops

. . . .

In This Chapter

▶ Getting to grow tasty salads all year

▶ Growing the cabbage patch family

▶ Trying crops you rarely see for sale

. . . .

Simply put, leaf crops are good for you. They are the most nutritionally important of all vegetables. As crops they vary from plants that need almost a year to mature to quick, 'baby leaf' plants that can be grown in the smallest garden and harvested after just a few months. These crops are for everyone and they include some of the best-loved (and most hated) veg.

In this chapter, I take you through tending the most commonly grown leafy crops, and introduce you to a few lesser-known ones as well. I walk you through the process of growing each plant from scratch, but remember that you also have the option in many cases of buying ready-grown plants to raise.

Selecting Succulent Salads

Eating raw food is the best way to get all the nutrients from your crops. Salad has a bad image in the UK, usually consisting of boring lettuce, hard tomatoes and tasteless cucumber. But you can find many more leaves to spice up your salads and energise your taste buds. Although the popularity of Iceberg types has transformed lettuce from limp and tasteless to crisp and, well, tasteless, and salads have been spruced up by bags of mixed leaves, you can do far better by growing your own. With tastes as varied as hot and spicy rocket and mustard, refreshing purslane and pea shoots, and the mouthwatering acid tang of sorrel, every salad you make can have its own distinctive character. (Check out the chapters in Part III for more salad suggestions.)

Making a hearty salad: Lettuce

For most people lettuce is the mainstay of any salad. A bigger and more exciting choice of varieties is available now than ever before, and you can grow all kinds as baby salad leaves, too.

People usually eat lettuce raw, but it also makes a surprisingly good soup and also tastes good after you lightly fry it in butter or add it, shredded, to fresh, young peas.

Green lettuce leaves are rich in betacarotene and vitamin C and red lettuce contains additional antioxidants. All types contain a little fibre, too.

Sowing and cultivating lettuce

When you've chosen the variety you want to grow, follow these steps to get going:

1. **Sow the seeds.** For a crop that's associated with summer, lettuce is odd in that the seeds germinate poorly if the soil is too warm; therefore, sow on cool days or in the evening in summer. Avoid sowing if the temperature is above 25 degrees Celsius. This advice is most important a few hours after sowing and watering, because the seeds absorb moisture.

   Lettuces often run to seed in hot weather, so try to avoid sowing large quantities at any one time. Growing lettuce for harvesting in early summer and early autumn is easier. You can sow a few varieties (mostly butterhead) in late summer for cropping in late autumn and early winter but these are only successful if you grow them in a greenhouse or polytunnel or under cloches (a transparent covering). Remember to choose an appropriate variety if you're sowing lettuce for autumn and winter use.

   You can treat the seeds in two different ways: sowing where they are to grow or in pots, trays and grow bags.

   > You can sow lettuce seed outside in rows from the end of March, as long as the weather isn't too cold. Sow about 1 centimetre deep in rows and cover. Seeds start to grow within two weeks.

   > Your other option is to sow seed in pots and trays and transplant the seedlings into cell trays, planting the seedlings out where they're to grow when they have three or four leaves. But lettuces don't always transplant well, so another option is to sow two or three seeds in each cell of a cell tray and then plant out the seedlings. This method often works well and is useful for sowing in summer when keeping seed rows moist in hot weather can be difficult.

Space most varieties of lettuce 20–30 centimetres apart, depending on the variety.

Lettuces prefer moist soil that is rich in organic matter and although best in full sun you can grow them in part shade, especially loose-leaf types. Keep them watered in dry weather and free from weeds or crowded, outer leaves may rot.

Lettuces are very susceptible to slug and snail damage and if you think that your seeds have not germinated, these little pests may be to blame. Protect your seedlings as soon as they start to appear.

2. **Cultivate your plants.** When the seedlings appear you need to thin them to give the remaining seedlings room to mature. When the seedlings are about 8 centimetres high, carefully transplant some to grow in another row. Choose a dull day to do this and water the row the night before. Lift the spare seedlings carefully, replant them immediately in their new home, and water them. The transplanted lettuce matures a week or two after the others. Alternatively, you can pull up and eat spare seedlings at any stage of growth.

Harvesting and storing your lettuce

The best time to harvest lettuce is just before you need to eat it. You can harvest all types of lettuce at any stage of development but hearted kinds are mature when the centre is full and firm to the touch. Most varieties 'stand' (in other words, remain at their peak) for a week or two but in hot or wet weather they may deteriorate or run to seed.

Choosing varieties

Lettuce is divided into four main groups:

✔ **Butterheads** are the typical soft-leaved cheap supermarket lettuce with creamy yellow hearts. They are quick to mature and are generally for spring and summer sowing. Once the staple of most salads, butterheads are now less popular.

- **All Year Round** has a compact habit and is good for early sowing under cover or outside in late spring.

- **Sangria** is a good choice for organic growers thanks to its resistance to disease and pests. Pale green hearts and red outer leaves make this a distinctive-looking variety.

- **Tom Thumb** is a compact variety, ideal for raised beds and pots.

✔ **Crispheads** (also known as **Icebergs**) are easily recognisable in supermarkets by their dense, heavy heads of crunchy, crisp leaves. Crispheads are easy to grow for summer and autumn cropping.

- **Lakeland** produces dense heads with a compact habit.

- **Sioux** has an unusual appearance, with red leaves that are most intense in hot weather.

- **Webbs Wonderful** is a traditional variety with small, dense heads. Webbs Wonderful was grown long before Iceberg-type lettuce became popular and is still available.

✔ **Cos** have upright, dense heads that are crisp and crunchy and essential for Caesar salad. They take longer to mature than other groups of lettuce, but are generally tastier.

- **Counter** produces dense, crisp, sweet heads and is resistant to many lettuce problems including mildew and tip burn (brown tips to leaves).

- **Little Gem** and **Bubbles** are mini-Coses, popular in supermarkets and ideal for small gardens because of their neat size – you can plant as close as 15 centimetres apart. Several 'improved' variants such as 'Little Gem Pearl' are available.

- **Lobjoits Green Cos** is a traditional favourite suitable for late sowing to harvest into winter or spring.

- **Winter Gem** is an ideal lettuce for autumn sowing for cropping in spring in a greenhouse.

✔ **Looseleafs** (also known as cut and come again) are adaptable and you can harvest them by picking individual leaves or cutting them off for re-sprouting. They don't form hearts. Looseleaf lettuces come in a wide range of foliage shapes and colours. Most crop for long periods and so are useful to fill gaps between other types that may not be ready.

- **Lollo Bionda** forms large heads of frilly green leaves. Not the best variety for eating, but looks great and withstands heat well.

- **Lollo Rosso** produces large heads of red, frilly leaves.

- **Salad Bowl,** easy and reliable to grow, is an old favourite with flabby, soft, green leaves.

Bouncing back: Cut-and-come-again crops

Commonly known simply as salad leaves or baby leaves, cut-and-come-again crops make up the salads that supermarkets sell in bags. These are the simplest crops you can grow, and they save you the most money. In recent years the number of varieties available has increased dramatically, giving you more options when choosing what to grow.

All cut-and-come again crops are for eating while the plants are small, which means they're the perfect crops to grow in containers, where space is at a premium, and when you need a crop fast! None of these crops are fussy about soil but try to avoid heavy, wet, clay soils, especially if you intend to sow early in spring or want to grow crops in late summer and autumn.

Adding a few tangy, home-grown leaves to shop-bought veg brings extra nutrients and excitement to your plate.

Most of these leaves are packed with vitamins, betacarotene and folic acid. Dark green leaves are more nutritious and rich in vitamin C, so eat them as soon as you pick them to get the greatest benefit.

Sowing and cultivating cut-and-come-again crops

1. **Sow the seeds.** You can grow most cut-and-come-again crops in the open ground, in pots and containers, and in grow bags, from spring to late summer.

   In pots, fill them with multipurpose compost, firming it gently and watering it well. Sow the seeds thinly, about 5 millimetres apart, and cover them lightly with compost. Water them regularly and the seedlings should appear in about a week, when sown in summer. This takes longer when the weather is cool.

   In the garden, sow the seeds thinly in rows and keep them moist at all times.

2. **Thin out your seedlings.** You can pull and eat crowded seedlings and then harvest individual leaves or shear off patches. Depending on the time of year, if you shear them off you should be able to harvest again in as little as one or two weeks.

3. **Keep plants well watered.** This helps ensure that they produce at least one more flush of fresh leaves for you to enjoy.

Harvesting and storing your cut-and-come-again crops

Some cut-and-come-again crops are naturally small plants whereas others are familiar plants that you simply crop when young. In many cases you can start to crop as little as six weeks after sowing. With care, you should be able to harvest cut-and-come-again crops, by shearing off the leaves, at least twice. Picking individual leaves from plants here and there takes longer but doesn't weaken the plants as much and they'll keep cropping for much longer.

Choosing varieties

You can choose from a wide variety of cut-and-come-again crops. I've named some of the most popular types below, but you can also include chard, mizuna, mustard, pak choi and spinach (all covered in full elsewhere in this chapter) in your list of cut-and-come-again crops:

- **Beetroot:** All beetroot leaves are edible, having a mild flavour, but growers now commonly sow it for harvesting as baby leaves. Bulls Blood is a popular ornamental variety grown for its deep red leaves and is a popular addition to salad leaf mixes. Beetroot has a long harvest period.

- **Cress:** In addition to the familiar cress sprinkled on salads as seedlings you can try Greek or wrinkled cress, which has 'bubbled' leaves with the same hot taste. Cress is quick and easy to grow.

- **Endive:** Although people usually grow endive as an autumn lettuce substitute, young leaves from seedlings add a bitter contrast to salad mixes. They are rather tough in texture but the frilly types such as D'Estale A Cuore Giallo are popular.

- **Lambs lettuce:** A popular leaf for autumn and winter use, lambs lettuce is easy to grow throughout the year, and despite its rather bland taste is valuable as a winter salad when little else is available. You can harvest individual leaves or leaf clusters, or cut the plant off at the base.

- **Land cress:** This substitute for watercress is easier to grow, hardy and long lasting. The rather tough leaves have a peppery taste. You can sow land cress throughout summer but you're probably best off sowing in summer for autumn and winter crops. Watercress itself is now available as seed to grow as baby leaves but it needs moist soil and, in most gardens, land cress is an acceptable substitute and far easier to grow. A variegated form of land cress exists that you can easily grow from seed, is just as tasty, and looks pretty in the flower garden, too. Both green and variegated plants sown in late summer and autumn provide leaves all through the winter and into spring but then produce clusters of yellow flowers in spring which you can discard.

- **Purslane:** Golden and green purslane are delicious but unusual salad greens. The rather straggly plants have fleshy stems and leaves that are crunchy and crisp. Start purslane off in a seed tray, because the seeds are tiny, and grow it under glass because it prefers warmth. You can plant the seedlings into patio pots in a sunny spot or grow them in a warm, sheltered place outside. Purslane has a long season after it starts to crop.

- **Radish:** Most radishes have rough, bristly leaves but you can also grow a leaf radish that has a hot, peppery flavour for adding to salads. You can sow them where they're to grow, either in pots, in containers, or in grow bags on the patio or in the open garden, making sure you keep them moist at all times to preserve their tenderness. Pick and eat them while they're young and before they get tough and too peppery.

- **Rocket:** Rocket is the most popular of all spicy salad leaves and is now available in a range of forms, with plain or frilly leaves. Most varieties have a hot, peppery taste that strengthens as plants age and when the weather gets hot. In hot weather rocket plants bolt quickly but even the flowers are edible. Sow a little and often throughout spring, summer and autumn.

The joy of growing salad leaves

If you only grow one crop – though I hope you try growing many more – make sure you grow salad leaves. A packet of mixed leaves seeds costs about the same as a standard pack of leaves in a shop but gives you the equivalent of twenty bags or more of fresh, tasty leaves.

You don't have to wait long for them to grow, and even if you don't have a garden, you can grow salad leaves easily in a container of multipurpose compost or even in a grow bag. No other crop is as easy to grow or rewards you more quickly.

✔ **Saladini:** Most seed companies sell several mixtures of salad leaves. Although traditionally called 'saladini' you can now buy these in various themes or tastes according to the mix of seeds. The most common are French or Provençal mixes with endive and chervil in with the usual lettuce and rocket, Oriental mixes with pak choi, mustard and other Chinese greens, and milder lettuce mixes. Some seeds in these mixes germinate after others so the mix of leaves varies as you pick them as the plants mature.

✔ **Salsola:** You rarely see this odd crop but it's worth a try. The leaves are crunchy with a distinctly salty taste but are rather tough so you're best using them sparingly in a mixed salad. Sow the large seeds directly where plants are to grow in late spring when the soil is warm. They take a long time to germinate. Salsola plants have a branched habit and long, needle-like leaves; although spindly at first, the plants quickly become bushy and crop well. Harvest salsola by pinching off the shoot tips.

✔ **Weeds:** Yes, weeds! Vegetable growers usually hate weeds but a few of them do have their uses. Some weeds are edible and the two most useful are bittercress – a common weed often found on cultivated ground, with a hot, peppery taste – and chickweed – which is very common on allotments. At its best in spring, chickweed has a mild, fresh taste. (Chapter 2 tells you more about weeds.)

Be sure to wash weeds well before eating to remove aphids. Also, although very few weeds are poisonous, please be absolutely sure that you correctly identify your weeds before you eat them!

Keep on growing: Winter salads

To grow salads for winter use you need to select the right plants and then protect them against the worst winter weather, so you need a greenhouse, a polytunnel or cloches. No crops grow much in winter, so to have leaves to harvest then, you need to sow seeds in late summer or early autumn, allowing the plants to grow until early winter.

Sowing winter salads

Here's how to grow miner's lettuce:

1. **Sow the seeds** in autumn. Miner's lettuce thrives on light, sandy soils. The plants grow to form mounds of pale green leaves.

2. **Harvest the leaves** throughout winter and into spring when the plant starts to flower. Miner's lettuce often seeds itself so after you've grown it once you may not need to sow it again.

Harvesting and storing your winter salads

All winter salad crops should be eaten immediately after you pick them because they don't store well. If you wash them, to rinse off any soil and slugs, you can keep them for a day or two in the fridge, but they start to lose nutrients as soon as you pick them – one big advantage of growing your own and eating them fresh!

Choosing varieties

Suitable crops for growing at this time of year include some lettuce varieties such as All Year Round, leaf beet, beetroot, land cress, lamb's lettuce and many oriental greens. (See the sections 'A taste of the East: Chinese greens' later in this chapter and 'Bouncing back: Cut-and-come-again crops' earlier in this chapter for the lowdown on growing these crops.)

Another crop to consider growing in winter is miner's lettuce (or claytonia). This plant has round leaves that are succulent and crisp with a mild taste.

Blooming lovely: Edible flowers

Although even contemplating eating flowers may seem strange, cauliflowers, calabrese and globe artichokes are actually flower buds and we drink teas containing jasmine and orange flowers added, so its not as unusual as it first seems. While the flowers I mention here are never going to become an important part of your daily diet, they can add some bright colours to your meals and those colours contain antioxidants that may do you some good.

You can eat the flowers of most herbs, such as thyme, rosemary, coriander and chervil, when they appear but you can also grow a few flowers specifically for eating too. You don't have to go to huge efforts to do this – just mix them between your rows of vegetables where they'll look pretty and attract beneficial insects such as hoverflies and bees to pollinate your beans and tomatoes, among others.

Small but perfectly formed: Microgreens and sprouts

Microgreens is the new, fashionable name for seedlings such as old-fashioned mustard and cress, and growers are also adopting this method of cultivation for radish, broccoli, cabbage, rocket, mooli and other seeds. We used to grow mustard and cress on wet flannel or perhaps in shallow trays of compost but the current practice is to sow them on shallow trays of *vermiculite* (inert, sterile expanded volcanic rock, available at garden centres, often mixed with compost for seed sowing). The plants grow quickly on the windowsill or in the greenhouse and you can shear them off after a few weeks when the seed leaves are expanded. In this way you can produce healthy salads all year round!

Seed sprouts are another way to raise a wide range of salad crops, including alfalfa, fenugreek, clover, and many beans and lentils. You can save money by sprouting lentils (not red split lentils), aduki beans and mung beans bought at the supermarket for cooking, which are far cheaper than the seeds you can specifically buy for sprouting. If you intend sprouting only a few seeds, the cheapest way to do it is with a clean jam jar. Put a teaspoon of seeds in the bottom, half-fill the jar with clean cold water and put a piece of cloth, such as muslin or fine netting, over the top and secure it with a rubber band. After 12 hours, drain the water out, add more water, and rinse again with fresh water. From then on you don't leave the seeds soaking in water again – just rinse them every 12 hours. That's all there is to it: no soil and no fertiliser – just add water! Alternatively, you can buy seed sprouters, the simplest of which are jars with screw-on plastic tops made of plastic with mesh in the lid. When you get more adventurous, you can buy stackable, layered sprouters that enable you to sprout a range of sprouts in a small area.

You can eat most sprouts, raw or lightly stir-fried and a valuable source of nutrients, within a few days. Most are best for eating before they get too large, when some, such as alfalfa and fenugreek, may become slightly bitter.

The *potager,* although literally a 'soup garden', is a term that applies to a veg garden that is both productive and attractive and combines flowers, vegetables and fruit, and is an ideal approach for small-space gardeners where veggies are on view all year. The flowers in a potager aren't restricted to edible flowers and you can have rows or clumps of flowers for cutting such as dahlias and cosmos.

Although you don't need to go as far as Homer Simpson (whose secret shame is to slip away somewhere quiet and eat handfuls of flowers), throwing in a few edible flowers is a great way of brightening up your salads, cakes and drinks. Flowers may not be the first crop you think of growing, and they're unlikely ever to comprise a large proportion of your diet, but try sprinkling some over a salad to make it look more tempting and maybe more appealing to children.

The best edible flowers to start with are as follows:

- **English marigolds** (*Calendula*) have a long history of use – the petals were used to colour rice and butter. Pick the petals off the flowers and sprinkle them in your salad. They have a spicy but pleasant taste.

- **Nasturtiums** (*Tropaeolum majus*) have a spicy, peppery taste. The leaves are edible too, but watch out for blackfly in the blooms. The leaves make great additions to sandwiches and you can drop the flowers onto salads or make a finely chopped egg mayonnaise and put a dollop of this into the centre of the flowers – it looks and tastes great!

- **Roses** of all kinds are edible but cut off the bitter, white, tough base of the petals. Rose petals are best coated with egg white, dipped in caster sugar, and dried as candied petals but you can add them to salads, too. Choose thin-textured petals and avoid the thick, rather leathery petals of big hybrid tea roses.

Other edible flowers include pansies and violas (just the petals), borage (cut out the black beak), most herbs such as rosemary, sage and lavender, and pinks (*dianthus*).

Never eat flowers bought for ornamental purposes because they may have been sprayed with chemicals. Also remember that they may contain pollen and not be suitable for people with some allergies.

Getting to Know the Cabbage Family

Brussels sprouts, cabbage, cauliflowers, broccoli, calabrese, Chinese greens (pak choi and mustards) and kale, along with turnips, radish, kohl rabi and swede (turn to Chapter 9 for more about these root crops) are often called *brassicas*. This group of vegetables includes crops that you can harvest more or less all year round if you stagger sowing and choose the right varieties, which makes them particularly valuable as sources of greens in winter and spring.

Although at first glance brassicas seem a diverse group, they're botanically related and have some common requirements. They all require full sun and a deep, fertile and well-firmed soil, especially Brussels sprouts, cabbage and cauliflower. All brassicas grow well on heavy, clay soils, and digging in some garden compost or well-rotted compost helps them along, especially on light, sandy soils. Most brassicas benefit from additional applications of high-nitrogen fertiliser, especially in spring or when they are young. Most importantly, all brassicas appreciate an alkaline soil, not only for healthy growth but also to suppress *clubroot* – the main soil disease that affects them.

Clubroot is a disease that spreads in the soil, so you're better off growing your own plants from scratch and not accepting gifts that have grown in the open ground, because they may harbour the disease. However, plants grown in containers and resistant varieties, such as the cabbage Kilaton, shouldn't pose a risk of disease. Kilaton is an F1 hybrid variety – these varieties often have great resistance to disease and are well worth considering, particularly when growing Brussels sprouts and cauliflowers (Chapter 3 tells you more about F1 hybrids). Also, you can help prevent the build-up of soil pests and diseases by making sure that you don't grow the same crop in the same soil for too long.

Brassicas also fall prey to other common problems such as mealy aphids, cabbage white butterflies and cabbage root fly.

Because a wide range of pests attack these crops, consider growing them under nets or fleece. Fine nets, held above the leaves, protect them from cabbage white butterflies in summer and pigeons in winter. Fleece is suitable for the smaller crops such as Oriental greens and protects them from butterflies, brassica whitefly and mealy aphids. (Chapter 7 gives you the lowdown on dealing with pests and diseases.)

Many people used to regard brassicas as too boring to consider growing, but the health benefits of eating them have made them increasingly popular. Not all are easy to grow – you may find that some are quite challenging – but that's part of the fun of gardening.

Eat brassicas as quickly as possible after harvest for the most nutrients. All these crops contain vitamins C and E and minerals, as well as betacarotene – nutrients and antioxidants considered essential for our health. Dark-coloured brassicas are the most nutritious; for example, loose, dark green cabbage is more beneficial for you than dense white cabbage. The way you cook food is also important – cooking veg for a short time means that it retains these health benefits better than when it's cooked for longer, as in boiling. Boiling isn't bad in itself – just be sure to use boiling water from the start, as little of it as possible, and avoid cooking the veg for so long that it loses its green colour. So that you can still benefit from the goodness in the water you've used, you can then use it for gravy and soup.

From Belgium with love: Brussels sprouts

Sprouts. You either love 'em or hate 'em. I spent many a childhood Christmas trying to avoid eating the dreaded green 'death balls', but eventually they won me over. Their subtle, nutty flavour when cooked well is something to savour, and because they're best for cooking and eating straight after harvesting, while small and tender, growing your own is well worth the effort.

Sprout tops (the rosette of leaves at the top of the plants) are a tasty and nutritious crop and you can remove them at any time when the plants are fully grown. Cutting the tops off autumn-maturing sprouts may even advance the swelling of buttons.

Most people boil their Brussels – for too long! Sprouts are far tastier, and more nutritious, if you only lightly boil them. If you fancy something different you can grate and eat them raw. To really enjoy these healthy veg, cook them for the minimum time and, if you're not vegetarian, try combining them with bacon, lard or chestnuts – they complement each other really well.

Brussels sprouts are a rich source of vitamins E and C and minerals such as iron and calcium and antioxidants.

Sowing and cultivating Brussel sprouts

So you've now chosen which variety to grow. Here's how to set about growing them:

1. **Sow the seeds in small pots or seed trays in a greenhouse, any time from late winter to mid-spring, depending on when the variety you choose matures.**

2. **Lightly cover the seeds with compost and, when the seedlings are large enough (when they start to produce their first true leaves between the seed leaves) transplant them into small (8 centimetre-diameter) pots or cell trays.** (Chapter 3 contains more information.)

3. **Plant your seedlings out where they're to grow when they have four or five leaves.** They need a lot of space, so plant the seedlings 75 centimetres apart, and deeply, and firm the soil around them well. Be sure to give them a good watering straight away.

4. **Keep your plants weed-free, and protect them from slugs, snails and rabbits**, especially when the plants are small (take a look at Chapter 7 for tips on how to do this). As older leaves die and yellow, pull them off and pick them up to prevent disease and slugs.

5. **Support your plants with stakes to keep them upright as they grow,** especially on windy sites.

You usually need to water your plants only in extremely dry periods.

Brussels sprouts have a long growing season, although modern varieties offer a choice of picking time from October to March. Early varieties occupy the soil for at least six months, and up to ten months for those harvested in late winter. Plants generally reach their full size before the buttons start to swell. If your soil is light, not well firmed, or is too rich in *humus* (decomposing plant material such as compost), old, cheap varieties may not form tight buttons. Loose buttons are perfectly edible but don't look quite as good on the plate.

Because sprouts take up space for a long time, sow salad crops between the plants when you plant them out. Salad crops mature in a few months and you can harvest them before the sprouts shade them too much.

Choosing varieties

You can choose from a number of different varieties of Brussels sprout when deciding what to grow, and I list here some of the best. The biggest difference between them is harvesting time.

- ✔ **Exodus F1** is a mid- to late season variety, straddling winter and spring, with excellent resistance to many common diseases, which makes it a good option for organic growers.

- ✔ **Falstaff** is a beautiful addition to your garden. This red sprout has attractive leaves and good crops of purple sprouts in late autumn and early winter.

- ✔ **Maximus F1** is unusual among modern varieties because the buttons mature over a long period from autumn to early spring.

- ✔ **Nelson F1** has strong, upright stems and an early crop of well-flavoured sprouts that make this a good choice if you want a crop from late summer until early winter.

- ✔ **Trafalgar F1** is notable mainly for the sweet taste of the buttons that may appeal to those who usually dislike them. You can harvest Trafalgar in midwinter.

Few other vegetables have been improved so dramatically by the introduction of F1 hybrids, which are generally smaller in size, uniform but vigorous, and more likely to hold a crop of tight 'buttons'. On the negative side, they also tend to produce buttons that all mature at the same time. So if you choose F1 hybrids select two or three varieties and grow a small number of each. The average F1 hybrid plant should produce about 850 grams of sprouts.

Harvesting and storing your brussel sprouts

You can pick your sprouts as soon as they're large enough to use. Although you can store them for a few days in the fridge or freezer, sprouts taste their finest when you eat them fresh, so clean, cook and eat them immediately to get them at their best. Although sprouts are now available from September onwards, they're most valuable as a winter veg and many people think they taste better after frosting.

A vegetable for all seasons: Cabbage

Cabbages are a great choice when growing your own veg. Unlike most crops, with planning and care you can harvest cabbages all year round. Therefore, you need never stop eating your own crops, even in the coldest months of the year.

Shredded and raw cabbage is good but most people usually boil it. However, cabbage retains its nutrients best when you cook it by steaming. Either way, cook cabbage for the shortest time, and by adding some butter and pepper you can really make it taste delicious.

Cabbage – especially the green outer leaves – is rich in vitamins C and E and betacarotene.

Sowing and cultivating cabbage

Here are the steps to take to sow and raise your cabbage plants. You sow them all in the same way as Brussels sprouts – in pots or trays – and just vary the sowing time according to the type of cabbage:

1. **Sow the seeds in small pots or seed trays in a greenhouse.** You can do this any time from late winter to mid-spring, depending on when the variety you choose matures.

   Summer cabbage. Sow the first seeds in early spring in a greenhouse. If you're growing F1 hybrids, which mature very uniformly, sow a few seeds of different varieties every month so that you avoid a glut of cabbages. Sow late summer cabbages in late spring and you can crop them well into autumn.

   Winter cabbage. Sow these seeds in spring.

   Spring cabbage. Sow spring cabbage seeds in mid- to late summer.

   Red cabbage. Sow these autumn and winter-maturing cabbages in spring.

2. **Lightly cover the seeds with compost and, when the seedlings are large enough, (when they start to produce their first true leaves between the seed leaves) transplant them into small (8 centimetre-diameter) pots or cell trays.** (See Chapter 3 for more information.)

3. **Cabbages prefer fertile soil so sprinkle some general fertiliser (at about 100 grams per square metre or as the pack states) before planting.**

4. **Plant your seedlings out where they're to grow, in a sunny spot, when they have four or five leaves.** The seedlings need a lot of space, and be sure to plant them deeply and to firm the soil around them well. Also give them a good watering straight away.

   Summer cabbage. Plant out the seedlings in late spring, 45 centimetres apart: they mature in a few months.

   Winter cabbage. Space the seedlings 45 centimetres apart: they don't mature until late autumn and winter.

Spring cabbage. Space plants 30 centimetres apart. For spring greens, plant closer; or sow directly in the soil where you plan them to grow and thin the plants to 15 centimetres apart in autumn. You can eat the small plants as greens as you thin them out.

Red cabbage. Space plants 30–45 centimetres apart. Red cabbage needs wide spacing because it's so leafy.

You can get a second crop from most cabbages after you cut the main head by cutting a cross in the top of the stem when you've cut the head. This technique enables several tufts of leaves to grow in a month or so, which you can use as tender spring greens at most times of the year.

Harvesting and storing your cabbage

The best way to harvest cabbages is to do it as you need to use them. However, by removing the outer, green leaves you can store the dense hearts in a fridge or other cool place for a week or more. You can store dense-headed cabbages and red cabbage even longer but their nutrient values decrease over time. You can also chop and freeze cabbage.

Choosing varieties

Cabbages come in all shapes and sizes, and are largely grouped according to the seasons in which they grow. *Summer cabbages* grow quickly and are the easiest to start with. Here are some varieties that I recommend:

- **Derby Day** is a reliable, really early, ball-headed variety for crops in midsummer.

- **Golden Acre Primo** is a famous cabbage suitable for all gardens because the plants are compact. The dense, tight heads are suitable for coleslaw.

- **Greyhound,** an older variety with pointed, dense heads, is still popular and grows quickly.

- **Hispi** is similar to Greyhound, with large, pointed heads and a tender, sweet taste. Perhaps the best-known variety, Hispi is the one to grow if you're not sure whether you like cabbage.

- **Kilaton F1** matures in late summer, producing large heads of dense leaves. Kilaton F1 is most notable for being resistant to clubroot disease.

- **Minicole F1** is the best choice for raised beds and small plots. You can space the plants just 30 centimetres apart, and they form dense, tight heads in autumn.

Winter cabbages have the longest growing season and take up your ground for a long time. However, they do include some particularly tasty varieties such as the Savoy types, which have wrinkled leaves. Here are a few recommendations:

- **January King 3** is a tough and dependable cabbage, with dense, large heads that stand well through winter until spring.

- **Robin F1** has beautiful, grey leaves tinged with purple, making it a traditional type of winter cabbage. It has large, dense, heavy heads that withstand winter weather.

- **Serve F1** is an adaptable Savoy choice that can mature from summer to autumn.

- **Tarvoy F1** is an ideal choice for colder gardens with 'Savoyed' leaves and dense heads that stand well in the garden for several months when mature.

- **Tundra F1** is a real crowd-pleaser. This hardy cabbage is part Savoy and has slightly crinkled leaves. Tundra F1 matures in late autumn and stands in good condition till spring.

Spring cabbages grow through the winter and you can harvest them in late winter and spring. You can crop immature plants as spring greens – as leafy heads before they've formed dense heads. Most varieties have pointed heads but some are round. Growing these varieties means that you keep your plot productive, because not much else can be harvested at this time of year. Here are a couple of spring varieties worth considering:

- **April F1** should be planted in late summer. You can crop as a spring green in early spring or allow to mature to dense, pointed spring cabbage later on.

- **Offenham 2 Flower of Spring** is the traditional spring favourite, with tasty loose leaves or dense, conical heads if allowed to mature.

Red cabbages are easy to grow and very ornamental, with purple, grey-flushed leaves. All red cabbages have round, dense heads, with the exception of Kalibos, a pointed, summer cabbage. I recommend these varieties:

- **Kalibos** is an old, recently rediscovered red cabbage with pointed heads that matures in summer. This large, leafy plant is ideal for summer salads so worth allowing some space for.

- **Rodeo F1** has medium-sized, round heads that last well when they've matured. You can harvest rodeo F1 from summer until the year's end.

Curly and cute: Kale

Kales are a primitive type of cabbage that are hardy and easy to grow. They are especially useful as spring crops, although you can grow kale for harvesting all year round. The mature leaves can be tough, but the tender young shoots are very tasty.

Spring crops of kale, of the new, tender shoots, are great for boiling (in as little water as possible) or steaming, and served up with butter or grated with cheese and grilled.

Sowing and cultivating kale

Kales are easy to grow, hardy, and a good choice of veg if your garden is cold and exposed. Here's how to go about growing it:

1. **Sow the seeds.** You can sow and harvest a few varieties, such as Red Russian, as baby leaves. In general, though, sow seeds from spring to summer in trays in the same way as for cabbages (see Chapter 3 for the lowdown) and other brassicas.

2. **Transplant your seedlings into pots or cell trays**.

3. **When the seedlings have four or five leaves, plant them out in full sun and fertile soil, just as you would cabbages, spacing them 30–45 centimetres apart to mature.**

Harvesting and storing your kale

Kale doesn't store well and you're best off picking it as you need it. Because of its hardiness, kale is most valuable as a winter vegetable, but old leaves are rather tough – though very nutritious because of their deep green colour. The best crop is in spring, of the new, tender shoots.

Choosing varieties

The simplest variety is Jersey Kale, which has large, plain leaves on tall stems that can reach 2 metres or more. Jersey Kale is a novelty that people mainly grow for the stalks, which they can dry and use as walking sticks. The most popular varieties are the *curly kales*, which have intensely frilled leaves, rather like giant parsley. Most curly kales are dwarf in habit and withstand winter weather well, providing a useful winter and spring crop. Some growers find it difficult to clean curly kale leaves of soil, and so although they're not as attractive as their curly cousins, the plain-leaved varieties do have their advantages. In addition to green-leaved varieties some, such as Redbor, have deep purple leaves.

Here are a few great varieties to consider growing:

- **Black Tuscan** is sometimes called *palm cabbage*, and has long, narrow, crinkled, dark green leaves (that you need to pick individually) but doesn't form a head. It withstands winter cold well.

- **Redbor F1** looks almost too good to eat. Redbor is a curly kale with intensely frilly leaves that become a brighter red in cold weather.

- **Red Russian** has slightly frilled leaves that are grey with purple veins and is an intermediate type of kale. Growers often like Red Russian, more for its baby leaves than as a mature vegetable.

✔ **Starbor F1** is more compact than most curly kales, with tender foliage that you can eat all year round. Starbor is especially valuable in spring.

Quick off the mark: Calabrese

Although most people don't make much distinction between calabrese and broccoli, gardeners need to know the difference. Calabrese is a quick-growing crop, usually maturing in three or four months, and the plants aren't frost hardy. Imports have made calabrese available in the shops all year long. At home you can harvest crops from midsummer till late autumn, which is what most people call simply broccoli. However, broccoli (better called *sprouting broccoli*) is hardy and takes longer to mature, usually not producing those tasty heads until the spring of the year after sowing.

Although susceptible to all the usual brassica problems (see the section 'Getting to Know the Cabbage Family' earlier in this chapter), calabrese is an easy and worthwhile crop to grow.

The best way to cook calabrese is to steam or cut it into small pieces and stir-fry. You can even eat (and enjoy!) it raw. Try to avoid boiling calabrese for too long or it loses its wonderful green colour.

Calabrese is rich in vitamin C, iron, calcium and folic acid.

Sowing and cultivating calabrese

To grow a good crop of calabrese, follow these steps:

1. **Sow the seeds in a greenhouse or propagator from early spring for early crops, through to midsummer for the last, autumn crops.** (Chapter 3 contains more information about doing this).

   If you're growing F1 hybrids, be aware that they mature rapidly and uniformly so only grow about a dozen plants of each type at each sowing, but re-sow frequently.

2. **Plant out your seedlings** when the plants have four or five leaves and space them 20–30 centimetres apart. For Ironman F1, though, space seedlings 60 centimetres apart. For Lucky F1, close planting of 25 centimetres apart results in small heads; you can double the spacing to achieve larger heads.

   Unlike other brassicas, because calabrese grows so quickly it doesn't grow well when sown in a seedbed and transplanted as 'bare-root' plants. Calabrese is best grown quickly in pots or cell trays, in fertile, moist soil. Don't allow plants to go dry at any time.

TIP

Choosing to save time

Although they look different, sprouting broccoli and cauliflower are very similar in their cultivation and nutrition. Both are worth growing if you have room, but they take up quite a lot of room for many months. If you're short of space – or time – stick to calabrese.

Harvesting and storing your calabrese

Calabrese is best for eating straight off the plants as soon as the heads are mature. Pick them while the heads are dense and before the tiny flower buds start to become obvious. If you pick them slightly early they'll be tender and the plants will produce sideshoots; pick them too late and they'll be less tasty. You can store any surplus in the freezer.

Choosing varieties

Varieties of calabrese vary widely. Some produce large heads, whereas others produce a number of small spears. Most varieties should also produce a second crop of thin, secondary shoots when the main head is cut.

Here are a few varieties to choose from:

- ✔ **Crown and Sceptres** is a useful variety that produces one, large head followed by many, smaller heads.

- ✔ **Ironman F1** is a vigorous variety that resists disease and produces large heads, just like the calabrese you see in shops.

- ✔ **Tenderstem Green Inspiration F1** is widely available in shops, and is usually quite expensive. Quick and simple to grow, it has slender stems that are tender, and produces a second crop after the first has been harvested.

Slow but superb: Sprouting broccoli

Sprouting broccoli is one of the slowest crops to mature and stays on your plot for about ten months. Even so, broccoli is well worth growing, not only because the young shoots of flower buds are nutritious and delicious, but also because it's one of the few green crops available in early spring.

COOKING TIP

To cook broccoli, you can boil it rapidly or steam and serve it with butter.

Broccoli is rich in vitamins, including B and C, and antioxidants. The green colouring of broccoli makes it especially nutritious; in particular it contains good amounts of folic acid.

Sowing and cultivating sprouting broccoli

Sprouting broccoli is simple to grow, and here's how to go about it:

1. **Sow the seeds.** Sow them from spring to summer in trays, as you would for cabbages and other brassicas. (Chapter 3 contains lots more information about this step).

2. **Transplant your seedlings into pots or cell trays, then plant them out when they have four or five leaves, as you would for cabbages.** The best site for them is one in full sun. Space the plants about 75 centimetres apart, because they grow to be large and leafy. If you're growing Nine Star Perennial, plant them 90 centimetres apart. With Bordeaux F1, though, you can space them as close as 45 centimetres apart.

Harvesting and storing your broccoli

Having successfully raised a crop of broccoli, the next step is to harvest and start eating it! The first harvest, in spring, is of the main, large heads. When you've cropped them, the plants quickly produce second and third crops of smaller shoots. You can encourage them along by treating the plants to a dressing of general fertiliser in spring.

Choosing varieties

Traditionally, you had to choose between purple- and white-sprouting broccoli. The white is slightly hardier and some consider that it has a better flavour. In recent years, breeders have developed compact F1 types that produce a crop without needing winter chilling, allowing you to grow purple sprouting broccoli for autumn and early winter harvest.

Plants take up a lot of space but modern F1 varieties are generally more compact and quicker to mature, and so are well worth the extra cost involved when buying seeds.

Here are a few of the more popular broccoli varieties to consider:

- **Bordeaux F1** is a modern variety that you can sow from early spring to midsummer for a long succession of crops.

- **Claret F1** is a superior, compact, modern variety for heavy crops of purple shoots in spring.

- **Early White Sprouting** is the traditional favourite with tasty spears from large plants, which you can pick for several months.

✔ **Nine Star Perennial** is a useful crop for busy gardeners because plants live for up to three years, vigorously producing a crop of white, sprouting broccoli every spring.

✔ **Red Arrow**, which is an improvement on the traditional 'Early Purple' and 'Late Purple', has large spears on relatively compact plants and a long harvest period.

A white shade of pale: Cauliflowers

If you want to feel really proud of your veg growing, try some cauliflowers. They have a reputation as being difficult to grow but F1 hybrids have made growing your own easier and more reliable.

With cauliflowers, a few varieties are suitable for growing all year round but otherwise you must choose your variety for summer and autumn harvest, winter harvest, or cutting in spring. Summer and autumn cauliflowers are the easiest to grow and don't occupy the soil for as long as spring-maturing types, producing a head (or *curd*) in as little as three months from sowing.

Cauliflower is delicious eaten raw and of course you can use it for the classic dish cauliflower cheese. Indian and spicy recipes are also good places to use cauliflower.

Cauliflowers aren't as rich in nutrients as other brassica crops because of their pale colour. However, they do contain fibre and vitamins, including vitamin C. The new yellow and purple varieties contain more beneficial nutrients, such as anthocyanins and betacarotene.

Sowing and cultivating cauliflowers

To grow your very own broccoli and cauliflower, just follow these easy steps:

1. **Sow the seeds.** Sow in trays and transplant them into pots or cell trays. You can sow most varieties in spring between March and May, summer cauliflowers in March, and autumn and spring cauliflowers in April and May. Ensuring that they don't suffer any check to their growth (in their pots or after planting out) is important, so keep them well watered. Though the curds hold for several weeks when the plant is mature, try to sow small quantities regularly to avoid having a glut of cauliflowers.

2. **Plant out the seedlings.** Plant them out, 45–60 centimetres apart, when seedlings have four or five leaves. Some cauliflowers are recommended for 'mini-veg' and you can plant these much closer. For example, plant Candid Charm 20 centimetres apart. This variety is also well suited to growing in raised beds. You need to water cauliflower plants as they grow, in dry periods, and they need a sheltered spot in full sun, and rich soil that you've improved with the addition of some organic matter.

3. **Protect your plants.** As they grow, draw up the soil around the base of the plants to keep them sturdy. Keep the plants tidy in winter, by removing any yellowing, lower leaves, and protecting the plants from the usual brassica pests.

   Protect plants when small from slugs, snails and rabbits and all the usual brassica pests. White cauliflowers often benefit from having a few, central leaves being bent over the curd as it matures to protect it from sun and maintain its pure white colour.

Harvesting and storing your cauliflowers

Cauliflowers are at their best for a short period only, so cut and eat them as soon as the curds are fully developed. If you leave them for too long they start to expand, become loose, and turn creamy coloured or grey and aren't then good to eat. You can freeze cauliflowers if you have too many to eat fresh.

Choosing varieties

Recent breeding has produced coloured cauliflowers with curds (the part you eat) in shades of yellow, orange and purple. All these types are summer and autumn maturing and are generally easy to grow. They may be more attractive to children who would otherwise turn their noses up at white cauliflowers.

Some of the best cauliflower varieties to grow are as follows:

- ✔ **Andes F1** has large, pure white curds and is suitable for sowing from early spring to summer for harvesting throughout summer and autumn.

- ✔ **Cheddar F1** has unusual, yellow curds that develop more colour when exposed to the sun and when you cook them. Crop Cheddar F1 in summer and autumn.

- ✔ **Clapton F1** has large, leafy plants and white curds, the big plus point being that it's resistant to clubroot. This variety matures in late summer to late autumn.

- ✔ **Graffiti F1** has brilliant, purple curds that develop their best colour when exposed to the sun. This variety produces compact plants that you can crop from early summer (from an early sowing) to late autumn.

- ✔ **Walcheren Winter 3 Armado April** is a hardy cauliflower for sowing in spring that matures the following spring.

Pretty in green: Romanesco

This beautiful vegetable looks rather like a green cauliflower designed by a mathematician and has lime-green 'spiralled' curds. The curds are nutty and tasty, and romanesco is worth growing just for its good looks.

You can use romanesco in the same ways that you would normally use cauliflower but the flavour is sweeter and they look far more impressive. I try to leave them in large pieces when serving them because they're so beautiful.

Although similar to cauliflower, because of its light green colour romanesco is more nutritious than its more familiar cousin.

Sowing and cultivating romanesco

To grow romanesco you can follow the same steps as in the 'Quick off the mark: Calabrese' section earlier in this chapter. Just sow romanesco seeds little and often and make sure that you water and feed your plants evenly. You can space plants 30–45 centimetres apart, according to which variety you choose and the size of head you require. Close planting results in smaller heads. The plants mature faster than cauliflowers and aren't hardy, so treat them like calabrese.

Harvesting and storing your romanesco

If you grow romanesco, cut it when you need it because you can only keep it for a few days in the fridge. Romanesco does freeze well, though, and because it's a late summer crop and growing it all year round isn't possible, freezing any surplus is worth doing.

A taste of the East: Chinese greens

Some of the best crops to cut your teeth on if you're a beginner to growing your own fruit and veg are *Chinese greens*. This wealth of intriguing and unfamiliar crops grow amazingly quickly, are healthy, and you can eat any part of them, even if they don't grow quite as you expect. All Chinese greens are quick-growing brassicas, although most are more closely related to turnips than to European cabbages.

Chinese greens are really adaptable in the kitchen. The large Chinese cabbage or Chinese leaves are sweet enough to eat raw in salads, either chopped or grated, and are equally good lightly boiled or steamed (for just a few minutes). A bonus is that they lack the pungency of traditional cabbage so may be a hit with children. Cooks usually steam or stir-fry pak choi for just a few minutes and then sprinkle soy sauce or oyster sauce and sesame seeds over the top. (There's something about the dark green colour of the leaves and crunchy stems that makes me crave these vegetables at times!) Mustards are best stir-fried but have a very strong taste so use them sparingly, in mixtures of leaves. Mizuna and choy sum are also best steamed or stir-fried.

Most of these crops contain plenty of vitamin C and folic acid. The darker the foliage the more iron and other beneficial compounds are present.

Sowing and cultivating Chinese greens

To become a grower of Chinese greens, just follow these steps:

1. **Sow the seeds.** The biggest problem with Chinese greens is that they can detect day length. If you sow them earlier than midsummer they're more likely to run to seed or *bolt* (in other words, produce flowers instead of leaves) and produce thin flowering stems than grow into mature heads or rosettes. You can see this tendency as a bonus, though, because these flowering shoots are tender, delicious and perfectly edible, whether raw or in stir-fries.

   Chinese greens require a moist, fertile soil, rich in organic matter. Make sure that you keep them well watered and that they can grow unchecked.

   Many Chinese greens are ideal for growing in raised beds or polytunnels, or under cloches or fleece, because they are an efficient use of space, producing heavy crops in a small area.

   > **Chinese cabbage.** Sow, from midsummer onwards, in rows. Ideally, sow the seeds where they're to grow because they don't like being transplanted. Sow the seeds along the row or sow three or four seeds every 15 centimetres along the row.

   > **Pak choi.** Sow from late spring to autumn. Sow where they're to grow in the same way as Chinese cabbage but you can thin them out to 20 centimetres apart. You can get a good crop in pots as well as raised beds and in grow bags.

   > **Mustard, mizuna and choy sum.** Sow in the same way as for pak choi.

   Stick with these safe sowing times when you start. Bolt-resistant varieties have recently been introduced that extend the growing season of Chinese cabbage, but drought, high temperatures, chilling and transplanting may all cause the plants to bolt.

2. **Cultivating the plants.**

   All Chinese greens suffer the same problems as other brassicas and are especially prone to slugs, snails and caterpillars. (See Chapter 7 for more on dealing with garden pests.)

   > **Chinese cabbage.** When the seeds germinate and are large enough to handle, pinch off the spares and leave one seedling per station. As the plants get crowded, pull up every other plant to eat as young leaves and allow the others to mature. Water the plants in dry weather and keep any weeds under control.

Pak choi, mustard, mizuna and choy sum. Keep plants growing fast at all times by thorough and regular watering. Give your plants liquid fertiliser once a week if you're growing them in containers.

Harvesting and storing your Chinese greens

You can strip the outside leaves from the large, solid heads of Chinese cabbage and keep them in a fridge for a few weeks, but use the other greens here as soon as you pick them because they're unsuitable for storing.

Choosing varieties

The best known of these greens are Chinese cabbages, with their large, heavy, barrel-shaped heads. They are easy to grow and generally mature in about two months. You can harvest Chinese cabbages from late summer through to autumn and longer if you grow them in a polytunnel, which protects the mature heads from wet and cold.

A couple of varieties worth looking at:

- ✔ **Orange Queen F1** has large heads with yellow inner leaves, and the plants are resistant to cool weather so it lasts well into autumn.

- ✔ **Richi F1** has large heads and is the best variety to choose if you want to try early sowing because it's more tolerant of hot weather than most other varieties.

Pak choi is another great Chinese green to grow. This tasty and healthy crop has a fresh, mild flavour, grows even faster than Chinese cabbage, and you can eat the plants at all stages of growth. You have two main types to choose from:

- ✔ Green-stemmed pak choi
- ✔ White-stemmed pak choi

Both have thick, swollen leaf stalks that may be white or green. The foliage is spoon-shaped and usually green, though purple-leaved varieties have recently appeared.

If neither Chinese cabbage nor pak choi floats your boat, you can choose from a host of other Chinese greens to grow. Take a look at these possibilities:

- ✔ **Mustard** is most commonly encountered in mixes of salad leaves. When small the leaves are peppery and crunchy. As plants mature the leaves become large, rather tough, and fiercely hot, although the attractive, metallic purple colour of the most common variety (purple mustard) is hard to resist. Red, Asian mustard is hot when young and blisteringly so as it ages. Green mustard is just as hot. Red Frills and Ruby Streaks have frilly leaves that are especially attractive.

✔ **Mizuna** is an attractive, easy-to-grow plant that forms clumps of finely divided, ragged foliage. Growers usually harvest mizuna at a young age by pulling a few leaves from each plant, but you can also cut mature plants in autumn. Mizuna has a pleasantly spicy, tangy taste and you can eat it raw or stir-fried. You can even eat the flowering shoots, too.

✔ **Choy Sum** is a fast-growing crop rather like broccoli. Each plant produces a thick, succulent stem with a few leaves and a cluster of buds that open to yellow flowers. You can cut and stir-fry choy sum at any stage of its growth.

Choosing Leaves You Won't See in the Shops

The number of leaves you can choose from when deciding what to grow can be overwhelming, but this section includes some of the easiest to grow and the most nutritious leaves. What they all have in common is that you rarely, if ever, see them in the shops, mainly because they don't travel or pack well.

Held in fond regard: Chard/leaf beet

This popular vegetable is rarely available in shops but is simple to cultivate and not fussy about soil type, although it grows best where the soil isn't too dry and poor. In fact, because chard/leaf beet is easier to grow, gardeners often choose it instead of spinach.

You can grow chard as a leaf for cooking or harvest the young leaves and add them to salads. The fleshy leaves are mild in taste.

Chard and leaf beet are rich in potassium, iron, magnesium and betacarotene.

Sowing and cultivating chard/leaf beet

Both vegetables are easy to grow, and here are the steps to take when growing your own crop:

1. **Sow the seeds.** Chard/leaf beet is biennial. If you sow in spring it often bolts when the hot weather arrives, but if you sow in late summer it provides leaves through autumn and again in spring before running to seed. Space the large seeds 8 centimetres apart in rows in the soil, and cover them with 1 centimetre of soil.

2. **Keep the plants well watered throughout the growing period.**

3. **Harvest your crop.** The usual method is to pick individual leaves off the plants. You can also shear off foliage from plants, although this weakens them and they take longer to recover and produce a second crop.

Harvesting and storing your chard/leaf beet

This crop is one that you really need to use as soon as you pick it. Especially in summer, the leaves start to wilt within minutes of picking. If you want to keep them after picking, wash them immediately, drain lightly, put them in a plastic bag and keep in the fridge for 24 hours at most. If you have too much to use immediately, lightly *blanch* (briefly cook) it in boiling water for a few seconds by pouring it over the leaves in a colander, let it cool, squash out the water, and freeze.

Choosing varieties

You can choose from two types of this vegetable: Swiss chard and leaf beet. Both are closely related to beetroot. Swiss chard is the most popular at present, largely because it's so ornamental:

- ✔ **Swiss chard** has thick leaf stalks that may be white, red (**rhubarb chard**) or yellow. You can buy mixtures or separate colours and they all look impressive when grown well.

  You effectively get two vegetables from this plant. Many people prefer the milder taste of Swiss chard to spinach, and by removing the leaf blade from the stalks you have a spinach substitute that you can steam or boil. You can also cook the thick leaf stalks by boiling, braising or steaming and although their taste is a little on the bland side, they are popular.

- ✔ **Leaf beet** is also called perpetual spinach and is basically the same plant as Swiss chard but has slim, green leaf stalks and usually smaller but more prolific foliage. Leaf beet usually has better quality leaves than Swiss chard.

Not just for sailors: Spinach

Spinach is an easy vegetable to grow but it bolts quickly, especially if the soil dries out and in hot weather. This tendency makes it tricky to grow to maturity but if you sow little and often you can easily get a constant supply.

Although you traditionally cook spinach lightly, the young leaves are delicious raw, perhaps in a salad, and have a mild taste. If cooking, be aware that spinach 'cooks down' dramatically, so pick lots! Wash it well to remove grit and cook in a minimal amount of water or steam for a short period – just until it shrinks. Press out the water, season and serve. Spinach is a natural partner for eggs and pasta and cheese.

Spinach isn't quite as rich in iron as Popeye once thought but it's still one of the best sources of this mineral and of betacarotene, folic acid and vitamin C.

Sowing and cultivating spinach

To grow your very own bumper crop of spinach, just follow these steps:

1. **Sow the seeds.** Spinach needs a cool growing season or it runs to seed. It grows best in rich, moist soil. Sow little and often in spring and through summer for summer crops or in late summer for picking through winter – be sure to protect with cloches. Don't transplant seedlings but sow where they're to grow. In hot areas grow spinach in semi-shade – the seeds don't germinate if the temperature is above 30 degrees Celsius. Spinach thrives in pots and containers and you can grow it under glass for early crops.

2. **Protect your crops.** Mildew is the most significant problem that affects spinach: select resistant varieties and keep plants moist as they grow to avoid this fungus.

Harvesting and storing your spinach

Picking spinach leaves individually from the plants is the best way to harvest this crop, but this can be longwinded! Cutting the leaves off in bunches is much easier, though this weakens the plants more. Spinach doesn't store well at all, so try to use it immediately or store and freeze it in the same way as for leaf beet.

Choosing varieties

You can choose from many different varieties of spinach. Here are a few of the more popular options:

- ✔ **Barbados F1** is resistant to mildew and has smooth, tender leaves.
- ✔ **Rhino F1** is an excellent, heavy cropper that's slow to mature and bolt.
- ✔ **Samish F1** is a small-leaved spinach, hardy and ideal for late sowings.

The crop of the future: Amaranth

Amaranths are rapid-growing crops popular both as leafy vegetables and for grain in warm climates, but you can grow them in the UK, especially in sheltered gardens or polytunnels.

You can pick the young shoots to eat as a spinach substitute. In fact, leaf amaranths and grain amaranths, which are grown for their nutritious seeds, are very similar and you can eat the leaves of both. Simply boil them for a few minutes, steam or stir-fry.

Sowing and cultivating amaranth

Sow the tiny seeds in rows in spring and thin them out to 15–30 centimetres apart as they mature. Plants grow large and may exceed 1.5 metres as they mature. They grow best in rich, moist soil. Pick them regularly and you can ensure that they become bushy and keep cropping.

Harvesting and storing your amaranth

When harvest time arrives, either pick off individual leaves or pinch out and harvest the centre of the young shoots. Use the shoots and leaves as soon as you pick them, in the same way as for spinach. Although some people eat amaranth leaves raw in salads, I find them too tough and rough and prefer them cooked – either lightly boiled or steamed.

Choosing varieties

You don't have a great deal of choice when choosing which variety to grow, and the usual offering is a mix that will contain both green and red-leaved varieties.

Poor-man's asparagus: Good King Henry

This unusual and uncommon vegetable has fallen from favour over the years as imported greens have become more common. But as a source of healthy greens in spring Good King Henry is useful and unusual because it's perennial, and so once planted you need to give it little attention. Plants are difficult to find, (you can sometimes buy them from herb specialists) but you can grow them from seed, which is available from a number of seed companies.

Good King Henry is a good substitute for spinach and you can use it in exactly the same way. Pick the shoot tips and young leaves, steam or boil, and serve with butter and pepper.

Good King Henry is rich in iron and some B vitamins.

Sowing and cultivating Good King Henry

Sow the seeds in spring where they're to grow or in trays: either is fine. Plant or thin them out to 25 centimetres apart. Good King Henry isn't fussy about soil or site but rich soil produces the best crops.

Harvesting and storing your Good King Henry

Don't crop in your first year. After that you can pick the young shoots and cook them like broccoli or asparagus, or pick leaves to use like spinach.

Chapter 9

Raising Root Crops

• •

In This Chapter

▶ Cultivating super staple root crops

▶ Growing unusual root crops to challenge your skills

• •

*R*oot crops include some of our most important staple crops. They provide veg that you can eat fresh in summer and autumn or store for use throughout winter, so are prime contenders for space on your plot every year. Despite this, root crops have a bit of an image problem – some people see them as dull and boring. How wrong they are! Among the common and more unusual root crops you can discover a wealth of delicious flavours, textures and colours. As a bonus, root crops are packed with nutrients, so are very good for you, and most are also full of sugar or starch.

Root crops are generally easy to grow but tend to grow best in light soils; some are less easy to grow well in clay soils. Even then all is not lost because you can grow many root crops in pots, so no matter how small your garden may be, the crops in this chapter are ones that you can grow.

Sowing Staples

Some staple root crops are less than glamorous. You may say that they have an image problem. After all, who gets excited about turnips? Well, it may just be you when you discover how sweet and tender they can be when you grow your own.

We rely on staple root crops to fill us up, but they have more claims to fame than you may at first think. These vegetables are usually high in carbohydrates, and so provide people with energy. But most vegetables that gardeners dig from their gardens are packed with other good things too and give much more than just energy – unlike many processed forms of carbohydrate, they're packed with vitamins and minerals as well. For example, potatoes contain fibre and vitamin C, carrots are a rich source of vitamin A, and experts now consider beetroot to be a superfood!

Another reason to be fond of root crops is that you can store them easily to use after most leaf crops and other veg have perished in the cold weather. You can leave some of them in the ground and harvest them when you need them, although others you do need to store, and most supply us with healthy eating well into winter and into spring.

Root crops are divided into *early* (as well as *second early*) and *maincrop* varieties. You most often see these terms referring to potatoes, and although the terms aren't as common with other veg, you may read the terms used again there. Generally speaking, early varieties mature quickly and as well as being useful for an early crop you can also use them for late sowings. This may seem like a contradiction until you remember that they're called 'early' because they grow quickly – so they also succeed when sown late. Maincrop varieties take longer to mature but generally grow to a bigger size, so give you more to eat. Maincrops are also the kinds that you may wish to store, if appropriate to the vegetable.

The humble spud: Potatoes

Potatoes are actually more interesting than you may think. As well as the familiar 'reds' and 'whites', potatoes also come in black and purple varieties. By growing your own, you can discover a whole new world of potatoes with different colours, shapes, textures and flavours. You may find yourself as excited as the Europeans who first saw potatoes being cultivated by the locals of Central America! No longer will you think of them as just plain old spuds!

Strictly speaking, the part of the plant that we eat isn't a root but a *tuber*, which is actually a swollen stem where the plant stores starch to feed the new plants that grow the following year until they're large enough to fend for themselves.

Potatoes have so many uses in the kitchen. To enjoy their taste to the full, leave their skins on when you cook them – much of the flavour of potatoes is in the skins and you get more fibre from them by eating the skins. While you may not want potato skins in your mash you can certainly leave them on for wedges and eat the skins when you bake them whole. If you grow new potatoes (early varieties), you don't need to worry about peeling them before cooking. Unusual-coloured potatoes often lose their colour when you boil them but may retain their colour when you fry them as chips or put them in the microwave.

People often think of potatoes as fattening and full of starch, but they're rich in magnesium and potassium, and also contain vitamins B and C. They also have fibre and are especially nutritious when you eat them with the skins still on.

The long history of the spud

People have cultivated potatoes for more than 7,000 years. However, they only reached Europe in 1586, where people didn't understand how to use them well at first. When Sir Walter Raleigh presented some to Queen Elizabeth I (he didn't actually introduce them to Europe – the Spanish got there first), her cook is said to have cooked and presented the leaves to her – not good for the royal digestion! Potatoes didn't catch on and come to be regarded as a valuable foodstuff for another two centuries. The most infamous phase in the potato's history was the Irish potato famine of the 1840s when 1.5 million people perished of starvation. The famine was caused by an over-reliance on one variety of potato that was prone to blight – just another example of why avoiding huge volumes of one crop and growing a diverse range of plants is important.

Sowing and cultivating potatoes

Potatoes are grown from seed, but not seed like most other crops. *Seed potatoes* are small tubers, grown in areas that are generally free from the main potato problems such as aphids, which spread virus diseases that reduce crops, and blight.

 Always buy certified, virus-free seed potatoes for planting. Never just plant some old potatoes from the shops that have sprouted. They may produce a good crop but may also be harbouring pests or diseases that are difficult to eradicate from your plot.

As an alternative to seed potatoes, you can sometimes buy micro-plants of rare varieties. Retailers grow micro-plants to be free from disease. Pot them when they arrive and grow them in a greenhouse. Each one gives a small crop the first year but the idea is to keep some to plant as seed the following year, and because these plants are sure to be free of problems you can safely save the tubers for the next season. This isn't the usual way to grow potatoes but is the only way to obtain some of the older, heirloom varieties.

After you've bought your seed potatoes, follow these steps:

1. ***Chit* your potatoes to allow them to develop short, sturdy shoots.**
   Chitting is a process that makes tubers produce short stems that have many sideshoots underground so that, in theory, they produce more potatoes (see Figure 9-1). Most gardeners use this process for all their potatoes, though it works best for early and second early varieties. Gardeners argue among themselves about how necessary chitting is, but I stick with tradition and do chit my seed potatoes.

First, identify the end of the seed with 'eyes' or tiny shoots in depressions. Second, take some egg boxes, shallow trays or seed trays and place the potatoes, 'eye'-end up in the tray, in a light, cool, frost-free place. Chitting generally takes about a month, depending on the temperature. Don't worry if the tubers shrivel – that's quite normal and doesn't affect growth.

You can plant the potatoes when the shoots grow to about 1 centimetre long. If the shoots get too long they're more likely to break off when you plant them. For crops of big tubers, you can thin the number of shoots on each tuber, leaving the three biggest and strongest.

Figure 9-1:
Chitted
potatoes,
showing
their short,
sturdy roots.

2. **Before planting, dig over and add some organic matter (see Chapter 4) to improve the soil.** Potatoes aren't fussy about soil but organic matter helps conserve moisture, which leads to better crops. You can add some general fertiliser just before planting too.

Potatoes are excellent in new plots – not because they tolerate poor conditions but because the digging required to plant and harvest them helps you clear the soil. They also have dense foliage that can help suppress some weed growth.

3. **Plant your potatoes (see Figure 9-2).** Dig out a trench or make individual holes in the soil for each tuber. If the ground is well prepared, making a slit with a spade and dropping in a tuber is fine. Plant most potatoes 8–15 centimetres deep. Space earlies 30–38 centimetres apart, and maincrop potatoes 40 centimetres apart. Rows should be 40–50 centimetres apart for earlies and up to 70 centimetres apart for maincrops, because maincrops make bigger plants.

Figure 9-2:
Planting chitted tubers, taking care not to damage the shoots, and covering them with soil.

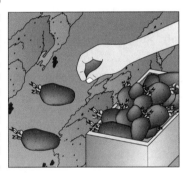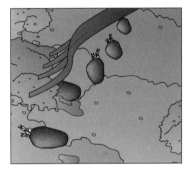

If you didn't get a chance to dig the soil over, take out a trench, add some organic matter to the bottom, and plant the tubers shoot-end up on this. Cover the tubers with about 15 centimetres of soil (Figure 9-2 shows how to do this), though this isn't too critical because you *earth up* the shoots (cover them with more soil) later on.

Plant early potatoes in March to April. Potatoes aren't hardy and frost kills anything above ground and so you don't want much top growth before the last frosts are likely in your area. Early April is a good average for earlies in most areas but late planting still results in a good crop. Plant second earlies and maincrop potatoes later in April.

Handle chitted potatoes with care so that you don't break the shoots off.

4. *Earth up* **your crop twice – early in the growing season (to protect the young shoots from frost) and as the shoots grow.** This involves using a hoe or spade to drag soil from between the rows, up, and over the shoots. Because the tubers are formed on the plant stems, burying them increases the crop. It also prevents light reaching developing tubers and turning them green, and acts as weed control.

5. **Water your crops in dry weather to prevent the tubers from splitting or growing hollow.** However, potatoes don't need watering in the early stages of growth, when just starting to appear through the ground.

If you don't have room for potatoes in your garden you can still enjoy a treat of new potatoes by growing them in bags or pots (old 80 litre compost bags are ideal but make sure that they have black sides inside). With this method you can grow potatoes on the patio or start them early in a greenhouse. This method is best for new (early) potatoes because they mature quickly, so need less watering and feeding and less time to grow. You can also grow new potatoes for Christmas in this way though you have to buy special 'late' seed potatoes, plant them in August, and grow them to maturity in a greenhouse, moving them from the patio to the greenhouse in October before they get frosted. You can buy potato grow bags and containers but the following method works fine – and saves you a small fortune!

1. **Roll down the bag to form a 'pot' about 30 centimetres deep and make some holes in the base.**

2. **Place 15 centimetres of compost in the base and plant three seed potatoes on it.**

3. **Cover the seed potatoes with another 10 centimetres of compost, water, sit back, and wait for the shoots to appear.** As they do so, unroll the bag and add some more compost. Keep doing this as many times as you like. Multipurpose compost is ideal because you'll have nice 'clean' tubers after using it, but it doesn't contain much plant food so, after the first month, apply a liquid fertiliser once a week.

4. **Make sure that your potatoes don't dry out.** Keep them watered.

5. **To check how your crop is doing, roll down the bag and look for the tubers.**

The chances are that you can grow a great crop of potatoes without any problems. However, you need to be aware of what can go wrong: the main problems are slugs (which eat developing tubers), wireworms (which burrow into the spuds) and potato blight (an airborne disease that rapidly causes the leaves to turn black and, in the worst cases, causes the tubers to rot in the ground and in storage). Blight can attack at any time from midsummer onwards, usually in warm, wet weather. See Chapter 7 for more details.

Harvesting and storing your potatoes

Potatoes vary in their harvest time depending on variety and season. Earlies are usually ready in July, and second earlies soon after. The flowers starting to open is usually a sign that you can dig up a plant and see how it's doing or at least pull back some soil to see if you have any decent tubers. If the tubers are big enough to harvest, start digging them. You don't need to rush or panic – they won't 'go off' if you don't dig them all immediately. All that happens here is that the tubers just get bigger and the skins tougher so they become a bit less easy to scrub and use as new potatoes.

Gardeners don't usually lift maincrops until the foliage starts to die down in late summer, after the flowers have opened and faded. You can harvest maincrop potatoes earlier but at that stage the tubers may not be full size, the skins are not fully developed, and they don't store well.

If you're harvesting potatoes to store them, choose a dry day and dig them up with a fork. Then carry out the following:

1. **Push the fork deep into the soil at the edge of the foliage, going under the plants to lift the root.** (If you stick the fork in too close to the stems you 'spear' lots of tubers and inevitably the biggest and best tubers come up on the tines of the fork!)

2. **Repeat this lifting and forking several times to make sure that you remove all the small tubers.** When you've worked out the right distance from the plants to fork, you may find cutting back the foliage a bit before you lift them makes it easier.

3. **Work along the rows and leave the tubers on the soil surface for a few hours to dry before putting them into paper sacks or boxes. Store them in a cool, dry, frost-free place.** Never use plastic bags because the potatoes will rot. Use any damaged tubers as quickly as possible.

4. **Check periodically while in storage in case the odd tuber has rotted.** If you don't remove it, rot will spread through the whole bag. Your own potatoes won't store for as long as commercial growers can store potatoes, but as long as you keep them cool and in a dark place, most types should store until well into the new year, at least before they start to sprout and shrivel.

If you're growing potatoes in bags or pots, you can rummage around and pull out the tubers or tip out the bag and harvest them in one go as soon as the foliage starts to turn yellow. Use the compost as a mulch on the garden or fill pots with it to grow a different crop.

All green parts of potatoes are mildly poisonous, so don't eat the leaves. In warm summers plants may produce 'potato apples' after the flowers. These are not edible. Also remember to discard any tubers that have turned green through exposure to light, or cut away any green areas before you cook them, because they contain toxins.

Choosing varieties

The most common method of classifying potatoes is by the time they take to grow, from planting to maturity, which usually also relates to how early in the season you can harvest them. The categories are *early (new)*, *second early* and *maincrop*. However, you sometimes see them listed according to their uses and you often see sections for salad potatoes (waxy-fleshed potatoes that you usually eat cold) in catalogues.

Early potatoes are the first to be planted and the quickest to mature. They need less space than other varieties because they have shorter stems. Earlies are also useful because you can plant a second crop, such as Chinese cabbage, after you've harvested them. People don't usually store earlies, but instead eat them fresh, although some do store well – just check the variety. Early potatoes are usually ready for lifting in July but always check a few roots first, by digging them up.

Here are some varieties of early (or new) potato:

- **Arran Pilot** is popular for its high yield, good flavour and general easy growing nature.

- **Colleen** is a fine-flavoured potato with cream flesh that is especially good for frying. This variety is resistant to blight and scab.

- **International Kidney** is a variety that people grow for the famous Jersey Royals – the best-known commercial new potatoes – with oval potatoes and white, waxy flesh.

- **Lady Christl** is one of the best varieties: easy to grow, it has cream flesh that doesn't disintegrate on boiling, and good flavour.

- **Orla** is a white-skinned, fine-flavoured potato with excellent resistance to blight and scab; it's especially good for organic growers.

- **Pentland Javelin** is a popular, standard variety that cooks and eats well, and which is resistant to scab.

- **Premiere** is a recently developed, easy-to-grow variety with firm, golden flesh, and resistance to blight.

- **Red Duke of York** has an excellent texture and flavour with yellow flesh and red skins.

- **Rocket** has white-fleshed, round tubers, and is possibly the earliest potato of them all, often ready 10 weeks after planting.

If you don't have much room to work with, choose earlies. They don't need much space, are in the ground for the shortest time, and usually miss the devastating potato blight. And because earlies are the most expensive variety to buy, you save the most money!

Second earlies bridge the gap between earlies and the maincrops and also often miss blight. Here are some of the most popular varieties:

- **Edzell Blue** has unusual, purple-blue skins with white flesh. This variety tends to disintegrate when you boil it, and so is best kept for baking.

- **Kestrel** is an excellent all-rounder. Easy to grow, and with some resistance to slugs, kestrel potatoes crop well even in dry seasons. Their attractive tubers have white skins with purple eyes, and taste great too. Kestrels are especially good for baking and roasting.

- ✔ **Smile** potatoes have attractive red skins with white 'smiles' above the eyes, and tasty flesh. They produce high yields.

- ✔ **Yukon Gold** is noted for its excellent flavour. The yellow-skinned, yellow-fleshed, oval tubers have a fluffy texture and are good for boiling, baking and roasting.

Maincrop potatoes are usually ready from September onwards and are the best types for storing. They include large and small waxy and floury tubers, and you're bound to find one you love in this list. Here are some of the varieties to consider choosing:

- ✔ **Arran Victory** has attractive, blue-purple skin that hides a pure white flesh. This variety has high yields and some resistance to blight.

- ✔ **Cara** has a creamy flesh, and makes a perfect potato for baking. Cara offers large yields of red-eyed tubers that have some resistance to blight.

- ✔ **Desiree** is desirable for its yellow, tasty flesh, red skins and big crops, and is best when roasted or chipped. This popular potato is resistant to drought but can get scab.

- ✔ **Golden Wonder** is a century old potato with dry, floury flesh, making it perfect for frying and baking. Golden Wonder has some resistance to slugs.

- ✔ **King Edward** potatoes have white tubers with red eyes. The excellent flavour of King Edwards makes them perhaps the best potatoes for roasting.

- ✔ **Lady Balfour** potatoes have white skins and cream flesh with good flavour. They're ideal for boiling, and with their good resistance to most common potato problems, they make an excellent choice for organic growers.

- ✔ **Maris Piper** white potatoes yield heavily, boil well and make good chips.

- ✔ **Remarka** potatoes have good resistance to most diseases and heavy yields of large tubers, making this variety a good all-rounder. Remarka has good flavour too and is excellent for baking and boiling.

- ✔ **Sarpo Mira** has exceptional resistance to blight, produces large weed-suppressing foliage, and delivers heavy yields of floury, red-skinned tubers.

- ✔ **Verity** potatoes are similar in appearance and taste to King Edward but with better resistance to blight and other diseases.

When you go shopping you see 'salad potatoes' for sale but you can easily grow your own at home. Salad potatoes are simply varieties – usually second earlies or maincrops – with a waxy texture that don't disintegrate when you boil them. Cooking and then allowing salad potatoes to cool before eating them is the ideal way to prepare them.

- ✔ **Charlotte** potatoes have yellow, waxy, tasty flesh and produce heavy crops.

- ✔ **Juliette** potatoes have an excellent flavour and attractive, oval, white-skinned tubers.

- ✔ **Mimi** potato plants produce masses of small, round, red-skinned tubers that have an excellent flavour.

- ✔ **Nicola** is a good easy-to-grow all-rounder with attractive, oval, white tubers with waxy flesh.

- ✔ **Pink Fir Apple** isn't an apple, but a potato plant with long, narrow, irregular tubers that have a superb taste. The downsides to this variety are that it's slow to mature and the large plants take up a lot of room.

- ✔ **Roseval** potatoes have red skins and creamy, waxy flesh with a fine taste. The plant produces good yields of irregular-shaped tubers, especially if you leave them to mature.

Plain and simple: Turnips

Surely one of the many vegetables that would benefit from a good PR campaign, turnips are perhaps the most humble of vegetables and are usually available only in shops as large, often wrinkled, sad-looking specimens.

Cooks use turnips mostly as a winter vegetable, peeling and boiling them until tender and serving with butter or wholegrain mustard. You can peel, dice, boil and serve larger roots as they are, or eat them mashed. Turnips are also an important part of many stews, and the young leaves are edible as a substitute for spinach, needing only light boiling or steaming. However, they grow quickly and by pulling them when young and small you can enjoy tender, sweet and delicious turnips in the summertime, too, perhaps grated and added to salads. Try them yourself and be surprised at how delicious they are.

Turnips are low in calories and carbohydrates. They contain moderate amounts of vitamins and minerals such as vitamin C.

Sowing and cultivating turnips

To get going with growing turnips, just follow these steps:

1. **Take out a *drill* (a shallow trench) 1 centimetre deep and thinly sow the seeds, spacing them 2 centimetres apart. Cover them with soil and water.** You can sow the first seeds in early spring under cloches or fleece, and quick-growing, early varieties from spring, through summer, and into early autumn to produce tender crops. Sow the larger, maincrop turnips, which include yellow-fleshed kinds, in late summer to produce roots that mature in late autumn. Rows should be 10 centimetres apart for baby turnips and 30 centimetres apart for maincrop turnips.

Turnips prefer a rich, firm soil, so avoid sowing immediately after digging the soil – allow it to settle first.

2. **As soon as the seedlings start to produce their first true leaves, thin the seedlings out to 10–15 centimetres apart, depending on how large you intend allowing the roots to grow.** If you're growing turnips just for the leaves, you don't need to do this.

3. **Don't let your plants go thirsty, and keep them free of weeds.** Turnips need a constant supply of water or they may run to seed or form small, woody roots. Water them in dry weather.

Harvesting and storing your turnips

Turnips are ready to pull as soon as they are bigger than a golf ball, which can be as soon as 6 weeks after sowing in summer. At this stage they are so sweet and tender you can eat them raw. You can continue to harvest them as they grow. Although turnips are hardy, they deteriorate in the soil over winter, so lift them by late autumn, twist off the foliage, and store them in damp sand or compost in a frost-free, cool place until required.

If you're growing turnips just for their leaves, you can harvest them with a knife or scissors. Each row produces two or three flushes of leaves.

Choosing varieties

Here are some of the best-loved varieties of turnip:

- ✔ **Aramis Squat** has purple-topped roots that mature quickly and make ideal baby turnips.

- ✔ **Atlantic** turnips have beautiful, squat roots, heavily flushed with purple. This variety is easy to grow, for sowing in spring and summer.

- ✔ **Purple Top Milan** is a standard, purple-and-white-skinned turnip, quick to grow and best used young.

- ✔ **Tokyo Cross** matures very quickly, with small, pure white roots. Tasty and tender, Tokyo Cross can mature in just five weeks. Sow from spring to late summer for regular harvests.

- ✔ **White Globe** is a standard variety with tender flesh and round (not squat) roots with purple tops.

Crunchy and colourful: Carrots

Carrots are a popular crop – useful in the kitchen and so tasty when you grow your own. Home-grown carrots are far superior to even the most expensive shop-bought carrots and by growing your own you can try more unusual varieties.

Carrots are an obvious choice of crop for organic gardeners, because you can't chemically prevent the most common carrot problems. Therefore, growing carrots can be a challenge at times but at least you know your crop is going to be fresh, free of chemicals and very tasty.

As well as tasting great, carrots are good for you, whether raw or cooked. They contain a lot of natural sugars, some fibre, and are rich in betacarotene (vitamin A) and traces of other nutrients.

Young carrots are more tender and sweet than old carrots, and taste their best when fresh and with the skins still on. Brush the roots rather than peel them to help retain nutrients, and steam or lightly boil them to avoid over-cooking. For a summer treat, par-boil them, and then sauté in butter with some fresh parsley, some honey or a splash of orange juice. Lovely!

Sowing and cultivating carrots

Carrots grow best in light, fertile, well-dug soils that you've manured in the previous year. The roots of carrots growing in clay soils aren't as perfect, and in stony soils, roots form odd shapes because they grow around obstructions. (If you have heavy or stony soil, try growing the shorter, stump rooted or round types.) Although improving the fertility of your soil is worthwhile, by adding some organic matter to improve moisture retention, fresh manure or too much fertiliser can cause the roots to fork.

As soon as you've chosen the variety you want to grow, you can get going with cultivating them. Here's how to do it:

1. **Fork over the soil a few weeks before sowing and avoid treading on the ground too much.**

2. **Take out *drills* (shallow trenches) about 1 centimetre deep and sow the seeds thinly along them.** If you sow too thickly you have to thin out the seedlings when they appear, which leads to attacks from carrot root fly. If the soil is dry, water the drill before sowing to help the seeds stick to the soil and provide moisture for germination. Leave carrots that you intend to use as baby roots with 3–5 centimetres between them; main-crop carrots need about 6–8 centimetres between plants to allow them to grow. Allow about 20 centimetres between rows. Cover the seeds and make sure that you keep the rows moist at all times.

   You can sow carrots between February and July, although most gardeners sow between March and June for harvesting between late June and October. For sowing at the earlier and later times of year, be sure to use fast-growing varieties.

   Carrot seed is small, so take care when sowing in windy weather in case the seed blows away.

They're carrots, Jim, but not as we know them

Although nowadays people think of carrots as being orange, they didn't look like this before the 18th century. The original, wild carrot had white roots, but natural variations were selected and early types were yellow or purple. People then developed a preference for orange carrots, which are the most valuable for supplying betacarotene, and this is what we now expect from our carrots. But many people are coming to realise that the more colourful our food, the more nutritious it is, and yellow and purple carrots and deep orange and red varieties, as single colours or a mixture, have been reintroduced and are gaining popularity.

Carrots don't germinate well in cold, wet soil so avoid sowing if the weather is cold and frosty – or if it's hot and dry, because keeping the soil moist enough is a chore. Carrots don't transplant well but you can sow early, stumpy carrots in greenhouse pots for extra early crops.

Lay horticultural fleece over your carrots for their entire lives to keep carrot root fly at bay (see Chapter 7 for more about pests).

3. **As the seeds germinate, keep the plants weeded by hoeing between the rows and weed by hand along with rows.**

4. **Thin out the seedlings to avoid overcrowding.** You can do this in stages and pull young carrots as they get crowded to leave the others to mature. Thin carrots on a dull day and water them immediately after, so the remaining seedlings are less likely to wilt.

Carrots are *biennials* (like onions and parsnips), meaning that they can potentially live for two years. However, we harvest them sometime in the first year, as soon as they've developed a tasty root packed with sugar. They form a root the first year but try to flower in the second when they use up all the sugar stored in the root. If a late cold snap in the weather, while the carrots are growing, makes the plants think that winter has been and gone, they stop making roots and produce flowers instead (known as *bolting*).

Harvesting and storing your carrots

You can harvest carrots as soon as they're big enough to eat! Doing so is easiest when the soil is moist, by holding the carrots at the base of the foliage and pulling them out. If they prove tricky to extract, push a fork into the soil 15 centimetres away from the row, lift the carrots in a block, and pull them up.

Washing carrots damages the skin and means that they can't be stored. If you intend storing them, handle them carefully and don't wash them. After you've pulled your carrots, the best thing to do with them is to snap off the tops, rinse them to remove the worst of the soil, and use as soon as possible. Leaving the tops on causes the roots to shrivel surprisingly quickly. For longer-term storage, at the end of the season you can remove the foliage and store mature, maincrop carrots in trays covered in old compost. You can store them for several months in this way. This process reduces slug and other damage that affects the roots if you leave them in the soil over winter. If this isn't possible, leave the carrots in the soil until you need them but cover the tops with old compost or straw to protect the roots from severe cold, and be prepared for some nibbles from rats, rabbits or smaller pests.

Choosing varieties

You can choose from a wealth of carrot varieties when deciding which one to go for. Here are some that I recommend:

- **Amsterdam Forcing Sprint** carrots are quick-growing, cylinder-shaped, 'baby' types; an established favourite but still popular. You can sow this variety until midsummer.

- **Autumn King 2** is a popular, standard, maincrop carrot with long, tapering roots.

- **Bolero F1** is a maincrop variety with smooth-skinned, bright orange roots and outstanding flavour.

- **Chanteney Red Cored 2** carrots are wedge-shaped, with good flavour.

- **Early Nantes** is a popular carrot that you can sow from early spring till midsummer; fast to mature and tender.

- **Favor F1** has cylindrical, bright orange roots with a sweet flavour; good as baby carrots or maincrop.

- **Flyaway F1** is a maincrop carrot, resistant to carrot root fly.

- **Harlequin F1** carrots are a mixture of maincrop carrots of slightly different sizes in a mix of white, cream, yellow, orange and purple roots.

- **Honey Snack F1** is a stumpy, pale orange carrot with an exceptionally sweet taste.

- **Nutri-Red F1** is an intensely coloured, long, tapering carrot that is well-flavoured, highly coloured, and rich in the nutrient lycopene.

- **Maestro F1** has long, blunt-tipped roots and strong foliage, and is resistant to fungal diseases and carrot root fly. A good choice for organic gardeners.

- **Parmex** makes the perfect patio carrot. Quick to mature, the round roots are idea for pots or grow bags.

- **Purple Haze F1** is a maincrop carrot with bright purple skins and bright orange flesh.

> ✔ **Resistafly F1** was bred for resistance to carrot root fly. The tapering, orange roots have good colour and taste.
>
> ✔ **Samurai** carrots have long, sweet roots with red skins and pinkish orange flesh.
>
> ✔ **Ulyses F1** carrots have long, tapered roots that resist bolting and stand in the ground over winter.
>
> ✔ **White Satin F1** carrots have long, sweet, juicy white roots.
>
> ✔ **Yellowstone** is a very vigorous carrot, with large roots that have yellow skins and flesh.

Sweet and nutty: Parsnips

Parsnips are a British winter staple and a valuable foodstuff because of the stored sugars in the roots. An easy vegetable to grow, parsnips suffer from few pests or diseases and the most common disease, canker, is unlikely to be a problem if you choose resistant varieties.

Frosted parsnips taste sweetest so don't harvest them until a couple of cold nights have passed. Cooks usually then roast parsnips but they are also great boiled and mashed with butter, on their own or with other roots. They also make good soup, especially if you add some curry powder. Remove the central core of older, tougher roots because it can be tough and fibrous.

Parsnips contain carbohydrates as sugars and starch, as well as helpings of vitamins E, C and B.

Sowing and cultivating parsnips

Parsnips need a long growing season to produce mature, large roots but you can lift them early to eat as small, baby roots at any time during the summer. They prefer moist, fertile, well-dug soil that isn't too compacted. Poor, dry sandy soils lead to thin, woody roots, and stony soils lead to twisted, oddly shaped roots. The crops need a sunny position, but aren't fussy about soil acidity, although canker is more common on acid soils. Avoid using fresh manure on your soil because it causes forked roots.

Here's how to go about growing parsnips:

1. **Rake the soil to a fine *tilth*, or texture, take out *drills* (shallow trenches) 1 centimetre deep, and water the drills before sowing.**

2. **Sow two or three seeds at points 10–15 centimetres apart.**
   Alternatively, just sow seeds thinly and when the seedlings get big enough to handle, thin them out to 10–15 centimetres apart. Space the parsnips that you intend to leave to mature at the wider end of this range. Space the rows about 30 centimetres apart.

If your soil is shallow or stony, make a deep hole with a crowbar, 10 centimetres in diameter at the top, fill it with good, fine soil and sow two or three seeds at the top. This ensures straight, long roots.

You can sow parsnips in early spring, when conditions are wet and cold, but germination is slow and erratic. Seeds germinate most quickly in warm soil, so help them along by covering the soil with cloches or polythene in early spring. Sowings as late as April or even May grow much more quickly.

Parsnip seeds are round, large and flat and very prone to blowing away, so avoid sowing on windy days.

Gardeners traditionally sow radish seeds along the rows with parsnips. The radish germinates quickly, so you can see where the row is before the parsnips start to grow and you get an early crop of radishes well before the parsnips are ready to harvest.

Buy parsnip seed fresh each year because it deteriorates quickly. Old seed germinates erratically or not at all.

3. As the seedlings grow, keep them free of weeds.

Carrot fly can sometimes attack parsnips. Chapter 7 tells you more about these pests. Also, be aware that parsnip foliage can cause skin allergies.

Harvesting and storing your parsnips

You can harvest parsnips at any stage but they taste most tender and sweet in winter after they've been frosted. Lift them to use as and when you require. If your soil is wet in winter, lift the roots by pushing a fork underneath to avoid them snapping, before the worst winter weather. Wipe, but don't wash, the roots, snap off the foliage, and store them in boxes of old compost to keep them moist.

Choosing varieties

Here are a few varieties of parsnip that I heartily recommend:

- **Albion F1** is a recent, disease-resistant introduction that has slender, smooth, well-flavoured roots.

- **Arrow F1** has slender roots that you can sow closely for baby parsnips.

- **Avonresister** is ideal for small parsnips, and is resistant to canker.

- **Countess F1** is one of the best all-purpose parsnip varieties with heavy yields of very sweet roots and a good resistance to canker.

- **Gladiator F1** parsnips have smooth-skinned, tender, tasty roots with a good resistance to canker.

- **Tender & True** is a reliable, tasty variety with resistance to canker.

The onion's big cousin: Leeks

Leeks are a great winter standby veg. You can leave them in the ground in winter until you need them and although they stay there a long time, taking up space, and need specific treatment, leeks are generally easy and rewarding to grow. They are traditionally a winter vegetable but modern varieties mature more quickly so you can enjoy them from autumn until spring, and the current trend for baby leeks means you can even eat them as a late summer veg. Make room for some in your plot!

Leeks are a biennial vegetable. You sow them one year, eat them while they have thick, tasty stems in late summer, autumn and winter, and in the second year they produce flower stems and are inedible.

Cooks usually cut leeks into sections, and then boil, steam, or add them to stews, but they're best slowly sweated in butter. They go well with ham and bacon as well as cheese and you can use them in all dishes that call for onions. Leeks make an especially fine quiche, with or without the ham. You can add them to Asian stir-fries too, sliced finely.

Much of the iron and vitamin C in leeks is in the leaves, which people usually don't eat – though you can use them in soup. Even so, leeks are rich in potassium, iron and other nutrients.

Sowing and cultivating leeks

Leeks grow in most soils but benefit from generous additions of organic matter such as garden compost or well-rotted manure. In poor, sandy soils, feeding leeks with liquid fertiliser to ensure good growth is a good idea. Leeks suffer, especially in winter, on poorly drained soils but grow well on improved clay. A deep soil is best because the roots grow so far down.

The usual way of growing leeks is to sow them, in a row, in the garden and then transplant them. You can also sow them in trays in the greenhouse for earlier crops but doing this isn't really necessary because it gives little time advantage over outdoor-sown seed.

Here's how to grow your own leeks:

1. **Take out** *drills* **(shallow trenches) 1 centimetre deep.**

2. **Thinly sow the seeds along the drill.** Do this in spring when the soil is warm. Sowing before March is pointless because sowings in April or early May give acceptable results. Because you need to transplant young leeks when they reach 15–20 centimetres high, make your rows of seedlings quite close – sowing several short rows about 15 centimetres apart works well.

If you want to sow early, in a greenhouse, sow the seed thinly in trays and, when the seedlings straighten up (they are crooked as they first emerge) and develop their second leaf, transplant them into trays, about 3cm apart, to grow on ready for their permanent positions.

3. **Keep the seeds watered and weed the rows to stop the seedlings being swamped.**

4. **If the seedlings are crowded, thin them out to 1 centimetre apart.**
   Seedlings need room to grow strongly so that the leek stems grow to about the thickness of a thick drinking straw or pencil when transplanted. The seedlings reach this stage at least two months after sowing.

5. **Transplant your seedlings.** Choose a cool, overcast day. The soil should be rich with added organic matter and recently dug, to make digging the holes for planting much easier. Use a string or line to mark out the row and make holes, 15–20 centimetres deep and 15–20 centimetres apart. Deep planting ensures a long length of blanched leek shaft and reduces the amount of watering you need to do. Wider spacing gives the leeks more room to grow into bigger mature leeks.

You can make holes in the soil with a trowel, but you then have to draw the earth up around the plants, so use a dibber or a long, straight handle instead.

The eatable white, blanched part of the leek is at the base of the leaves, and is called the *shaft*. Although leek varieties vary, the length of the shaft depends largely on how deep you plant them in the first place. You can draw soil up around the base of the plants as they grow but avoid getting soil between the leaves or this may end up between the layers in the shaft as they grow and give you gritty leeks.

Water the seedlings in the row and then, using a fork, lift a clump of young plants. Separate them carefully and drop one into the base of each hole. If you find they don't drop easily to the bottom you can trim the roots, but this isn't always necessary. If the seedlings are very big, you can also trim the top of the foliage off, but again, the more foliage you leave, the better the plants grow, at least initially. As soon as you've transplanted a row, go along and water the plants by filling the hole with water. As the water drains away some soil settles around the roots.

For baby leeks, sow very thinly in rows and pull them for use when they reach the size of spring onions or slightly thicker, during summer.

Harvesting and storing your leeks

You can harvest leeks at any stage but most gardeners leave them until they have a diameter of at least 3 centimetres. They don't increase in size after the end of October.

Because leeks are so deeply rooted you have to push a fork deep in the soil beside the row and lift the whole plant from the base. Take care not to damage the long, soft shaft as you harvest them. In fact, you don't even need to harvest and store leeks – they are hardy and, even if severe cold damages the foliage, the edible part of the leek remains intact.

Choosing varieties

Here is a rundown of some of the most popular varieties of leek:

- ✔ **Autumn Giant 3 Albana** is winter hardy, and has long shafts with little bulbing at the base.

- ✔ **Bandit** is a hardy, adaptable variety with blue-green foliage that you can harvest until late spring without bolting.

- ✔ **Carlton F1** is a tender, tasty leek with long, smooth, straight shafts and fast growth.

- ✔ **Lyon 2 Prizetaker** has long, thick white shafts and is good for eating in autumn and early winter.

- ✔ **Malabar** has very broad foliage that is resistant to rust (see Chapter 7 for more about rust). This variety is good to eat from autumn to spring.

- ✔ **Musselburgh** is a traditional, hardy variety of leek.

- ✔ **Sultan** has dark, rust-resistant foliage and long, dense, slender shafts and is a good choice for eating from autumn to spring.

So good, they make you cry: Onions and shallots

After potatoes, onions must be the most valuable and adaptable of all vegetables. Useful as both a flavouring and a vegetable, onions are ready for use soon after harvest and store well for use throughout winter and into spring. Shallots have smaller bulbs than onions and grow in a different way. (You plant a shallot bulb of the size you would eat and it splits as it grows into 8–12 similar bulbs.) They have a milder flavour than onions, and are easier to grow, so ideal for beginners.

Most people usually fry onions and shallots and add them to cooked dishes, though you can also bake them, whole, in their skins. You can eat mild onions and shallots raw.

Onions and shallots have small amounts of a wide range of vitamins and minerals.

Sowing and cultivating onions and shallots

Onions need a fertile, rich soil that isn't too acidic, in full sun. Poor soil produces smaller bulbs and small, pickling onions or shallots may grow better. Digging in organic matter several months before planting and applying a general fertiliser prior to planting increases yields.

When you've chosen your onion variety, get out to your growing beds and follow these steps:

1. **Sowing or planting.** You have three options here:

   In the greenhouse, thinly sow seeds in late winter and early spring in seed or cell trays. Ideally, keep the temperature at 18°C for them to germinate. If sowing in cells, sow four to six seeds per module. As the seeds grow, you can leave them as a small clump to grow on and eventually plant them together to form a cluster of small bulbs. Alternatively, remove all but one seedling as they grow to produce regular or large bulbs later in the season. If sowing in a seed tray, transplant the seedlings when they have two leaves carefully into cell trays, one per cell, and grow them at a minimum temperature of 10°C. By late March they should fill the compost in the cell with roots and you can plant them outside, 15–25 centimetres apart, the wider spacing for clusters of seedlings and extra large onions. Choosing this option and sowing under glass means that you should get larger onions.

   In the open garden, sow seeds in March or April, as soon as the soil warms up, avoiding both very dry and cold weather. In cool weather cover rows with cloches or polythene before sowing to warm the soil. Take out drills 1 centimetre deep and sow the seed thinly along the rows or sow a pinch of seed every 15 centimetres. Cover them with soil and keep it moist until the seedlings appear through the surface. Thin them out as soon as the seedlings have two leaves and are growing strongly. Water the row first and then remove spare seedlings, leaving the remaining ones 8–15 centimetres apart. Closer spacing results in smaller onions.

   In the open garden, plant sets in March or April, 8–15 centimetres apart. Sets are more prone to bolting than onions from seed, often caused by a cold snap after growth has started, and so, unless planting heat-treated sets, don't plant too early or if the weather is likely to turn wintry. Plant sets with a trowel – don't just push them in because this compacts the soil beneath the bulb and pushes the set out of the soil as the roots grow. Keep sets well watered. Because sets are easy to handle and space evenly, they're the easiest way to grow onions, even despite the bolting problem.

Birds sometimes pull sets out of the ground, confusing the dry 'tail' of the bulb for a leaf a worm is dragging into the soil, so cut off any long tails before planting. For the first couple of weeks after planting, check frequently and replant any our feathered friends have pulled up.

Early sowings give heavy crops of larger bulbs.

Onions frequently bolt, often due to drought, cold weather and erratic spring weather.

2. **Keep onions free from weeds, and watered in dry weather.** Until mid-July they need plenty of nutrients and moisture. After that date they usually don't make any more leaves but the bulbs start to swell.

Soon after this stage the foliage flops over and the leaf tips may turn yellow. You can then bend over the foliage to prevent it flopping over the bulbs – gardeners usually bend the leaves over in the same direction for neatness.

Shallots need similar growing conditions and cultivation to onions but are easier to grow and tolerate poorer soils. Each bulb splits as it grows and forms six to ten replacement bulbs.

Here's how to go about growing shallots:

1. **Plant the bulbs in early spring 20 centimetres apart, with 40 centimetres between the rows.** Plant with a trowel (don't push the bulbs into the soil) so that just the top of the bulb is visible.

2. **Keep the plants free from weeds throughout their growth.** Weed by hand; careless hoeing can damage developing bulbs.

Most people grow shallots from bulbs in this way, but you can also now grow shallots from seed. The bulb method is simplest, but growing from seed is still easy. Just sow the seed like onions and thin the seedlings to about 5 centimetres apart. Each seed then produces one shallot.

Harvesting and storing your onions and shallots

By late July, the leaves are largely yellow and you can break the roots to stop growth and help the ripening of the bulbs. Push a fork under the plants and lift the soil immediately under the bulb to sever the roots. After a few more weeks the onions and shallots should be almost dry. Pull up the onions or shallots, shake off excess soil, rub off the roots, and lay them on the green-house bench, on wire netting or shelves with good air flow. Alternatively, lay them on the soil and cover with a cloche to keep them dry and allow them to ripen.

Store onions and shallots in a frost-free, cool, dry, airy place, keeping some shallot bulbs to plant the following year. Use any damaged bulbs or those with thick necks (where the foliage grew out of the top of the bulb) immediately because they don't store well.

Choosing varieties

You're not short of options when it comes to onions and shallots. You can grow them from seed or from *sets* (small, immature onions). Sets are easier to grow, less prone to onion fly, more reliable than onions from seed in areas where summers are short and cool, and you don't have to prepare the soil as well as for seed. However, you have less choice of varieties among sets, they are more prone to bolting than onions from seed (although heat-treated sets usually give better results), and are more expensive than seed.

Sets also provide an easy way to grow spring onions. Soon after planting, before the bulb starts to swell, you can pull young onions from sets and peel off the outer layers of the set to reveal what looks like a spring onion. Red onion sets work especially well for this method.

Here are some of the most popular onions that you can grow from seed:

- **Ailsa Craig Prizewinner** is a reliable, traditional, golden-skinned and round variety that stores well.

- **Albion** is an unusual variety with round bulbs and pure white skins and flesh.

- **Hytech F1** is a uniform, firm, brown-skinned onion with strong flavour. Hytech F1 stores well, and is also available as sets (see below).

- **Kelsae** is the variety to pick if size matters to you! Kelsae are large, sweet onions that win shows as well as votes in the kitchen.

- **Long Red Florence** onions are long, spindle-shaped bulbs with red skin and flesh and a mild, sweet flavour.

- **Napoleon F1** is a uniform, vigorous variety with good yields of pale-skinned, slightly flattened bulbs; stores well.

- **Owa** are unusual, long, club-shaped bulbs.

- **Red Baron** onions are attractive, round and red-skinned with strong taste. This variety stores well and is also available as sets.

- **Sweet Spanish Yellow** onions are large and round with a very mild flavour, and are ideal for eating raw.

Here are a few onions that you can grow from sets:

- ✔ **Centurion F1** makes an excellent choice for an early crop in all seasons and stores well.

- ✔ **Hyred F1** is the best red onion, with heavy crops of strong onions that store well into spring.

- ✔ **Sturon** are thin-necked bulbs that store better than most. The medium-sized bulbs have a good flavour.

- ✔ **Stuttgart Giant** is a popular, traditional variety that makes good crops of rather flat, well-flavoured bulbs, and stores well.

Here are some worthwhile varieties of shallot to consider growing:

- ✔ **Ambition F1** is an easy-to-grow seed-raised shallot, slow to bolt, and with great taste.

- ✔ **Golden Gourmet** is an improvement on the old Dutch Yellow variety, with better yields and bulb size and shape.

- ✔ **Hative de Niort** is the exhibitor's choice with perfectly shaped, slender-necked bulbs.

- ✔ **Jermor** produces rather elongated bulbs with bright, brown skins and pink flesh.

- ✔ **Langor** shallots are long with golden copper skins and pink flesh.

- ✔ **Red Sun** shallots are red-skinned with good shape and size and a mild, spicy flavour. Plant this variety late to prevent bolting.

- ✔ **Topper** produces heavy crops of golden bulbs with pinkish flesh; stores well.

Go east for early onions

If you want to get a head start with your onions, Japanese onions such as *senshyu semi-globe* (good crops of round, straw-coloured bulbs in early July) are useful because you can harvest them at least a month before most spring-sown or spring-planted sets. However, they need fertile, well-drained soil to ensure good growth, and are prone to downy mildew in some areas, especially if the winter is wet and mild. Sowing time is critical because if you sow too early they bolt the following spring and if you sow too late the plants aren't big enough to survive the winter weather. In most areas mid-August to early September is fine. Germination is usually rapid and reliable because the soil is warm and moist. Autumn-planted sets are now available that are slightly easier to grow than Japanese onions.

Pretty in purple: Beetroot

Tasty beetroot is a popular choice partly thanks to its bright colouring, which shows that it's high in healthy antioxidants. Indeed, seed companies say that beetroot always ranks among their bestselling vegetable seeds. Beetroot isn't difficult to grow and by growing your own you can harvest when it's young and tender. You can also try growing something unusual such as yellow or white beet.

Before you do anything in the kitchen with your beet, twist the foliage off the roots instead of cutting them to prevent coloured juice bleeding from them. (Wear gloves as you do this because beet stains your skin.) You can then cook, freeze or pickle the beet. Beetroot needs boiling for more than an hour to make it tender, unless you harvest the beet when small. You can also bake beet in its skins in the oven and peel when cooked to intensify the flavour. Test that the beet is cooked by pushing a sharp knife into the centre of the root. Beet is also delicious pickled and you can use raw beet in salads by grating it. Beet is also increasingly popular as a salad leaf, and is closely related to leaf beet (chard).

Beetroot is high in carbohydrates, mainly as sugars, and is high in potassium and folic acid. In recent years the antioxidant value of this vegetable's highly pigmented flesh has won it many new fans.

Sowing and cultivating beetroot

Beetroot adapts to varying conditions but grows best in full sun and in moist, rich, neutral soil; hot, dry, poor soil results in small, thin, woody roots, and if your soil is very acid you need to add lime to improve it (Chapter 5 gives you the details on how to do this). Also, well-dug, deep soil is a good place for growing large, long beet.

Any check to growth, perhaps a cold snap after an early sowing or drought at any stage in growth, causes beetroot plants to bolt.

1. **Prepare the soil by forking, and rake the soil to a fine tilth.** Forking helps to improve the soil if it has become compacted.

2. **Take out *drills* (shallow trenches) 1 centimetre deep and about 30 centimetres apart if you're sowing more than one row.**

3. **Sow the seeds.** You can do this throughout spring and early summer, starting in March with protected sowings under cloches. Beet seed is large and most varieties have seed clusters with two or three seeds. Sow the seeds 3–5 centimetres apart.

   If you're growing beet for its leaves, to use in salads, sow regularly in pots or rows in the soil and pick individual leaves, or use a knife to harvest the crop, cutting off the foliage just above soil level. Plants re-grow several times although the roots don't grow large.

4. **Cover the seed with soil and water well.**

5. **If more than one seed in each cluster grows, pull out the spares when they are large enough to handle.**

6. **Water the rows well in dry weather and pull up weeds to prevent the small seedlings from being smothered.**

Harvesting and storing your beetroot

You can harvest beet as soon as the roots are the size of a golf ball. Pull up every other beet in the row to give those that you leave room to develop further. You should be able to hold the foliage at the base and simply pull the roots out of the soil but you may find larger and longer beet easier to remove by pushing a fork into the soil under them to loosen the soil before pulling.

Be sure not to leave frost-hardy beet in the ground all winter. Lift the roots after the first frost, twist off the foliage near the top of the plant, and pack the roots into boxes of compost and store in a cool place such as a shed for the winter.

Choosing varieties

- **Boltardy** is a traditional variety with evenly coloured roots and resistance to bolting, and it's a good variety for early sowing.

- **Burpees Golden** has mild, tender flesh that is orange when raw but golden when cooked.

- **Chioggia (Barabietola di Chioggia)** has round roots with pale red skins. The flesh inside has alternate white and red rings.

- **Cylindra** has long, cylindrical roots that grow partly above the soil. Cylindra is good for slicing and pickling and stores well.

- **Golden Detroit** has round roots with sweet golden flesh. The leaves are especially tender and work well as a spinach substitute.

- **Kestrel F1** is an early, dark-fleshed beet with sweet, fine flesh.

- **Monogerm** varieties are a recent introduction. They differ from older types of beet in that each 'cluster of seeds' only contains one seed. This advantage means that you don't have to thin out and remove the other two or three seedlings at each place seed was sown.

- **Moneta Monogerm** has round roots with deep crimson flesh. This variety is slow to bolt, even from early sowings.

- **Monorubra Monogerm** has long, cylindrical roots with fine, crimson flesh.

- **Pablo F1** has well-flavoured roots of uniform size and rich colour.

The Swedish turnip: Swede

Closely related to the turnip, the swede is a staple root vegetable widely available in shops and as the famous 'neeps' of Scotland. Swedes typically have yellow flesh and top-shaped roots with a red or purple upper part, and modern varieties are free from the unpleasant bitterness that people often associate with them.

Compared with other vegetables, swedes can be difficult to cultivate, and they're prone to most of the common brassica diseases. However, by taking note of the main rules of not sowing too early and making sure they don't go short of water while they're growing, you could end up with a bumper crop.

Small swedes are the most tasty and tender. Peel, slice and boil, and then mash them with butter for a really tasty treat. You can also boil, mash and mix swede with carrots, potatoes or squash. Cut the swedes into smaller pieces than the potatoes because they take longer to cook. You can also dice swede and add it to stews; diced swede freezes well.

Swede is relatively low in nutrients with few carbohydrates (calories) but some Vitamin C and B.

Sowing and cultivating swedes

Along with other brassicas, swedes need firm soil, and in poor, dry or light soils they are likely to run to seed or produce small, woody roots. Although they need well-drained soil they must have a constant supply of moisture. If they dry out and are then watered, the roots are liable to crack. Swedes grow best in full sun or, in dry soils, in light shade.

Here's how to go about growing your own swedes:

1. **Take out seed drills 1 centimetre deep and 45 centimetres apart.**

2. **Sow the seeds thinly in late spring in cool areas, and in early summer in warmer areas.**

3. **Thin the seedlings to 25 centimetres apart when they have two or three leaves.** The seeds germinate quite fast but swedes have a long growing season and the foliage is large and bulky.

4. **Firm the soil around the remaining plants after thinning.** Swedes cannot be transplanted.

5. **Keep the plants well watered as they grow.** This helps to avoid dry soil and stressed plants, and the resulting mildew.

Harvesting and storing your swedes

Swedes are ready to harvest from autumn onwards. They are hardy so you can leave them in the ground until you need them but, if slugs or wireworms are a problem in your garden, lift the swedes in late autumn, when fully grown. Cut off the foliage and fine roots and store them in damp compost in a cool place where they should last until late winter.

Choosing varieties

Choose your variety to suit your needs. Some modern kinds are resistant to clubroot and mildew.

- ✔ **Angela** swedes are attractive and have exceptional flavour and some resistance to mildew.

- ✔ **Brora** has unusual, deep purple tops with exceptionally sweet, tasty flesh.

- ✔ **Invitation** has colourful roots that are resistant to clubroot and mildew.

- ✔ **Marian** is a popular swede with colourful skin, sweet flavour, and resistance to clubroot and mildew. Marian is an excellent variety for beginners.

- ✔ **Virtue** has highly coloured purple tops, fine texture without fibrousness, and some resistance to mildew.

Quick and easy: Radish

Pungent and colourful, radishes are among the easiest and quickest of all vegetables to grow and are often the first veg that many people attempt. The large radish seeds are easy to sow, germinate readily, and can be ready to harvest in little more than a month after sowing. They make a good choice for container gardens, growing well in pots and grow bags, and come in a wonderful array of colours – not just red. You can grow radish for winter and even grow one with crunchy, tasty seedpods.

Radishes are perfect for *catch-cropping* – sowing in gaps between another crop being harvested and another being planted.

People usually eat radishes raw. You can slice, grate or eat them whole and add them to mixed salads. Large, autumn and winter radishes are especially useful grated in winter salads.

Considering how easy they are to grow, radishes are surprisingly good for you. They contain few calories but have vitamin C, iron and some protein, as well as other minerals.

Sowing and cultivating radishes

Radishes grow best in sun or part shade in moist, fertile soil. In dry, poor soil they run to seed quickly and mature more slowly, with tough, pithy, hollow roots that taste hot and unpleasant.

To begin cultivating radishes, just follow these steps:

1. **In the open garden or in raised beds take out drills about 1 centimetre deep.**

2. **Sow seed thinly, about 1 centimetre apart.** The seeds are large and easy to space out. Radishes are easiest to grow if you sow them in spring and late summer when the weather is cooler than in midsummer. In the hottest months growing radishes in semi-shade is the best way forward.

   Sow small amounts of seed regularly because even varieties that are supposed to 'hold' well or retain their crispness when mature soon go pithy and old.

3. **Cover the seed with soil and water well.** In early spring, sow under cloches so the soil is warmer and growth is quicker. Weeds aren't usually a big problem because they can hardly grow as quickly as the radishes!

4. **Thin out the seedlings to 1 centimetre apart if they are sown thickly.** The plants don't form good, succulent roots if they're too crowded.

Radishes are a favourite meal for the flea beetle, which can do great damage to your plants. Chapter 7 tells you more about dealing with them.

Harvesting and storing your radishes

Except for winter radishes, which you can store like carrots and parsnips, eat radishes as soon as possible after harvesting because they don't store well. Trim off the leaves immediately after harvesting or the roots will quickly shrivel and lose their plumpness.

Choosing varieties

You can choose from a whole array of radish varieties. Here are some that people grow to use in salads:

- **Amethyst** has bright purple skin and white flesh, and is slow to run to seed.
- **Celesta F1** has bright red roots with white flesh and is resistant to disease and pithiness (in other words, becoming hollow and fluffy).

✔ **Fluo F1** is similar to the French Breakfast type with improved vigour and long, white-tipped, red roots.

✔ **French Breakfast** has long, cylindrical roots with red skin and white tips.

✔ **Pink Beauty** has pinkish red, round roots with white flesh.

✔ **Prinz Rotin** has bright red roots with white flesh that is slow to become tough.

✔ **Rudi** is an exceptional variety for poor soils and early sowings with crisp, round red roots.

✔ **Scarlet Globe** has bright red, round roots with white flesh.

✔ **Sparkler** is a popular variety with red, round roots with white tips.

The following varieties of radish make great winter vegetables:

✔ **Black Spanish** has large, black-skinned roots with dense, crisp, white flesh and produces tasty seedpods if you leave them to flower the following year. Round and long-rooted types are available.

✔ **China Rose** has large, cylindrical, pinkish red roots and dense, white flesh.

✔ **Mantanghong F1** is an unusual winter radish to sow in summer. The green and white roots have crisp, sweet, deep pink flesh.

✔ **Mino Summer Cross F1** has pure white skins and flesh, and fast-growing roots that mature in about two months from sowing.

✔ **Mooli** has long, white, tender roots that grow partly out of the soil and can weigh as much as one kilogram. Sow in midsummer and harvest in autumn. Mooli isn't winter hardy.

✔ **Munchen Bier** is an unusual radish that people grow for its seedpods and not the roots. To make the plant run to seed quickly, sow seed thickly and don't thin the seedlings. The long-tailed pods appear after flowering, and are sweet and mildly hot when young. Pick before they become tough and fibrous.

Enjoying Exotic Vegetables

If you feel adventurous, you can try growing some less familiar vegetables that aren't difficult to grow but provide variety to your plot and your diet. Some are almost impossible to buy in the shops, so these vegetables really are worth growing if you fancy a new taste sensation.

Space invaders: Kohl rabi

No other vegetable looks quite like kohl rabi – an unusual vegetable that is a little like a turnip. But whereas turnips are really swollen roots, kohl rabi is a swollen stem studded with leaves and growing above the ground, so you don't even have to get dirty harvesting or preparing it!

Kohl rabi isn't as popular as it deserves to be, mainly because shops rarely stock it and those that do often sell large, tough, unappetising specimens. Therefore, kohl rabi is a crop that's definitely best to grow yourself; and you can confound your friends when they see it on your plot!

Kohl rabi, when young, is delicious, sweet, and crisp and you can eat it raw – usually grated and added to salads. But you can also use it as you would cabbage and cook it in the same way as turnips – the best way to use older roots.

Kohl rabi is low in calories but rich in minerals and vitamins.

Sowing and cultivating kohl rabi

Kohl rabi grows best in full sun or light shade, and because it grows quickly, it's an ideal vegetable for raised beds or pots, where it grows happily in multipurpose compost as long as you regularly apply liquid fertiliser. Kohl rabi isn't fussy about soil, but rich soil that you've improved with organic matter is best because this crop needs to be grown quickly to be tender and tasty.

Here's how to go about raising a crop of kohl rabi:

1. **Fork in some organic matter to increase the fertility and amount of moisture in the soil.** This approach helps the kohl rabi to grow quickly and so to be tender and sweet.

2. **Take out *drills* (shallow trenches) 1 centimetre deep and 30 centimetres apart.**

3. **Sow from March to July**. The seeds germinate quickly but are prone to damage from flea beetles, which eat small holes in the seed leaves, in common with most other brassicas (Chapter 7 has more about flea beetles). Keep the soil moist.

4. **Thin the seedlings out to 8–10 centimetres apart when they have several leaves and are growing well**.

5. **Keep the plants well watered.** If the ground is dry, the roots don't swell and they get tough and woody. When you water them again they split.

Harvesting and storing your kohl rabi

Harvest kohl rabi when it's no bigger than a tennis ball, about two months after sowing, when the vegetable is at its most delicious and tender. Old roots are tough and fibrous and have a strong taste. This crop doesn't store well.

Choosing varieties

Here are a few of the most popular varieties of kohl rabi:

- ✔ **Azur Star** has bright purple roots and is very quick to mature.

- ✔ **Kolibri F1** has purple roots that stand well when mature.

- ✔ **Logo** is a fast-growing variety with white roots and good resistance to bolting.

- ✔ **Quickstar F1** has greenish white roots that are slow to go woody but fast to mature.

From Florence with love: Fennel

Florence fennel is a form of the herb fennel that has thick, fleshy, sweet leaf bases forming a kind of bulb, which is the part you eat. This delicious and unusual vegetable is generally free from pests and quick to mature, but can be tricky to grow. You do need to get the timing right. You can't produce Florence fennel all year round, but you can produce masses of it from midsummer onwards.

Young fennel is tender enough to eat raw, grated in salads, but its flavour may be too strong for some. Cooking gives it a milder taste. Cut the roots in halves or in quarters, along the length, and parboil, drain and sauté in butter. Delicious! Florence fennel is also good with cheese and fish dishes, and you can use the feathery foliage just as you would use the herb fennel.

These tasty, swollen leaf bases are a good source of potassium, with some vitamin C and other minerals.

Sowing and cultivating Florence fennel

Florence fennel grows best in moist, fertile soil and in warm weather. This plant hates transplanting and any shock to its growth causes it to bolt. Early sowings also bolt readily, due to the increasing day length and the risk of chilly nights.

1. **Prepare the soil by forking it over, removing weeds, and incorporating some organic matter and some general fertiliser.**

2. **Take out drills, 1 centimetre deep.**

3. **Sow the seeds, from late spring to late summer.** Cover them with soil.

4. **When the seedlings appear, thin them to 20 centimetres apart to mature.** You can use the seedlings that you remove as salad leaves.

5. **As plants grow, water them in dry weather and keep rows weed-free.** Drought causes bolting and prevents the formation of thick, tender bulbs. Weeds swamp the delicate, feathery foliage of Florence fennel, and compete with it for light and water. Weed by hand because hoeing can cause damage to the developing bulbs.

Because you can harvest plants only for a relatively short period, sow a short row of seed regularly throughout the summer to avoid gluts and famines.

Harvesting and storing your Florence fennel

Fennel is ready for harvesting as soon as the leaf bases are thick and swollen, which may be as little as 10 weeks after sowing. Plants don't stand in harvestable condition for long, and bolt and produce flowering stems quickly in hot weather, so use them as soon as they're ready. Simply pull the plants up, trim off the foliage from the top, and cut off the roots to leave the edible, swollen leaf bases. You can store them, after trimming off foliage, for a week or so in the fridge but fennel doesn't keep well otherwise.

Choosing varieties

Here are a few varieties that I recommend:

- ✔ **Amigo F1** has squat, bulky bulbs, and was bred for its resistance to bolting.

- ✔ **Cantino F1** is fast growing and good for late sowing to harvest in September and October.

- ✔ **Goal F1** is a quick-growing variety with large, pure white bulbs.

- ✔ **Fennel de Firenze** is the standard, common variety with large, slender bulbs.

Sleek and slender: Salsify and scorzonera

Salsify and scorzonera are an odd pair of vegetables. Gardeners don't commonly grow them and they're a bit of a fuss to prepare. But most gardeners try them once and if you have a taste for the unusual, they may be just your thing. You can be certain that your dinner guests will have no idea what you're feeding them!

These vegetables are useful for their long, slender roots, which have white skins in salsify and black skins in scorzonera. Gardeners raise them in a similar way to parsnips and carrots, from seed, sowing where they are to grow. Both vegetables are hardy and need a long growing season and you can leave them in the ground, in autumn and winter, until you need them for cooking. If you leave them in the ground until the second year, the plants produce tall stems and flower: lilac in salsify and yellow in scorzonera. These flowers are attractive to bees but the unopened, young flower buds make tasty food for humans too – steamed and eaten! Unfortunately, you don't have much of a choice when it comes to varieties and you generally have to take the one you see offered in most catalogues.

Salsify is often called the vegetable oyster because of its delicate taste and soft texture when cooked. Scorzonera is similar. Both are the kind of veg that you either relish or hate. I suggest tasting some before you grow them if you're a fussy eater. When you're ready to use them in the kitchen, remember that the cut surface of both roots discolours in the air so cut off the foliage and the thin root tips, scrub the roots, and soak in water with lemon juice added until you're ready to use them for cooking. Cooks usually then cut the roots into sections and boil for about 20 minutes until tender, and then peel and serve them with butter and pepper or cheese sauce.

Growers cultivate salsify and scorzonera primarily for their taste but a bonus is that they contain inulin, a sugar that diabetics can usually eat.

Sowing and cultivating salsify and scorzonera

Both crops prefer a light, sandy soil free from stones, which cause the roots to twist and bend. Heavily manured soils also lead to forked roots, which are fiddly to prepare and to dig out of the soil. The good news is that both plants are free from any serious pests.

Follow these steps for both vegetables, and you should have an unusual crop to be proud of!

1. **Sow the seeds, 1 centimetre deep in rows about 40 centimetres apart.** Sow in mid-spring when the soil is warming up.

2. **Keep plants free from weeds as they grow.**

3. **Thin the seedlings out to about 20 centimetres apart in the rows after they have three or four leaves.**

Harvesting and storing your salsify and scorzonera

The roots are ready to harvest in late summer and autumn onwards. Never attempt to pull them up – instead, push a fork or spade into the ground beside the rows and carefully pull the roots up by the foliage as you loosen the soil around them. The roots are thin, very long, and snap easily. Dig them as you need to use them, from October until March.

Not such an ugly duckling: Celeriac

Celeriac isn't going to win any beauty competitions but it's the tops when it comes to being useful and delicious! Celeriac is basically a celery in which the swollen root is the end product, rather than the crunchy stems. It's much easier to grow than celery and is a tasty and adaptable autumn and winter vegetable. Although celeriac has a long growing season, the fact that buying it in the shops isn't always easy means that celeriac deserves serious consideration as a contender for space on your plot.

Celeriac is versatile in the kitchen. You can grate the peeled roots (which may be substantially smaller than the unpeeled roots!) and add them to salads, boil and mash them on their own or with carrots and parsnips, roast them, or add them to stews. The flesh discolours when cut, so always put prepared, uncooked celeriac in water and lemon juice.

Celeriac is rich in magnesium and other minerals.

Sowing and cultivating celeriac

Celeriac needs a moist, rich, fertile soil with plenty of organic matter, but the plants aren't too fussy. As long as your soil isn't too dry and sandy, and you can water in dry weather, you should get a decent crop.

Celeriac tolerates light shade as long as the plant isn't dry at the roots, but plants growing in rich soil in full sun produce the biggest roots. Celeriac is suitable for deep beds and raised beds but isn't really productive enough for growing in pots.

Here's how to grow a bumper crop of celeriac:

1. **Sow the seeds.** Celeriac needs a long growing season and isn't completely hardy, so sow the seeds in mid-spring, in a greenhouse or indoors. The seed is tiny, so sow it carefully in a pot or seed tray and lightly cover with compost or perlite. Keep the tray in a temperature of about 20°C and keep the compost moist. Germination takes about two weeks.

2. **When the seedlings have produced a leaf in the centre of the seed leaves, carefully transplant the seedlings into trays, spaced 2–3 centimetres apart or, preferably, into cell trays so they don't suffer root disturbance when planting them out.** Water carefully but don't allow the seedlings to dry out at any time.

3. **Plant the seedlings out in the garden by late May, when they should have filled the cells or small pots with roots.** Plant them about 25 centimetres apart in rows with 40 centimetres between the rows.

4. **Keep the soil free of weeds and moist.** If the plants dry out they may run to seed.

5. **If you're growing an older variety, snap off the side shoots on the main root.** This method ensures a neat, globular root that's easy to peel and use. Modern varieties tend not to produce side shoots – even so, watch out for side shoots growing from the main root.

Harvesting and storing your celeriac

Celeriac roots are ready to harvest when they are 10 centimetres in diameter or larger – usually in autumn. Though the roots withstand some frost, they aren't winter hardy and, to be able to use them throughout winter, you need to lift in autumn, cut off the foliage, and store the roots in damp compost in boxes in a cool place until you need them.

Choosing varieties

Here are a couple of celeriac varieties that I recommend:

- ✔ **Brilliant** is a newer variety that has flesh that doesn't discolour when you prepare it for cooking.

- ✔ **Monarch** is the standard variety and has relatively smooth, globular roots. Monarch doesn't usually produce side shoots.

Sweeter than the average: Sweet potatoes

This vegetable, and not the 'other' potato, was the one that explorers first introduced from the Americas to Europe; the Elizabethans were more familiar with this than the common potato that was introduced later on.

The sweet potato can be difficult to grow in cool climates because it needs high temperatures to do well and to form tubers. Polytunnels can provide a suitable environment, but this vegetable is unlikely to thrive outside except in warm, mild areas.

You can use sweet potatoes in the same way as common potatoes: boil and mash, roast them, make them into chips, or add them to stews.

Sweet potatoes have more calories than common potatoes but are a good source of starch, especially for people who can't eat potatoes or other staples. Varieties with orange flesh are especially rich in betacarotene and all types contain vitamins B and C and potassium.

Sowing and cultivating sweet potatoes

Sweet potatoes are frost-tender and need warm, humid conditions and protection from sub-zero temperatures. They prefer acid soils improved with lots of organic matter rich in nutrients and holding plenty of water. They grow best in full sun or part shade (if warm and sheltered). They do grow in raised beds and pots but the foliage and stems are large and take up a lot of room so your total crop from that area may be disappointing. The rampant, sprawling stems do, however, smother most weeds.

If you grow your sweet potatoes in a polytunnel, remember that plants growing under cover are prone to red spider mite (see Chapter 7).

Sweet potato plants grow from *slips*, which you can buy. Slips are young shoots cut from sprouted tubers and you have to root them when they arrive, before you plant them to grow a crop. Alternatively, you can grow your own slips from a bought tuber for eating if you can't find a supplier of slips. Either way, follow these steps:

1. **Plant tubers horizontally in pots or trays of multipurpose compost in spring and keep them in a warm place.** You should get 8 to 10 shoots from each tuber.

2. **When the shoots are 20 centimetres long, cut them off at ground level, trim off the lower leaves, and root them in gritty compost. If you've ordered slips, treat them the same way as soon as they arrive.** A mix of equal parts multipurpose compost and perlite is ideal. Keep the cuttings shaded and in a warm propagator to root.

3. **At the end of May, when the danger of frost is past, put the plants out into the soil.**

Alternatively you can plant small tubers directly in the soil in late May. Plant them in a sunny spot outside, in a greenhouse border or in the polytunnel, and keep them watered at all times. Pinch out the growing tips if the stems become too long and spreading. You can apply a general fertiliser to the soil before planting or throughout the growing season. If you've planted the tubers in containers, give a general, liquid fertiliser once a week throughout the growing season.

Harvesting and storing your sweet potatoes

Harvest your tubers before the first frost because both the stems and the tubers are sensitive to cold. Sometimes the foliage turns yellow to show that the plants have stopped growing and that the tubers are ready to harvest. Dig up the plants, taking care not to impale the tubers on the fork, and store them in a cool, frost-free place until needed.

Choosing varieties

Seed companies are the best places to look for sweet potatoes, which are usually sold as unrooted cuttings, or slips. However, few varieties of sweet potato are available in the UK. **Beauregard** is the most commonly available variety, but even this is hard to find. Those tubers that you can buy for planting aren't usually labelled, so you don't know the variety, and because they are imports from warmer countries they may not be the best to grow in our cool climate. You rarely have much – if any – choice.

Chapter 10

Growing a Selection for All Seasons

*F*ancy some sunshine on your plate? This chapter introduces you to some crops that many people associate with the Mediterranean. Although some of these plants aren't at all Mediterranean in origin, they are an intimate part of French, Italian and Spanish cooking. You can get a special sense of achievement when you pick your own aubergines, tomatoes and squashes, and add the excitement of warmer climes to your diet.

Growing Tangy Leaf Crops

Endives and chicories are crisp, tangy and slightly bitter alternatives to some of the more usual summer salad leaves. Apart from their distinctive taste, these crops, along with radicchios, are useful for late summer, autumn and winter use, and their wide range of leaf shapes, colours and textures makes them an adventurous cook's dream. All three are easy to grow, sown from July onwards, and have rather tough, bitter leaves that improve with blanching.

Something to end up with: Endive

Endives are less popular in the UK than in the rest of Europe, but these attractive plants are a great salad crop and a worthy addition to your plot. Endives come in a wide variety of types but the most common have heavily lobed or deeply cut leaves, and all have a distinctive taste.

Cooks normally use endive raw, in salads, to give some bite, and the slightly bitter, refreshing taste combines nicely with the sweetness of orange slices, apricots and grapefruit. You can lessen the bitter taste of the leaves through blanching (see the 'Sowing and cultivating your endives' section below).

Endives have moderate amounts of vitamin C and iron.

Sowing and cultivating endives

By adding lots of organic matter to light soils, you can provide endives with the type of environment they like best. You can grow them in light shade, especially as baby leaves, but they grow best in full sun. They often bolt in hot, dry weather, so always keep them well watered.

Here's the drill for growing endives:

1. **Sow seed thinly in *drills* (shallow trenches) 1 centimetre deep.** Sow most varieties from late June to August, and bolting-resistant varieties earlier. You can also sow from spring to summer if you're growing for young, baby leaves to pick early.

2. **Thin out the seedlings to 20 centimetres apart as they grow.**

You can decrease the bitterness of the leaves through *blanching,* or in other words, by protecting the leaves from light. Do this to your endives when they're fully grown, a few days before harvesting, by placing an upturned plate or other disc over the centre of the plant or by tying the outer leaves together to shade the centre. Alternatively, you can buy some varieties that are naturally self-blanching, at least to some extent, such as Glory.

Harvesting and storing your endives

You can cut endives as small leaves or, more usually, when mature and blanched. Because they wilt rapidly and don't store well, cut endives immediately before use.

Choosing varieties

Here are three great varieties of endive to consider growing:

- ✔ **Cornet de Bordeaux** is a frost-resistant variety good for winter use.

- ✔ **Glory** has very frilly leaves, and you can sow this variety from spring to summer and harvest it as individual leaves or as a complete head.

- ✔ **Natacha** also has traditional, frilly leaves. This variety is resistant to bolting so you can sow it from late spring onwards for summer use.

Two of a kind: Chicory and radicchio

Both chicory and radicchio are easy to grow. Their delicious bittersweet leaves pep up salads through the late summer, autumn and into winter. Chicory, because it has to be grown to form roots, then dug and the shoots produced in a shed over winter, takes more effort than radicchio but tastes more tender and not quite as bitter. But radicchio is colourful (the colour develops best in cool weather) and useful for winter salads. You can grow both of them as baby leaves, though they develop their best taste and looks if you leave them to grow to maturity.

Like most salad leaves, chicory and radicchio are low in calories and contain iron, magnesium and vitamin C.

Sowing and cultivating chicory and radicchio

Both crops grow in any reasonable soil but you can help them along by adding in some organic matter to avoid the soil drying out in summer, when plants are more likely to bolt. For best results, grow them in full sun.

All you need to do is to sow seeds thinly in rows 1 centimetre deep where the plants are to grow. At first, the leaves are thin and upright but as plants mature they develop their characteristic shape and colour. Red-leaved varieties develop their best colour when the weather gets colder.

To lessen the bitter taste of chicory you can blanch by digging up the roots and forcing them in winter to produce *chicons,* or shoots (see the following section).

Harvesting and storing your chicory and radicchio

Harvesting witloof chicory is more involved. These plants make lots of leaves and look scruffy. As soon as they've been frosted in autumn, dig up the roots to force them (or produce the crisp new shoots or chicons) as and when you need them. To do this:

1. **Dig up the roots carefully and trim off the leaves**, about 1 centimetre above the top of the root.

2. **Trim the thick roots** by cutting off the base so they're about 15 centimetres long.

3. **Put five to seven plants**, depending on how many fit, in a 15-centimetre wide pot and pour compost around them, firm in gently, water, and put in a warm but dark place. Make sure that they don't dry out at any time.

According to how warm you keep them, the white, torpedo-shaped chicons appear in one or two months. You can cut these off when they're the size you want and discard and compost the roots.

For a succession of crops, you can dig up and force roots throughout winter. None of these crops store well but, when cut and trimmed of the outer leaves, they keep in good condition for a week in the fridge.

Choosing varieties

You can choose to grow *leaf chicory* (for eating straight after cutting from the plant in the garden) or *forcing chicory*, also known as *witloof chicory* (to produce chicons). Sugar Loaf (sometimes known as Pain de Sucre) is the leaf chicory to look out for. This variety looks like a Cos lettuce, has dense, crisp heads of sweet leaves, and makes a superb salad crop to use in autumn – or later if you grow it in a polytunnel. Zoom F1 is a good forcing chicory, and is an improved form of a traditional favourite.

If you plan to grow radicchio, here are a few options for you to consider:

- **Augusto** has round heads of red leaves, and is slow to bolt.
- **Palla Rossa Bella** is a standard variety with round heads of dark red leaves and white veins.
- **Rouge de Trevise** is an unusual, non-hearting type with long, pointed leaves that you pick individually as required throughout autumn.
- **Treviso Precoce Mesola** produces oval heads of dark red leaves.

Enjoying Flavoursome Summer Crops

With the warmth of the sun to get people gardening and make plants grow, summer crops give gardeners the results they crave. Summer crops grow fast and quickly fill both kitchens and tums, and are some of the most delicious of all the crops you can grow. Among their number, summer crops include tomatoes – the most popular home-grown crop of all.

A bit saucy: Tomatoes

No better moment exists in the whole of the gardening calendar than the day you pick your first, fresh, sun-ripened tomato. You may think I'm exaggerating but honestly, nothing you buy in the shops comes close to the taste.

To-mato or not to-mato? That was the question

Tomatoes are so familiar to us that we take them for granted but when explorers first introduced them to Europe from the Americas they were greeted with suspicion. This was probably because the fruits looked too good to eat and they're closely related to poisonous native plants such as deadly nightshade.

Today we expect tomatoes to be red but in fact the first tomatoes were yellow. In the past few years seed companies have embraced unusual tomatoes in exciting colours, sizes and shapes, so now you can grow your own tomatoes that come packed with flavour and add excitement to your salads and pasta dishes.

Tomatoes are the most popular of all home-grown crops but so often gardeners try to emulate what the supermarkets sell us and grow dull, boring, round, red tomatoes. A whole new world of tomatoes lies out there, waiting to be discovered; they can be green, striped, orange, yellow, pink, black, and red, and they vary in weight from 5 grams to more than a kilo! Whether you want a tomato for canapés, burgers, making sauce, or just to show off to the neighbours, a variety just right for you is out there. So even if you don't grow anything else, grow tomatoes.

People usually eat tomatoes raw but you can, of course, cook them in a multitude of ways. Although you can freeze tomatoes whole, they are then only good for cooking and for convenience I suggest you stew the tomatoes, make sauce, soup or juice, and freeze this.

Tomatoes are really good for you. They contain few calories and are rich in vitamins A, B and C. Along with watermelons and pink grapefruit, tomatoes also contain lycpopene, which experts associate with reducing cancer. Lycpopene is also fat-soluble, so drizzling some olive oil over tomatoes is doing you good!

Sowing and cultivating tomatoes

You can grow tomatoes from seed or buy ready-grown plants in spring from most garden centres, although their range of varieties is usually very limited. So if you want something unusual, or want to save money, growing your own plants is worthwhile.

You can grow tomatoes outside, in a greenhouse or polytunnel, or in small, covered, 'mini' greenhouses on the patio. Most varieties grow just as well outside as in a greenhouse, providing they have a sheltered, warm spot. You may see adverts for tomatoes that you can grow on your windowsill at home, but this method is fraught with problems and so I don't recommend it.

Tomato seeds are easy to grow, and the plants aren't fussy about soil type, but a fertile, well-dug soil with plenty of organic matter is ideal. Cold, wet, waterlogged soils aren't good for this crop. Full sun is essential.

You can grow tomatoes in various ways. If you grow them in pots, each pot should ideally be big enough to hold 15–20 litres of compost. Any multipurpose compost is suitable. You can also grow tomatoes in the open ground or in your greenhouse border. The advantage of growing them in the soil is that supporting them with canes is easier. Also, they're less likely to dry out, need less regular feeding, and so are easier to care for.

Here's the procedure for growing tomatoes:

1. **Sow the seeds thinly in pots or trays of multipurpose compost, cover with perlite or compost, and put in a propagator in a temperature of about 20°C.** Germination takes about two weeks.

   Unless you have a greenhouse that you heat to 10°C or above, delay sowing until mid-March. If you sow the seeds too early they don't grow well or grow too big before you can plant them outside.

   Packets of F1 hybrid seed may only contain five or six seeds whereas common varieties may contain 100 or more. Count on at least 50 per cent germination, and so sow only a few seeds of each variety. Tomato seed keeps quite well for at least a year, so you can sow the rest the following season.

2. **When the seedlings start to produce their true leaves from the centre of the seed leaves, carefully transplant them into 8–9-centimetre pots.** Plant them deeper than in the seed tray, almost up to their seed leaves. They form extra roots from the buried stem.

3. **Water immediately but sparingly until they start to grow.** Keep them in a warm propagator; moving them into a cold greenhouse at this stage causes a check to their growth. Keep them in good light so they grow sturdily. Apply more water as they grow and, after a few weeks apply a general purpose, liquid fertiliser once a week.

4. **When you see the first cluster of flowers appearing in the tip of the plant you can plant them out in their final growing position.** This should be about 8–10 weeks after sowing. If you plant them into their large pots or into the ground before this stage they often grow quite tall before producing their first truss.

   Tap the flowers or shake the plants to help pollination. Tomatoes are self-fertile but shaking them dislodges the pollen and helps fruit to set. Spraying plants with water on hot days can also help.

Perhaps the most popular method of growing tomatoes is in grow bags, with each bag supporting a maximum of three plants. Here's how to prepare the bags:

1. **Follow steps 1 and 4 above, setting your seedlings aside for grow bags rather than pots.**

2. **Shake the contents of the bag to loosen the compost.**

3. **Lay the bag down in its intended location and cut three holes for the plants in the top.** You don't need to cut away the whole of the top.

4. **Push the soil to one side with a trowel or your hand, make a hole, and plant the tomato, deeper than it was in its pot.**

5. **Cut two holes between the three plants and push an empty pot into each for pouring the water into for the plants.** This process prevents water flowing over the side of the bag, washing away compost.

To give the plants more root room, cut the base out of a pot, cut a hole in the bag the same size as the base of the pot, and push the pot into the bag. Fill the pot with compost and plant into this; carry out for all three plants. The extra volume of compost, which retains more water, makes the plants easier to grow.

Tomatoes growing outdoors are very prone to blight. Chapter 7 gives you the lowdown on this, and other, plant diseases.

General care

Indeterminate varieties need support. You can tie them to canes as they grow, or suspend strings (from the greenhouse roof or from an overhead, horizontal support) and tie this around the base of the stem, twisting the string around the plant as it grows. Remove side shoots from the base of every leaf as they grow to stop the plants getting bushy and harder to control. If you don't, you get more trusses of fruits, but they're small ones that don't ripen by the end of the season.

Plants in pots and grow bags need regular feeding at least once a week with a high potash fertiliser or a tomato feed (containing calcium to help prevent blossom end rot). Because plants in pots and grow bags dry out quickly when they are mature, they also need regular watering. Although not essential, plants in the greenhouse border or outside may benefit from extra feeding.

As plants grow the lower leaves naturally turn yellow. Remove them to prevent fungal diseases such as botrytis (grey mould), but don't be over zealous in removing the lower leaves or be tempted to remove them to hasten the ripening of fruits. Warmth rather than direct sun causes ripening and if the fruits receive too much sun they get scorched and develop hard patches at the top that don't ripen.

Try to avoid irregular watering too, because this can cause blossom end rot – sunken, black patches at the ends of the fruits. Also, if plants get dry the skins of the fruits harden and when you water the plants again the fruits swell and the skins crack. Some varieties, such as Sungold, are more prone to this problem than others.

Ripening

Tomatoes often seem reluctant to ripen, usually thanks to the weather, notably temperature. Cool weather, rather than lack of sunlight, is a common reason why tomatoes fail to ripen as early as you'd like. Variety is another factor. Small-fruit varieties usually ripen earliest because the fruits rapidly reach full size. Bush varieties usually ripen early. Beefsteaks are usually late developers. Look out for details of ripening times in catalogues and be sure to grow at least one early ripener.

At the end of the season you're likely to have some full-size, green tomatoes at risk of rotting rather than ripening. Pick these off and keep them indoors in a warm place to ripen. Placing them in a plastic bag with a ripe banana can help speed ripening.

Harvesting and storing your tomatoes

Ideally, pick your tomatoes when fully ripe, just before you want to eat them. Most varieties change from green to red or whatever their final colour. Large beefsteaks also become soft when ripe. Pick them off by bending the stem, just above the fruit, at the 'knuckle' where the stem bends. When you lift the fruit, it usually breaks off easily here when ripe. If left too long, some fruits may split.

You can't store tomatoes for long in their fresh state and they don't freeze well, but you can make sauces and soup and freeze it for later use. You can also use them for chutneys and pickles that you can then store.

Choosing varieties

Tomatoes come in determinate and indeterminate types. With *determinate tomatoes* (also called *bush tomatoes*), as the first stem grows, a flower cluster appears in the shoot tip. That stem stops growing and side shoots grow from lower on that stem and also end in a flower cluster. Side shoots may grow off these too but because every stem ends in flowers and, later, fruits, the plant makes a mounded bush and never gets taller. These types of tomato are often ideal for cool climates because they tend to crop early but over a short period. Some have a low, weeping habit and are suitable for window boxes and hanging baskets.

Indeterminate varieties (sometimes called *cordons*) have a stem that grows indefinitely. Clusters of flowers appear on the side of these stems. At the base of every leaf a side shoot tries to grow but you pinch or cut these out to maintain the vigour of the main stem. Growing outside, you can expect the fruit on these types to ripen on four or five flower clusters, or *trusses*. Indoors, in warmer conditions you may get five or six trusses but, if conditions are warm enough, each plant can live for a year or more and produce 20 or more trusses!

Tomatoes vary in shape, size and colour, and you can find something for every taste. Yellow varieties, for example, tend to be less acid in taste, whereas pink and black toms usually have good, rich flavour.

Here is a list of some varieties that deserve your consideration. All are suitable for growing indoors (in a greenhouse, mini-greenhouse, or polytunnel) as well as out, unless stated differently.

- ✔ **Beefsteak** tomatoes are large, juicy, fleshy fruits, sometimes with excellent flavour. They can weigh 500 grams (and more) and you only get two or three fruits per truss.

  - **Big Boy F1** tomatoes are large, red, tasty fruits weighing up to 450 grams. An indeterminate variety, for greenhouse cultivation.

  - **Brandywine**, with its large red fruits and few seeds, is the finest-flavoured tomato of all according to many people. Several strains exist – all are good but sometimes slow to produce fruits. Indeterminate.

  - **Marmande** is a rather ugly, ribbed, small red beefsteak but with excellent flavour. Semi-determinate.

  - **Mortgage Lifter** produces good crops of large tomatoes with greenish 'shoulders' and an excellent flavour. Indeterminate.

- ✔ **Cherry** tomatoes are popular bite-sized fruits, and tend to be the sweetest type. Easy to grow, each truss usually has at least a dozen fruits and often many more.

  - **Gardener's Delight** is a standard, old red cherry with good flavour. Some seed strains aren't as good as they should be, so quality can be variable. Indeterminate.

  - **Nectar F1** has long trusses of small, tasty, sweet red fruits, and is resistant to disease. Indeterminate.

  - **Sungold F1** is one of the very best for flavour, producing heavy crops on strong plants. The orange fruits are rather prone to cracking. Indeterminate.

  - **Sunset F1** produces sweet, bright orange fruits. Indeterminate.

  - **Sweet Million F1** produces big trusses of sweet, tasty, 15-gram red fruits. Indeterminate.

  - **Tornado F1** produces masses of sweet, thin-skinned red fruits. A determinate variety for outdoors.

  - **Tumbler F1** is the most popular bush tomato for tubs and baskets with lots of sweet red fruits. A determinate variety for outdoors.

- ✔ **Cherry plum** tomatoes are currently very popular, and generally more fleshy, with fewer seeds than cherry tomatoes but just as tasty and sweet.

- **Floridity** produces large clusters of sweet, slender, early-to-ripen red fruits that taste really sweet. Indeterminate.

- **Ildi** produces huge trusses with masses of small, grape-sized, flavoursome yellow fruits. Indeterminate.

- **Santa F1** is the best known cherry plum tomato, producing heavy crops with up to 50 firm, sweet and tasty red fruits per truss. Indeterminate.

- **Sweet Olive F1** is an excellent, strong-growing variety with early, heavy crops of tasty, bright red fruits. Indeterminate.

✔ **Plum** tomatoes are long, blocky fruits with few seeds and firm flesh, and are better for paste and sauce than for salads. Lemon is a variation on this shape.

- **Britain's Breakfast** is a very special variety with massive trusses of red lemon-shaped fruits, ideal for paste, soup or grilling! Indeterminate.

- **Roma VF** plants are vigorous, with heavy crops of solid, almost seedless red fruits. Semi-determinate, and an outdoor grower.

- **San Marzano** produces heavy crops of large red fruits with good flavour. Semi-determinate.

✔ Some of the popular standard varieties are:

- **Ailsa Craig** is an old-fashioned, popular, red tomato choice with good flavour. Indeterminate.

- **Alicante** is an old budget variety but still good with reliable crops of tasty red toms. Indeterminate.

- **Fantasio F1** is an excellent all-rounder with resistance to many diseases, including blight, and large, 200-gram red fruits of good flavour. Indeterminate.

- **Ferline** is most famous for good resistance to blight but is also a very tasty variety with large, rather flat red fruits. Indeterminate.

- **Nimbus F1** is excellent for early, round, red toms with good flavour. Indeterminate, and an indoor grower.

- **Shirley F1** produces heavy crops of 80-gram red fruits. Reliable in cold and cool greenhouses and in less than ideal conditions. Indeterminate.

- **Stupice** is a rather straggly plant that produces very early pink, deliciously flavoured fruits. Indeterminate.

- **Sub-Arctic Plenty** plants are small and semi-bushy and produce small, round red fruits. Choose this variety if you live in a cold area or want the earliest crop in the neighbourhood! Semi-determinate, and an outdoor grower.

- **Tigerella** produces small fruits that are subtly striped with orange on red, are thin-skinned, and have a rich flavour.

- **Vanessa F1** produces heavy crops of slightly flattened red fruits, and is resistant to disease and irregular watering. This variety is popular as a 'vine-ripening' tomato – the fruits remain in good condition for several weeks after they ripen. Indeterminate, and one for the greenhouse.

- **White Beauty** produces large, round fruits that ripen to creamy white, and that have a good, low-acid flavour that many find more digestible than other tomatoes. Indeterminate.

You can also buy

✔ **Currant tomatoes**, have very small fruits – about the size of blackcurrants. They are great for salads but take a lot of picking! The plants are also usually difficult to control.

✔ **Pear tomatoes**, which are the shape you'd expect and are usually tasty and fleshy with lots of fruits per truss.

✔ **Sausage** (yes – sausage!) **tomatoes**: only a few of these varieties exist, in various colours, with long, cylindrical fruits; they're usually best for making paste and sauce.

Spicing things up: Peppers

Crunchy, sweet, colourful and good for you, sweet (bell) peppers aren't difficult to grow in a warm, sunny spot outside or in the greenhouse. Most peppers start out green and ripen to yellow, orange or red, but whatever the colour they all need the same sort of treatment and all are attractive plants as they grow and look pretty when covered in fruits. Sweet peppers are usually rather square or 'blocky' in shape, but can also be long and horn-shaped.

You can eat peppers raw but they can cause wind. Cooks often fry or stuff and bake peppers, creating some mouth-watering dishes with rice and dried fruit, among other dishes. Roasting them works wonders, too – put them under a grill and turn now and then. When the skin blisters, put them into plastic bags to cool, and peel off the charred skin, then cut out the centre and scrape out the seeds. You can then eat them cold or in a variety of hot dishes such as on pizzas and in rice dishes and couscous.

Peppers are rich in vitamins A and C as well as in antioxidants.

Truth…or just an old gardeners' tale?

With so many varieties of tomato, and so many colours, do they really taste different? The answer is yes, but other factors also affect their taste. Growers largely accept that, if you keep plants in perfect conditions and feed them heavily, they produce huge crops of poorly flavoured fruits; if plants have to struggle a bit they produce better-tasting fruits. Taken further, this idea suggests that fruits taste better if the plants are a bit dry as the fruits ripen. The trouble is that different fruits on the same plant are ripening as others are developing, and drought causes blossom end rot. So be careful not to take this idea to its extreme.

Some gardeners also believe that fruits taste better if you grow plants in soil rather than in bags or pots of compost.

Huge differences exist in the taste and texture of tomato varieties, but they all taste better if you allow them to ripen fully on the plant. Always pick them ripe and preferably warm from the sun, and eat them as soon as possible!

Sowing and cultivating peppers

Sweet peppers are rarely as productive as you expect or want. Unless you start plants very early and have warm, sunny conditions you're unlikely to get more than ten fruits per plant. Varieties with large fruits may only produce four or five fruits in a poor summer. Much depends on the weather, on the variety, and on how well you grow your plants. So, if you like peppers, grow plenty of plants!

Peppers need warmth and sunlight. They aren't fussy about soil but must have a constant supply of nutrients and moisture to do well, especially early in the season when the plants build up their stems. If they are starved of water or food they tend to produce a single stem with a single pepper at the top. If you leave this stem to develop, the plants make hardly any other growth and you end up with a pitifully small crop. So be sure to feed plants with a tomato fertiliser at least once a week.

To get it right, just follow the same steps as for tomatoes (in the preceding section), sowing peppers in early spring and protecting them against cold and poor light in dull, cold springs. Remember that peppers, like tomatoes, don't tolerate frost and they grow slowly in cold temperatures. If you don't heat your greenhouse, delay sowing until late spring (April), so the plants grow without a check; however, you don't then get peppers until later in summer. Peppers take longer to germinate than tomatoes but seedlings should appear after three weeks. A temperature of 22–25°C is ideal. To save time and effort you can buy small pepper plants in garden centres in April and May but the range of varieties is limited.

Some gardeners claim that sowing the disc-shaped seeds on their edges helps germination.

Time for some crops

Some seed catalogues give a time period – such as 85 days – next to a variety. This is the number of days you can expect to wait for the first ripe tomatoes, peppers or other crops after planting the young plants or seeds in your green-house or garden. Catalogues also provide this information for some other crops too, such as sweetcorn and squashes, helping you to predict when you can enjoy the fruits of your labours (excuse the pun!). For example, because you can't plant out tomatoes or peppers in the garden until late May, an 85-day variety is likely to crop in late August.

Harvesting and storing your peppers

Yellow, orange and red peppers are green before they begin to ripen but most change to either red, yellow or orange. Picking them off the plants while still green leads the plants to produce more peppers and a heavier crop than if they were to carry the fruits to maturity.

If you don't keep your plants well watered and fed, allowing the peppers to ripen reduces cropping substantially.

Cut off the peppers when they're fully grown, either ripe or green, with a sharp knife or secateurs, as you need them. Peppers store for a week in the fridge if necessary but using them straight off the plant is best.

Choosing varieties

Here are a few tasty varieties of pepper to choose from:

- **Barrancio** are compact plants, ideal for patio pots, with masses of small, orange fruits.

- **Gypsy F1** is an early, reliable, compact variety with long fruits that ripen to red. This variety grows best in a greenhouse.

- **Jumbo F1** is a large plant with huge, red fruits up to 25 centimetres long. Grows best in a greenhouse.

- **Red Knight F1** is a compact plant with large, crisp, sweet red peppers. Grow this variety in a greenhouse.

- **Redskin F1** is a very compact plant with lots of large, thick-walled red fruits. Grows best in a greenhouse or on the patio.

- **Sweet Orange Baby** is a compact, bushy plant with masses of miniature, orange fruits, ideal for stuffing with cream cheese! This variety grows best in a greenhouse or out on the patio.

Feeling hot: Chillies

Sunshine and summer heat sum up chillies. Not only are these fiery fruits packed with hot taste, from mild to painfully hot, but also you can grow chillies large and small and in a variety of colours and shapes. If you grow your own, the choice is all yours.

Although chillies are strictly perennial, gardeners usually grow them as annuals from seed every spring. Most varieties are very productive and, unless you're a chilli addict you only need a few plants.

Be cautious when cooking with chillies and add a small amount at first. Adding more later is always easier than trying to salvage a dish when you've used too much!

Sowing and cultivating chillies

Sow and cultivate chillies the same way as for sweet peppers, although they're more productive. Both plants like plenty of warmth, and grow in the same way, so follow the same guidelines as in the preceding section about peppers and you can't go wrong.

All chillies are suitable for growing in pots or grow bags. Apart from dwarf varieties, they usually need support as they grow.

Harvesting and storing your chillies

Like sweet peppers, chillies change colour as they ripen. They usually start green or purple and ripen to red, orange or yellow. The flavour changes with the colour, too. As they ripen they become sweeter and the flavour more complex, though they don't necessarily get hotter. If you pick off fruits when unripe, the plant is more likely to produce more flowers and fruit than if you allow them to ripen and develop fully, but the difference isn't as marked as with sweet peppers because chillies are naturally more productive and some varieties produce hundreds of tiny fruits.

The best way to store chillies is to dry them. Simply lay them on the windowsill to dry out. Alternatively, you can make a spicy sauce with chillies, peppers and tomatoes and freeze it for adding to dishes later on in winter.

Chillies contain *capsaicin*, which gives the fruits their hot taste. Capsaicin is difficult to wash off with water and the sap from the fruits remains on your fingers for some time after handling.

Choosing varieties

In the way they grow, chillies are very similar to sweet peppers, but they vary a lot from neat, dwarf plants 30 centimetres high to 1 metre or more, so check the variety before planting out. Here are some of the best-loved chilli varieties. All are happy in both greenhouse and patio environments, unless otherwise stated.

- ✔ **Apache F1** are compact plants with heavy crops of red fruits that hang from the stems. Good for pots on the patio.

- ✔ **Boule de Turquie** is available under various names. The large, tall plants produce lots of round, thick-walled, medium-hot chillies that are late to mature. One for the greenhouse.

- ✔ **Demon Red** are dwarf plants with upright, tiny, fiery fruits that are good to use fresh or dried.

- ✔ **Habanero (Scotch Bonnet)** are large plants that come in several forms; they all have lantern-shaped fruits that are among the hottest of all chillies. Likes a greenhouse environment.

- ✔ **Hungarian Hot Wax** are large plants with long, attractive fruits that are mild in flavour and which ripen from green, through yellow, to red.

- ✔ **Jalapeno** is a popular, conical, medium-hot chilli that you can use green or red. Jalapenos typically have a netted pattern of 'cracks' on the skin and are compact plants.

- ✔ **Super Chilli F1** are dwarf plants with masses of upright, small, very hot fruits that ripen to bright red.

Deep purple: Aubergines

Aubergines are perennials but gardeners usually grow them as annuals. In all but the warmest areas they crop better in greenhouses, although modern kinds, especially those with small fruits, do well in patio pots. Aubergines usually don't crop until late summer and results vary according to the weather, but they're attractive plants worth growing. The spiny shrubs with grey-green leaves and attractive, large flowers are generally free from diseases but young shoots are vulnerable to aphids and red spider mite, especially when growing in a greenhouse.

With their mild flavour and soft texture when ripe, you can add aubergines to a wide range of dishes and cuisines. Cooks traditionally slice and sprinkle aubergines with salt for an hour to extract excess water and bitterness before cooking. You can then add them to curries and other Oriental dishes or to tomato and pepper dishes. A basic component of moussaka, aubergines are also delicious just fried in olive oil. They do absorb a lot of the oil though, so watch the calories!

Aubergines are low in calories (until you fry them in olive oil!) and rich in potassium and calcium, but have only a little protein and vitamin C.

Sowing and cultivating aubergines

Aubergines aren't very tolerant of bad growing conditions and need warmth and good light to do well. They appreciate soil improved with organic matter and enriched with a general fertiliser before planting. After planting, hope for warm, sunny weather to be in with a chance of a good crop!

1. **Sow seeds in early spring in the same way as for tomatoes and peppers.** (See preceding sections.)

2. **Transplant the seedlings into cell trays or small 8-centimetre pots.**

3. **When they fill the cell trays or small pots with roots and have four or five mature leaves, plant out the seedlings into 20-centimetre-wide pots, beds or grow bags (three per bag).**

4. **Water carefully at first while the plants are young and when overnight temperatures may be low.** Keep watering as they get established.

5. **Soon after planting, especially in containers, apply a liquid tomato fertiliser once a week.** Aubergines respond well to feeding.

6. **Stake your plants to support them. If they grow as a single stem, pinch out the growing tip when the plants are 30 centimetres high to prevent one large fruit developing early, at the expense of branching.** Doing this results in a better crop. No other training is necessary but the shortening of long shoots keeps plants tidy.

   If you grow your plants on the windowsill and they become 'drawn' and spindly, pinch out the tips after they have four or five leaves. This encourages them to produce side shoots and make bushy plants.

Aubergines make attractive patio plants, particularly dwarf F1 hybrids. The large flowers and shiny fruits look beautiful. Put one plant in a 12–15-centimetre pot at first and then re-pot into a 22–25-centimetre pot as it grows.

Harvesting and storing your aubergines

Aubergines are ready to harvest when they're full-size and firm but not hard – give them a light squeeze to check. You must pick them before they start to wrinkle or they produce large seeds and are unpleasant to eat. You can pick aubergines young, before they're fully developed, but they may then be too firm and a bit chewy! Ideally, pick them just before you need to use them but, because aubergines are for eating after cooking, fresh-from-the-sun picking isn't vital. Aubergines don't store well but you can cook and freeze them or use them for delicious chutneys.

You say aubergine, I say brinjal

Some people commonly call aubergines by another name – *eggplants* – because some varieties have egg-shaped, white fruits, and some people refer to them as *brinjal.* Whatever you know this plant as, it probably originated in India. Other, unusual, orange aubergines come from Africa.

Choosing varieties

Some popular varieties of aubergine include the following:

- **Baby Rosanna F1** produces masses of small, bitter-free fruits on compact plants.

- **Early Long Purple 2** is an improvement on the older Long Purple variety, with heavier crops of long fruits.

- **Fairy Tale F1** is a beautiful plant with large, lavender flowers and large fruits striped in shades of purple and white. They taste good and are great for patios.

- **Mohican F1** are dwarf plants with masses of large, oval, white fruits. Picking young increases the amount of crops.

- **Moneymaker F1** is a popular variety that crops well in our unreliable climate. This variety has large, chunky fruits that taste just great.

- **Ophelia F1** is a compact, prolific variety with small, pretty fruits, and is ideal for patios. The fine-tasting fruits aren't bitter.

Cool as a . . .: Cucumbers

An essential part of any salad, cucumbers are almost as easy to grow as tomatoes but they tolerate more shade and generally need more heat, especially in the early stages. To grow the long, green cucumbers you buy in shops you really need a greenhouse but other, usually shorter, kinds do grow outside in sheltered places such as a patio. If you grow them well, cucumber plants can be highly productive and you only need a few to provide you with all the cucumbers you want throughout summer.

Most people eat cucumbers raw but you can also lightly fry them in butter and make them into a good soup, for eating chilled.

Cucumbers are nutritionally poor with only small amounts of vitamins B and C and few calories.

Sowing and cultivating cucumbers

You can grow cucumbers outdoors, in a greenhouse, or in a cold frame. Cucumbers are unusual because the traditional greenhouse types produce fruits without being pollinated. If the female flowers are pollinated by the males they produce fruits with seeds that are usually swollen at one end and taste bitter. So, removing the male flowers regularly, each morning, is necessary with traditional varieties. Recent F1 hybrids are usually all-female and don't produce male flowers, and so you don't need to undertake this time-consuming activity. These seeds are much more expensive but the cost is worthwhile because they're usually very resistant to common diseases too.

Greenhouse types need a warm, partly shaded and humid environment to grow well. You may hear that you can't grow cucumbers and tomatoes in the same greenhouse; this advice isn't quite true but tomatoes do prefer more sun and less humidity than cucumbers.

You can grow cucumbers in grow bags (two per bag), in pots or in the greenhouse border. They like a rich, moist soil and forking in lots of organic matter keeps them contented. Cucumber plants are climbers so they also need support. You can tie them to a cane as they grow or support them on strings. To do the latter, tie a string to a horizontal support near the top of the greenhouse, bring it down, and tie loosely around the base of the plant. As the plant grows, twist it around the string.

In addition to the greenhouse types, you can also grow outdoor or *ridge* cucumbers that don't usually have this complication – you just let them grow and fruit. However, the cues they produce are shorter, have thicker skins, and are often prickly. They taste great though, and are worth a try if you're not too bothered what your cues look like.

Outdoor cucumbers are generally easier to grow, but only plant them outside when the last night frost is past and the nights are warm. Again, add plenty of organic matter to the soil before planting and mulch the soil with more compost. The stems are rather brittle and susceptible to damage by strong winds and strong sunlight if you take them straight out of a greenhouse and plant them outside, and so support plants with pea sticks (twiggy sticks), plastic netting or chicken wire. Most varieties grow to about 1 metre high and gardeners usually allow them to ramble freely.

Cucumber plants are prone to damage by slugs and snails, and vulnerable to fungal diseases such as powdery mildew and root rots when young, especially when they're cold and receive too much water. Chapter 7 gives you some pointers for dealing with these problems.

Carry out the following steps, and look forward to a crop of cucumbers to be proud of!

1. **Sow the seeds in April.** Cucumbers grow rapidly so don't be in a hurry to sow them too early. They die in temperatures below 10°C, so if you take them out of a warm propagator and put them in a cold greenhouse in early spring they're likely to die. Delaying sowing until April when conditions are perfect is a wise move.

   Fill small pots lightly with compost and push one seed, on its side, to about 1 centimetre deep. Add extra compost to cover if necessary, water well, and place in a propagator at about 21°C. As soon as the seedlings appear, open the vents and reduce the temperature slightly to avoid the seedlings becoming spindly. Keep them well watered at all times.

2. **Plant out the young seedlings (in pots, grow bags, or in the soil) when they have three or four leaves.** Because they're prone to rotting, plant them slightly above the compost level and mound fresh compost up around the stem. The buried stem produces roots that help the plant to establish and to recover if the excessively wet lower compost damages the original roots.

3. **Water very sparingly at first but don't let them dry out.** When they start to grow strongly they need plenty of water, so a few weeks after planting start applying a high-potash liquid fertiliser once a week. Lack of water or feed halts the formation of new fruits.

4. **Pinching out.** Older greenhouse varieties ramble about and branch, and you need to *pinch out* or remove the shoot tips to prevent them getting out of control. Modern outdoor types don't need pinching out – they grow as a single stem. You can tie this stem to a cane or to a vertical string. In the garden, you can allow outdoor types, which are generally more vigorous, to scramble over netting.

All-female cucumber varieties may produce male flowers if the plants are poorly grown and stressed.

Harvesting and storing your cucumbers

You can pick and eat cucumbers at any stage but allowing them to mature before picking is best. However, they don't continue to improve if you leave them on the plants after they reach full size, and may turn yellow or golden. Cucumbers are still edible at this stage but you need to peel them and remove the seeds from the centre. Cucumbers don't store well.

Choosing varieties

Outdoor or 'ridge' cucumbers tend to be shorter and more prickly than greenhouse types. However, they're easier to grow and some people think they have better flavour. You also have a greater variety of outdoor types to choose from, so not having a greenhouse is no great disadvantage (note that you don't need to remove the male flowers of any of these types):

✔ **Adam F1** is a fast-maturing variety with heavy crops of tiny cucumbers, or *gherkins*.

- ✔ **Burpless Tasty Green F1** is a good-quality, long green cucumber growing on vigorous plants that are resistant to mildew.

- ✔ **Crystal Apple** is an unusual but easy-to-grow variety with small, round, white cucumbers with bristly skin. This variety crops heavily and is very tasty.

- ✔ **Marketmore** is a reliable variety in all seasons, producing good-quality cucumbers with dark green skins.

- ✔ **Swing F1** plants are resistant to disease and produce heavy crops of short, crisp cucumbers.

These F1, all-female, greenhouse types are the best to choose for heavy crops and disease-free plants – ideal for the organic gardener:

- ✔ **Bella F1** is resistant to most common cucumber problems and has heavy crops of long, slim, dark green cucumbers.

- ✔ **Carmen F1** is an exceptional variety with long, straight cucumbers that win at flower shows and taste great. This variety is resistant to disease and crops heavily.

- ✔ **Luxury F1** produces heavy crops of long, smooth cucumbers on disease-resistant plants.

- ✔ **Passandra F1** is a disease-resistant plant with good crops of mini-cucumbers.

- ✔ **Socrates F1** is a healthy plant with masses of mini-cucumbers, and the best of this type.

- ✔ **Zeina F1** produces heavy crops of small, mini-cucumbers on vigorous plants. You can also grow this variety outside in sheltered spots.

Smashing Pumpkins and Squashes

Of all the crops that you can grow in the garden, pumpkins and squashes are the most exciting. Everything about them is on a big scale. The seeds are large and easy to handle, the plants are big and bold, the flowers are showy, and the fruits can be too big to lift! Forget radishes to get kids into gardening – give them a pumpkin plant or even a courgette and they're sure to be hooked.

Although the fruits vary in size, colour, shape and use, all the plants look similar, with large leaves and, usually, bristly stems. They all need lots of warmth, sunshine and water throughout their lives, and few plants respond to extra care with watering and feeding quite like these.

When is a pumpkin a squash?

Even experienced gardeners, and botanists, put on a puzzled frown when it comes to working out their squashes. This is because people have been eating them for thousands of years and have selected so many different kinds. The basics are that there are summer squashes and winter squashes, and all grow in the same way and like the same conditions. The difference is that summer squashes, such as courgettes, are for eating in summer when immature and with soft skins, and winter squashes should stay on the plants to mature so that the skins to go hard and growers can store them for use throughout winter. There, that was easy! From a nutritional point of view, summer squashes, which are largely made of water, don't have much to offer but winter squashes are rich in nutrients and are a really valuable winter food.

Prolific producers: Courgettes

Second only to tomatoes in popularity with home gardeners, courgettes are well worth growing. Attractive, fast-growing plants, courgettes are easy to prepare for the kitchen, useful in many different dishes, and they usually crop heavily. In fact, your main problem may well be knowing what to do with them when you have a glut!

In the shops, courgettes are always dark green and long, but if your grow your own, you suddenly have a new world of exciting colours and shapes to choose from. So courgettes must be high on your list of crops to grow.

Courgettes have a mild flavour and a high water content. You can eat young fruits raw, chopped or grated (the yellow-fruited types tend to have firmer flesh that's better than the greens for eating raw). Courgettes are delicious when you slice and fry them or drizzle them with oil and put them under the grill. You can even pick them the day the flower opens, dip them in batter, and fry them, complete with the bloom. You can also grate and add them to muffins and cakes. Don't boil them.

Courgettes are low in calories and most other nutrients too, but contain some minerals and vitamins A and C.

Sowing and cultivating courgettes

Courgettes, like marrows and all other squashes, benefit from lots of moisture and nutrients. Unless you're lucky enough to already have really rich and fertile soil, fork in lots of compost or well rotted manure, mulch heavily, and water frequently.

When is a courgette a marrow?

Courgette or marrow? Basically the two are the same thing. If you leave a fruit on the plant too long it grows into a marrow and if you pick a marrow when small it counts as a courgette. But you're best off buying seeds of varieties bred for the specific crop, because courgettes are bred specifically to be compact and to produce masses of fruits. Marrow plants tend to be less compact, often trail, and don't produce as many flowers as courgette plants. Their fruits are also less densely textured and don't make for such good eating when young.

Here's how to proceed when you're ready to get going with your courgettes:

1. **Sow the seeds.** Because they're frost-tender, sow seeds no earlier than a month before the last frost is likely. Fill small pots with compost and sow a seed, on its side, in each pot. If you're short of space, sow two seeds per pot and pinch out the weaker seedling if two appear so that you don't have empty pots where any seeds fail to grow.

   Seeds germinate best in a temperature of 21°C. After they've germinated, move them immediately to a warm, well-lit spot such as a windowsill or a heated greenhouse in good light or the seedlings will become drawn and liable to snap – they are very brittle.

2. **Plant out the young plants about four weeks after sowing.** Do this only when all risk of frost is over and the weather is mild, and protect them from strong winds in their first few weeks if you've raised the plants in the greenhouse or on the windowsill. Space plants 60–80 centimetres apart, depending on the variety, with each plant in a shallow depression in the soil to make them easier to water, unless your soil is heavy and poorly drained, in which case it may be better to plant on a slight mound. Planting the seedlings through a weed-supressing mulch can help save on watering (see Figure 10-1).

   Some gardeners fill pits in the ground with compost and manure, cover with soil, and plant into this prepared ground to make sure that the plants have enough water and nutrients.

3. **Water plants regularly after planting and protect them from slugs and snails.** Chapter 7 contains all you need to know about controlling these pests.

Well cultivated plants grow strongly and flower before long. However, plants commonly produce only male flowers when young, possibly because of cool weather. Therefore you don't get any courgettes for a while, but you can't do anything about this. Cold, wet weather may cause the flowers to rot at the ends of the young fruits and you can't avoid this either, except by picking the courgettes when very young or carefully pulling off the flowers.

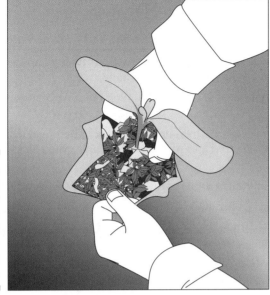

Figure 10-1:
Planting
your
seedlings
through
a weed-
suppressing
mulch.

Courgettes suffer from mildew and cucumber mosaic virus, and are also popular treats with badgers and rats. Like all squashes, though, courgettes are resistant to attack by rabbits and most other pests, and so are a good choice for plots where rabbits are a problem. Chapter 7 tells you more about dealing with problems and pests.

Harvesting and storing your courgettes

Cut and eat your courgettes when they're small. You don't need to leave them until they get to the size you see in the shops. In fact, courgettes are at their most delicious a day or two after the flowers open. If you leave the courgettes to get large, they rapidly become marrows and the plants don't produce as many flowers and fruits. Courgettes don't store at all well, nor do they freeze well, so be sure to use them fresh, when in season.

Choosing varieties

You're not short of options when it comes to choosing a variety of courgette to grow. Here are a few that I recommend:

✔ **Ambassador** is a popular commercial variety with heavy crops of dark green courgettes.

✔ **Black Forest F1** has dark green fruits and is an unusual, compact, trailing variety that can be trained up a trellis or post.

✔ **Clarion F1** produces torpedo-shaped courgettes and has an open plant shape that makes picking easy. Many people consider the pale green fruits to have the best flavour of all courgettes.

✔ **Defender F1** is an early, heavy cropping variety with dark green fruits and resistance to disease.

✔ **Golden Dawn lll F1** is a reliable, tasty, and early yellow variety.

✔ **One Ball F1** are bushy, compact plants with round, yellow, delicious fruits. One of the best to eat raw.

✔ **Orelia F1** is a reliable and heavily cropping plant with bright yellow, long fruits.

✔ **Partenon F1** produces dark green fruits. This variety can make fruits without being pollinated and so is ideal for early crops and for growing under glass.

✔ **Romanesco** is an Italian variety with ridged fruits and good flavour.

✔ **Rondo di Nizza** is a prolific variety with pale green, round fruits.

✔ **Soleil F1** produces heavy crops of bright yellow courgettes on compact, vigorous plants. Resistant to mildew.

✔ **Sylvana F1** produces long, dark green fruits. Bred for cool, northern climates, this variety has a good resistance to disease.

Get ready for a glut: Marrows

Almost embarrassingly easy to grow, marrows are also great fun to grow. Although definitely better to eat when young and not overly large, marrows are still edible as they get close to being giant-sized, making this is a crop that children love to grow. Marrows aren't a crop for those with sophisticated taste buds, but make a good standby, and they usually crop well in any season.

Cooks usually boil marrows, allowing them to drain well before serving, but this vegetable has little flavour (a good cheese sauce can add some!). Another traditional way to serve marrows is to cut them into rings 8 centimetres wide, scoop out the seeds, parboil them, and stuff the centres with spicy cooked minced beef and bake for a while. The skin of young marrows is edible but is too tough to eat on mature, older marrows.

Sowing and cultivating marrows

Marrows need exactly the same treatment as courgettes, so just follow the instructions in the preceding section to have a bumper crop of marrows on your hands. However, because marrows can suffer from damage or rot if their underside is in contact with wet soil for prolonged periods (in common with winter squashes), support developing fruits with a piece of wood, an old seed tray or a piece of carpet as they grow.

Harvesting and storing your marrows

You can cut and eat your marrows at almost any stage, from slightly bigger than a courgette to mature fruits with tough skin. Some people leave their spectacular, heavy fruits on the plants to become large and gnarled but they're best for eating when considerably smaller. So unless you're going for something special at the village show, harvest your marrows when they are less than 40 centimetres long. This way your plants keep on producing and you can enjoy them much more.

You can store mature fruits for winter use but they become so stringy and unpleasant that doing so is hardly worthwhile. If storage is important, grow a winter squash instead.

Choosing varieties

Most varieties of marrow are bushy but some are trailing and these can take up a lot of room. Here are a few, bushy varieties that I can recommend:

- ✔ **Badger Cross F1** is a tidy plant with good crops of dark and light green striped fruit, and is resistant to disease. Tiger Cross F1 is similar.

- ✔ **Bush Baby** is a useful variety with small, short marrows on compact plants. Good for containers.

- ✔ **Hasta La Pasta F1** is a modern 'vegetable spaghetti' (see the nearby sidebar). You can boil or bake the mature fruits whole for about 40 minutes, and then cut open and fork out the stringy flesh to mix with butter and pepper. They're delicious and easy to grow.

Not just for Halloween: Winter squashes and pumpkins

Delicious, nutritious and, most of all, fun to grow: winter squashes and pumpkins are invaluable for autumn and winter meals. They're easy to grow, but most varieties are greedy for space and so generally more suitable for allotments, where they cover the ground, suppress weeds, and give you a useful crop. If you want to grow them in your garden you may find it helps to train the clambering stems over arches and up fences. Keeping winter squashes and pumpkins in pots watered enough is tricky because they're very thirsty, but with care and effort you do get rewarded. And not only are all these crops tasty and nutritious – a big pile of squashes in September is just about the best-looking harvest you can get.

Vegetable spaghetti

Old marrows aren't as good to eat as young ones because the flesh gets stringy. In fact, I hate them! But growers cultivate vegetable spaghetti specifically because it *is* stringy. When the skins are starting to toughen, the vegetable is ready to harvest and the flesh inside is all 'strings'. Although solid when you cut the marrow open, you can fork out the strings and fluff them up. Vegetable spaghetti sounds odd, but as long as you add plenty of seasoning, the taste is delicious. I heartily recommend it, and kids love it!

Pumpkin flesh contains more water than winter squashes and less flavour, and works well with spices and sugar for pies, or made into soup. Winter squashes are more adaptable and you can roast them, or boil and mash them, sometimes with potatoes. You can also add them to stews and make them into soup. Squashes usually have dense, hard, orange flesh with a nutty flavour but this varies widely.

All squashes are resistant to rabbits and so make ideal vegetable choices for allotments and large gardens overrun with these furry pests!

Most winter squashes have very dense flesh and hard skins. Cutting them with a sharp knife can be dangerous, so take great care when peeling and preparing them.

Sowing and cultivating winter squashes and pumpkins

All these plants need a soil enriched with organic matter including well rotted manure. Giving them too much fertiliser is almost impossible (as long as you're sensible), although an excess of nitrogen encourages leaf growth, which hides the fruits.

Most of these plants are trailing and take up a lot of room. You can train some up arches and trellises, but the heavy fruits can make this impractical. If you train them along the ground instead, the stems can root, therefore strengthening the plants and helping to feed your crops.

If you want giant pumpkins, you need to restrict the number of fruits on each plant. Generally a plant doesn't support more than three or four pumpkins but you need to remove the others when one has set if you want a giant. Remember that each plant can cover several square metres of ground, and so you need to decide whether you can afford this luxury! Other winter squashes such as butternut squashes should produce about six fruits per plant.

Because of the size of the plants, most aren't suitable for growing in containers. But, if you're prepared to water and feed regularly, you can grow a small-fruited variety such as Baby Bear up a trellis on a patio.

Sow your pumpkin seeds as for courgettes (see the 'Prolific producers: Courgettes' section earlier in the chapter). Scatter a general fertiliser such as pelleted chicken manure on the soil before planting. When you plant out your seedlings, in general space the plants 1 metre apart and mulch them with any organic material you can find. Keep them watered in dry weather to keep the plants growing.

Harvesting and storing your winter squashes and pumpkins

You can eat all these squashes and pumpkins before they're fully mature. However, they don't develop their full flavour until fully grown and ripe, so leave them on the plants for as long as possible, ideally after the foliage has started to die, but before they get frosted. Frost ruins the fruits. Remove them from the vines with the stalk intact – cut it off the vine and never snap the fruit off the stalk or it isn't going to store well. Use any that have holes in the skin or are damaged straight away, rather than storing them.

Winter squashes and pumpkins store well – you can keep them stored away until March. Those that you intend to keep for long-term storage last much longer if you keep them for a week or so at room temperature before storing at lower temperatures. Never let the storage temperature fall below 5°C or they may suffer damage.

Choosing varieties

Here are some great varieties of winter squash:

- **Barbara Butternut F1** is an unusual, green-striped squash, good when young fruit and steamed or fried, or left to mature.

- **Buttercup** produces small, round dark green fruits with dense flesh and flat tops and base. Buttercup has excellent flavour and stores well.

- **Cobnut F1** is the earliest of all squashes to mature, with good quality, 1 kilogram fruits.

- **Crown Prince** fruits are large and heavy with blue-grey skin and orange flesh. Very tasty and store well.

- **Delicata** is a fine-flavoured, long squash with pale skins and green stripes. Good for storing.

- **Festival** produces small, striped, squat fruits with pale flesh. This variety has a nutty taste and stores well.

- **Golden Hubbard** produces large, spindle-shaped fruits, with golden, warty skin, which store well and taste great. Blue Hubbard is similarly good.

- **Harrier F1** is a butternut squash bred for cool summers, with fine-textured fruits that store well.

- **Turk's Turban** produces ornamental fruits in the shape of a cottage loaf, with orange and striped skin and tasty orange flesh. Stores well.

✔ **Uchiki Kuri** is an onion-shaped fruit with hard skins. The fruit has dense, hard, orange flesh and excellent flavour, weighs about 1.5 kilograms, and stores well. Blue Kuri is similar, with grey skin.

Here are some varieties to choose from the pumpkin world:

✔ **Atlantic Giant** is the one to grow if you want huge pumpkins to impress the neighbours! It doesn't taste great, but it looks fantastic!

✔ **Baby Bears** are perfect, small bright orange pumpkins. Good for lanterns and more importantly for eating – the hollowed fruits make perfect bowls for pumpkin soup.

✔ **Jack of all Trades** are the perfect pumpkins for Halloween, with bright orange skins and a round shape, though the flavour isn't as rich as most.

✔ **Jaspee de Vendee** produces round, large, pale gold fruits with sweet, tender flesh that's good enough to eat raw. Excellent for pies!

✔ **Moschata Muscade** produces flattened, ribbed, waxy fruits that are no good for lanterns, but excellent for eating.

Chapter 11

Planting Pods and Grains

. . . .

In This Chapter

▶ Getting to grow delightful beans

▶ Propagating peas worth making a fuss about

▶ Gaining delicious grains

. . . .

*N*othing beats the satisfaction of walking along your rows of peas, picking a pod, and popping the fresh, sweet peas in your mouth, or sitting on the patio shelling broad beans on a sunny day in preparation for a fresh, home-grown meal. These treats, and more, are yours if you grow some of the many peas and beans available.

Peas and beans are among the easiest of all veg to grow and most varieties crop prolifically, so they're a sensible option too. From the strong and distinctive taste of broad beans to the sweet crisp pods of mangetout peas, you can discover a whole world of flavour here and be picking your own beans from early summer to autumn if you plan carefully. Even better, most of these crops freeze well so you can save any surplus for use later in the year. All in all, these are crops that you just can't ignore.

Growing grains is something we usually leave to farmers, but a few may well find their way into your garden. Although gardeners aren't likely to grow maize for grinding into flour, sweetcorn (which is maize developed for eating when immature, before the sugar turns to starch) is definitely one to try. If you're feeling adventurous, I include a couple of others that you may want to try as well.

Nurturing Nutritious Beans

Beans are among the easiest of all vegetables to grow. They grow quickly and among their number are included broad beans, which thrive in most gardens and are among the hardiest of all vegetables. Many varieties, such as runner beans, crop over a prolonged period and you can find different kinds suitable for every size and type of garden.

Beans are delicious to eat and useful in the kitchen. To boot, beans contain more protein than most other vegetables, and so are good for you, too. Beans are also good for your soil because their roots add the plant nutrient nitrogen to the soil, providing nutrients later crops will appreciate. You just can't lose!

Healthy and hardy: Broad beans

Broad beans are well worth growing because the ones you grow at home taste so much better than those available in the shops. Broad beans are the hardiest of the beans and possibly the easiest to grow. However, because you need to allocate a reasonable amount of space for a good number of plants to get a worthwhile crop, broad beans make a better choice for larger gardens and allotments than for patios or small gardens. A metre can produce about 600 grams of beans, although much depends on how well they grow and at what stage you pick them.

Cooks usually boil broad beans but you can also steam them. Young beans are delicious cold with spring onions and French dressing, especially when you remove the skins after cooking them. Broad beans are traditionally served with gammon and parsley sauce.

Broad beans are rich in vitamins A, B1, B2, E and C, and in folic acid.

Sowing and cultivating broad beans

Broad beans are very tolerant of most soils. They generally prefer heavy soils, including clay, but don't grow well in soils that are waterlogged or wet in winter and spring. Digging over the soil before sowing or planting and adding organic matter is a good way to improve drainage in spring and help retain moisture in summer, when the pods swell and the beans need water. The deep roots of broad beans also work to improve soils, with the nitrogen-fixing bacteria in the nodules supplying nutrients.

After preparing your soil, just follow these steps:

1. **Take out a shallow trench with a spade, scooping the soil about 5 centimetres deep and placing it to the side of the trench.**

2. **Put the seeds in the trench, roughly 20 centimetres apart.** You can space them evenly in a double row in the trench or just scatter them so that they fall roughly 20 centimetres apart.

   You can sow broad beans in the autumn or spring. Make autumn sowings in late September in northern areas or October in colder areas, so the seedlings have only a few leaves showing when winter sets in. If they're too big they may not survive the winter cold. Autumn sowings benefit if you cover them with cloches in cold areas or during cold weather but even with this protection you may lose a few plants in winter. However, the advantage of sowing at this time of year is that the plants grow better root systems, making spring growth more vigorous, and you get an earlier crop than you would from spring sowings. Sow only the hardiest varieties, such as Aqualdulce, at this time of year.

Alternatively, you can sow broad beans in spring – as early as February in warm areas but March is generally early enough. Although broad beans are hardy and tolerate cold temperatures, sowing in cold, wet soil has no advantage over sowing when the soil is warmer because the seeds are unlikely to germinate; if they do, the plants will grow very slowly.

If you want a regular supply of broad beans, sow them in batches, about a month apart, from March until June.

3. **If sowing in autumn or early spring, cover the seeds with soil, water the rows and cover with cloches to provide a little shelter from the cold.**

   Alternatively, you can sow seeds singly in pots or cell trays and keep them in a cool greenhouse. (Don't start them too early – late February is early enough or the plants will be too big before the weather outside is suitable for planting.) When they're about 10 centimetres high, you can plant them out, 20 centimetres apart.

4. **Protect your seedlings.** When seedlings appear they're vulnerable to attack by pea and bean weevils (refer to Chapter 7), which eat small round holes from the edges of the leaves. This damage is usually only superficial.

5. **Give your seedlings some support.** Put some canes at 1-metre spacings along the rows and at the ends, and tie twine around them to make a supporting cage for the stems.

   This step isn't usually necessary for most dwarf varieties.

6. **Pick the tops off the plants, immediately above the uppermost flowers when they open, to reduce blackfly attacks upon the stems and the developing beans.** You may feel that you need to spray with an insecticide as well. If you do, take care not to spray during the day when bees may be pollinating the flowers.

7. **Regularly water plants in dry spells when the beans are forming.**

All bean and pea seeds are vulnerable to rodents. They may dig up the seeds before they germinate or eat the seedlings. If rodents are a problem for you, either cover the rows with chicken wire, tucking it well into the soil with no gaps, or place a few humane traps nearby and check them daily. Germinating seeds in a greenhouse and planting out seedlings can also help.

Buddying up to bacteria

'Good' bacteria occurs naturally in soil, but you can augment it by buying packs of beneficial bacteria (from seed companies or garden centres) that promote healthy plant growth and add nitrogen to your soil for your crops. You add this bacteria to seeds before sowing to inoculate the plants with beneficial bacteria, an especially good idea on poor soils.

Harvesting and storing your broad beans

You need to pick a surprising number of pods to get a meal! Some gardeners pick broad beans when they're small (about 10 centimetres long) and eat them whole, but most people leave them to mature and shell them and eat the beans inside. The lower beans on the plant, which develop from the first flowers, are ready for picking slightly earlier than the rest, but in general the picking period is quite short.

Feel the pods and check that the beans are swelling, and then pick one and open it. If the beans have gaps between them and the pods are green, they're tender – if the pods are starting to turn spotty and crammed tight, the beans are edible but tougher.

Taking the beans out of the pods is a sensory delight, but although the interior of the pods is soft and velvety, they can stain your hands. Broad beans freeze well, so you can store them for a long time without losing any of their goodness.

After harvesting, pull up the plants or cut them off at ground level and compost them. The roots that you leave behind add nitrogen to the soil, benefiting the next crop to grow on that spot.

Choosing varieties

You can choose from *longpod*, *shortpod*, *green-seeded* and *white-seeded* varieties of broad bean when deciding which type to grow. Longpod varieties, with up to eight seeds per pod, grow earlier and are hardier whereas shortpods, with four seeds per pod, have the finer flavour. Some people consider the green-seeded varieties to have a better flavour than those with white seeds, but modern varieties have blurred the distinctions. Here are some of the best:

- **Aquadulce** is a white-seeded longpod variety, best for sowing in autumn for the earliest crops.
- **Imperial Green Longpod** is a green-seeded longpod variety that produces heavy crops of tasty beans on tall plants. Masterpiece Green Longpod is similar.

- ✔ **Jubilee Hysor** is a white-seeded shortpod bean, the heaviest cropping of the shortpod types.

- ✔ **Listra** is a white-seeded shortpod, with heavy crops of upright pods that are easy to pick. Suitable for late sowing.

- ✔ **The Sutton** is a white-seeded shortpod. You can sow this dwarf, heavily cropping, hardy variety in autumn in mild areas, if you protect it under cloches.

- ✔ **Verdy** is a green-seeded shortpod. The stocky plants produce heavy crops of tasty beans.

- ✔ **Witkiem Manita** is a white-seeded longpod variety that crops heavily. Suitable for late sowing.

- ✔ **Witkiem Vroma** is a white-seeded longpod variety that produces heavy yields of tasty beans early on in the season.

Going continental: French beans

French beans are so easily available in the shops all year round that they may not seem an important home crop. But French beans are easy to grow, crop readily and heavily, and taste far better if you cook and eat them straight after picking. You can also enjoy interesting varieties that you just can't buy in the shops.

In contrast to broad beans, French beans are well worth growing in pots or on the patio, with even just a few plants giving you a useful crop. Also, they have the advantage over runner beans that their flowers are self-pollinating so you don't have any problems with the flowers opening but not setting pods.

 Small, tender beans are best for steaming or lightly boiling, whole or cut in half – just 'top and tail' them. You don't need to slice or *string* them (remove the tough fibre down the side that occurs in older beans). You can chop older beans into sections and cook them with tomatoes and onions.

Your own baked beans

The beans in your tin of baked beans are haricot beans, which are basically French beans. The difference is that the varieties grown for their seeds, such as haricot (mature dried) beans and flageolet (mature but fresh) beans, have pods that, although edible, aren't as tender and tasty as the varieties we now grow for their immature pods, which we call French beans. The few dual-purpose varieties aren't as tender as modern French beans. On the other hand, if you leave French beans to get old on the plants, either by accident or design, the beans inside the pods are perfectly edible so you need not waste them.

You cook flageolet beans like peas, by boiling or steaming but for a longer time, and they're excellent additions to stews or, when cool, to salads. You need to soak dried haricot beans before cooking.

Dried beans (the seeds in the pods) contain 21 per cent protein but the fresh, green pods (with tiny immature seeds) contain only a tenth of that. However, they do contain vitamins A, B1, B2, B6 and E, biotin and folic acid.

Sowing and cultivating French beans

French beans are generally easy to grow but their sensitivity to cold temperatures is the most common cause of failure. Make sure that they have rich, light, warm soil to grow in; germination may be a problem in heavy, cold, clay soils. You can help your French beans along by adding in organic matter to improve soil fertility and by keeping them well watered in hot, dry spells.

You need to make sure that your French beans also have protection from cold winds. Climbing varieties are especially vulnerable to cold, drying winds, and so in exposed sites the dwarf varieties are more reliable.

Here are the steps to follow to grow yourself a bumper crop of French beans:

1. **Sow the seeds.** If you want an early crop, sow the seeds in cell trays or pots in a greenhouse at a temperature of at least 10°C, and preferably higher. Sow two seeds per cell or pot, about 2 centimetres deep, water them well, and while not letting them dry out, avoid the temptation to keep the compost sodden. Never be tempted to sow seeds early outside, even under cloches – the seeds are more likely to rot than to germinate. In general, April is early enough to be sowing, indoors or out, because the plants can't stand frost and can't grow outside until late May at the earliest.

   Alternatively, you can sow seeds outside from late April to mid-July for a succession of crops. Sow them 5 centimetres deep and 15 centimetres apart. The closer spacing is necessary because not all the seeds germinate. Alternatively, you can sow two seeds per station, 20 centimetres apart. Use fast-growing, early varieties for late sowings so that they mature before the first frosts of autumn.

2. **Plant out those seedlings growing inside.** French bean plants are sensitive to frost so don't plant them outside until all danger of frost is past – usually late May – and make sure you acclimatise them to outside conditions for a few days before planting by putting them outside during the day, bringing them back in at night. Plant them 20 centimetres apart, in double rows. At the same time as planting you can sow some seeds in the same row to give a longer cropping period.

   If you're growing a climbing variety of French bean, plant them at the base of canes spaced 30 centimetres apart. Climbers easily reach 2 metres high and need the canes for support. Also, sowing seeds at the base of canes when you plant out the seedlings is a good move, because they have longer growing and cropping periods.

Dwarf varieties don't need any support but the pods of some types can touch the soil, making them vulnerable to slug and snail attacks (Chapter 7 tells you how to deal with these pests).

Harvesting and storing your French beans

Although most people grow French beans to use fresh, and generally pick them when still young, tender and stringless, the plants also develop beans that you can use as pulses (haricot and flageolet beans) in winter stews and casseroles.

Dwarf varieties produce their crops over several weeks. By picking the beans when young and tender, as well as making sure that you keep the plants watered, you can prolong the cropping season.

Climbing varieties have a much longer cropping period. Picking the beans when young (by snapping them off to avoid damaging the plants) and not allowing them to get coarse and 'beany' can substantially increase the crop. If you leave the beans to mature, especially at the end of the season, you can pick and use the seeds as fresh flageolet beans.

When small and tender, French beans freeze well. If you allow bean pods to mature completely and the beans inside to go dry, though, you can dry and store them for later use. To do this, spread them on a baking sheet and place them in a dry, warm place for a few days before storing them in jars or tins.

Choosing varieties

Dwarf French beans are the most popular with gardeners because they need no support, are ideal for all gardens, and grow well in containers. A wide variety of types exists, including purple and yellow-podded varieties which can give your meals added interest. They also crop a bit more quickly than the climbing types. But climbing French beans crop over a longer period and have bigger crops, so you may think the additional work of putting up supports is worth the effort. The choice is yours but all are rewarding and tasty.

- ✔ **Berlotto Firetongue (Berlotto lingua di Fuoco)** produces colourful pods streaked with red. You can use these beans fresh, but shelling them first and using them as fresh beans or dried haricot is better. This variety is also available as a climbing form.

- ✔ **Delinel** produces good crops of slender, tasty beans and has excellent flavour.

- ✔ **Fandango** produces long, slender pods. This variety has good resistance to disease and is reliable in poor, cool weather.

- ✔ **Golden Teepee** produces good crops of bright yellow pods held above the foliage. Tasty and attractive.

- ✔ **Masterpiece** is a traditional favourite, with flat pods.

- ✔ **Purple Queen** produces purple pods that are easy to see and pick. Round and stringless, purple queens turn green through cooking.

- ✔ **Purple Teepee** produces heavy crops of slender, purple pods held above the foliage. The pods turn green during cooking.

- ✔ **Safari** produces heavy crops of tasty, Kenyan-type, slender beans.

- ✔ **Sunray** produces slender, stringless, tasty pods and has exceptional resistance to most diseases.

- ✔ **Valdor** produces heavy crops of slim, stringless, bright yellow pods with good flavour.

Climbing French bean varieties are especially good in patio pots for their pretty flowers and attractiveness, but mostly because of the heavy crops they produce. They make a good option if you've had trouble with runner beans in the past because the flowers produce pods even without bees visiting them, so you can be sure of a good crop.

- ✔ **Cobra** produces vigorous plants with heavy crops of round, stringless beans and attractive, purple flowers.

- ✔ **Goldfield** is an unusual, vigorous variety with heavy crops of long, flat, gold pods.

- ✔ **Limka** produces flat beans a little like early-cropping runner beans.

- ✔ **Marie Louise** is a heavy cropping, tasty variety, best for use as shelled or dried beans.

- ✔ **Nektar Gold** produces masses of bright gold, slightly flattened, stringless pods. A reliable variety, even in poor weather.

- ✔ **Pantheon** beans are long, flat and stringless like runner beans, but are much earlier to mature and easier to grow. Hunter is a similar variety.

- ✔ **Soissons** is the best bean to grow for flageolet beans. The pale green seeds have good flavour.

Sprinting up the canes: Runner beans

Most gardeners consider runner beans to be the best-tasting of all the beans, and for many, summer starts only when the first runner beans are on the plate! Runners usually need more preparation in the kitchen than French beans do, but their taste and the heavy crops they produce more than make up for that. Although not without their problems, runner beans are usually reliable plants and are among the most productive of summer vegetables.

Cooks usually prepare runner beans by removing the edges of the beans with a knife and cutting the beans into thin slices before boiling or steaming them until tender, but not so long that they lose their fresh green colour.

When runner beans fail to set

Runner beans aren't difficult to grow but sometimes the flowers do not set and produce beans, for several possible reasons:

✔ **Dryness at the roots.** Plants that are short of water don't form beans or the small beans that do form fall off and don't mature.

✔ **Birds.** Sparrows often attack the flowers of red-flowered varieties, to get the sweet nectar, and prevent bean formation.

✔ **Bees.** Bees aren't adapted to pollinate the flowers of runner beans and often chew the backs of the blooms to get to the nectar without effectively pollinating the flowers.

✔ **Hot weather.** Ironically, although runner beans are subtropical plants, high temperatures in midsummer prevent the flowers from setting. As the weather cools they set more beans. Spraying the flowers with water is often a good idea in hot weather.

In areas where beans often fail to set well, try white-flowered varieties instead, as these often set more effectively.

The large, swollen roots that runner beans produce are not edible.

Runner beans contain A, B and C vitamins and folic acid.

Sowing and cultivating runner beans

Runner beans need a soil that never dries out and is rich in organic matter, with some lime (they generally grow better in neutral or alkaline soil rather than acid). The traditional way to prepare the soil is to dig a trench in autumn, where the beans are to grow, and fill it, over winter, with organic matter and old plants cleared off the allotment. The next step is to fill this trench in, perhaps after adding some manure, to make a mound. Try to avoid very cold, windy spots because strong wind damages the foliage and prevents bees from visiting the flowers.

Except for the few dwarf varieties, runner beans need poles or canes 2.4 metres long to grow up.

Just follow these steps to get going with your runner beans:

1. **Prepare the soil with lots of organic matter.** Dig in as much as possible. Spent mushroom compost is ideal because it contains lime, which runner beans need.

2. **Sow the seeds.** Runner bean seeds are large and easy to handle, but resist the temptation to sow them until after the last frost. Early plants that bloom at the hottest time in summer often don't set beans until the weather cools. Even so, many people sow their seeds in pots in a greenhouse.

Sow two seeds on their ends (which end doesn't matter), 4 centimetres deep, in 8-centimetre-diameter pots of multipurpose compost. Keep them in a temperature of at least 10°C, moist, and in good light. The seedlings are ready to plant out when they begin to climb – about a month after sowing.

Alternatively, you can sow the seeds 5 centimetres deep, where the plants are to grow. Be sure not to sow out before the last frost is forecast.

3. **Place canes in the soil for the plants to grow up.** Arrange them in a double row, with canes 30 centimetres apart in rows 45 centimetres apart, tied to horizontal canes about 1.5 metres from the ground. Alternatively, arrange in a wigwam with about eight canes in a circular pattern tied together 1.5 metres from the ground. By tying them so far from the top, you can easily see the beans from the overhanging canes.

4. **Plant out the seedlings, one plant at the base of each cane.** Runner beans are frost-tender so don't plant them out until after the last frost of spring.

Seedlings are very vulnerable to attack from slugs and snails so use your preferred method to keep these pests at bay as soon as you plant out the seedlings (Chapter 7 tells you about methods for controlling pests).

To maintain a prolonged crop, sow a seed with each seedling you plant.

5. **Make sure that the plants don't go short of water at any time, and mulch the rows to retain moisture.**

6. **Pinch out the tops of the plants when they reach the top of the canes to encourage shoots lower down and to control the growth of the plants.** You don't usually need to tie them to their canes.

Note that if you're growing a dwarf variety, sow or plant them 30 centimetres apart without canes (dwarf varieties don't need this support). You can pinch out the tips of the shoots when they reach about 30 centimetres in height, but generally they don't need any other special care. However, the pods do rest on the soil and so mulching with straw helps to keep the pods clean and reduce the number of slug attacks.

Runner beans make good crops for small gardens. You can grow them in large tubs of multipurpose compost. Just remember to add some slow-release fertiliser and put a wigwam of canes in the tub for them to grow up. You can even plant in some sweet peas to add extra colour and help attract pollinating insects, too.

Harvesting and storing your runner beans

Runner beans crop over a long period but if you allow pods to mature and develop 'beans' (seeds), you're likely to get fewer crops – the more you pick, the more you get. So unless you're trying to grow large beans for the local show, you're best off picking them while they're young and immature. Runner beans freeze well, so you can store them until you need them.

Choosing varieties

Here are some of the best varieties of runner bean:

- ✔ **Aintree** is a stringless, slim, tender bean. The plant produces good crops, even in hot weather.

- ✔ **Hestia** is a dwarf variety with red and white flowers. Good for patio pots and exposed positions.

- ✔ **Lady Di** has smooth, long, stringless pods with good flavour. Lady Di is a heavy cropper that sets well.

- ✔ **Painted Lady** is popular for its red and white flowers and good flavour, but the beans aren't as long or prolific as other varieties.

- ✔ **Red Rum** is a popular scarlet runner with early and heavy crops. Tolerant of poor weather conditions.

- ✔ **Snow White** is a white-flowered, dwarf type for pots that produces prolific, tasty pods.

- ✔ **Sun Bright** is a late, less vigorous variety with yellow foliage and red flowers. Very ornamental, with decent crops of beans.

- ✔ **White Apollo** has white flowers and heavy crops of long, slim, tasty pods.

- ✔ **Wisley Magic** produces long, smooth, slender pods and heavy crops of tasty beans.

Producing pleasing pods: Peas

Peas are a summer treat for gardeners, thanks to the sheer delight of picking and eating fresh peas, young and sweet, straight off the plants. In contrast, 'fresh' peas in supermarkets never taste as good as your own.

Varieties exist to suit every garden, from dwarf kinds that are ideal for pots and small plots and tall kinds that need staking but which have bigger crops. Even better, you can easily grow your own mangetout peas and crunch your way along the rows munching on them before you even get back to the kitchen!

The most delicious way to eat peas is raw, straight from the plant! Boiling for a short time is the usual way of cooking them, but the French method of frying them lightly with onion and shredded lettuce in some butter is also delicious.

Fresh peas (not mangetout peas) contain considerable protein as well as vitamins A, B1, B2, C, E and K, and folic acid.

Sowing and cultivating peas

Peas aren't too fussy about soil fertility but they don't grow well if the soil is waterlogged. An ideal location for growing peas is in a slightly alkaline soil, improved with organic matter, and in full sun.

1. **Sow the seeds.** You can sow peas from spring to early summer. In mild areas you can also make an autumn sowing for early crops, but these only succeed in well-drained soils and if you can protect the plants from pigeons and extreme cold.

   The most usual way to sow is direct in the soil, either in a single row or, more often, in a double row. To do this, take out a broad trench with a spade or Dutch hoe, about 5 centimetres deep, and scatter or place the seeds about 5 centimetres apart in the rows. Then cover them with soil and water well. If you're sowing more than one row, base the spacing on the height of the variety, but in general, space at least 45 centimetres apart.

   Alternatively, you can sow early in the greenhouse (see Figure 11-1). To do this, fill lengths of guttering (short enough to handle easily when full of compost) with multipurpose compost and sow the seeds 5 centimetres apart, about 2 centimetres deep. Water and keep the seeds warm and free from rodents, and when the seedlings are about 8 centimetres high you can plant them out. Make a trench in the soil and slide the compost and plants out without disturbing them. Cover the compost with a little soil, water well, and make sure that you protect them from pigeons.

Figure 11-1: Sowing early in the green- house using lengths of guttering.

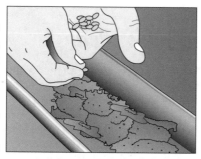

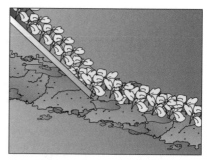

Sowing seeds in compost in lengths of guttering for an early crop.

When the seeds have grown just slide the whole row into the prepared soil.

2. **When most varieties get a little larger, you need to give them some sort of support.** Peas vary greatly in height so check the pack! Gardeners traditionally support pea plants with *pea sticks* – twiggy stems made from hazel, birch or beech, but any twigs are suitable – by pushing them in between and around plants in the rows. If you don't have any twigs to hand, you can use pea netting, supported on canes.

3. **When the peas are in flower and the pods are swelling, keep them well watered.** This improves the quality of the crop. At other times, peas don't need a lot of extra watering

Pea shoots and *tendrils* (the curly bit at the end of the leaf) are also edible and taste delicious. Sow a row of peas for harvesting as pea shoots, cutting the shoots off as soon as they reach 10 centimetres high. A second crop should be produced by the seeds a few weeks later. You can sow in containers full of compost on the windowsill for shoots all year round.

Rodents, pigeons, pea moths and pea and bean weevils all love peas, so be sure to protect your plants from attack. Chapter 7 tells you about dealing with these pests.

Harvesting and storing your peas

You can pick mangetout and sugarsnap peas over a period of several weeks when they're immature, in the case of mangetout peas when they're flat and before the peas inside start to swell. Sugarsnaps will be swollen with small peas inside. Other peas tend to crop over a shorter period.

Check the quality of the peas daily so that you pick them when the pods are full but before they start to become pale, wrinkled and veined on the outside, which is a sign that the peas inside have become hard and bitter and lost their sweetness.

If you need to store peas the best way is to freeze them, but why do that when frozen peas are so cheap to buy? Make the most of them while they're fresh. When you have finished picking all the peas, pull them up and add the plants to the compost heap.

Choosing varieties

Catalogues sometimes label peas as *round-seeded* or *wrinkled*. In general, round-seeded peas (such as Meteor and Pilot) are less sweet and have more starch but are hardier and suitable for early sowings. Those varieties with wrinkled seeds (such as Delikat) are less hardy but much sweeter. However, although not all catalogues give this information, they do say when to sow and give general characteristics. Although some peas are sweeter than others, the key to tender, sweet peas is to pick them young and small and not to let them get large and tough.

Early peas give you the earliest crop of peas and are the best for impatient growers!

✔ **Kelvedon Wonder** is a popular, heavy-cropping variety with good flavour and resistance to mildew. Grows to 45 centimetres.

✔ **Little Marvel** produces heavy crops of fine-tasting peas. Good for sowing under cloches. Grows to 50 centimetres.

- ✔ **Meteor** is a tough, hardy variety for early sowings in cold and exposed gardens. Grows to 60 centimetres.

- ✔ **Misty** produces heavy crops of tasty peas over a long period. Grows to 60 centimetres.

- ✔ **Pilot** is possibly the hardiest pea – in mild areas you can sow this variety in autumn for early crops – and one with a long cropping period. Grows to 120 centimetres.

- ✔ **Spring** is an early, wrinkled seed pea with heavy crops of sweet peas. Grows to 60 centimetres.

- ✔ **Starlight** is an early maincrop variety with heavy crops of easy-to-see-and-pick pods and good resistance to mildew. Grows to 60 centimetres.

Maincrop peas take longer to mature than the early types but generally produce bigger crops and you can pick them over a longer period. They include *petit pois*, which is a type noted for its small, sweet and tender peas.

- ✔ **Alderman** is a tall pea with heavy yields. This variety is late to crop but produces pods over a long period. Grows to 180 centimetres.

- ✔ **Ambassador** has excellent resistance to all common pea diseases and produces heavy crops of short pods. Grows to 70 centimetres.

- ✔ **Ceresa** is a short, self-supporting pea with many small, petit pois per pod. Grows to 50 centimetres.

- ✔ **Greensage** is an exceptional type with big pods and sweet, delicious peas. Grows to 75 centimetres.

- ✔ **Onward** is a reliable, heavy-cropping pea with big pods of tasty peas.

- ✔ **Waverex** is a popular, traditional petit pois type with long, well-filled pods. Grows to 75 centimetres.

As well as regular peas and the smaller, sweeter petit pois, you can choose to grow mangetout or sugarsnap peas to eat whole – pod and all. Here are a few varieties that are just as easy to grow and well worth trying:

- ✔ **Carouby de Maussane** produces extra sweet, large, flat pods. Grows to 150 centimetres.

- ✔ **Delikat Sugarsnap** is a very sweet, round-podded mangetout pea. Grows to 75 centimetres.

- ✔ **Ezetha's Krombek Blauwschok** is an unusual pea with attractive purple flowers and pods that brightens up your salads. Grows to 180 centimetres.

- ✔ **Oregon Sugar Pod** is the most reliable mangetout type, with a good resistance to many diseases. This variety has a long season of picking. Grows to 100 centimetres.

- ✔ **Sugar Ann Sugarsnap** is an early producer of really sweet pale green pods. Grows to 100 centimetres.

Growing Glorious Grains

Growing most grains, such as wheat or barley, takes a lot of time and space, and the end result is very similar to anything you can buy; therefore, most grains aren't the best use of your resources as a grow-your-own gardener. However, a few grains are definitely worthwhile crops to grow on your plot, and I tell you about them in this section.

Sweet as sugar: Sweetcorn

The most important grain for growing at home or on the allotment is sweet-corn – no one bothers with rice or wheat! Sweetcorn is a form of maize that you eat while the grains are immature and before the sugar in the kernels gets converted to starch. You can grow few more delicious crops than your own, fresh sweetcorn.

Sweetcorn tastes great after boiling it for a few minutes and serving up with butter as corn on the cob. You can also strip it from the cobs with a knife and cook it as a vegetable, perhaps mixing it with peas. You can also try cooking sweetcorn on the barbecue, but perhaps the best way is to eat it raw, straight off the plant!

Sweetcorn is rich in sugars as well as vitamins A, B1, B2, B6, E and K, and has significant fibre, too. However, the sugar in the luscious kernels starts to turn to starch as soon as you pick them.

Sowing and cultivating sweetcorn

Sweetcorn is the only grass (grain) grown as a vegetable at home and is unusual among our crops in that the wind rather than bees pollinates the flowers. For this reason, gardeners grow sweetcorn in blocks rather than in rows so that the wind is more likely to blow the pollen shed by the male flowers at the top of the plants onto the developing (female) cobs lower down on the plant.

Sweetcorn needs a warm, sheltered spot and isn't fussy about soil, although light soils are better than heavy clay. Adding organic matter to the soil improves growth and crops.

Traditionally, sweetcorn had a long growing period and was unreliable in British summers, but modern varieties crop much more quickly and have made growing sweetcorn possible in most areas. Here's how to do it:

1. **Sow the seeds.** Sweetcorn isn't frost-hardy, and so don't sow too early: if sowing in the greenhouse, about a month to six weeks before the last spring frost is likely should be fine; if sowing outside, aim for just before the last spring frost. Because sweetcorn doesn't germinate well in cold soils, most gardeners sow seeds in cell trays or pots in a greenhouse or on the windowsill. A temperature of about 22°C is ideal.

   Some seed is expensive and most varieties are F1 hybrids. Packet contents vary from less than 30 to more than 100 seeds, and knowing that each plant produces two cobs – or three if you're lucky – enables you to work out how many plants you need. Sow one or two seeds per pot or cell tray, about 2 centimetres deep in multipurpose compost. If two seeds germinate where you've sown two, pull out the weakest one as soon as possible. If you sow only one per pot you end up with quite a few empty pots because only about 75 per cent of seeds germinate.

   Alternatively you can sow seeds in the garden where they're to grow, but the ground must be warm first. Many gardeners choose to warm the soil by placing cut, plastic lemonade bottles over the soil for a few weeks, usually in late April, before lifting and sowing under them. Make sure that the seeds don't dry out and that the plants don't cook under these mini greenhouses.

2. **Plant out the seedlings, after acclimatising them to outside conditions, when they're about 15 centimetres high and are filling the pots or cells with roots.** Equally space the plants 30–40 centimetres apart, in blocks. The plants around the edge of the blocks may not get effectively pollinated, and so in a block of nine plants (planted 3x3) only the central plant may have complete pollination. For this reason, the larger your block of plants, the better your results are likely to be. Where pollination isn't complete, the cobs are gappy and missing many of the juicy kernels you're growing them for.

3. **Water your plants regularly.** Sweetcorn don't crop well if they're short of water.

Although sweetcorn is basically easy to grow, as the cobs ripen they attract the unwanted attention of a variety of wildlife. In the past, I've lost the lion's share of a crop to rats and mice, and badgers also attack ripening cobs. Chapter 7 gives you some tips on dealing with these pests.

Harvesting and storing your sweetcorn

Telling when sweetcorn is ready to eat is sometimes tricky, but easy when you know how. As soon as the *silks* (the tassels at the ends of the cobs) turn brown you can start to check for ripeness. Pull back some of the leaves (sheaths) around the cob to expose some kernels and push your thumbnail into a kernel. The cob is ready if the juice inside is milky, but if the juice is watery it needs more time, in which case just cover up and leave for a few more days.

You can harvest the cobs by snapping or cutting them off the plants. Each variety ripens over a short period and the lower cobs are ready first. Always pick the cobs immediately before you intend to use them because they lose sweetness after picking – although modern, supersweet varieties last better. To unwrap the cobs, pull back all the leaves, wipe off the silks, and snap off the stem.

Choosing varieties

- **Ambrosia F1** cobs are a white and gold, bicoloured variety, early to mature and good in cool seasons.
- **Honey bantam Bicolour F1** has yellow and white kernels, and is very early to mature.
- **Incredible F1** has long cobs packed with gold kernels and is resistant to rust.
- **Indian Summer F1** is an unusual variety with kernels in white, gold and purple.
- **Lark F1** has the advantage of extra tender kernels and is easy to germinate.
- **Ovation F1** is early to mature and has large cobs.
- **Passion F1** is a particularly sweet and tender variety.
- **Quick Treat** is fast to mature, with sweet, short cobs.

A couple of other varieties are good for certain culinary uses:

- **Mini Pop F1** is the best variety for mini-sweetcorn.
- **Strawberry Popcorn** produces short cobs with red kernels, and is often grown for popcorn.

Something different: Amaranth and quinoa

Amaranth and quinoa (pronounced *keen-wa*) may be unfamiliar to some people. Because they're rather unusual and don't feature in most seed catalogues, you have little choice of varieties and not many of those are ideal for growing in Britain. However, if you have space and fancy trying something unusual, why not give them a go?

Amaranth and quinoa are closely related to each other and are useful for their small seeds, which grow in large heads at the top of the plants. Both crops are generally easy to grow and as a bonus you can also eat the leaves as a substitute for spinach.

Quinoa is related to the common weed *fat hen* and is a staple grain in South America. Amaranth is similar but is a larger, coarser plant. Some people grow certain forms of amaranth specifically for their leaves.

Be sure to thoroughly wash these grains first (quinoa has a bitter soap-like coating that you need to wash off before use). You can then boil them in water until they're plump and use them like rice.

Both these crops are nutritious. Quinoa has more protein than any other grain (14–18 per cent) and more fat, making it especially nutritious. It contains no gluten but is rich in lysine and methionine. Amaranth is also high in protein and has similar nutritional value.

Sowing and cultivating amaranth and quinoa

Both crops prefer a well-manured soil in full sun, and neither are fussy about soil type.

Here are the simple steps to take after finding your site and preparing the soil:

1. **Sow the seeds.** Cell trays are ideal. Sow a pinch of seed in each cell, cover with a little compost, water, and germinate in a greenhouse at a temperature of 21°C.

   Amaranth and quinoa plants aren't frost-hardy, so don't plant them out until mid-spring, after the last frost, when the plants are about 15 centimetres high.

2. **Plant out the seedlings 20–30 centimetres apart.** Wider spacing results in bigger plants with larger heads of seeds, but these plants are then more prone to *lodging* or falling over in autumn when the heads of seeds get very heavy.

The plants are easy to look after and don't need any special treatment, but results do vary with the season.

Harvesting and storing your amaranth and quinoa

Both crops are usually ready to harvest in late September, and this is the most difficult part of the process. As soon as the seed heads are ready you need to cut off, dry, and *thresh* them (remove the seeds from the stems and husks by rubbing against a sieve) to remove the seeds from the chaff. When fully dry, you can safely store them away for use in winter. Depending on how well the seeds have dried they should store at least until spring.

In prolonged wet autumn weather the seeds may start to germinate in the heads and sparrows often strip the plants of seeds before you get a chance to harvest them.

Chapter 12

Branching Out: Growing Unusual Vegetables

. . . .

In This Chapter

▶ Discovering the attraction of artichokes

▶ Making room for delicious and unusual vegetables

▶ Challenging your skills and taste buds with something different

. . . .

*W*hichever way you look at them, some vegetables just aren't easy to categorise. So that you don't overlook these tasty misfits, this chapter assembles some of the most worthy contenders for space on your plot: flower buds that taste delicious, knobbly underground tubers that take longer to scrub than to eat (but taste delicious), edible leaf stalks, and pods full of sticky goo!

If you're intrigued, you're bound to be keen to try some of these weird and wonderful foodstuffs. What all the vegetables in this chapter have in common is that they taste infinitely better if you grow them yourself. Some are so unusual that you never see them in your local supermarket, so the *only* way to try them is to grow them yourself. This chapter shows you how.

Achieving A+ Artichokes

Artichokes are frequently confusing, always intriguing, and decidedly exotic. In this section I tell you about the two basic types of artichoke, and I throw in a rather odd, third type as well!

Globe artichokes and Jerusalem artichokes are related, but not closely, and couldn't be more different, both in the parts that we eat and in their cultivation. In globe artichokes, which are basically a souped-up thistle, we eat the young flower bud. (To be accurate, the globe is a collection of flowers surrounded by fleshy *bracts*, or scale-like leaves). In Jerusalem artichokes, which are related to sunflowers, the edible part is a tuber dug up from the ground. And while globe artichokes are a gourmet treat, Jerusalem artichokes could be a staple. They crop heavily, but have never really become very popular, partly because of their taste. Neither type is difficult to grow, but they both take up a fair bit of space and so aren't ideal for smaller plots.

Going global: Globe artichokes

Globe artichokes (*Cynara cardunculus*) are attractive, large plants with coarsely cut, silvery grey leaves. They can easily reach 2 metres high and 1.5 metres across and don't look out of place in herbaceous borders. Each plant produces several flowering stems with up to ten globes, which are ready for cutting over several weeks.

To cook this delicious vegetable, all you need to do is snap the stem off the base of the globe and boil the globe in water (adding in some lemon juice to prevent browning) for about 30 minutes. You eat artichokes by peeling off the outer scales first to get to the fleshy bases nearer the centre. Scrape off the flesh with your teeth and, when you get to the centre, scoop off the fluffy, white 'choke'. This should come off easily, leaving you with the solid base – the best bit! Serve with melted butter. The only downside of eating globe artichokes is that you end up with a pile of debris many times bigger than the original globe!

Artichokes contain iron and potassium, and are mildly diuretic. They also contain a special sugar, and drinking water while eating them makes the water taste sweet.

Sowing and cultivating globe artichokes

Globe artichokes need a rich and fertile but well-drained soil in a sunny spot. They don't tolerate wet, heavy soils and waterlogged soil in winter is fatal. If you have heavy soil, planting your artichokes on mounds to prevent rot damage may be worthwhile.

You can grow artichokes in one of two ways. The quickest method is to buy plants of good, named varieties, although these aren't easy to find and virtually all plants in garden centres are grown from the same seeds that you can buy. So, because globe artichokes grow easily from seed, you're best off starting with a packet yourself if you want to save money. However, seed doesn't always breed completely true and the resulting plants will be variable in the quality of the globes, some being of good quality and others spiny and not quite so fleshy or good to eat.

To grow your globe artichokes from scratch:

1. **Sow the large seeds in early spring, in trays, and in a temperature of about 20°C in the greenhouse or on the windowsill in your house.** The seeds sprout quickly, and so as soon as they're big enough, transplant them into small pots.

2. **Plant out the young plants after about three months. Space them about 1 metre apart and protect them from slugs and snails at this vulnerable stage.** (Chapter 7 gives you tips on dealing with these pests.)

3. **Keep the young plants free of weeds and water them well in dry weather to make sure they get established** (they may die in dry weather if you allow them to fend for themselves).

After planting and when established, artichokes generally take care of themselves. They have deep roots and rarely need watering in summer, although they appreciate a drink in dry weather. In the first year, remember to remove the flowering stem as soon as it appears, to build up the strength of the plant. However, you can let one globe develop – just for a taste!

After a few years, you'll find many side shoots have developed at the base of the plant, making it overcrowded, so you need to divide it. Take a sharp spade and cut off the side shoots, with as much root as possible, trim off the outer leaves, and replant the young side shoots, watering them well until they're established.

In cold areas, globe artichoke plants may benefit from a covering of straw or fleece through the winter to protect them from extreme cold. Put this netting on only in late December, and remove it in early spring after the worst of the cold has passed. In autumn, cut down the flowered stems and old leaves to tidy up the plants. In spring, remember to mulch the plants with compost and add some general fertiliser to boost growth for the year ahead.

Artichokes have few real pests but blackfly often cover the leaves and the flowering stems, although they rarely cause much damage unless they get into the globes. You can find help for dealing with these pests in Chapter 7.

Harvesting and storing your globe artichokes

The top bud on the stem is the first one ready to harvest. You need to harvest globe artichokes as soon as the green scales start to open, but no later. Cut them off, leaving a piece of the stem attached to form a handle. As the lower, smaller buds are ready, cut them too. If you leave them too long the buds become large purple flowers that are attractive to bees but no good to eat.

Some globes have fierce spines on them which you're unlikely to want so select the best plants when they produce their first globes and discard the poor ones. Use artichokes as soon as you pick them because they don't store well.

Choosing varieties

Here are a few good varieties of globe artichoke to consider growing:

- ✔ **Green Globe** is the most common green variety.

- ✔ **Purple Globe Romanesco** produces beautiful purple-scaled heads.

- ✔ **Violetto di Chioggia** produces purple and green heads.

Gone with the wind: Jerusalem artichokes

Few crops are as easy to grow as Jerusalem artichokes (*Helianthus tuberosus*). They are hardy, grow almost anywhere, and nearly always crop well; all this with the minimum of effort!

Jerusalem artichokes are a perennial sunflower and in long summers they may open their small, yellow flowers, although this isn't guaranteed. The plants grow strongly with upright stems. Gardeners often plant them in rows as a windbreak because the stems grow to 2 metres or more by the end of summer.

Jerusalem artichokes have rather knobbly roots that are fiddly to peel. After peeling, cooks usually slice, boil or steam, and serve with butter or a white sauce. With their slightly smoky, and earthy but pleasant flavour, Jerusalem artichokes also make great additions to soup or to stews.

As well as inulin (a carbohydrate that the stomach can't digest, making them low in calories), Jerusalem artichokes contain fructose, potassium and phosphorus. They also contain vitamins A, C, B1 and B2, are low in calories, and devoid of starch, making them suitable for diabetics.

Ironically, for a plant that makes a great windbreak, protecting other plants from draughts, wind is an infamous problem with the tubers, which are renowned for the disconcerting flatulence they often produce soon after having been eaten! This can be severe and embarrassing but many people say that regular consumption reduces the severity of the problem. This is a real pity because the flavour of the tubers is interesting and delicious, so don't let this put you off planting and enjoying this really simple crop.

Sowing and cultivating Jerusalem artichokes

Jerusalem artichokes aren't fussy about soil and grow in most places, but they don't like waterlogged soils. If your soil is light and dry, adding as much organic matter as possible leads to better crops in rich soils that stay moist all season.

Jerusalem artichokes grow from tubers, rather than from seed, and because they aren't prone to any major pests and diseases you can use the tubers that shops sell for consumption. Alternatively you can buy tubers for planting. These steps tell you where to go next:

1. **Plant the tubers where they are to grow, as soon as possible in spring, 15 centimetres deep and 30–45 centimetres apart.** The tubers are knobbly – so simply plant them on their sides – and hardy, so you have no worries with frost.

Identity crisis

Jerusalem artichokes are actually native to North America and have nothing whatsoever to do with Jerusalem, which is in the Middle East! Native Americans had long cultivated the crop, which they called *sunroot,* before explorers brought it to Europe. The word *Jerusalem* comes from the word *girasol,* meaning sunflower in Italian, and the plant is called *artichoke* because people thought the taste of the tubers was similar to globe artichokes.

2. **Pull soil around the base of the stems in summer to protect from pests any tubers that may develop near the surface.** The tubers aren't poisonous when left in the light, unlike potatoes.

3. **Water the plants in dry weather.**

4. **In early autumn, cut the stems back to 1.5 metres high to prevent flowering and to direct all the energy into tuber production.**

Harvesting and storing your Jerusalem artichokes

You can start harvesting as soon as the leaves start to turn yellow in autumn. You don't need to lift and store the tubers as you would with potatoes – just dig them up as you need them. However, slugs attack tubers in the soil and so in heavy soils where slugs are prevalent, lifting them all in autumn may be a good move. If you do lift your artichokes, store them in damp compost or sand to prevent them from rapidly drying out and shrivelling.

After harvesting, Jerusalem artichokes can become a problem if you accidentally leave a few tubers in the ground, and can almost become a weed, so try and lift them all if you want to grow something else in the soil the next year. However, this need not be a problem if you're happy to leave them in the same space for several years. Crop rotation isn't important with Jerusalem artichokes because they're so tough and generally unaffected by problems.

Choosing varieties

Here are a couple of the most popular varieties:

- **Fuseau** is the most common variety, good for its smooth tubers.

- **Sunray** is best known for its relatively dwarf size and regular flowering.

A taste of the east: Chinese artichokes

Chinese artichoke (also known as *crosne* and *gan lu zi*) is unrelated to the other artichokes and in fact is related to mint. A very easy crop to grow, it's a hardy, upright plant with coarse, dark green leaves and small pink flowers that bloom in summer. Chinese artichoke spreads rapidly by underground stems and on these, the small, ribbed tubers form. Only about 5 centimetres long, these tubers look almost like grubs, but taste lovely.

Chinese artichokes have a pleasant, delicate, nutty flavour, and you need about 30 tubers per serving. Because you can't peel the tubers, try using a nail brush to scrub them, making sure that you get all the grit from the fissures. Then they need very quick cooking: steaming or boiling them for more than five minutes makes them go soggy and unexciting. Alternatively, you can fry them in butter so they retain their crunch.

The tubers contain starch for energy, like potatoes, but are unlikely to become a major part of your diet because preparing them is so fiddly!

Planting and cultivating Chinese artichokes

This vegetable is a very easy crop to grow in sun or partial shade. However, because the tubers are so fiddly to prepare, growing them in light, humus-rich soils gives you a huge advantage (cleaning heavy, clay soil from the fissures in the tubers is a tricky job even for the most experienced kitchen hand!). If you have heavy soil you may be better off growing this crop in pots of multipurpose compost, simply for the ease of harvesting.

Chinese artichokes grow from tubers rather than from seed, and you can buy these at some garden centres. When you have your tubers, just plant them 8 centimetres deep and 30 centimetres apart, in spring, exactly where you want them to grow. Apart from watering them in dry weather, you need do nothing else other than sit back and watch your plants grow!

Harvesting and storing your Chinese artichokes

In autumn, cut the tops down to near ground level. The tubers are hardy and you can safely leave them in the ground, digging them up as and when you need them. However, slugs may attack the tubers if you leave them in the soil for long, so check out Chapter 7 for ways of guarding against their attacks.

If your crops were planted in the ground, fork over the soil carefully when you harvest them to avoid leaving some tubers behind. If you do, you then get a crop in the same place the following year. Because Chinese artichokes have no serious pests, reusing the soil isn't a real problem unless you need that land for growing different crops the following year.

Choosing varieties

Chinese artichoke is one crop for which no varieties exist. Fortunate, therefore, that the sole type of Chinese artichoke tastes so good!

Growing Culinary Treats

The trio of vegetables in this section are some of the most delicious and fabled types on the planet! I include one that's easy but requires an investment of time and space, another that challenges all your gardening skills, and a third that's so rare you've probably never eaten it – and yet is easy to grow. So for a really rewarding experience, get growing and enjoy the challenge and the taste.

The highlight of spring: Asparagus

For many gardeners – and indeed for anyone who loves their food – the first asparagus of the season is a treat almost beyond compare. Perhaps the fact that the season is so limited explains the excitement (the cropping period is usually only about six weeks long); or perhaps it's the delicious taste or the fact that eating asparagus is such a good excuse to consume butter and rich sauces!

People often associate asparagus with luxury and yet this vegetable isn't hard to grow, and an asparagus bed should remain productive for several decades. The sooner you start, the sooner you can enjoy your own succulent spears.

Asparagus is best when you cook it immediately after cutting. Steaming or boiling works best, ideally upright so the tops of the spears are out of the water, for about ten minutes, until a sharp knife easily pierces the stems.

Asparagus is both delicious and nutritious! It contains vitamins A, B1, B2, B6, C, E and K, as well as biotin, folic acid and nicotinic acid.

Sowing and cultivating asparagus

The most important consideration when growing asparagus is where to plant it in soil that's free from perennial weeds. Asparagus is a long-term crop, so think ahead before you plant and, if necessary, wait a year before doing so to enable you to clear the soil of weeds. Removing bindweed, ground elder, creeping thistle and mare's tail, for example, from the soil after planting asparagus is very difficult.

Because asparagus needs good drainage it grows best in light soil. although it does grow in well-drained heavy clay soils, too. Therefore, in light soils you can plant asparagus on flat ground but if the soil is heavy or rather wet, you need to plant on mounds (ridges) 15 centimetres above the natural soil level. Prepare the ground well beforehand, by digging in lots of organic matter.

You can grow asparagus from seed or buy one-year-old *crowns* (roots) to give you a one-year head start. Garden centres usually sell crowns, but often keep them too warm, leading to the crowns sprouting in their packs. So, if you choose to grow crowns, the best option is to order them from a specialist supplier (see Chapter 3 for a list of these).

Here's how to grow a bumper crop of asparagus:

1. **Depending on the method you choose, either plant crowns or sow seeds and then plant out the seedlings.** Each plant produces only a few spears at any one time, so you need to plant a minimum of 20 plants or crowns to be able to provide enough for a meal for two or more people.

   • **Sow seeds in spring, soaking them in warm water for 24 hours beforehand.** Sow one seed per small pot and keep in a temperature of 20°C until they germinate.

   At first the seedlings look like stalks of grass but, at three or four months old, they're ready to plant out, 40 centimetres apart.

   • **If you're planting crowns instead of seeds, do so in early spring, setting them out 40 centimetres apart with 1 metre between rows if possible.** Take the top 8 centimetres off the top of the ridge (on heavy soils), spread the roots of the crowns evenly over the soil, and cover them with the soil you removed.

2. **Keep the plants free from all weeds, especially in the first year and water them in dry.**

3. **At the end of autumn, cut down the stems to ground level.**

4. **In the second year, spread, to a depth of 5 centimetres, compost or well rotted manure and some general fertiliser around the plants just as they start to grow.** Keep them free from weeds.

Apart from slugs and snails, the other major pest that affects asparagus is asparagus beetle – a small, black beetle with red and yellow spots, whose larvae strips the foliage off plants and weakens them. You can use sprays based on bifenthrin to control them.

Harvesting and storing your asparagus

Although you may be able to harvest a few spears in the second year, during May, you're best off waiting until the spring of the third year to allow the plants to build up strength and get established. The cropping period then is from early May to mid-June – a period of about six weeks.

You can cut the spears when they're about 15 centimetres high, by pushing a sharp knife under the soil. Try to go over the beds every few days, cutting the spears when they've grown to about 15–20 centimetres above the soil. After mid-June allow all the shoots to mature and don't cut them, so that the plants can build up strength for the following year.

Part of the joy of this crop is that its season is short, and because asparagus doesn't store well, you need to try and eat it as soon after cutting as possible. You can freeze asparagus but it isn't very good.

Choosing varieties

Asparagus plants are male or female. Most gardeners consider modern, all-male varieties of asparagus to crop more heavily than older varieties. Female varieties produce small, red berries that may seed into the beds, making them crowded and diverting the plant's energies from building up the crowns.

Here is a handful of good asparagus varieties:

- ✓ **Backlim F1** is an all-male variety, with thick spears and high yields.

- ✓ **Connover's Colossal** is an established variety with thick spears of excellent flavour.

- ✓ **Gijnlim F1** is an all-male variety that crops very heavily and is early too, beating most other varieties for the first crop of the year.

- ✓ **Jersey Knight F1** is a vigorous, all-male variety with heavy crops of purple-tipped spears.

- ✓ **Stewart's Purple** is one of the new purple varieties that often taste sweeter and have less fibre than the green types. Steaming retains the purple colour.

Stick to it: Celery

If you fancy a challenge, try growing celery – one of the most difficult vegetables to grow well. You can choose from two basic types: trench celery, which is the most difficult, but also the most hardy and delicious; and self-blanching celery, which is the most popular because it grows more quickly and involves less work. Both are ready at about the same time, in late summer and autumn.

Most people usually eat celery raw but it's also excellent when chopped and boiled or braised in stock. Celery also makes a good addition to stews and you can make it into soup.

The thick base at the bottom of the celery is rarely present in shop-bought celery but tastes delicious. You can enjoy it as a treat if you grow your own.

Celery is famously low in calories and contains vitamins A, B1, B2, B6, C, E and K.

Sowing and cultivating celery

Celery needs a rich, moist and, slightly acidic soil that never dries out. For celery to grow well, you need to add lots of organic matter to that soil to add nutrients and help retain moisture. Here's what you need to do next:

1. **Sow the small seeds in pots or trays, covering with vermiculite or perlite (expanded rock particles). Keep them in a propagator at a temperature of about 20°C.** Celery needs a long growing season, and therefore sow in spring, in the greenhouse or on the windowsill.

2. **When the seedlings produce their first true leaf, transplant them into small cell trays or seed trays 2 centimetres apart.**

3. **Plant out the seedlings in late spring when the last frosts are likely to be over.** The way to do this depends on which type of celery you grow:

   • **Self-blanching celery.** Gardeners usually plant self-blanching celery in a block, 25 centimetres apart in all directions so that the foliage at the top of the stems keeps some light off the stalks. These plants are sensitive to the cold, so cover them with fleece if frost is forecast. Water the plants regularly and keep weeds under control, although as the plants crowd together they tend to keep weeds under control naturally. Pull off old leaves as they die.

   • **Trench celery.** Dig a trench about 15 centimetres deep and 30 centimetres wide and plant the seedlings in the base, about 40 centimetres apart. Being in a trench it's easy to water the plants by flooding the trench. They must never be short of water. Try to keep weeds under control at all times.

   In late summer, when the plants are almost fully grown, remember to *blanch* the celery to make the stems white and more tender. Pull or cut off dead leaves and any side shoots at the base of the plants. Cut out and wrap some newspaper, corrugated cardboard or thick black plastic around the whole length of the stalks, leaving the leaves free at the top. Tie it firmly in place and fill in the trench, earthing up the soil around the stems. The blanching material protects your celery from cold until it's ready for harvesting and eating a month later.

Harvesting and storing your celery

Self-blanching celery is a vegetable to use in autumn and early winter before the first frost damages it. You can harvest trench celery as you need it through the winter, however, but it tastes better before Christmas.

When harvesting, dig up plants, remove the blanching material, pull off the outer leaves and any slugs, and wash them well. Trim the roots and leaves and you can then eat them straight away!

Choosing varieties

Here are a few good varieties of self-blanching celery:

- ✔ **Loretta F1** is a tall variety with a sweet flavour and thick, smooth stems with reduced stringiness.
- ✔ **Octavius F1** is a strong grower with green stalks. This variety is slow to bolt in dry conditions.
- ✔ **Victoria F1** is bred specifically for the UK climate, and produces pale, crisp stems with good flavour.

If you prefer trying your hand at the trickier, but tastier trench celery, consider growing these excellent varieties:

- ✔ **Solid Pink** is an old variety with red-tinged stalks and good flavour.
- ✔ **Hopkins Fenlander** is a crisp, tasty variety with white stems when blanched, and stands cold in early winter better than most, so is ideal for late crops.

Beside the seaside: Seakale

Seakale, or *Crambe maritima*, is more often seen as a feature of flowerbeds than on dinner plates, which is a shame because blanched seakale makes a tasty treat, and an unusual one, too. To blanch it, all you do is put an upturned pot over the mature plants in spring so the new leaves are deprived of light and are tender. As a bonus, seakale is an easy-to-grow perennial vegetable that you can harvest for many years without much effort, so do consider giving it some space on your plot.

Seakale's thick, rubbery, grey leaves are inedible when mature, but the blanched leaves and flower stems taste great. Try steaming them, and serving with sauce or butter.

Seakale is low in calories and contains some vitamin C.

Sowing and cultivating seakale

Seakale needs full sun and a very well-drained, light, and sandy soil. It doesn't tolerate wet soils, and being a brassica is susceptible to clubroot (see Chapter 7), and so a limy soil is also preferable.

Most people grow seakale from seed. However, if you can find them, you can also try growing seakale plants from *thongs* (root cuttings). Thongs produce a harvest more quickly than seeds.

Here's how to grow a crop of seakale:

1. **Sow seeds in individual pots or cells in spring in a tray filled with loam-based seed compost.** Keep them in a temperature of 18°C or more.

2. **Plant out in early summer when the plants have filled the pot with roots. Set the plants 45 centimetres apart.**

   If you're using thongs, plant them where they are to grow, 45 centimetres apart, with the tops just below the surface.

3. **Water your plants well and keep them free from weeds in the first year while they establish.**

4. **In autumn, remove the dead foliage.**

5. **To produce a crop, blanch the plant after the second season. Cut off the foliage, and cover the crowns with straw in autumn. In late winter or early spring, before you see signs of new leaves growing, cover the plant with an upturned, large pot (with the drainage hole covered) or a forcing pot (similar to an upturned pot, designed for rhubarb).** A month or so later, the plant produces creamy white, often pink-tinged leaves that you can cut off and eat.

Mature plants produce domes of honey-scented, small white flowers. The plants benefit if you remove these as quickly as possible, before they open, so they don't waste energy producing flowers and seeds that they don't need.

Harvesting and storing your seakale

You can cut off the blanched leaves when they're about 25 centimetres high. You can even cut and eat the creamy white, pink-tinged developing flower stems, too. When harvesting your seakale, take care not to remove all the leaves. By removing the pot and allowing at least a third of the leaves to mature you enable the plant to regain its strength again for the following year. Seakale doesn't store well.

Choosing varieties

Seakale is such a minor crop that few varieties have been developed. The only variety you're likely to find is Lilywhite, which has less pink colouring in the blanched leaves than wild seakale.

Trying Something Different

While just a few vegetables make up the majority of the food that most people eat, lots of other rarities exist just waiting for you to discover them. These rarities may be new and unexplored, at least in the UK, or were once popular but have since fallen from favour, usually because of an unusual taste or a need for long preparation. Perhaps the time has come to give these a try. Not all of them will be a hit with you but you may discover something you really like and find it becoming a regular on your plot.

A blast from the past: Cardoons

Few people eat cardoons (*Cynara cardunculus*) nowadays but it's an easy vegetable to grow and if you forget to harvest it, your garden becomes all the more beautiful, producing large heads of purple flowers, very like artichokes. Cardoons are very closely related to globe artichokes but, instead of eating the flower buds, you blanch and eat the leaves.

Cardoons are large plants and take up a lot of space, and so they work best in large gardens or on allotments.

Cardoons have a mild flavour but are a useful late-autumn vegetable. Cooks trim and chop the thick, white leaf stalks into 4–5-centimetre sections and poach them in stock or parboil and fry them. Alternatively, many people boil them, in water containing added lemon juice, and serve them with butter or white sauce, or added to tomato and pasta dishes.

Cardoons contain some vitamin C and minerals and are low in calories.

Sowing and cultivating cardoons

Cardoons prefer a well-drained soil in a sunny spot, and you can grow them in exactly the same way as for globe artichokes. Growing from seed and avoiding the plant producing flowering stems works best, because these stems make the crop inedible. If you prefer, you can buy young plants but cardoons are easy to grow from seed and plants aren't commonly available.

Here are the steps to take:

1. **Sow seeds in early spring in a temperature of about 20°C exactly as you would with globe artichokes.** (See 'Going global: Globe artichokes' earlier in the chapter.)

2. **Transplant the seedlings into small pots and keep them in good light.**
   You can do this when they've filled the pot with roots, which is usually when the plants have three or four leaves.

3. **Plant seedlings 40 centimetres apart where they are to grow.**

Harvesting and storing your cardoons

At the end of the summer, remember to prepare your plants for cropping by tying the leaves together in a tight bundle and wrapping newspaper or cardboard around them. In this way you blanch the leaves by excluding light from the centre of the plants. Blanching takes about two months, after which you can dig up the roots and cut away the outer foliage. The inner, pale leaf stalks, that look like giant but slightly felty celery, are for eating.

Cardoons aren't a crop that you can store.

Choosing varieties

Sadly, you have no alternative varieties of cardoon to choose from – just the one, common form exists. You can buy the seeds from most seed catalogues – often, oddly, in the herb section.

Going gumbo: Okra

Okra (also known as *lady's fingers* or *gumbo* and botanically as *Abelmoschus esculentus*) is a beautiful plant that you see rarely in gardens and allotments but, with care, you can grow it at home. This tender, annual plant grows from seed each year and the large, yellow, attractive flowers come just before the long, five-angled pods. Okra is a plant for the greenhouse or polytunnel in most areas but in mild areas you can grow it outdoors in a sheltered spot.

You can eat okra whole or, with older pods, by slicing it. You can fry or add okra to sauces where its mucilage thickens the liquid. This sounds unpleasant but is a useful quality. You can also add okra to chutneys, use it in Indian cuisine, or coat it in breadcrumbs for deep frying as is done in the American southern states.

Okra is low in calories and rich in vitamins A and C and many minerals, including calcium, phosphorus, potassium, magnesium and iron, as well as folic acid and thiamin.

Sowing and cultivating okra

Generally, you cultivate okra in a similar way to peppers and tomatoes, in pots of multipurpose compost, in grow bags, or in the open ground. If you go with the latter option, improving the soil beforehand with plenty of organic matter helps. The plants don't need training other than staking as they grow to stop them falling over, but they do need warmth and plenty of sun, water and feeding. Dry conditions lead to poor growth and in cold weather only a few fruits form. In cold, wet weather the fruits grow very slowly.

Here are the steps to take for cultivating a crop of okra:

1. **Sow seeds in early spring in a temperature of 20°C in a propagator kept in a greenhouse.**

2. **When the seedlings appear, transplant them into cell trays or small pots and grow in light, warm conditions.**

3. **When the plants are 15 centimetres high, you can plant them out, making sure that they're not frosted; while growing, keep them as warm as possible.** Don't take them out of the greenhouse until late May at the earliest. For best results and a decent crop, you need to grow them, throughout their lives, in a greenhouse or polytunnel.

Okra plants are prone to red spider mite under glass, to aphids and to whitefly. Chapter 7 offers tips on dealing with this unwelcome attention.

Harvesting and storing your okra

You can cut the pods off the plants when they're less than a week old – after the blossom drops. If you leave them any longer they become tough. Use them as soon as possible because they rapidly wilt and shrivel.

Choosing varieties

Here are a couple of worthwhile varieties:

- ✔ **Burgundy Red** is a good variety to eat and to look at, with red stems and pods.
- ✔ **Clemson's Spineless** is the standard variety, with green pods.

Pretty and dainty: Asparagus peas

If you see photographs of this pretty little plant you may just be tempted to try it, especially when you read that the pods taste of asparagus. But although asparagus pea is attractive and easy to grow, don't expect to grow fat on this dainty vegetable – the pods are small and crops are light.

You don't need to do anything with asparagus peas other than topping and tailing the pods, and steaming or boiling them for a few minutes. The downside is that you need hundreds of them to feed a family!

The pods contain some minerals and vitamins A and C. The mature seeds contain protein but few people eat these.

Sowing and cultivating asparagus peas

Asparagus peas prefer a light soil and a warm, sunny spot but prefer not to be too dry, so digging in organic matter before planting is beneficial. The plants trail and don't need support. After a while, they produce deep red flowers that develop into the edible pods. The plants have a long cropping season, continuing to grow and produce flowers and pods over many months.

Here's how to sow a productive crop of asparagus peas:

1. **Sow seeds 1 centimetre deep either where the plant is to crop, or in pots.** If you choose the former, sow the seeds 10 centimetres apart in single or double rows, in late spring. If you go with pots, sow three seeds in each one, in mid-spring. Keep them in a temperature of 21°C.

2. **If you've sown the seeds in pots, plant out the seedlings, 20–30 centimetres apart, when they're about 10 centimetres tall.**

Harvesting and storing your asparagus peas

Asparagus peas get tough quickly, so you need to pick over your plants regularly. The pods are small and have four, leafy ribs along the sides and are ready to pick when they reach about 3 centimetres long. If you leave them to grow longer they become tough and stringy. At the end of the season you can simply pull up and compost the plants.

Choosing varieties

Sadly, no alternative varieties of asparagus pea plant are available, but at least that means you don't have to spend time agonising over which type to grow!

Part IV
Growing Your Own Fruit Salad

'That's the one drawback with growing coconuts.'

In this part . . .

Growing your own strawberries, pears or peaches may seem an impractical dream, but you can grow at least some fruits in any garden. Even traditional allotment crops such as gooseberries and redcurrants can find their place in the smallest garden or in pots on the patio. Seemingly exotic crops such as peaches and apricots are hardy and, with the introduction of new varieties, are getting easier to grow. With a little planning, your garden can be delighting you with fruit from June to October and, with apples and pears, for even longer. If you fancy picking your own sweet strawberries, exotic Cape gooseberries and aromatic melons, or sinking your teeth in the soft, melting flesh of a pear, content in the knowledge that you've grown them, start reading here.

Chapter 13

Fruit in a Flash: Planting Quick-Growing Fruit

In This Chapter

▶ Making summer special with strawberries and raspberries

▶ Growing quick fruits from seed

▶ Cultivating scrumptious melons of all sizes and flavours

*Y*ou may think that the only way to grow your own fruit is to hope that your parents planted an apple tree for you. However, while some fruits do take a while to start producing a decent crop, others will give you something to smile about within as little as a few months. For example, if you want an easy fruit that gives you something delicious to eat within a few months you can start with strawberries. Success here can give you the confidence to move onto other fruits that take a little longer to produce their crops and that need a bit more care, including pruning. Raspberries are the perfect crop to move onto next and when you've succeeded with these, which is more or less assured if you follow the advice I give you in this chapter, you'll be well on your way to growing all sorts of tasty and healthy fruits.

Growing fruit is a never-ending journey, but every step is full of sweet treats.

Creating Summer Treats

Summer fruits – especially strawberries and raspberries – are perhaps the most keenly anticipated of all crops, and unlike many other fruit, they can give really quick results. You can have strawberries ripe in your garden within just a few months from planting and, if you pick the right varieties, you can have raspberries the same year you plant them, too.

Succulent and summery: Strawberries

Nothing beats the taste of your own home-grown strawberries. You can choose to grow your own for their freshness or for the joy of picking them at their peak of ripeness. But, for me, the main reason for growing strawberries is that you can choose varieties that actually have taste! I never understand why out-of-season, imported strawberries are so popular. So many of these varieties taste nothing like strawberries and have the texture of turnips! Commercial growers select those varieties for heavy cropping and resistance to disease rather than taste, but by growing your own you can choose 'uncommercial' varieties that shops don't sell because they're too soft and don't travel well, but that taste delicious.

Of course, you can make strawberries into jam or cook them on their own or with other fruits (especially rhubarb) to make some delicious puddings and tarts, but they're surely best for eating fresh!

Strawberries aren't just delicious, they really are good for you. Five large strawberries contain as much vitamin C as an orange and they also contain iron and fibre, B vitamins including nicotinic and folic acid, biotin and antioxidants. Grow them and enjoy!

Planting and cultivating strawberries

You can buy strawberries in many ways. You can find them in garden centres at any time of the year, although the choice of varieties they offer is usually very limited, and you can buy potted plants by mail order at most times of year. Fruit specialists that offer the widest variety of choice may also sell potted plants but more often sell bare-root, young plants in a bundle without any soil. Unlike potted plants, which you can leave in their pots for several weeks, you need to plant these bare-root plants straight away. Another method is to buy some increasingly popular cold-stored runners to plant between spring and mid-July, which crop within two months. *Runners* are young plants on trailing stems.

If you choose to grow alpine strawberries you can buy them as plants or grow them from seed. You can also grow a few normal strawberries from seed but these are generally inferior to plants, and so you're best off giving the seeds a miss. (Jump to the 'Choosing varieties' section later on for the lowdown on different types of strawberry.)

Along with most soft fruit, and especially raspberries, checking that you buy only certified, virus-free stock is vital. Both fruits are prone to virus diseases that reduce vigour and cropping and buying cheap plants that may carry disease is a waste of money and time. If in doubt, buy only from fruit specialists.

Strawberries are very adaptable and grow happily in hanging baskets, pots and grow bags, although you can achieve the heaviest crops by planting them in the garden bed. Plants usually crop moderately in the first year, best in the second year, and then less in the third year, after which you can discard or replant them. In pots and containers their cropping life is shorter because of the restricted room and nutrients in the compost.

The ideal soil for strawberries is slightly acid and free-draining. Chalky and heavy soils aren't ideal, although they do support crops if you first improve them with grit and organic matter. Try also to plant them in a site in full sun, to enable the plants to grow well and the berries to ripen fully. A nearby source of water is useful because the plants often need extra water in early summer to help the fruits swell if the weather is dry.

Here are the steps to follow to grow strawberries from bought plants:

1. **Prepare the soil well, whatever its nature and condition, by removing all perennial weeds and digging in lots of organic matter before planting. Add some fish, blood and bone, or other general fertiliser, a week before planting.**

2. **Plant out your strawberry plants.** If you're planting them in your garden, the best time to do this is between March and September. (Try to avoid planting between October and February because they don't make growth at that time and the small plants are vulnerable to winter damage.) Space the plants 40 centimetres apart with rows 90 centimetres apart. This arrangement enables you to get easily among them for picking and routine care. On heavy soils, pull the soil into slight ridges and plant on the raised parts to improve drainage around the crowns of the plants, especially in winter.

Make sure that you don't plant strawberry plants too deeply – the crown, where the base of the plant connects to the roots, should be just below soil level. When planted too deeply they don't thrive. If planting bare-root plants, use a trowel to make a hole deep enough to take the roots without bending them, spread the roots out well in the hole, replace the soil, and firm it well with your hands or knuckles.

Alternatively, you may grow your plants in a container. Varieties vary in plant size but generally six to eight plants fill a large grow bag, three plants are ample for a 40-centimetre basket, and a single plant needs a 20-centimetre diameter pot. Strawberry pots, despite their name, aren't ideal because watering can be difficult, but you can buy stacking pots that are far more effective.

If you decide to grow strawberries in a container, the good news is that you can plant them all year round, using a good-quality compost such as John Innes No 3.

3. **After planting, water the plants immediately, and keep the young plants free of weeds and water them regularly.** Be especially attentive to plants in containers and any that you planted between April and September when high temperatures cause fast growth and make the need for water that much greater.

4. **Depending on when you planted your plants, remove/leave the first blooms.** If you planted them in spring you may want to remove the first flowers that appear, to allow the plants to concentrate on growing. If you planted cold-stored runners, where the point is to get a fast crop, you can leave the flowers on to produce a quick crop. If you planted your strawberry plants in late summer, when fruits may not develop fully because of the impending frosts, removing any flowers that appear in September or October is definitely a good plan because those fruits wouldn't have a chance to develop.

   Bees pollinate these flowers and, unless a late spring frost strikes, when the centre of the blooms turn black (putting fleece over the plants if they are in flower may prevent this), fruits will develop soon after the petals drop from the flowers. Misshapen fruits are the result of uneven pollination and although you can do little to prevent this, the fruits are still edible.

5. **Protect the fruits as they develop.** The fruits often hang onto the soil and get dirty. Gardeners usually spread straw around the plants but you can buy 'mats' or just use cardboard or newspaper.

   Also remember to protect the fruits from slugs and snails. As soon as the fruits start to turn red they attract the attention of blackbirds who peck at as many fruits as they can find. Netting is the best protection, but don't leave any gaps or the cunning birds are sure to find a way in!

You can also grow strawberries from seed – a useful way to raise alpine strawberries, which are smaller than normal strawberry plants but have an intense flavour. They should produce a few fruits the first year and lots for the following years. Here are the steps to follow:

1. **Fill pots with multipurpose compost, water thoroughly and sow the seeds thinly but evenly on the surface.** Do this in spring.

2. **Cover the seeds with a little compost and put the pot in a warm place, such as on a windowsill or in a propagator, in a temperature of about 20°C.**

3. **Transplant the seedlings into small (8-centimetre) pots.**

4. **When, after a few months and in early summer, the seedlings have filled the compost with roots, plant them in the garden in full sun or part shade.**

You can *force* strawberries (or in other words, bring them into growth early) to get an early crop if you grow some in pots and bring them into a cool or cold greenhouse in February or March, after you've subjected the plants to cold temperatures for a few months over winter. They grow more quickly in the greenhouse and flower and fruit earlier. Make sure you water and give them liquid fertiliser once a week to sustain growth and check that the greenhouse door or vents are open when the plants are in flower to allow bees to pollinate the flowers and ensure a crop of fruit.

Harvesting, storing and propagating your strawberries

You can pick strawberries as soon as they're fully ripe, which means going over the plants every day for two or three weeks. Afterwards, you can store them in the freezer, but defrosted strawberries go mushy. Frozen strawberries are best for smoothies, whizzed up while still cold.

After you pick the fruits, the plants usually start to produce runners. Unless you need to grow more plants, cut off these runners straight away to stop them diverting energy from the main plant. If you leave runners to root and grow, they crowd the beds, meaning that you get smaller fruits more prone to mould because of the dense mass of foliage. By late summer the plants look miserable and their foliage may be covered with grey mildew.

Because a strawberry plant is only really productive for two or three years, you may well want to propagate new plants yourself so you can keep on enjoying them for another few years! You do this by *rooting* the runners that grow from the main plants: by leaving some to run across the soil and root where they want or by rooting them in pots. If you let them run free you have to wait until September before you can carefully dig them up, cut off the runner, and move them to the new bed. A better option is to sink a pot of compost in the soil where a plantlet is growing on the runner, peg the plantlet in the compost with a bent wire, and nip off the end of the runner to stop it making yet more plants! Keep the pot moist at all times, and after a month you can lift the pot from the soil and sever the new plant from its mum.

Strawberries are prone to virus diseases spread by aphids (greenfly) that reduce yields dramatically. Don't propagate from any plants that show yellow mottling of the leaves or look stunted – sure signs that greenfly have paid your plants a visit. Chapter 7 tells you more about pests and diseases.

Any time after cropping, remember to shear the leaves off, rake up the straw, and give a high potash fertiliser, and healthy new growth will appear. You can add the straw and leaves to the compost heap. You may need to tidy the plants again in autumn and spring, removing runners and dead leaves that encourage slugs.

Choosing varieties

Basically three types of strawberry exist. The most popular are the summer-fruiting varieties, followed by perpetual strawberries, the 'day-neutral' kinds, and the tiny alpine strawberries.

Summer-fruiting strawberries are the most varied group. You can choose from early, mid-, and late season varieties, and between giants, some with excellent flavour, and old-fashioned types with smaller, but delicious berries. Many are suitable for forcing, to obtain crops a month earlier than you get outside in the garden. Summer-fruiting varieties usually crop between mid-June and late July, each over a two- or three-week period. Here are some of the best:

- **Alice** is a late variety with attractive, sweet and juicy orange-red berries and with good resistance to disease.

- **Cambridge Favourite** is a mid-season variety with heavy crops of well-flavoured fruits.

- **Elsanta** is a mid-season variety and the most popular strawberry of all. Elsanta produces heavy crops of orange-red, firm berries of reasonable flavour, but it isn't particularly resistant to disease.

- **Florence** is an excellent late variety, resistant to diseases and pests, with heavy crops of fine flavour.

- **Gariguette** is an early variety. This French strawberry is a weak grower and has light crops but the slender, dark red berries have soft flesh and an amazing flavour.

- **Mae** is an early variety that has more berries than most other early strawberries. The soft, sweet, juicy berries have good flavour.

- **Rhapsody** is a late variety with lots of good qualities including health, heavy yields and excellent flavour.

- **Royal Sovereign** is an early variety that does well on heavy soils and is tops for flavour but isn't a heavy cropper and is prone to disease.

- **Sonata** is a mid-season variety. Another alternative to Elsanta, Sonata has bigger berries, is more able to cope with wet and hot weather, and has a sweeter flavour.

- **Tenira** is a mid-season variety that crops heavily in the first year but then declines rather quickly. The attractive berries have good flavour, and the upright growth holds them off the soil.

Perpetual strawberries produce a few flowers and fruit over many months, from summer into autumn, if you water and feed them well. Gardeners often remove the earliest flowers to prevent fruiting, so that the plants have plenty of energy to crop in autumn, when other varieties finish cropping.

- **Aromel** is an old variety still popular because of its good flavour, although it's not a heavy cropper and can get mildew.

- **Bolero** is a vigorous plant with excellent-quality fruits that have good flavour.

- **Calypso** has large, juicy fruits with good texture and flavour. This variety has compact growth that crops well and is resistant to disease.

- **Flamenco** has heavy crops of large, sweet berries and is resistant to disease.

- **Mara de Bois** is an exceptional variety that has heavy crops of berries with wonderful, rich flavour, and is resistant to mildew.

Everbearers, or *day-neutral strawberries*, are the type available in supermarkets all year round and, if you keep them warm enough, in pots or grow bags in a greenhouse in the UK, they can crop at any time. In fact, they crop over such a long period that gardeners usually discard them after a year because the plants exhaust themselves. You can buy day-neutral plants only from specialists.

When you compare day-neutral strawberries to some of the other varieties, they seem tough and tasteless to me, but are worth growing (six to eight plants in a grow bag or one in a 15-centimetre pot) if you want fresh strawberries in December or March. Here are a couple of varieties:

- **Diamante** is a very compact plant that produces heavy crops over at least three months.

- **Selva** produces firm, deep red fruits. Some single plants have produced more than 3 kilograms of strawberries!

Alpine strawberries are small plants with tiny berries that aren't particularly juicy but are packed with flavour. They're tougher than ordinary strawberries but don't produce runners, so are easier to maintain. Gardeners grow alpine strawberries to add some variety to the more normal types, and to add some good old-fashioned taste. You can grow them from seed.

Here are a couple of nice varieties:

- **Alba** produces tasty, white fruits that birds ignore.

- **Baron Solemacher** is the standard alpine strawberry with aromatic, small fruits.

Fruit for the masses: Raspberries

People grow their own fruit for various reasons: perhaps for freshness or for the knowledge that what they grow is free from chemical sprays. However, one alternative and very good reason to grow raspberries is that they are just *so* expensive in the shops! Raspberries aren't designed to be sold in supermarkets. You have to squeeze the fruit gently to pick it and because raspberries are so delicate and susceptible to damage in transit, you have to buy more packaging than fruit in the shops! Even then you often find a good number of squashed berries, so by growing your own, you really do get much better raspberries than those you could buy in the shops.

Many people choose to blow a raspberry at supermarket prices and put them at the top of their lists of fruit to grow. They crop well, are hardy, produce a crop in a relatively short time, and most importantly, raspberries are delicious and good for you! Their fruits have a bit more tang and more obvious pips than strawberries, but raspberries are a wonderful treat for the summer.

Raspberries are best for eating fresh. You can make good jam and conserves with them, but raspberries are surely best with cream and meringues. They make a great addition to smoothies, too!

Raspberries are low in calories and rich in vitamins A, B1, B2, B6, C, E and K, as well as antioxidants and folic and nicotinic acid.

Planting and cultivating raspberries

Raspberries prefer a slightly acid, well-drained soil and don't do well in very alkaline soils or any that are wet or waterlogged in winter. To give your plants the best chance of doing well, digging in as much organic matter as possible before you plant is a good idea. This preparation improves the soil and can help to make it more acidic. Garden compost, well-rotted manure, leaf mould and recycled compost is all suitable but avoid mushroom compost because it contains some lime, which raspberries don't like. A sunny spot is best, but summer raspberries do tolerate a little shade. Autumn raspberries need full sun because the sun is weaker at that time of year, when the berries are ripening. Remembering to remove all perennial weeds before you plant is important because they're difficult to remove afterwards.

Raspberries aren't grown from seed, but from stems called *canes* which get dug up and planted to establish new plants. Garden centres usually sell canes bare-root, from autumn to spring. Sometimes they sell pots of canes to keep the roots moist. These pots are a good buy while the plants are dormant but don't buy them when they're in leaf because you can't separate them without causing damage. When you have your canes ready, just follow these steps:

1. **Plant the canes 40–45 centimetres apart in rows.** If you're planting more than one row, space these 2 metres apart. Make sure the roots are 5 centimetres below the soil surface. Planting any deeper may prevent growth. Early spring is the best time of year to plant raspberries.

2. **Give the plants some support!** All varieties, except autumn raspberries, need some sort of support. Spacing fence posts 2–3 metres apart with horizontal wires 1 metre and 1.5 metres above the soil works fine. You can tie the canes to these with twine in spring as they grow.

3. **Water your plants regularly.** This is especially important in the first season.

4. **After planting, cut down the canes (see Figure 13-1).** Otherwise leave them for the first year. After planting, mulch with more compost or manure.

By the end of the year the canes may be tall, in which case you can take the tops out to keep them at less than about 2 metres. The plants shouldn't need additional feeding the first year but, if the soil is poor and sandy, it may be worth giving a dressing of pelleted chicken manure in spring to add some nitrogen for the first season. In following years, giving a high potash fertiliser and another mulch, each spring, is well worthwhile.

Raspberry beetle can be a problem with raspberry plants, resulting in maggots in the fruits (see Chapter 7 for advice on dealing with this pest). Autumn varieties are rarely affected, because they ripen after the insect has finished breeding. Birds are the biggest problem, though. Blackbirds strip the ripe berries from the plants and you need to drape net over the plants or grow them in a fruit cage to beat these feathered fiends.

If you feed and mulch your plants well and dig out shoots that grow too far from the main row, your raspberries should crop well for about ten years. After that, cropping starts to decrease and you need to plant new canes in new soil.

Harvesting and storing your raspberries

Raspberries ripen over many weeks and you need to go over the plants every day and pick the ripe fruits, squeezing them gently as you pull them from the plant. They freeze well after picking – more so than strawberries – although they do lose their texture.

Raspberries may contain the small maggots of raspberry beetles but you can easily remove them by soaking the picked fruits in cold, salty water for a few minutes, which makes the maggots crawl out of the fruits, and then rinse them in cold water before eating.

Growing raspberries in pots

You can grow autumn raspberries in pots but be prepared for a lot of work. You need to fill a large pot at least 60 centimetres wide and deep with lime-free John Innes compost, and put in three to five canes. Remember to water the plants at all times and feed them well. By doing this you should get a reasonable crop for a few years.

Choosing varieties

You can choose from two basic types of raspberry: *summer-fruiting* and *autumn-fruiting*. Summer-fruiting is the most common type, with berries ready to harvest in July and August. They have a very simple method of growth, which is common to many other summer fruits, including blackberries and tayberries. The stems are *biennial*, which means they live for two years. In the first year they grow up from the soil, reaching their full height. You leave them over winter without pruning, unless they grow too tall, in which case you can trim the tops off to keep them at less than about 2 metres. In the following year these upright stems produce short side shoots that flower and produce the fruits. After picking the fruits, any time from autumn to winter you can cut back the stems to the ground. By then, a new set of upright canes have grown and these crop the next year. You may need to thin them out so that they're 15 centimetres apart and, because new shoots grow up from the roots some distance from your main row, you may need to dig up stems that grow in the wrong place.

In short, if you plant summer raspberries in the spring of year one, you'll be picking some more in the summer of year two and lots more in year three!

Some raspberry varieties are *spineless*. No – they aren't as cowardly as they sound! Whereas most raspberries have small thorns up the canes and on the leaves, which can make picking and pruning a painful process, some modern spineless varieties have no thorns or very few, so are easier and more pleasant to handle.

Here are some of the most popular varieties of summer-fruiting raspberry, which are ready to pick in July and August:

- ✔ **Glen Ample** is a spineless, mid-season producer of very heavy crops of large berries over a long period. I highly recommend Glen Ample, but it does need good soil to thrive, and doesn't like cold areas.

- ✔ **Glen Lyon** is a spineless, mid-season variety that produces heavy crops of tangy, bright red fruits. Avoid planting Glen Lyon in heavy or poor soils.

✔ **Glen Magna** is a late variety, and is almost spineless. The large crops of big, dark red fruits have excellent flavour.

✔ **Glen Moy** is an early, spineless variety. The easily manageable, upright canes produce heavy crops of large, well-flavoured, berries.

✔ **Glen Prosen** is a spineless mid-season heavy-cropper with exceptional flavour and compact canes.

✔ **Leo** is a late, healthy variety with heavy crops of medium-sized, tasty berries.

✔ **Malling Minerva** is a spineless early variety that produces high yields. This compact variety is resistant to most problems and the medium-sized berries taste good.

✔ **Octavia** is a very late, slightly spiny variety that produces heavy crops of tasty berries all the way up the sturdy canes.

✔ **Tulameen** is a late, vigorous raspberry with attractive, tasty berries and an exceptionally long picking season – usually of six weeks.

Autumn-fruiting or *primocane* varieties used to be less common than the summer varieties but are becoming very popular now for several reasons. Unlike traditional raspberries, autumn fruiters send up shoots from the soil in spring that not only reach their full height in one year but also start to produce side shoots in July or August of the same year; these produce berries from late summer until the first frosts of autumn. After picking, you need to cut the stems down to the ground, as I show in Figure 13-1. Simple!

Figure 13-1:
Cut down the canes immediately after planting. At the end of the season, simply cut all the canes back to ground level.

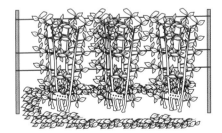

Autumn varieties also tend to be more sturdy and need less support than summer raspberries. They also make the best choice for growing raspberries in containers, although this takes some doing. The good thing to remember is that if you plant them in spring you can expect a small crop the very first year and a good crop in the second.

Here are some good varieties to consider:

- ✔ **Autumn Bliss** canes are sturdy and rarely need support. This variety produces heavy crops of large berries in August and September.

- ✔ **Fallgold** or **Allgold** produces tasty, sweet, yellow berries of medium size for almost two months that are more attractive to birds than other varieties!

- ✔ **Himbo Top** is an almost spineless Swiss variety that crops heavily, and has huge berries that you can pick for two months.

- ✔ **Joan J** is an exceptional spineless variety with large, well-flavoured berries. The fruit is bigger and the crops heavier than with Autumn Bliss.

- ✔ **Polka** is a vigorous new variety with large, bright, tangy berries for harvesting over a very long season. Very hardy and easy to grow.

Never accept unnamed, old canes from friends, no matter how attractive some free plants may seem! Raspberries are prone to viruses spread by aphids, which cause the leaves to have yellow mottling and the yields to be lower. Modern varieties are often resistant to some viruses and to the aphids, and so are much better to grow in the long term.

Growing Fruit from Seed

If time is of the essence and you want quick results, this section is for you. Here, I introduce you to a few plants that produce a crop within a few months from sowing seeds. Most of them need a greenhouse or polytunnel to do well but they may survive and crop on a warm, sheltered patio. All are worth a try and may well become regular residents of your garden.

Not just a pretty face: Cape gooseberries

An annual or short-lived perennial (*Physalis edulis*) from South America, cape gooseberry gets its common name from the fact that it was enormously popular among the residents of the Cape of Good Hope. With their protective, papery husks, cape gooseberries hardly look edible until you tear or split them, and peel them back to reveal the round, golden fruit inside. Yes, this beauty is the fruit that restaurants leave on your plate, often dipped in sugar or chocolate, to distract you from the dullness of the dessert you ordered!

If you've successfully grown peppers or tomatoes, you can succeed with cape gooseberries, too; in general, they need similar cultivation. The plants are tall and branching, with attractive, yellow flowers among the furry leaves. Just a few plants can produce a small crop of fruits over several months which is enough for most people, unless cape gooseberries are your favourite fruit.

The golden, acidic but sweet fruits are tasty to eat raw, though they aren't to everyone's taste. The gooseberries also make good jam or look and taste good in fruit salads where they provide a dash of colour and contrasting flavours to savour.

Cape gooseberries are rich in vitamin C and contain vitamins B1, B2 and A, and nicotinic acid.

Sowing and cultivating cape gooseberries

Cape gooseberries are tender and intolerant of frost. They need sun and warmth and aren't reliable outside. However, you can grow them in a warm, sunny spot on the patio and they also do well in pots or grow bags (three to a bag), where you need to water and feed them like tomatoes. They do give better crops in the greenhouse or in a polytunnel, however.

Here are the steps to take if you fancy growing a crop of this exotic fruit:

1. **Sow seeds in pots or trays in a greenhouse or on the windowsill in mid-spring, in a temperature of 20°C.** The seedlings grow quickly so you don't need to sow too early.

2. **When the small seedlings are big enough to handle, transplant them into cell trays or 8-centimetre pots.**

3. **Continue to grow under cover in a warm well-lit spot. If the plants are to go outside, gradually harden them off over a period of 2 weeks beforehand.**

4. **By late May, when frosts should be over, you can plant out the plants where they are to fruit.** Plants usually grow to about 1 metre high and need spacing 40 centimetres apart, though smaller varieties are available (see the 'Choosing varieties' section later on).

5. **Put stakes in the soil to support the plants. Tie the plants to the stakes as they grow.** You don't need to pinch out the tips or sideshoots – just let them grow naturally.

6. **Keep the plants well watered.**

Cape gooseberries are also easy to grow in pots and grow bags, if you prefer. Just put two or three plants in a grow bag or one plant in a 20-centimetre-wide pot, make sure you water them freely, give them liquid fertiliser every week as they grow, and you should see a healthy crop.

A cape gooseberry by any other name. . .

Cape gooseberries are a type of *physalis* related to the common garden plant *Chinese lanterns* (which is also edible) and *tomatillos*. Tomatillos are grown in the same way as cape gooseberries but the larger fruits, which split the husk, are either green or purple and slightly sticky. In Mexican cuisine, cooks use tomatillos raw to make true salsa and they have a refreshing, acid flavour.

These plants don't suffer from any particular problem apart from the usual greenhouse pests of red spider mite and whitefly. On the allotment, rodents often seek them out. Turn to Chapter 7 for advice on keeping these pests at arm's length.

Harvesting and storing your cape gooseberries

Cape gooseberries ripen over many months and in the greenhouse you can usually start picking them from July through to the first frosts. You can tell when they're ready to pick because the husk around them turns a straw yellow. You may find that they drop off when ripe. The fruits don't deteriorate much if they get over-ripe, although they may split, which doesn't matter a great deal because the husk protects the fruit.

A useful feature of cape gooseberries is that you can store them for several months, as long as you leave the husks in a cool place.

Choosing varieties

Few varieties of cape gooseberry exist, and most suppliers, including garden centres and catalogues, list them as 'golden berry':

- ✔ **Pineapple** is a dwarf variety.
- ✔ **Golden Berry** is the standard variety and produces lots of fruit on a tall plant up to 2 metres high.

Unfamiliar but useful: Huckleberries

Garden huckleberries (*Solanum melanocerasum*) are the most unusual of the fruits you can grow from seed and are unfamiliar to most gardeners. Unrelated to the American huckleberry (which is actually like the blueberry), this small, black fruit looks exactly like the weed black nightshade – a name that inspires fear in many people – but is an infinitely better plant to have growing in your garden and a really useful, if not especially flavourful, fruit!

Although some people do grow huckleberries year after year, other gardeners consider this plant a waste of time. As well as the weed-like appearance, the other problem is that, as fruits go, the huckleberry is virtually inedible raw and even when cooked it doesn't have much flavour. Even so, huckleberries crop within a few months, crop heavily, and are easy to grow. So if you fancy a change, give the huckleberry a go.

You may wonder whether huckleberries are worth growing, especially if you only have a small plot. Well, they make a great choice of fruit for certain dishes for example, they make extraordinary ice cream! For a bit of extra variety in your diet, you can also use them in muffins instead of the more usual blueberries. You can even grow them for using as a dye. Because their taste isn't very distinguished, however, huckleberries are perhaps best for stewing with other fruits such as apples, although their strong violet hue dominates anything you cook them with. You can then make them into pies or freeze them for later use.

Huckleberries are low in calories and very rich in vitamins such as C, antioxidants, and minerals such as calcium, magnesium and phosphorus.

Sowing and cultivating huckleberries

Huckleberries aren't fussy about soil, but grow best in a fertile soil in full sun. The plants don't gain anything from being in a greenhouse and prefer being outside.

Here are the steps to follow to grow a crop of huckleberries:

1. **Sow the seeds thinly in pots of multipurpose compost, in a temperature of 20°C, in a propagator, in late spring. Cover them with perlite or compost.** The plants grow very quickly.

2. **Transplant the seedlings into cell trays when large enough to handle.** Keep them moist as they grow and start feeding with a general liquid fertiliser about three weeks after transplanting.

3. **In late spring, when the plants are established and about 10 centimetres high, plant them outside, 30 centimetres apart.** They usually tolerate light frosts.

4. **Water the plants regularly until they get established in the soil, after which they usually are able to look after themselves, even in dry weather.**

As the plants grow, remember to keep the area free of weeds and to protect them from the ravenous appetites of slugs and snails (see Chapter 7 for tips on how to do this).

Harvesting and storing your huckleberries

After producing small, white flowers, clusters of about ten small, green berries that ripen to black appear on the plants. Each plant produces many hundreds of berries that you need to pick when they're black and soft to the touch. They taste better if you leave them on the plant until frosted, although you may not be able to do this in mild areas. The berries remain edible for several weeks after they ripen. At the end of the season you can just pull up the plants and add them to your compost heap.

You can store huckleberries in the fridge for at least a week after picking them.

Take care not to pick and eat green berries because they can be toxic at this stage.

Choosing varieties

Unfortunately, no alternative varieties of huckleberry exist, so you're limited to the one type available, which you may see for sale as 'wonder berries.'

More varied than you might think: Melons

Melons are so familiar, as the ubiquitous honeydew variety, that many people have no idea that other types are available. The virtue of honeydews is that they store well, and so shipping them around the world to supermarkets is easy for the people who grow them. However, nice though the honeydew is, hundreds of other types of melon exist and most have a much better flavour. Orange-fleshed cantaloupes, for example, and the old-fashioned musk melons, with a network of corky ridges on their rind, are much more distinguished but they need eating as soon as they're ripe. These varieties don't travel well so to enjoy them you need to grow them yourself.

Melons need to be eaten raw as soon as they're ripe. You can enjoy them on their own, perhaps drizzled with coulis, or combine them with other ingredients to make delicious dishes. For starters, melons are a natural soul mate for Parma ham. For puddings, you can create lovely melon sorbets or put together one of a thousand different varieties of fruit salad, using melon as a key ingredient.

Melons contain few nutrients but do have some B and C vitamins.

Sowing and cultivating melons

Melons are annual plants. They prefer a soil that's rich in organic matter and that retains moisture. They tolerate a little shade and you can grow them under tomatoes, although they prefer more humidity than do tomatoes. You can train melons up netting or canes but allowing them to trail over the ground is easier and makes training easier, too.

Unfortunately, melons are very prone to fungal diseases. These diseases kill the roots or rot the stems at soil level, and so the plants need warmth and lots of water – but not too much – as they grow. They rarely succeed outside and need a greenhouse, polytunnel or cold frame, ideally heated to at least 18°C, in which to grow.

You grow melons from seed, and you may be tempted to take the seeds out of a melon you've bought and try to grow your own from there. You can get the seeds to grow easily enough, but because all melon fruits you buy are imported and have grown in areas with much warmer summers than in the UK, you may well waste your efforts growing a plant that never produces a decent fruit. Instead, I always recommend buying seeds of a named variety that's likely to produce a good crop.

Here's what to do:

1. **Sow two melon seeds in a 8-centimetre pot full of compost, on their sides, in the centre, about 1 centimetre deep.** Keep the pot in a temperature of about 25°C and keep the seeds damp but not wet. Melons grow quickly, and seedlings should appear within two weeks.

   Melons don't tolerate frost, so if you're sowing in an unheated greenhouse, don't sow any earlier than mid-April. If you do have a heated greenhouse, you can sow a few weeks earlier than this.

2. **If both seeds germinate, pinch off the weakest seedling.**

3. **When the plants have two or three true leaves (in addition to the two seed leaves), you can plant them out, in the greenhouse border, in grow bags (two per bag) or in pots.** If you plant them in the border, improve the soil with as much organic matter as you can beforehand.

   To plant out, draw up the soil into small mounds about 10 centimetres above the rest of the soil and make a hole in these mounds to plant your melons, 5 centimetres deeper than in the pot and about 45 centimetres apart. The mound ensures that the plants don't get too wet around the 'neck' and the deep planting allows the stem to form more roots. Make sure that the plants don't dry out, but don't keep the soil too wet, especially at first when the soil may be cold. If growing in pots or grow bags you need to apply liquid fertiliser once a week as the plants are growing. You can feed plants growing in the soil too but it's not essential.

4. **When the plants have formed four leaves, pinch out the growing tip.** This technique makes the plants produce four side shoots and you get a melon on each of these. Melons are mean with their fruits and as soon as one fruit starts to develop, the plant stops bothering with the others, and so the idea is to get four melons – one on each stem – to grow at the same time.

5. **Pollinate the flowers.** This isn't as tricky as it sounds! Small yellow flowers appear along the stems and the females, which produce melons, have a small, often hairy, tiny melon behind them. When you have a

female flower open on each stem, take a soft, small paintbrush and rub it into male flowers and then into the females to pollinate them. Alternatively, you can adopt the less sophisticated method of pulling off a male flower, stripping off its petals, and shoving it into the centre of the female – this method works just as well!

Try to do this procedure every day for a few days, to get four melons 'set' at roughly the same time. Within days the tiny melons start to swell.

6. **Make sure that your plants are never short of water or food.** As the melons start to ripen, you can water less. This speeds up ripening and gives the fruits a sweeter flavour, although the plants look dreadful!

7. **As the plants grow, remember to pinch out the growing tips and the tips of any side shoots to control the amount of foliage.** You also need to pick off any more melons that start to form when you're sure your four have started developing.

Melons are very prone to whitefly and red spider mite (see Chapter 7 for tips on keeping on top of this problem).

Harvesting and storing your melons

When things go to plan, each plant should produce about four fruits of roughly 10–15 centimetres in diameter. They vary greatly in their appearance as they ripen, with some changing colour from green to yellow or gold and others retaining a grey or green skin. You can tell if a melon is ripe by gently pressing at the flower end and if it gives slightly your melon is probably ripe. However, a better giveaway that a melon is ripe is the divine scent it then gives off! This scent is something you don't experience with anything you find in a shop, but as soon as you walk into the greenhouse you can tell that a melon is ripe by the sweet, aromatic fragrance that greets you!

Apart from honeydew varieties, melons don't store very well. You can freeze melon, but I don't recommend doing so. You're much better off enjoying them when still fresh.

After harvesting all four melons, you can pull up and compost the plants.

Choosing varieties

Here are a few great varieties of melon:

- ✔ **Ambrosia** is a quality variety with golden flesh and fine flavour.
- ✔ **Antalya F1** is reliable and easy to grow, with yellow skin and pale flesh.
- ✔ **Blenheim Orange** is an antique variety that survived because of its orange red flesh and exceptional flavour. However, this variety needs heat and growing it can be a challenge!
- ✔ **Castella** is a reliable, fairly easy-to-grow canteloupe melon with fine-flavoured, orange-fleshed fruits.

> ✔ **Edonis F1** is an easy-to-grow, early–to-mature variety that produces small fruits with pale orange flesh and fine flavour.

> ✔ **Sweetheart F1** produces small, orange-fleshed fruits, is the easiest to grow and is the best for beginners. You can even try growing it outside.

Crunchy and juicy: Watermelons

Watermelons aren't closely related to other melons – you see when you grow them that the pips are scattered among the crunchy flesh rather than all in the centre. If you enjoy eating these fruits, you've probably also noticed that the flesh is crunchy rather than soft, though packed with juice. However, watermelons grow in more or less the same way as other melons and both crops are fond of summer heat and sunshine.

Watermelons are wonderful fruits to eat fresh, after chilling them in the fridge, and you can blend them as well to include in tasty summer smoothies.

Despite its sweet taste, watermelon is low in calories and a rich source of the antioxidant lycopene, as are pink grapefruits and tomatoes. The flesh contains reasonable amounts of vitamins A, B1, B2, B6, C and K, and folic acid.

Sowing and cultivating watermelons

Watermelons aren't as fussy about soil as other melons and are easy to grow, providing that you can give them warmth, sun and plenty of water. They aren't generally suitable plants for growing outside in the UK, where summers aren't warm enough, but they are good crops for a polytunnel or greenhouse. Because they don't need high levels of humidity in the air, watermelons make better companions for tomatoes than regular melons or cucumbers.

Watermelons grow quickly, and in general you should expect one or two melons per plant. Here's how to grow them:

1. **Sow the large, flat seeds on their sides in small pots, two seeds per pot, about 1 centimetre deep. Keep them in a temperature of about 25°C, in good light, to enable the seeds to germinate.** Don't sow the seeds until late April or your seedlings will be getting straggly in their pots by planting time.

2. **If both seeds grow, pinch out the weaker of the two.**

3. **Before planting out the seedlings, improve the soil where they're to grow by adding organic matter and general fertiliser to provide nutrients.**

4. **Plant out the seedlings, about 80 centimetres apart, and pinch out the growing tip when four leaves are showing.** Take this step at the beginning of May in a warm greenhouse but no earlier than late May in an unheated greenhouse or polytunnel.

5. **Decide whether to let your plants grow vertically or sprawl across the soil.** Watermelons are large, rambling plants with large, deeply divided foliage. You can grow them up strings, trellis or netting or let them sprawl across the soil. If you train them upwards you need to carefully support the heavy fruits by putting some netting (similar to the netting that you buy oranges in) around the fruits and tying it to supports. If you grow them up trellis or strings, train them so they make a single shoot which grows to at least 2 metres. You don't need to worry about doing any further pinching out or training and when plants start to grow strongly, they form side shoots at the base naturally. Allowing the fruits to grow on the ground is easier, although they then have a pale bottom where they rest on the soil.

6. **Water plants regularly to promote growth.**

7. **Pollinate the small yellow flowers that appear.** You can do this in the same way as for melons (check out the 'Marvellous melons' section earlier in the chapter).

Watermelons are likely to be affected by whitefly and red spider mite. Chapter 7 is the place to look for help in dealing with them.

Harvesting and storing your watermelons

Watermelons don't have the distinctive aroma of ordinary melons to tell you when they're ripe. The way to check is to knock the fruits with your knuckles. Ripe watermelons sound hollow and when you hold them you're able to feel that the contents are under pressure. When you carefully push a knife through the rind after picking one, the rind suddenly splits, perhaps violently, which is a good sign that you have a sweet and juicy melon to look forward to! After picking all the fruits, you can just pull up and compost the plants.

Watermelons should store for many weeks in a cool, frost-free place.

Choosing varieties

Few varieties of watermelon are commonly available in this country. Here are two of the best:

- ✔ **Blacktail Mountain** produces large fruits weighing up to 5 kilograms, with deep green rind and deep red flesh. Experts bred this variety to tolerate cool night conditions.

- ✔ **Yellow Baby** is an unusual, yellow-fleshed variety with 4-kilogram fruits and an excellent flavour.

Chapter 14

Very Berry! Growing Berries, Currants and Nuts

Certain fruits tend to get a little overlooked. Berries and currants, for example, are packed with goodness and are among the most important fruits in our diet, and yet very few people eat any, let alone enough. Other fruits suffer from an image problem: if you're like I used to be, you probably think of gooseberries as green blobs of acid that become edible only when you boil them with their own weight in sugar and cover them in custard. But ripe gooseberries can be as sweet as nectar. You may also think that you can get all the blackberries you want from roadside bushes, but the types you can grow in your garden are sweet and juicy without so many pips. Other fruits just aren't very familiar to many people: by digging a little deeper (sometimes literally!), you can discover a wonderful range of fruits that you never see in the shops, and to enjoy these you need to grow them yourself. These fruits include my favourite of all, the mulberry.

As well as these delicious fruits, if you have room for a tree then you have the possibility of growing nuts for yourself. Some need a lot of room but they take very little work and if you want to leave something for the future you can make few better choices than a planting a nut tree.

Within this chapter you can discover plants with tastes to tantalise, delight and surprise. As a bonus, most of them are easy to grow when you know how, so read on . . .

Growing Healthy Berries

Most of the berries I introduce to you in this section take up little room and so are easy to squeeze into a small garden. Gooseberries are small, spiny shrubs and the other berries here are sprawling climbers that need support to keep them tidy. You can train blackberries and hybrid berries such as loganberries against fences and walls, where they take up little space while producing good crops of fruit that you just can't buy in the shops.

Gardeners grow all these fruits from plants rather than from seed because seedlings are very variable and although you may get a plant from them that crops well, most are mediocre. Also, you have to invest several years of cultivation on these plants before you get a crop. To avoid lavishing time and space on plants that you may later have to remove, buying and cultivating named varieties as plants is the best way to approach growing them. You can then be sure that the plants have both desirable and known qualities.

The berries here are all useful and versatile: you can eat them all raw or cooked, and they freeze well so you can enjoy them all year round.

Dark and delicious: Blackberries

Blackberries are always delicious and, by growing your own rather than foraging in hedges, you can be sure of sweet, juicy berries. The plants are easy to look after, hardy, have few problems, and generally crop well. They even tolerate a little shade, though for the best crops and the sweetest berries, they do need to see the sun. You don't have to wait too long for a crop either – you should get a small crop the year after planting (if you plant them in spring) and a normal, heavy crop in the third year.

Blackberries, and hybrid berries, are attractive when in flower and you can include them in ornamental gardens, trained on a wall or over an arch. Thornless varieties are best for growing this way.

You can enjoy eating blackberries raw but the traditional method is to cook them with apples. Just a few impart their flavour to the apples and enliven dishes of plain stewed apple. Together, they make wonderful pies and crumbles! Blackberries are also excellent for jams, jellies and smoothies and even for making wine.

Blackberries are rich in vitamins A, B1, B2, B6, C and E, and nicotinic acid and antioxidants.

Planting and cultivating blackberries

Blackberries thrive in most soils and aren't bothered by heavy clay or lighter soils, although as with any plant you get better results if you improve the soil beforehand by digging in some well-rotted manure or other organic matter and make sure the soil is free from weeds. Although the most compact varieties are worth trying in large pots on the patio, because of the natural vigour of the plants they grow best in the open ground. Blackberries do tolerate a bit of shade but a spot in full sun is best.

1. **Get going with the planting.** Dig a hole where the plant is to grow in the open ground or close to a fence (but not a north-facing fence), depending on how you plan to train them. Place the plant into the hole, spreading the roots out carefully (if the plants are bare-root) and at the same depth as in the original soil (you can tell this from the soil on the stem).

   Planting distance varies according to the variety. You can plant some types as close as 2 metres apart but others are much more vigorous and need at least twice that amount of space! You can find out how to space your plants by looking at the general height and vigour of the variety. Most suppliers state the ideal planting space, but as you train these fruits and control them you can control their size. The minimum space they need is 2 metres.

   Most people buy blackberry plants in pots and you can plant these all year round, but if you buy them in winter as bare-root plants you need to plant them immediately.

2. **Provide your plants with support.** Blackberry plants are generally large and have sprawling stems, so you need to provide them with some support as they grow.

   For this support, you need to erect fence posts (or use the ones already there if growing against a fence) or other stout poles 2–3 metres apart, with the plant set midway, and install strong wires horizontally on these at heights of about 80, 120 and 160 centimetres above the ground. You can tie the long stems to these as they grow, to display the fruits. Three wires are usually sufficient, at least 2 metres long so that each plant spreads over an area of about 2 metres high and wide. These wires can accommodate six shoots from the base. If the plant produces more shoots you can tie two to a wire.

   Sometimes shoots grow so long that they overhang the ends of the wires. You can shorten them to fit the wire framework but you need to check the vigour of the variety before planting – some varieties spread to 4 metres wide, with stems that grow 2 metres high in the first season, and so you need wires 4 metres wide to accommodate the plant after its second year.

3. **Mulch the soil with garden compost or well-rotted compost after planting and apply a general fertiliser such as fish, blood and bone.**

In future years, remember to mulch annually in spring to feed the plants and help retain soil moisture. You can also apply a fertiliser to encourage growth and cropping but avoid applying too much nitrogen, which causes excessive, leafy growth and makes the plant more prone to fungal diseases such as cane spot. Ideally, apply a high-potash fertiliser such as sulphate of potash – about 50 grams per plant in April. Keep this fertilising up, and a plant should crop well for at least ten years.

4. **Water the plants regularly and keep the area free of weeds.**

5. **Train your plants as they grow.** Like summer raspberries and most hybrid berries, blackberries fruit on the stems that were produced in the previous year, and this affects the way that gardeners train and grow them.

In the first year your plant should produce several long, trailing shoots that grow from the base of the plant, from below the soil or the base of the stem. You can train these shoots upwards at first but, by late summer, when they stop growing, tie them to the horizontal wires, both sides of the centre, so that the plant produces fruits all along the stem (or stems) in the second year. As these stems are producing flowers and then fruits in their second year, the plant is also producing new, long stems from the base that crop in the third year. You can train these stems upright at this stage. As soon as cropping finishes, you can cut out and remove the fruited stems at the base and tie in the new stems in their place. This process continues every year.

6. **Protect the berries from birds as they start to ripen.** The simplest way to do this is to drape netting or fleece over the plants as soon as the first berries start to turn red.

Blackberries root where their stem tips touch the soil. Although this tendency is a useful way to propagate plants, it also means that untrained plants can become an untamed thicket if you're not careful. Also, be aware that if birds eat the berries they also thank you by staining your hard surfaces and spreading seeds that later pop up in your borders! Uneven ripening can be another problem with blackberries; Chapter 7 tells you how to deal with it.

Harvesting and storing your blackberries

Blackberries crop from late July to September, depending on the variety. Each variety crops for several weeks and you need to pick the berries as they ripen and turn black and juicy. Blackberries freeze well.

Choosing varieties

You may hear that growing varieties with large berries means compromising with flavour. Not so. Although some varieties do have better flavour than others, even the least flavourful are sweet and generally much better for eating than some pippy plants you find in hedges. You need to select your variety carefully, though, because some are spiny monsters that take over your garden if you neglect them. Other varieties are neat, easy to control, and have no spines at all – the best if you have a small garden because you can easily pick them without getting torn to shreds!

Here are some varieties worth considering:

- **Ashton Cross** is a late, spiny variety that produces exceptionally heavy crops on vigorous plants. The berries are medium-sized and have exceptional flavour.

- **Black Beaute** is a mid-season, almost spineless variety that produces heavy crops of good-flavoured berries that are twice the size of most other types.

- **Chester** is a late, spineless, compact variety with upright growth and heavy crops of berries over many weeks with a very sweet taste.

- **Fantasia** is a mid-season, spiny variety. A good choice if you want massive crops of large berries, but bear in mind that Fantasia is a vicious monster and needs loads of room!

- **Helen** is a very early, spineless variety with compact growth and heavy crops of fruits with good flavour.

- **Kotata** is an early, spiny variety, exceptional because of its wonderful flavour. Displays vigorous growth and heavy crops of lustrous, large berries.

- **Loch Ness** is a late, spineless, exceptionally compact plant with an upright shape – ideal for small gardens. The fruits are large and flavourful.

- **Veronique** is a late, spineless variety that produces heavy crops of nice berries on upright, compact plants and is unusual mainly for its large, deep pink flowers.

- **Waldo** is an early, spineless variety – possibly the best for small gardens. Waldo plants have compact growth but heavy crops of large, shining fruits with great flavour.

Apical dominance

Apical dominance is a natural phenomenon where plants want to grow upwards and if a blackberry or other climbing plant stem is trained upright, only the buds at the tip of the shoots grow. But if a cunning gardener ties the shoot close to horizontal, most of the shoots along the whole length of the stem sprout, because none is higher than the rest. This reason is why gardeners tie blackberries and other berries, as well as climbing roses and wisteria, to horizontal wires – to ensure that all the buds along the stem grow flower buds and then fruits, vastly increasing the crop.

It takes two: Loganberries

The loganberry is a popular hybrid cane fruit raised by Judge Logan in California in 1881 as a cross between a raspberry and a blackberry. Many people consider it to be the world's first hybrid berry.

Loganberries have large, deep red fruits with a good, sharp flavour on plants that grow and look like blackberries and which are very vigorous. They crop well, although some people dislike them as a raw fruit because they retain their white core when you pick them, like blackberries and unlike raspberries.

You can eat loganberries raw but not as enjoyably as raspberries because the fruits retain their plug, which is firmer than the flesh, when you pick them. However, loganberries are excellent for cooking, stewing, cooked desserts, jams and jelly, and make a great addition to summer pudding. You get about the same amounts and types of nutrients from loganberries as you do from blackberries.

Planting, cultivating, harvesting and storing loganberries

Follow the same steps I give you in the 'Dark and delicious: Blackberries' section earlier in the chapter, and you can't go wrong.

Choosing varieties

LY654 is the standard variety of loganberry. The plant is spineless and the large fruits are deep red and juicy and taste delicious – sweet but acid with a complex range of flavours – and they ripen earlier than blackberries.

Other unusual berries

Most of the hybrids I list here are crosses between blackberries and raspberries and come from various countries around the world, with varying degrees of popularity. Most are spiny plants with stems covered in prickles but a few have smooth stems without prickles and may be better in gardens where children have access. Few are available in garden centres; specialist stockists are the best places to locate them.

Some of these hybrids have red fruits and are similar to loganberries, whereas others are closer to blackberries. Some have exceptional flavour and others crop earlier than most black-berries, thus extending your season of picking, so are definitely worth considering.

In all cases you plant and cultivate these berries in the same way as for blackberries (see the earlier 'Dark and delicious: Blackberries' section). Don't underestimate the vigour of some of these plants, though: some grow into bigger plants than others and most need plant-ing at least 2 metres apart. Breeders have developed thornless varieties for very good reason – because the long, arching stems, when set with large thorns, can cause serious damage. Be prepared to train and regularly tie them in to their support. A sylvanberry that I planted against a greenhouse regularly makes stems that reach 6 metres down one side and would do the same the other way if the green-house was big enough!

After harvesting, you can eat all these berries raw or cooked. Try sylvanberries with raspberries and tayberry ice-cream for some-thing unusual. Nutritionally, they're all very similar to blackberries.

- ✔ **Boysenberries** come from a spineless plant that produces heavy crops of black berries with rich, acid and sweet flavour.

- ✔ **Karaka Black** is a new fruit from New Zealand with huge, black berries almost 10 centimetres long with a rich, sweet flavour. This unusual plant is compact and crops from July to September. Highly recommended!

- ✔ **Marionberries** come from a spiny plant. Sometimes classified as a blackberry, this hybrid is vigorous and has heavy crops of loganberry-type fruits that ripen over two months.

- ✔ **Sylvanberries** come from a spiny plant, and this hybrid is the first to ripen, doing so before most blackberries. The large, black, tangy but sweet fruits crop over many weeks.

- ✔ **Tayberries** come from a spineless plant, and are rather like loganberries but with larger, sweeter, red fruits. Buckingham is the only variety generally available. Recommended.

- ✔ **Veitchberries** come from a spiny plant. This blackberry-raspberry cross is vigorous and crops later than most. The fruits have a rich, intense flavour.

Although not a hybrid, another unusual berry worth considering is the **Japanese wineberry**. A separate species (*Rubus phoenicolasius*) rather than a hybrid, this is an ornamental plant with red bristles on the stems. The small, reddish berries are sweet and tasty.

Not to be left out: Gooseberries

All things considered, gooseberries are probably the easiest summer fruit to grow. They are hardy, easy to prune and train, grow in most soils, tolerate a little shade, and birds and wasps usually leave the fruits alone.

Unfortunately, gooseberries have something of an image problem – many people regard them as acidic and almost inedible. This perception is largely because gardeners, before the advent of imported fruits and desperate to have some sort of fruit from their plot, picked the immature fruits early in the season when they contain little sweetness and are edible only after stewing them with copious amounts of sugar. But leave gooseberries to properly ripen and they can taste sweet and delicious.

Gooseberries are great for stewing, for making jams and chutneys, and in pies, fools and even wine. Fully ripe dessert gooseberries are also delicious raw.

Gooseberries are rich in vitamins A, B1, B2. B6, C and E, biotin, folic acid and nicotinic acid.

Planting and cultivating gooseberries

Gooseberries are tolerant of most soils as long as they're not waterlogged. Chalky and even clay soils are fine, but a rich, moist soil is best. In very dry, sandy soils mildew is likely to be a problem (see Chapter 7 for tips on dealing with this problem). Gooseberries are hardy plants and are great choices for exposed and windy gardens where other fruit may struggle. A gooseberry bush should continue to crop well for more than ten years.

You can train gooseberries against walls or grow them in pots on the patio. However, gardeners usually grow them as bushes on a single stem for at least 15 centimetres from the ground and then train them as a spreading bush. You can also grow them as standards with a taller, single stem, about 60 centimetres high and as *cordons*, training a single stem with short side shoots, which is an ideal way to grow several varieties against a fence in a small space.

Here are the steps to take after buying your plants:

1. **Add well-rotted compost to the soil before you plant your gooseberry bushes.**

2. **Plant your bushes 1.2 metres apart. If buying or training cordons, plant these 40 centimetres apart at a 45° angle to 'slow the sap' and encourage heavier crops than you get if you plant them vertically. If planting in a pot, choose a 30-centimetre-diameter pot for the first few years and use John Innes No 3 compost for potting.**

When planting, dig out a hole large enough to take the roots, roughly 30 centimetres deep and wide. Spread the roots of bare-root plants evenly around the base of the hole. Add a little soil and, holding the plant by the stem, shake it so that the soil works its way between the roots. Add some more soil and repeat the shaking and pull the plant up, if necessary, so that the dark mark on the stem, where the old soil level was, is at the new soil level. Add more soil to fill the hole and then firm the soil by gently treading on it around the plant.

3. **Give a thorough soak with water and put a mulch of compost around the plant.** You may then need to prune the plant, cutting off any broken stems, back to a bud, and shorten any weak stems or those that are growing so that they cross against each other.

4. **If training a young plant, cut back the main leading shoot to about 20 centimetres each year, so that it slowly increases in height until the plant reaches the height you want (up to about 1.2 metres).** Each August, shorten all the side shoots to about 5–7 centimetres. In this way you create a narrow plant that crops heavily and you can easily see and pick the fruits.

The small, green gooseberry flowers bloom soon after the leaves appear, and are pollinated by early-flying bees in spring. The plants usually have no problems setting fruits and are self-fertile, so just one plant produces fruits.

Gooseberry bushes need pruning after the first year. Pruning consists of removing any shoots that appear from below the ground and trying to keep the centre of the bush open – often described as a goblet shape. Figure 14-1 shows where to make the cuts. You prune in this way because the main pest – gooseberry sawfly – lays its eggs in the centre of the bushes where the grubs can start to feed unseen, and to prevent a congested centre where the main disease – American Gooseberry mildew – can establish, encouraged by a lack of air movement. You can prune after August until late winter by which time you'll have picked the crop.

When pruning, try to shorten any long growths by about half to keep the bush neat, cut away some shoots in the centre of the bush, and remove the tips of shorter shoots to encourage flowering. At this time you can also give a feed with sulphate of potash to encourage flowering next season.

Harvesting and storing your gooseberries

Picking gooseberries can be traumatic because of the spines but not if you grow some of the thornless varieties now available (see the following 'Choosing varieties' section). You can pick the fruits when small and not yet ripe when they are best cooked and eaten with custard or another source of sugar. If you leave gooseberries until they are ripe, when they either change to red, pale green or yellow according to the variety but always remain translucent and soft, they taste sweet and pleasant raw. Gooseberries don't store well in this raw state but you can stew and freeze them or freeze them raw for adding to smoothies.

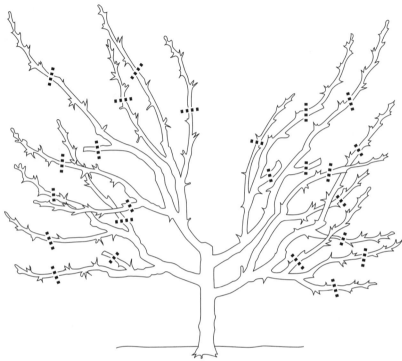

Figure 14-1:
Going over the bush in winter to shorten the longest shoots ensures your plant keeps a neat, even shape with no long branches to catch you when picking the fruit.

Choosing varieties

Don't accept any plants you see simply vaguely labelled 'gooseberry– red' of unknown kind, but instead make sure that you buy a named variety that completely suits your requirements. You can choose from dozens of varieties, and they vary enormously. Modern varieties have many advantages over some of the older ones, with increased resistance to disease, although all varieties are susceptible to sawfly (see Chapter 7).

Here are some varieties to consider:

- ✔ **Careless** is a standard, easy-to-grow variety with heavy crops that are good for cooking.

- ✔ **Greenfinch** is a new mildew-resistant variety with heavy crops of well-flavoured fruit and fewer spines than most.

- ✔ **Hinnonmaki Red** orHino Red is a dual-purpose variety for dessert or cooking with heavy crops of red fruits. This variety is resistant to mildew. Hinnonmaki Yellow is similar but has yellow fruits.

- ✔ **Howard's Lancer** is a fine variety with yellow berries and an exquisite flavour. This variety thrives on most soils.

- ✔ **Invicta** is worth planting because it has very heavy crops and is resistant to mildew. The pale green fruits are best for cooking.

- ✔ **Leveller** produces large, golden fruits of good flavour. It needs good soil to do well.

- ✔ **Lord Derby** produces huge, dark red, sweet fruits with exceptional flavour.

- ✔ **Martlet** is a reliable, tasty, red-fruited gooseberry that is resistant to mildew. This variety is better and bigger than the popular alternative Rokula.

- ✔ **Pax** is a very popular choice because it's (almost) spineless and has good crops of red, sweet fruits.

- ✔ **Worcesterberry** is actually a thorny hybrid of a gooseberry and an American species, and has small, black berries and little to recommend it.

Everyone's favourite: Blueberries

Blueberries (or highbush blueberries to give them their complete name) were a rarity in British gardens just a decade ago but are now amazingly popular. Part of this surge of interest is undoubtedly because experts herald them as a 'superfood', thanks to the antioxidants they contain, but also because blueberries are one of the most ornamental fruit bushes. The attractive, often blue-green leaves are sometimes tinged bronze in spring, and their small, bell-shaped flowers in spring are also pretty. The plants are at their most beautiful in autumn when the leaves turn scarlet, crimson and gold before they drop. All these features mean that blueberries are also now popular as patio plants.

Most people eat blueberries raw in a variety of ways – stewing them, mixing them with apple and other fruits, making them into jams, smoothies and pies, or adding them to cakes, to name just a few ideas. Blueberries are perhaps most famously used to make muffins.

The fruits are rich in vitamin C and high in antioxidants.

Planting and growing blueberries

Although blueberries are self-fertile, you get the best crops by planting and keeping two or more plants, of different varieties (two plants of the same variety don't have the same effect). They cross-pollinate each other, which seems to aid fruit setting.

Blueberries are usually available as potted plants that you can replant at any time of year. They grow best in full sun, with most growing to about 1 metre high – considerably larger than most people expect. Many gardeners grow blueberries in pots because of their precise soil requirements, but if your soil is acid, you can try them in a border. Few garden soils are sufficiently acid for blueberries to thrive, but if you can grow rhododendrons and azaleas well, you may well have success with blueberries, too. They make attractive additions to the shrub border and crop for at least a decade.

As well as an acid soil, blueberries need a soil that never dries out – they need plentiful moisture at all times. You can encourage this condition by adding copious quantities of organic matter to the soil before planting, to improve moisture retention. Leaf mould is excellent but moss peat is also good and closely matches the soil that blueberries naturally grow in. However, if you prefer not to use peat, you can acidify the soil by digging sulphur chips into the soil before planting and adding them as a dressing each year to make sure that the soil remains acid. You can also make the soil more acid by using acidic fertilisers such as sulphate of potash or sulphate of ammonia (in moderation). Avoid bonemeal, which is alkaline.

Here's where you go next:

1. **Plant your blueberries.** If you're planting in the soil, space them a minimum of 1 metre apart. Blueberries are hardy and winter cold doesn't bother them, so you can plant them at any time of year.

   If growing in pots, use a pot about 20 centimetres wide for the first year and then re-pot into a 30-centimetre pot for the next two years. Eventually you may need a larger pot, up to 45-centimetres across. Use an *ericaceous compost*, which is usually based on peat or recycled materials, and add some loam to it. Ideally, use a mixture of equal parts lime-free John Innes and standard ericaceous compost.

2. **Ensure your blueberries are never short of water.** Water potted plants regularly and in hot weather water those in the open garden, but be sure that you don't waterlog the soil. Try to use rainwater rather than tap water, especially in hard-water areas.

   During spring and summer, plants in pots need regular feeding too, and the best way is to give an acid, liquid plant food once a week while the plants are growing.

Birds are exceptionally fond of blueberries and in most areas you need to cover your plants with fleece or netting or you don't get a crop at all! Another danger is late spring frosts, which can damage new shoots and the flowers, so if you see late frosts forecast, cover your plants overnight with fleece.

You don't need to prune blueberry plants regularly, but you may need to remove the tip of the occasional, long shoot to keep plants in a balanced shape. After a few years, when the branches may start to become crowded, you can cut out a few of the oldest each year to give the younger stems more room to grow.

Harvesting and storing your blueberries

Blueberries crop over many weeks and often months. The first berries to ripen are usually the largest in size but even the smallest taste great. Pick them as soon as they ripen, when they change from green to black and become soft. You can't store blueberries for long after they ripen but they freeze wonderfully.

Choosing varieties

Here are some popular varieties of blueberry to consider:

- ✔ **Bluecrop** is one of the most popular, with heavy crops of medium-sized berries and good flavour.
- ✔ **Bluetta** is one of the earliest of all varieties, with large, tasty berries.
- ✔ **Chandler** is a recent variety, notable mainly for the huge size of its berries.
- ✔ **Goldtraube** is one of the latest to ripen, with heavy crops of tasty berries.
- ✔ **Nui** is an early variety with large fruits and very good flavour.
- ✔ **Ozark Blue** is a late variety with large berries.
- ✔ **Top Hat** is the best for growing in containers because of its compact size, reaching only 60 centimetres high. This variety produces heavy crops of tasty berries.

Bilberries are a British native plant with fruits that are similar to blueberries but much smaller. Bilberry plants are sometimes available for sale but they don't produce serious crops in a garden situation.

Time for Christmas: Cranberries

The idea of growing cranberries is an attractive one and the plants themselves are pretty and small. However, these plants don't produce much of a crop in the average garden and, like blueberries, they need a very acid soil. Consider cranberry plants as ornamentals that give you a bonus of some berries. The attractive pink flowers have turned-back petals and the name 'cranberry' may derive from 'crane berry' because of their beak-shaped flowers.

Cranberries are acidic and not particularly juicy fruits, and aren't really very palatable raw. Some people add just a few to stewed apples, to add flavour and colour, and to juices (although you need a huge crop to get enough to make juice from them), but you most commonly see them in relishes or cranberry sauce. You can use this sauce on anything from goat's cheese toasties to yoghurt and muesli, and if you don't add it to your turkey at Christmas, you're missing out on a treat!

Cranberries are rich in vitamin C and antioxidants, and have some medicinal qualities.

Planting and cultivating cranberries

Gardeners usually buy cranberries as small, potted plants, but they grow naturally in cold, windswept areas with waterlogged, peaty soils (not the sort of conditions found in most domestic gardens), and are completely hardy.

To grow cranberries you can follow the same steps that I describe in 'Everyone's favourite: Blueberries' earlier in this chapter. However, although cranberries have few problems when you get the growing conditions correct, few garden soils are sufficiently acid or wet enough for cranberries, so pay even more attention to watering because cranberries don't tolerate dry soil for even short periods.

You don't need to prune cranberry plants regularly, but you can give them a light trim in spring to keep them neat if necessary. Also, because they need similar conditions to blueberries, but are low, creeping plants, you can plant a cranberry to grow over the soil of a blueberry in a pot. Two crops in the space of one!

Harvesting and storing your cranberries

Cranberries ripen in autumn and remain edible for many weeks afterwards, both if you leave them on the plant and when you pick and keep them in the fridge.

Choosing varieties

Here are three popular varieties of cranberry:

- ✔ **Cranberry C N** is a spreading plant with large, red fruits.
- ✔ **Early Black** is an unusual variety because of the dark colour of the fruits; very vigorous.
- ✔ **Franklin** is a compact plant, ideal for pots, with heavy crops of small berries.

Scandinavian delight: Lingonberries

Whereas the commercial cranberry is North American in origin, lingonberries come from Northern Europe. The two plants are very similar, and have a similarly acidic taste, but lingonberries have small, fragrant, pink, bell-shaped flowers, and the actual berries are much smaller, appearing in small clusters. The plants are more bushy and upright and even more attractive, and they make a nice container plant for the patio in sun or part shade. A single plant doesn't produce much of a crop, and so you need to invest in several to harvest a decent quantity.

You can add the small lingonberries to fruit salads or mix them with cranberries and blueberries for jams and sauces.

Planting, cultivating, harvesting and storing lingonberries

Lingonberries need similar treatment to cranberries – just follow the same guidelines and you can't go wrong. As lingonberries grow, they form a dense bush, about 20 centimetres high in a pot, and after a few years you can cut out a few of the oldest stems to give the new growth room to develop.

Choosing varieties

Unfortunately, no alternative varieties of lingonberry are available. At least you won't lose any sleep deciding which variety to grow!

Coaching Currants

The redcurrant and the blackcurrant are the two basic types of currant. You prune them differently but otherwise redcurrants and blackcurrants have similar requirements. Both are easy to grow, hardy, crop well in most situations, and are forgiving: even if you get the pruning wrong, or forget to prune them at all, they soldier on for years, growing and fruiting. But of course, treat them correctly and they repay you handsomely for your efforts.

Better than blueberries: Blackcurrants

Strange as it sounds, most people have never eaten blackcurrants and know them only through juice or jam! But experts have given us a reason to pay them more attention – they've discovered that blackcurrants are actually richer in antioxidants than blueberries. Also in their favour, blackcurrants are easier to grow and crop well in almost every situation, too.

All the colour of blackcurrants is in the skin – the flesh is actually pale green. Cooking releases their rich purple colour. Most cooks use currants for jams, syrups, stews, juices and smoothies, with apples and other fruits, as an alternative to blueberries in muffins, and as an essential ingredient in summer pudding. Raw, off the bush, they have a distinctly odd, rather 'adult' taste, being acidic and not that sweet, at least when you compare them to strawberries.

Blackcurrants deserve the title of superfruit more than most others, being rich in vitamin C and containing A, B1, B2, B6, E and K, biotin, and folic acid and nicotinic acid. Blackcurrants are also a rich source of antioxidants, more so than blueberries, although cooking and processing reduces their effectiveness.

Planting and cultivating blackcurrants

Blackcurrants are much easier to accommodate in the garden than blueberries because they don't need any special soil conditions. However, blackcurrants are vigorous plants and they always grow best in rich soil, so improving the site by deeply digging in organic matter before planting is always a good move. Because they grow rapidly, need lots of feeding, and are rather dull plants to look at, blackcurrants are less suitable for growing in pots on the patio than in the soil. You stand your best chance of getting good crops by planting them in a sunny spot, although they do tolerate a little shade. More sun, though, ensures that the fruits develop as much sugar as possible as they ripen, so taste sweeter. Most varieties grow to a similar height – about 1 metre tall – in maturity and you can expect them to crop reliably for at least ten years.

Blackcurrants flower early in spring when they're susceptible to frost damage. Experts have bred new varieties to overcome this problem, by having flowers that are frost-resistant or flowering later than older varieties. The best thing to do is just avoid planting blackcurrants in an area prone to late frosts.

You can grow your own blackcurrants by starting out with bare-root plants (the best option) or potted plants. Plant bare-root plants in the same way as for gooseberries (see the earlier section 'Not to be left out: Gooseberries') but deeper than they were originally, either in the pots or in the soil they were grown in (you can tell by the mark the soil has made on the stem). Although varieties differ in size, you're generally fine to plant them at least 1.2 metres apart, and they grow to about 1 metre high.

From here, you need to take several steps to cultivate your blackcurrant plants successfully:

1. **Cut back the young plants hard to about 15 centimetres high in winter or spring, so that you get a constant succession of shoots from the base or from below the soil, as I show in Step I of Figure 14-2.** In the first year you want to see several new shoots growing. Blackcurrants differ from gooseberries and redcurrants because they don't have a permanent bush with a single stem. Also, blackcurrants aren't grafted so the shoots that grow from below ground aren't suckers and will produce fruits.

2. **Blackcurrants are greedy plants, so give them a general feed of pelleted chicken manure or fish, blood and bone in spring.**

3. **If you want, in the following winter you can cut the tips off the shoots to even up the height.** Aside from this, you don't need to do any other pruning at this stage. (See Step II of Figure 14-2.)

   The stems bear flowers and fruits early in year two. As the currants develop, more long stems grow up from the base of the plant throughout summer and these bear the crop the following year.

4. **After picking the fruits** (see the following 'Harvesting and storing your blackcurrants') **you can cut off the shoots that fruited near their base (see Figure 14-2), but leave the new shoots, which will crop the next summer.**

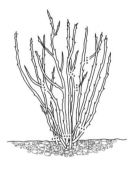

Figure 14-2: Pruning your blackcurrant plants.

Prune blackcurrants hard straight after planting to encourage lots of new shoots.

The new shoots produce a crop in the next year.

After several years, bushes get crowded with stems and you need to cut out the oldest, twiggiest branches at ground level.

Blackcurrants are sometimes affected by mildew but this should be less of a problem when the soil is rich and moist. Selecting a resistant variety helps, too. A more serious problem is big bud mite (see Chapter 7), although this problem isn't inevitable.

Harvesting and storing your blackcurrants

You have a choice when it comes to picking and pruning. You need to cut out only the stems that have carried fruit and leave the new shoots intact for cropping next year. If you think you may get confused, pick the fruits with secateurs! Simply cut the branches that are bearing fruit, close to the base. Then take them to the garden table and pick off the fruits, and shred and compost or discard the prunings.

If you don't want to pick all the fruits in one go, though, you can just pick them off the plants as and when they ripen. Then, at any time between harvest and late winter, go over the plants and cut out the fruited stems. You can usually identify these by their duller and darker colour, and their short side shoots – the new stems have no (or very few) side shoots.

Blackcurrants freeze well, and so you can store them away in your freezer for up to a year.

Choosing varieties

Here are some of the most popular varieties of blackcurrant:

- **Ben Hope** is a proloific- and late-cropping, vigorous variety that's resistant to diseases and is especially suitable for poor soils. Most of the Ben series, bred in Scotland, are worth trying.

- **Ben Sarek** is a recent introduction and one of the best. These very upright, compact plants with very big crops produce frost-hardy flowers and large, early fruits, and are resistant to mildew.

- **Big Ben** is one of the latest cropping varieties, and produces huge, very sweet berries. Resistant to mildew.

- **Ebony** is a new variety and sports the largest berries of all, but is most important because of the low acidity of the ripe berries, which taste delicious raw.

- **Foxdown** is resistant to most diseases, making it an ideal choice for organic growers. Foxdown is an upright plant that produces long strings of berries with good flavour.

- **The Raven** is an old variety that makes a huge bush. This variety is notable for its exceptional flavour and huge berries, but isn't good for small gardens and produces only moderate crops.

- **Wellington XXX** is an old established variety, and the most common of all, but it's not good for small gardens because it takes up more space than most. A spreading bush with good, early crops of tasty berries.

For something a bit different, you can also try growing the jostaberry. This gooseberry/blackcurrant hybrid is thornless and produces larger fruits than most blackcurrants. The black fruits are rather acidic but still pleasant, especially when cooked. The jostaberry usually crops well and is a trouble-free plant to grow. It needs exactly the same conditions and cultivation as blackcurrants.

Summer jewels: Redcurrants and whitecurrants

Both red- and white currants make great additions to fruit salads and as garnishes for desserts and lamb dishes. Both make wonderful cordials, juices and jelly – white currants especially make a beautiful pale pink jelly – and they're essential ingredients for the classic summer pudding.

Red- and white currants have a similar nutritional value to blackcurrants, with vitamins A, B1, B2, B6, E and K, biotin and folic and nicotinic acids Redcurrants, because of their bright colour, contain more antioxidants than white currants.

Planting and cultivating red- and white currants

You plant red- and white currants in the same way as for blackcurrants and gooseberries (check out the earlier sections in this chapter on these fruits for guidelines). However, you do prune them differently. In fact, pruning red- and white currants is more similar to pruning gooseberries.

Redcurrants produce their fruits on short stems running from the main branches. You can start pruning at the end of the first year, any time after August, cutting back the main shoots by about one third of their length. After that, side shoots grow and these produce the flowers and fruits. So in the summer of the second year and every summer after that, cut the new side shoots back to about 5 centimetres long.

In spring, give a dressing of a general purpose fertiliser. Mulch with compost each spring and give a feed with a high-potash fertiliser.

Both red- and white currants are prone to blister aphids that feed on the growing tips and under the leaves, causing the leaves to curl and develop bright red, puckered areas. Chapter 7 tells you how to control these pests.

Harvesting and storing your red- and white currants

Redcurrants are ready to harvest when all the fruits in each cluster have turned red and translucent. White currants also turn transparent and have a yellow tinge. Both are soft and delicate, and don't store well after picking, but you can preserve them either by freezing or by making them into jellies, cordials or juices.

Choosing varieties

Some of the most popular varieties of redcurrants:

- ✔ **Junifer** is an early-cropping new variety that produces heavy crops of (relatively) sweet fruits. Easy and reliable.

- ✔ **Laxton No 1** is also an early-cropping variety. Laxton is the standard and most common variety and produces heavy crops of large berries.

- ✔ **Red Lake** crops in mid-season. This variety flowers late, and so misses the last frosts and has heavy crops of large berries.

- ✔ **Redpoll** is a very late cropper. From different breeding, this new redcurrant has massive strings of fruits and out-yields almost all others.

- ✔ **Redstart** is a late-cropping variety that crops very heavily, producing medium-sized fruits with good flavour.

If you decide to grow white currants, keep a lookout for these varieties:

- ✔ **Blanca** is a late cropper. This new variety is popular in Europe because of its heavy crops of sweet, large berries.

- ✔ **White Pearl** or **White Transparent** crops in mid-season. The long bunches of pale yellow fruit have excellent flavour.

- ✔ **White Versailles** crops early. The most common variety of white currant, it's still possibly the best, with a compact shape and good flavour.

If you're lucky, you may also find pink currants for sale, though they're very rare indeed. Snap them up immediately if you see them because they have a sweet taste and a very beautiful appearance.

Trying Something New: Growing Unusual Fruits

Some of the fruits in this section are difficult to grow, need high temperatures to crop, or take a very long time to produce fruit. But the quirky quartet of fruits that follow each have their own special merits, and deserve a try if you fancy growing something a little different. In this section I include the new, the ancient, the healthy, the aromatic, the curious and the delicious, and although three of them are actually trees, you may be able to fit at least one in your garden.

Getting going with Goji berries

In recent years, few fruits have hit the headlines quite like the goji berry (*Lycium barbarum*). Familiar to the Chinese as *gou qi cai*, the goji berry's fame is largely down to the great claims that have been made about the health benefits of its small, orange berries which are largely available as dried berries and have a taste somewhere between raisins and tea! Hardy and easy to grow, the arching goji berry shrubs reach about 2 metres high and wide. They have small leaves, a few thorns, and small purple flowers that appear just before the clusters of oval, scarlet berries.

The goji berry is such a new crop that not many people know what to do with it! You can eat the berries dried, in smoothies or delicious fruit salads, or raw, when they have the greatest nutritional benefit.

Goji berries are exceptionally rich in amino acids and vitamin C. They also contain betacarotene, converted in the body into vitamin A and other antioxidants.

Planting and cultivating goji berries

Most people buy potted goji berry plants to cultivate. Goji berries aren't fussy about soil and although they grow well in dry soils, they may be prone to mildew in these conditions. The plants grow best in full sun, but their scruffy appearance and size make them a less-than-ideal choice for pots on the patio. A single plant will produce about 1 kilogram of berries when fully grown.

Goji berries are related to tomatoes and potatoes, both important commercial crops, and some people worry about imported bare-root plants from China carrying diseases that may affect UK crop plants. So, to be on the safe side, stick to potted plants, grown within the EU, usually from seed.

Here are the steps to take if you fancy growing goji berries:

1. **Plant the shrubs 1.5 metres apart in a sunny spot at any time of year.**

2. **Mulch with compost each spring and give the plant some general fertiliser.**

   The plants grow arched, sprawling and untidy, but you don't need to do much in the way of formative pruning. The flowers and fruits appear in year two on arching branches made the previous year, so resist the temptation to tidy the plants up too much in winter.

3. **After several years, get into the centre of the plant with a pair of loppers and cut out a few of the oldest stems to open up the bush and give more room for the new shoots.**

Harvesting and storing your goji berries

Goji berries are such a new crop in the UK that few people have picked or eaten them fresh. The soft berries don't store for long after picking because of their softness, but you can lay them on trays to dry in the sun or a cool oven, and store.

Choosing varieties

Unfortunately, goji berries are one of those fruits where you don't get to choose between a multitude of different varieties. No named varieties of goji berry are available.

Here we go: Mulberries

The mulberry grows to be a beautiful, sizeable tree that often looks much older than its true age. It has handsome foliage of variable shapes and quickly forms an interesting, gnarled shape. The tree casts a dense shade and you can expect it to be about 3 metres high after ten years, although it can grow to twice that, or even higher. So plant with care – you don't want to have to try and move it after ten years because you've planted your tree in the wrong place.

Mulberries come in white and black forms, and black is the one to go for if you want fruit. The black mulberry is easy to grow in most soils, is self-fertile, and the fruits – which ripen over many weeks – look like blackberries. These fruits are packed with juice and are very fragile, which is the reason why you never see them for sale in shops – they don't transport at all well. Therefore to experience what I consider to be the king of fruits, you have to grow them yourself. Mulberries are sweet but acidic when fully ripe, and have a wonderfully rich and complex flavour – quite unlike any other fruit.

Mulberries are delicious raw, on their own or with cream, and they make vivid ice-creams and sorbets. You can also make good jam with mulberries, and they taste great cooked or mixed together with other fruits.

Mulberries are rich in sugar with moderate amounts of vitamin C. Their rich colours are a sign that they contain high levels of antioxidants.

A king's folly

The white mulberry is the preferred food of the silk moth and King James I planted 100,000 mulberries in the 16th century in an attempt to establish the silk trade. Unfortunately for him, he imported black mulberries and his scheme wasn't a success. But his efforts did leave a legacy of black mulberries, which have far bigger and tastier fruits than the white mulberry, so it wasn't all bad news!

Planting and cultivating mulberries

People usually buy mulberries as young trees about 1.2 metres high, in pots. Be prepared for these trees to set you back a considerable sum! The high cost of mulberry trees – usually at least £30 – seems odd because they're easy to propagate from large (1-metre) cuttings. However, this is a tree, and should therefore live for at least a century, giving good value for money.

You can plant your tree in any well-drained soil, in full sun, ideally in a warm, sheltered place. Because the fruits tend to fall from the tree when ripe, planting the tree in a lawn is a good idea, so that you can easily collect the fruits from the ground when they fall. Stake the tree for its first few years and water it regularly until it gets established. You don't need to give your tree any real attention from this point on, apart from light pruning to shape the tree when it's young.

Remember not to plant mulberries near any pale paving in your garden. The fruits stain everything, including your fingers when you pick them and your clothes if you get them on fabric.

Mulberries are 'intelligent'! More than any other tree, mulberries come into leaf very late in spring and somehow they usually 'know' not to come into leaf before the last frost. Though not infallible, the mulberry tree seems a useful plant to have in your garden.

Harvesting and storing your mulberries

Despite their long lifespan, mulberries start to crop at an early age and you should see the first berries after about three years from planting and decent crops after five years. When ripe, the berries fall onto the ground from where you can collect them, or you can also pick them directly off the tree if you go over it every day.

Choosing varieties

Not a great deal of difference exists between the few varieties of mulberry available. **King James** is the most common variety and it crops well, with fruits that ripen through red to rich deep purple when perfectly ripe.

Scents of pride: Quinces

The quince is a rather old-fashioned, attractive and unusual fruit that many people plant purely as an ornamental tree, but the fruits are decorative, fragrant and useful in the kitchen. Quinces are usually small trees, about 4 metres high and wide, with twisted and rather gnarled branches and large leaves that are deep green above and usually silvery underneath. In late spring they produce large, white flowers, often tinged with pink, followed by large, knobbly, pear-shaped fruits. These fruits are softly felted and ripen to gold, in late autumn, and hang on the trees after the leaves fall. Quinces aren't a fruit to eat raw but they have a powerful aroma and are well worth growing for their fragrance alone – a dish of fruits is superb for perfuming a room.

You need to first cook quinces to make them edible. Raw quinces are hard and very astringent and make your mouth pucker! Cooks usually grate and add them to stewed apple, to which they give a wonderful depth of flavour and fragrance. You can also use quince to make a beautiful pink jelly and because of the high *pectin* (a setting agent) content, it's a useful fruit for adding to other jams and jellies to improve setting.

Quinces contain minerals, especially potassium, and vitamin C.

Planting and cultivating quinces

The UK is the northern limit of where quinces thrive, so, to give them their best chance of producing a successful crop, avoid planting them in cold, northern gardens or at high altitudes. Quinces dislike damp areas, and are more likely to grow and crop well in southern and sheltered areas of the country, particularly in the east where summers are hotter and drier. They aren't fussy about the type of soil you plant them in, as long as it's not too damp.

Quince plants themselves are usually available as small trees, pot-grown or bare-root, and you plant them in the same way as apples (see Chapter 15). Quinces are self-fertile and so you need only one tree.

After planting, you can trim any long shoots by about half their length to encourage a better shape and better branching. In subsequent years you may need to prune lightly to shape the tree, because they naturally try to grow into strange shapes! Water the tree often in the first year until it establishes itself. Also remember to water the tree in dry weather to reduce the likelihood of mildew affecting the leaves, although this is rarely a problem.

Harvesting and storing your quinces

Pick the fruits in late autumn before the frosts arrive and damage them. These fruits are hard and they last for many months in good condition if you store them in a cool place.

Meet the japonica

The 'proper' quince is related to, but is a different plant from, the ornamental flowering quince or japonica (*Chaenomeles*) that many gardeners commonly plant as a spring-flowering wall shrub. However, although the fruits of japonica don't possess quite the same aromatic properties as quince, they are perfectly edible and useful in the same ways as quinces. Japonicas often fruit heavily and the golden fruits are ornamental. If you want to grow japonicas for their fruits, avoid the double-flowered varieties, which rarely produce fruits, and stick to the more common red-flowered varieties.

Choosing varieties

You have only a few varieties of quince to choose from and to be honest they're all rather similar. The two most common, which are both likely to produce a decent crop in the south of the country in most seasons, are:

- ✔ **Meeches Prolific**, which is the most common variety and has small, yellow, pear-shaped fruits.

- ✔ **Vranja**, which has large, pear-shaped fruits that are a golden yellow colour when ripe but it produces few fruits at a time.

Much maligned: Medlars

The poor medlar is not a fashionable fruit these days! In centuries past, the medlar was a useful fruit in autumn when few others were available, but isn't really to modern tastes. The fruits are an ugly, dull brown and they have to be almost rotten (or *bletted*) before you can eat them. However, as a link to the past, a curious delicacy, and an attractive small tree with pretty, white flowers and attractive autumn colour, medlars deserve a place in your garden.

Medlars aren't a fruit to eat fresh. After you leave them to go brown and soft (take a look at the 'Harvesting and storing your medlars' section later on), however, you can squeeze out and eat the flesh raw. The taste of medlars is then sweet, vinous, and aromatic, and people traditionally eat them with biscuits and cheese and also make them into jelly.

Because you don't eat medlars fresh, they aren't rich in vitamins by the time you eat them, but they do still contain sugars and minerals at that stage.

Planting and cultivating medlars

Medlars are hardy and thrive in most areas. They don't mind too much what soil you plant them in, as long as it's not too damp. You can usually buy them as small trees, growing in pots or as bare-roots, and you plant them in the same way as apples (check out Chapter 15).

Medlar trees are self-fertile (in other words, they produce a crop even if you have just one tree) and usually set a good crop of fruits. They normally grow to a small size – about 3 metres high and 4 metres wide – and so you don't need to prune them regularly except to tidy the shape of the tree, which is naturally spreading and untidy.

Harvesting and storing your medlars

You need to pick the fruits as late as possible but before the first frost of autumn arrives, and then store them in your shed or outhouse. Keep them 'flat face' down on a layer of straw or sawdust to prevent damage until they go soft or *bletted*, which is when they're ready to use, and don't store any them any longer.

Choosing varieties

Although few varieties of medlar exist, and they're all rather similar, here are the most common varieties:

- ✔ **Dutch** has the largest fruit of all but is usually considered to have a poorer flavour than Nottingham.
- ✔ **Nottingham** is the standard variety and forms a low, spreading tree. The fruits are small but have the richest flavour.

Going Nuts

You need a fair bit of space to grow your own nuts (no sniggering at the back), but despite the fact that you can store them for many months, nuts are especially delicious when you eat them fresh. In this section, I look at the two easiest types to grow in your garden: walnuts and hazelnuts. Neither are affected by serious pests or diseases but you may have to battle with squirrels to enjoy your harvest!

A long-term challenge: Walnuts

Walnuts grow to become large trees. Most varieties reach about 8 metres high after 20 years and live for at least a century, and so they make a good investment! Majestic and attractive, many people value them as much for their timber as for their nuts. However, walnuts aren't suitable for small gardens because of their size and the dense shade they cast, and the leaves, when they drop in autumn, can stain your paving, and the falling nuts also make a bit of a mess. The fleshy green case that covers the nuts splits and this flesh can also stain paving and your hands.

Walnuts are high in calories and loaded with vitamins A, B1, B2, B6, D, E and K, linoleic acid, phosphorus and some protein. These nuts are especially delicious when freshly picked (called *green walnuts*) but they also store well for at least a few months. You can eat walnuts raw and add them to cereals, breads and cakes.

Planting and cultivating walnuts

Walnuts prefer a deep, rich soil and a warm site sheltered from strong, cold winds and late spring frosts, which can damage the new spring growth. They don't thrive in cold, upland areas. Trees produce both small female flowers and thick, green catkins as male flowers. But for the heaviest crops, planting two different varieties to ensure effective pollination is the best way forward, except for a few, newer varieties such as Buccaneer.

Most people buy walnuts as potted plants. Buying a named variety is essential if you want a tree that will produce a good crop. Popping a nut in a pot instead of buying a plant may give you a free tree but you'll be waiting at least a decade for it to start cropping and the crop and the quality of the nuts will be variable.

Here's what you need to do to get potted walnut plants off to a good start:

1. **Prepare the planting hole well, digging down at least 60 centimetres deep and wide and mixing in plenty of organic matter.**

2. **Put a stake alongside the plant to keep the roots stable as the tree gets established.**

3. **Backfill the hole until at the right depth, so that you can then plant the tree with the top of the root ball level with the soil.**

4. **Water the young tree immediately and then regularly in dry weather, especially in the first season.**

From this point, the tree doesn't need much aftercare, and you don't need to do a great deal of pruning. When it's established, the tree needs little maintenance.

Harvesting and storing your walnuts

Walnuts drop in autumn and the fleshy protective coating splits in half. You can peel this off immediately or put the whole nuts in damp sand to rot the flesh, although this process can be a bit messy. The walnuts you see in shops are carefully dried so that they store for long periods. Your walnuts aren't going to store as well and I recommend using them by Christmas.

Choosing varieties

Here's a rundown of three popular varieties of walnut:

- **Broadview** is a popular variety with heavy crops, but may produce better crops with a pollinator such as Buccaneer.
- **Buccaneer** is a standard, self-fertile, heavy-cropping variety.
- **Rita** is a new self-fertile variety with compact growth but heavy crops.

Ideal for smaller gardens: Hazelnuts

The hazelnut (*Corylus avellana*) is smaller than most other nut trees. It's a small, multi-stemmed tree that grows to about 3 metres high. Although wild hazels do produce nuts, buying and planting a named variety is worthwhile if you're hoping for a good crop. Filberts (*Corylus maxima*) are slightly different because they have longer nuts but grow in the same way and need the same treatment. Fresh hazelnuts (or *cobs*) are softer and more milky in taste than bought nuts, and they taste delicious.

You can eat hazelnuts raw, add them to cakes and cereals, or ground them in a blender and use them in a variety of desserts.

Hazelnuts are high in calories because of their high oil content and rich in vitamin E, minerals and amino acids. Many people consider them to be at their best when you eat them as soon as the husks around the nuts are turning brown and the nuts inside are soft and milky in taste.

Planting and cultivating hazelnuts

Hazelnuts grow well in most soils to about 3 metres high, and tolerate a little shade but crop best if you plant them in a spot in full sun. These trees are generally hassle-free – the biggest problem you're likely to have is squirrels and possibly mice stealing nuts before they're ready for harvest.

Here's are the steps you need to take:

1. **Prepare the soil well by digging out perennial weeds and adding organic matter.**

2. **Plant each tree about 4 metres apart, water them well, and be sure to water the young trees through their first season until they get established.** Although hazels are partially self-fertile, you get better crops from planting two hazels or cobs of different varieties.

3. **In the first few years, prune the main shoots growing from the main stem back by about half their length.** This encourages side shoots to grow that bear flowers and nuts. Try to create a spreading shape with an open centre – a bit like a goblet.

By the third spring you should see the yellow catkins (male flowers) appearing, and the tiny, red, female flowers that develop into nuts. At this stage you don't need to prune except to cut out a few of the older branches every year to keep new branches growing; do so in late winter after the catkins have dropped.

The cut branches are valuable for staking peas and beans and any long branches make good bean poles.

Choosing varieties

Here are four good varieties to consider when choosing which hazelnuts to grow:

- **Butler** is a vigorous tree, suitable for windy and cold sites, producing high yields of large nuts.

- **Cosford Cob** is a good variety that produces showy catkins and heavy crops of large nuts with good flavour. Also, Cosford Cob is a good pollinator for most other varieties, and so makes an ideal choice for your second tree.

- **Di Giffoni** produces heavy crops of very large nuts on exceptionally compact trees.

- **Kentish Cob** or **Lambert's filbert** is a heavy cropper with large, pale brown nuts.

Chapter 15

Caring for Slow-Growing Tree Fruit

....

In This Chapter

▶ Considering your options

▶ Planting apples for months of healthy fruit

▶ Working towards the perfect pear

▶ Making your garden home to juicy stone fruits

....

Some fruits are an investment in time as well as money. Unlike most 'soft fruits', which often crop in their second year, apple, pear and plum trees make you wait a few years more before you can expect to see a reasonable crop. Every cloud has a silver lining, though, and the good news is that you can then expect a harvest every year for the rest of your life! Growing any of the fruits in this chapter really is planting for the future.

Many people are put off planting tree fruits because they imagine that they need an orchard to do so, but you don't need to give over quite that much space. Indeed, few gardeners happen to have a half-acre spare for creating an orchard! Thankfully, most apples and some other fruits are now available on special roots called *rootstocks*, which control the vigour of the trees so that they don't grow too big, or give increased vigour so that the tree will be just the right size. You can also train fruit in ways to take up even less space. For example, growing three different apples in the space of a 2-metre-wide fence panel, giving you fruit over several months, is possible, and you can even grow most of the fruits in this chapter in pots, to create your very own 'patio orchard'!

A good reason for growing your own tree fruits is that doing so enables you to experience the varied tastes of unusual varieties, types that you can't buy in the shops. Even better, you can pick and eat them at the peak of ripeness, when they taste their best. You don't have to compromise the look of your garden either. The blossom of apples and pears, peaches and cherries is as pretty as any other flower, and can enhance the beauty of your garden as well as making it productive. The advantages of growing your own become all the more obvious when you choose to grow peaches and apricots. These fruits seem exotic but, thanks to new, easy-to-grow varieties, are easier to cultivate than ever before and are a joy to pick and eat at the height of juicy ripeness.

Avoiding feast and famine

Healthy trees – potted or planted in the garden – set heavy crops of fruit if the spring weather is good. Apple trees and other fruits automatically adjust their crop according to the amount they can support, so in June a significant number of fruits naturally fall off the tree. (Dry weather increases the amount that fall.) After this initial fruit drop you may need to thin the fruits further. Thinning the fruits is important. As an average, allow only one or two fruits to develop in each cluster. If you allow them all to develop you get a big crop of small fruits. Even more importantly, heavy crops place such a strain on the tree that it can't make much growth, meaning that that you get a very poor crop the following year. This leads to *biennial bearing*, meaning that you get alternate years of feast and famine.

Looking at Seed and Rootstocks

Gardeners could grow any fruit from a seed or pip, but usually only do so for those fruits that grow on short-lived plants. Several problems with growing from seed make it an unpopular option. The two major problems are:

- Getting a crop from a seedling as opposed to a bought plant (that will have been grafted, as with most tree fruit, or grown from a cutting, in the case of most soft fruit) takes a long time.

- You can have no idea what the quality of the fruit is like until it's produced. The fruit won't be the same as the tree from which the fruit was taken. With the way that new varieties are produced, a plant grown from a pip of a Granny Smith won't produce Granny Smith apples.

Of course, someone, at some time, has to grow fruit from seed or no new varieties would appear, but these breeders have to grow possibly hundreds of seedlings for ten years or more – until they produce fruit – before they can see if any of them are worth keeping, and this isn't something that many people have room for.

Instead, gardeners don't grow apples and other tree fruits from seed but use *grafted* plants instead. Grafting is where growers cut and 'stick' pieces of the stem of an apple variety onto another plant with roots (the *rootstock*), and the two plants then unite and form one plant. When you buy a tree you see a bend in the stem, near the base, where the two are joined.

Be sure not to plant apples and other grafted trees too deeply. The join between the rootstock and the top apple at the base of the tree must always stay above the soil surface. The rootstock controls the growth and size of the tree and if the join is buried the top part of the apple forms its own roots and the controlling influence is lost.

Experts have bred special rootstocks that make the tree vigorous, of moderate growth, or very small. The ultimate size of the tree you grow depends not just on the apple variety but on the type of rootstock from which it grows. So by choosing the right rootstock you can be sure of your tree reaching the right size for your garden.

As well as controlling the size of the plant, *dwarfing* and *semi-dwarfing* rootstocks encourage the tree to fruit at a younger age. So you don't have to wait five or six years for your first apples – often trees try to fruit in their second year.

Although you don't usually have a choice of rootstocks when buying peach, nectarine and apricot plants, the plants that you buy will still have been grown in this way.

Deciding on Tree Types

Before you buy an apple or other fruit tree, you need to think about where and how you're going to plant it, because different shapes of tree suit different situations. If you plan to plant it in a lawn or a border, a bush or standard tree may be the answer. Against a fence, however, you may prefer cordons or a fan. The great thing is that you have a choice, and that you can train trees in a wide range of shapes and sizes (see Figure 15-1).

Cordons

In most gardens, *cordons* – trees with a single stem – are by far the best and most suitable way to grow apples and pears. Gardeners typically plant cordons at an angle of 45 degrees to slow the sap and encourage flowering along the whole length of the tree. The angle also means that you get a longer stem and thus more fruit. As well as producing heavy yields, cordons also enable you to grow a wide selection of apples, pears and some other fruits in a tiny area. You should be able to get as many as three individual cordons on a 2-metre fence panel, although you can use them just as effectively as a living screen, supported on posts and wires, to divide up your plot, or instead of a fence with your neighbour.

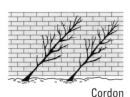
Cordon

Standard

Half-standard

Bush

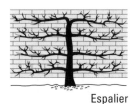
Espalier

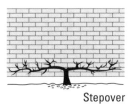
Stepover

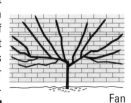
Fan

Figure 15-1:
You can train fruit trees in a variety of ways to suit your needs and your garden.

You can buy ready-trained cordons but young plants (often called *maidens*) are easy to train yourself. To train a cordon:

1. **Set three horizontal wires – at 80 centimetres, 120 centimetres, and 180 centimetres above the ground – against a fence or on a row of 2-metre tall tree stakes and tie one cane for each tree onto these wires. Set the canes at 45 degrees, about 60 centimetres apart at ground level.**

2. **Plant each tree and tie it to a cane, taking the top out of the growing tip to encourage it to make side shoots.** (See Step I of Figure 15-2.)

3. **In the following year and every winter afterwards for about four years, let the tree grow and cut off about half to one-third of the new growth at the top of the main stem, until the cordon reaches the top of its cane.** This slows its progress and makes sure that the tree forms side shoots all the way up the stem. The lower part of the cordon starts cropping before the stem reaches the top of the cane.

4. **Every August, cut all the side shoots off the main stems, back to four leaves (see Step II of Figure 15-2). When the main stem has formed and reached the top of the cane, reaching a length of about 240 centimetres, you need to do only the August prune from then on (see Step III of Figure 15-2).**

You may also see for sale *minarettes* or other single-stemmed apple, pear and sometimes plum trees, which are basically vertical cordons on dwarfing rootstocks. Gardeners usually plant these vertically rather than at an angle of 45 degrees. You also have the option of buying ballerina trees, which look like cordons but are genetically predisposed to creating this shape. Ballerina trees naturally form a single stem with very short side shoots, but you can't buy your favourite apples as Ballerina trees – only a few varieties from which to choose are available, and this limits their usefulness and popularity.

Year 1   Year 2 onwards

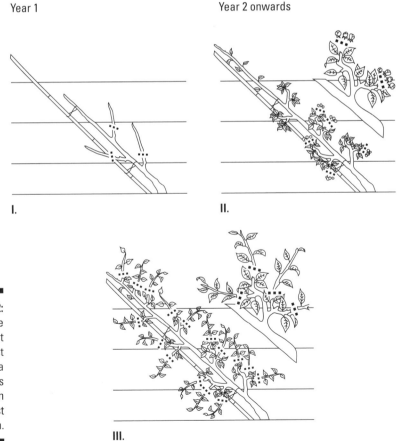

I.   II.

Figure 15-2:
Cordons are the simplest and easiest way to fit a lot of trees into even the smallest garden.

III.

Standards and half-standards

Although not the most popular types of tree, standards and half-standards are the 'typical' apple tree shapes. The bare stems, 1–1.8 metres high with branches on top, grow to form large trees, and you need a ladder to pick their fruits. This tree shape will have been grafted onto vigorous rootstocks (see the section 'Looking at Seed and Rootstocks'), but the advantage is that you can grow them in grass or in the border.

Standards and half-standards are ideal for apples, pears, plums and damsons and are also suitable for cherries if you can protect the fruits from foraging birds. In mild areas this tree shape can also be suitable for apricots.

If you decide to plant a standard apple during winter, shortening the main branches by about half is a good way to increase the number of branches, and therefore the amount of fruit that the tree produces. This method delays fruiting by a year but gets you more apples in the long run! You can also help your tree by cutting back any thin twigs to two or three buds to strengthen their growth. Do this in winter for about two years and after that concentrate on summer pruning to stimulate fruiting.

Bushes

Planting a bush is a more popular method of growing apples, and is a good way of growing most of the fruits in this chapter, too. Bushes have branches down to almost ground level, are usually grafted onto semi-dwarfing root-stocks, and most are restricted to about 2 metres in height, making all the fruits easy to pick. Planted at least 2 metres apart, bushes are ideal for small gardens and you can even grow them in pots.

Bushes like the same kind of pruning treatment as standards.

Espaliers

Espaliers are a little complicated and less popular than other types of tree. They consist of a single, upright stem with a series of horizontal branches (usually three to five) trained on either side. However, espaliers are another way to get a lot of fruit from a small space. By this method a single tree could cover an area of about 2 metres square – the size of a fence panel and an area that you would need three cordons to cover. Espaliers are most appropriate for apples and pears.

You can buy ready-trained espaliers and although they usually cost upwards of $40, they will save you several years' work training your own. Growing your own espalier is fairly simple but you can't expect to see any fruit for at least three years and completing the training takes about five years. Here's how to do it:

1. **Set horizontal wires to train the branches against – ideally at 60, 90, 120, 150 and 180 centimetres above the ground – to provide five layers of branches.**

2. **Plant your young (or *maiden*) tree, tie it to a 2-metre cane and cut it off about 50 centimetres from the ground in winter.** Three branches will grow; if more than three grow, you can just cut the extras off.

3. **In July, tie the central, upper shoot to the cane and carefully bend the two outer shoots to the left and right, to the lowest wires.** Summer is when the shoots are most flexible.

4. **When winter comes along again, cut the vertical stem off just below the 90-centimetre wire.** This may mean cutting off most of the growth but you must be brave!

5. **Shorten the two horizontal shoots by about half to encourage side shoots to grow.** These will bear the fruits in a year or two.

6. **In summer, bend the new growth from the ends of the horizontal stems to the wires. You also need to tie down your two new shoots to the 90-centimetre wire and train the third up to the 120-centimetre wire.**

You can then repeat this process until your framework is complete, and then regularly summer prune in August.

Stepovers

You may be forgiven for referring to *stepovers* as 'tripovers'! Gardeners often plant them as an ornamental edge to vegetable plots, and train them in the same way as espaliers, but they have a single layer of branches, about 30 centimetres off the ground, either side of the main stem. Stepovers crop well, but are irresistible to birds and even snails. In addition, stooping to prune and pick the fruit isn't always convenient. You can buy them or train them yourself in the same way as the first layer of an espalier. Gardeners usually only apply this shape to apples and pears.

Fans

Fans aren't as popular for apples as they are for peaches and plums. Gardeners train fans so that, from a central, low point, a dozen or so main stems radiate out like the spokes of a wheel. Fans are appropriate for growing against a fence or wall, where they can look very attractive, or for training against horizontal wires on upright stakes as you would set up for cordons and espaliers.

You can buy ready-trained fans or train a young plant yourself, as with espaliers, to save a lot of money. To do this:

1. **Set about 12 180-centimetre canes, secured on horizontal wires, radiating out from the central point in the ground.**

2. **Plant the young plant at that point and cut it back to about 40 centimetres high, as shown in Step I of Figure 15-3.**

3. **Equally space out the three or four shoots that grow in summer but remember to pull two shoots down to the lowest canes of the fan.**

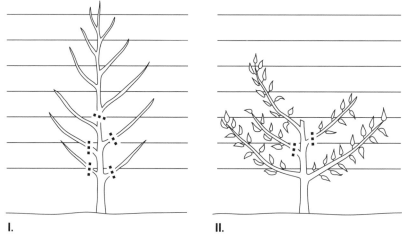

Figure 15-3: Fan-training a tree takes several years but it will be productive and attractive.

I.

II.

4. **In winter, cut all the shoots back to three or four buds, as shown in Step II of Figure 15-3.**

5. **You should then get about a dozen shoots that you can train to the canes, and in the next winter, you need to prune these back by half.**

6. **Take one of the shoots that then grow from the ends of each of these pruned stems and train that along the canes and summer prune all the rest.** After all that, hey presto – you have a fan!

Anchoring Apple Trees

Apples are one of the most popular fruit plants to grow and – when they're established – one of the easiest to look after. No longer do you need a ladder to pick them, and you don't need to put up with gluts of maggoty apples. With clever planting and selection of varieties, you can have just the sort of apples you like from your very own garden.

Apples are usually grouped as dessert or culinary (cooking) apples. Dessert apples are usually sweeter and less acidic than culinary apples but of course, some people like to eat acid apples. I, for one, don't like Granny Smith apples but they are popular, and devotees of this apple might find some culinary apples delicious! Most culinary apples ripen and get sweeter as they age; some are popular for eating raw at this stage, and are called *dual-purpose*. The same applies to other fruits such as pears, plums and cherries.

Apples are surely the most adaptable of all fruits. As well as the amazing diversity in the flavour of the different dessert apples you eat raw, you can cook them in so many ways. Although you can use dessert apples, cooks in the UK tend to prefer cooking apples. Different varieties vary widely in the way they cook – some retain their firm texture and others cook to a light fluff. Fluffy apples are best for baking and stewing. Just think back to what you liked eating most as a child and apples will feature somewhere: apple pie, apple crumble, apple strudel, apple snow – the list goes on, and by growing your own apples you can make your tarte tatin the best ever by choosing just the right variety to make your dish special.

Famously, apples are good for you. They contain a complex mix of good things such as many minerals, soluble fibre, biotin, folic acid, and reasonable amounts of vitamin A, B1, B2, B6, C, E and K.

Rummaging around rootstocks

The four most commonly used apple rootstocks are:

- ✔ **M27**, a very dwarfing rootstock that severely restricts the vigour of the tree, and which rarely gets taller than 2 metres, making it ideal for small gardens and patio pots. Trees growing from M27 rootstock always need to be staked and aren't a good companion for poor soils. Because of the small size of the trees, the crops aren't huge – you can expect about 6 kilograms per tree – but the individual apples are big.

- ✔ **M9,** a dwarfing rootstock that restricts growth less severely and is also good for small gardens and pots, with trees growing no bigger than 2.5 metres high and wide, so you should be able to pick all the apples easily. M9 trees generally need staking throughout their lives, but are the best choice for most gardens, soils, and pots, although they aren't ideal for very poor and dry soils. Yields from mature trees are around 15 kilograms, depending on variety.

- ✔ **M26**, a semi-dwarfing rootstock that usually results in a tree about 3 metres high when mature. M26 makes a better choice for trees growing in poor or dry soils, although the trees do need staking at first. Crops are heavier than on M9 trees, but they can be slow to start growing.

✔ **MM106,** a semi-vigorous rootstock that results in trees about 4 metres high and wide, used for standard and half-standard trees rather than bushes and cordons. MM106 can be useful for poor soils but is generally too vigorous an option if you have a small garden. Although the crops are heavier than on other rootstocks, because the trees grow larger, they may take longer to start cropping as the tree develops its network of branches.

Other rootstocks, such as MM111 and M25, are too vigorous for the average garden, so avoid them unless you have a few acres to spare!

Because apples are grafted onto a rootstock, wouldn't it be great if someone came up with the idea of grafting several types of apples onto one stem. You would then be able to plant just one tree without worrying about pollination and wouldn't be faced with massive crops of apples all ripening at the same time. Three types of apple on one tree! It sounds a great idea. Well, someone has already thought about it and created *family apple trees*. The reality isn't quite as good as the fantasy because the three different varieties often grow at different rates and need slightly different pruning. And the trees never look quite right! However, family apple trees are popular and are worth planting, although you're restricted to the three varieties that have been combined by the grower. Some specialists offer a range of family trees.

Keeping the doctor away: Growing apples

Apples are hardy, adaptable plants but because of their heavy crops, the trees take a lot out of the soil, and therefore need good soil preparation and feeding. They grow in most soils and are happy in a clay soil and on chalk. In fact, they may not crop quite as well on very acid soils.

Apples are hardier than pears but generally grow and crop best in a sheltered spot out of cold winds, especially in spring. They also need sun, not so much to grow well but to form flower buds, ripen their fruits, and develop sugars. Shelter from strong or cold winds is especially important in spring because bees, who pollinate the flowers, don't fly in cold conditions.

Planting and cultivating apple trees

You can buy apple trees in garden centres, but remember that their plants are usually potted and more expensive than plants stocked by a specialist. If you do buy potted plants, avoid any that have weeds or moss on the top of the compost or any that have roots crowding the surface. These plants have been in the pot for too long and don't grow well. Also look at the growth if you buy in summer – a healthy tree should make at least 30 centimetres of new growth. If the new growth looks stunted, the tree may be pot-bound and not vigorous.

Garden centres and other outlets such as supermarkets also sell bare-root *root-wrapped* trees in bags of damp peat to keep the roots moist. These trees can be fine but, in supermarkets, where conditions are warm, they often start to sprout in the middle of winter. Avoid these trees like the plague! I've also seen trees that have dried out and are completely dead for sale in spring and even in summer, long after they should've been put on the bonfire.

The best time to plant apple trees is early spring, but any time from November to March is fine. You can plant potted trees at any time, in a similar way to bare-root trees. However, you can't spread out the roots of potted trees when planting in summer because damage to the roots while the trees are in leaf often means that the trees don't grow as well. If you plant a potted tree in summer, remember to water it thoroughly and regularly.

Apples generally have flowers that can't pollinate themselves (which they need to do so the apples can form) and need another variety to pollinate them. If you live in a suburban area and your neighbours have an apple tree, you may be lucky and find that it pollinates your tree. But to be on the safe side try to plant at least two apple trees.

Several problems can befall your apples tree. Most, such as mildew and scab aren't going to harm them much or reduce cropping and you may wish to ignore them, in which case make sure your tree has ideal growing conditions and water and feed it well, and the tree may well recover without further intervention. Some insect pests can be more of a worry – the last thing you want is to bite into an apple and find half a maggot staring back at you! Chapter 7 has more details about dealing with these pests.

Growing apple trees in the ground

Here's how to do it:

1. **Before planting, remove all perennial weeds and dig a large planting hole, ideally 1 metre wide and 60 centimetres deep. Put plenty of organic matter in the hole and replace and firm the soil to leave a hole 30 centimetres deep.**

2. **If planting a bare-root tree, soak the roots in a bucket of water for an hour before planting. If planting a potted tree, give it a good soak of water an hour or so before planting to make sure all the compost in the pot is moist.** Wetting the root ball after you've planted it is almost impossible!

   If you plant your tree in a lawn, keep an area at least 1 metre in diameter free from turf to reduce the competition from grass roots.

3. **Place your tree into the hole and spread the roots over the soil, having first cut off any damaged roots with secateurs.** Ensure that the level is correct by placing a cane across the hole and making sure that the original soil level of the tree is at the new soil level. When you're satisfied, put some soil on the roots and shake the tree to work the soil among the roots. Then add more soil until the hole is almost full. Firm well with your foot and water very thoroughly.

4. **Stake the tree.** The best way is to hammer a stake in, at 45 degrees to the tree, and tie it with a tree tie to the trunk, about 60 centimetres above ground level. The stake should be on the leeward side of the tree to support it against the prevailing winds. This method of staking keeps the roots stable as the new roots start to grow, but allows the trunk to flex, which helps it to thicken.

After planting your tree, you need to devote a little time each year to keeping it in good condition. I'm always amazed at how many people take a crop off their trees every year and yet hardly ever consider feeding their fruit trees. So, every spring remember to spread a general fertiliser around the tree and mulch the soil surface; your tree will thank you for it.

As well as feeding your trees, you also need to prune them. No subject strikes fear into the heart of gardeners more than pruning (more apples and other fruit trees are prevented from fruiting by wrong pruning than due to any other reason), but the basics are very simple.

You may want your tree to grow fast to start with – for example, when you're training it as a fan or espalier – but after your tree is as big as you need, you then want to make it flower and fruit and not grow so fast. This situation is where summer pruning comes in, which is the only pruning that mature trees really need. In general, you can do it in August, when the tree has stopped growing, and prune all the shoots back to about four leaves. It's that simple. Those buds then slowly mature and some develop into flower buds.

Pruning a plant hard and cutting it back a lot makes it grow more strongly, especially if you prune in winter. If you have a large, overgrown apple tree and you prune it hard with a saw in winter, it produces lots of tall, upright stems the next year and no apples. Within two years your tree is as big as it was before you pruned, but will have no apples. So don't do it!

Growing apple trees in containers

Although the most usual way to grow fruit trees is in the ground in the garden, you may be surprised to hear that you can also grow them in pots! This isn't a new idea – gardeners have been growing fruit in pots for centuries. Most tree fruits are suitable, not just apples, but look out for trees that have been grafted onto dwarf rootstocks (usually clearly labelled).

Any plant in a pot depends on you at all times for water and food. So although you can enjoy advantages, such as having the fruit by your back door, you must never neglect them even for a few days in summer or they'll die. Growing fruit trees in pots may be convenient, but its not a labour-saving method!

If you're planting your apple tree in a pot, here are the steps to follow:

1. **Choose a pot and add some compost.** In the first year a 30-centimetre diameter pot – with a drainage hole – is ideal, and John Innes No 3 compost is perfect for potting. Put the tree in the pot (having soaked the roots first to make sure the roots and compost are moist) and add soil around the roots or root ball and firm gently.

2. **Stake the tree.**

3. **Water your tree regularly and apply a liquid feed every week from spring to late summer.** An alternative way to feed is to apply a controlled-release fertiliser to the compost at potting time and every spring thereafter.

4. **After one or two years, re-pot the tree into a 45-centimetre diameter pot and the next year into a 60-centimetre diameter pot. After about the fifth year, you can re-pot one more time into a slightly bigger pot.** This will be your tree's final pot and you need to top-dress the compost in subsequent years. (To do this, every spring scrape away the top 5 centimetres of compost and replace with fresh compost. After about 10 years try to find a garden to plant the tree in so that it doesn't start to deteriorate.)

Harvesting and storing your apples

Different apple varieties are ready to harvest at different times. As a rule, you can tell if an apple is ready to pick by cupping it in your hand and lifting it upwards. An apple that snaps off easily is mature and ready to pick but, according to variety, may not be at its best for eating. Some late apples need storing for a month or more, by laying them in shallow boxes in a cool, dark place, before eating. You can also store small numbers of apples in your fridge to keep them at their peak. So, by growing a few varieties for harvesting and storing at different times, you can be eating your own apples from August to December, or possibly even longer. Remember that apples are versatile and you can cook and freeze them, cut them into rings for drying in a cool oven, or even make them into cider or wine!

Choosing varieties

Apples are peculiar because each one needs pollen from a different variety to produce a fruit. Therefore, to get a good crop you need to have at least two apple trees that flower at the same time. The same applies to most tree fruits, including pears, plums and cherries (although not peaches or apricots).

Fruit growers have made things easy for gardeners by grouping varieties according to when they flower and giving each group an identifying letter – A–D – or number – 1–4. These two identification systems are the same and are interchangeable, and similar groups apply to other fruits such as pears (but don't think that a pear from pollination Group 2 (or B) will pollinate an apple in Group 2!) So, all you need to do is buy two different trees from the same group so they can pollinate each other. Even better, because the groups overlap a bit and flowering time varies with the season, trees in adjacent groups pollinate each other to some extent. So if you want three trees and you choose two from Group B (or Group 2) and one from Group C (or Group 3), you have nothing to worry about. Some apples, such as Falstaff, may be listed by sellers as self-fertile, enabling you to get a crop even with a single tree, but you get a much better crop if another apple to pollinate it is nearby.

The one fly in the ointment is a small group of apples called *triploids*. Triploids don't make fertile pollen and need two pollinators, so if you plant one, you also need to plant two other, non-triploid, apple trees, remembering that the triploid doesn't pollinate the other two. This may seem an unnecessary complication that you can do without, but triploids include the delicious Blenheim Orange, marvellous Jonagold and indispensable Bramley varieties, and so may be worth going the extra mile for.

The other important factor when it comes to choosing a variety, apart from flavour, is resistance to disease. Although many modern varieties are much less prone to most of the common apple diseases than older varieties, gardeners are sometimes suspicious of them because the names are unfamiliar. Growing your own gives you the chance to be brave and try something different, instead of a familiar variety such as Cox. Many new apples are not just easy to grow and heavy croppers, they have a really good taste, too. And if you want to grow organically, the newer varieties are much easier to manage.

When choosing a variety, avoid cheap apple trees. Your apple tree should last a lifetime, but most cheap apple trees are poor-grade plants that no one else wants. Avoid buying apples simply named 'red' or 'green', and choose carefully – you want your tree to be with you for a long time.

Going back to our roots

You may hear people say that the best apples in the world grow in the British climate. Indeed, most famous varieties of apple were bred originally in Britain. But you can be forgiven for doubting this fact after seeing the apples available in supermarkets that get shipped in from around the world. This situation may be a necessity if people want to eat apples in May, but from August until the New Year you can buy British apples.

Here are a few of the very best varieties of *dessert apples*, which are great for giving you dependable crops of really tasty apples to eat raw.

- **Blenheim Orange** is an easy-to-grow and disease-resistant, dual-purpose variety that produces large fruits (popular as cooking apples) with delicious, slightly acid, yellow flesh. (Triploid; pick in October for eating in December.)

- **Braeburn Helena** produces large crops of hard, crisp apples, growing best in warm areas. The ordinary Braeburn doesn't always grow well in the UK and so choose the clone Helena. (Pollination group C; pick in October for eating in November.)

- **Charles Ross** produces large, red fruits with crisp, juicy flesh and wonderful flavour, similar to Cox. This variety performs well in colder gardens and on poor soils and is resistant to disease. (Pollination group C; pick for eating in October.)

- **Cox Self Fertile** has the same great flavour as ordinary Cox but is less susceptible to disease and more reliable. Ordinary Cox is also difficult to grow and only suitable for warm areas. (Pollination group C; pick in September for eating in October.)

- **Discovery** is an easy-to-grow, popular, sweet and tasty apple with red skin and crisp, white flesh, stained with red under the skin. (Pollination group B; pick for eating in August.)

- **Fiesta** is a delicious, easy-to-grow apple that has Cox in its breeding. The large, pale yellow, red-flushed fruits have crisp, white flesh and store well. (Pollination group B; pick for eating in September.)

- **George Cave** is a green, rather acid apple with a red flush. This variety is hardy and reliable, and produces large crops of crisp apples. (Pollination group B; pick for eating in August.)

- **Greensleeves** apples resemble Golden Delicious but have good flavour and the trees crop well. This variety is partly self-fertile and hardy and easy to grow. (Pollination group B; pick for eating in September.)

- **Herefordshire Russet** is a new and easy-to-grow *russet* (a fruit with dull, brown skin) that has crisp, juicy flesh with a complex, delicious, nutty flavour. This variety crops well, is self-fertile, and stores well. (Pollination group B; pick in October for eating in November.)

- **Jonagold** produces heavy crops of large apples that have yellow skin with a red flush, and yellow, crisp, juicy flesh with a delightful, sweet flavour. (Triploid; pick for eating in October.)

- **Katy** apples are juicy and red-flushed with excellent flavour, and make a good choice for colder gardens. (Pollination group B; pick for eating in September.)

- ✔ **Kidd's Orange Red** is a fine, crisp apple with a Cox flavour. This variety is hardy, resistant to disease, and good for northern gardens (unlike Cox). (Pollination group B; pick in October for eating in November.)

- ✔ **Meridian** is a cross between Cox and Falstaff that combines the qualities of both, resulting in an apple that has the fine flavour of Cox but which is easier to grow and produces heavier crops. (Pollination group B; pick in September for eating in November.)

- ✔ **Red Falstaff** is a hardy, partly self-fertile apple that always crops well, even in colder areas. The red apples have great flavour and crisp flesh. This faultless apple stores well, is healthy, and is resistant to disease. Falstaff is similar but not as colourful. (Pollination group B; pick for eating in October.)

- ✔ **Redsleeves** is a red-flushed, crisp apple with good flavour. These compact, partly self-fertile trees crop heavily. (Pollination group B; pick for eating in September.)

- ✔ **Scrumptious** are delicious, early-cropping apples with a complex flavour. The trees have compact growth, are self fertile, and make excellent pollinators for other apples.

- ✔ **Spartan** is a beautiful, hardy and heavy-cropping apple with polished, deep red skin, crisp white flesh, and an intense, sweet, grapey flavour. (Pollination group C; pick for eating in October.)

- ✔ **Sunrise** are attractive, red-flushed, yellow apples with crisp, juicy texture and good, aromatic, complex flavour. These trees are reliable and crop well. (Pollination group B; pick for eating in August.)

- ✔ **Sunset** is a recent variety that produces heavy crops of attractive apples with a Cox-type flavour, but is much easier to grow. These trees have a compact habit. (Pollination group B; pick for eating in October.)

- ✔ **Winter Gem** produces big, reliable crops of large, red-flushed fruits with crisp flesh and sweet taste that store well. These trees are hardy and suitable for all areas. (Pollination group B; pick in October for eating in December.)

If *cooking apples* are on your gardening wish list, take a look at these choice varieties:

- ✔ **Arthur Turner** trees produce very pretty blossom and large, pale green apples that cook to 'fluff' and are good for baking. The trees crop well and are partly self-fertile. (Pollination group B; pick for cooking from August onwards.)

- ✔ **Bountiful** produces attractive, yellow apples flushed brown with a sweet flavour that you can eat raw after storage. These reliable trees crop very heavily. (Pollination group B; pick for cooking in October.)

✔ **Bramley's Seedling** is the most popular of all cooking apples with its large, flat, waxy fruits, that are green with a red flush. Bramley's Seedling is a vigorous tree, but isn't easy to grow as a cordon. (Triploid; pick for cooking in October.)

✔ **Emneth Early (Early Victoria)** is a beautiful, red-flushed apple with white flesh that cooks well. This variety crops heavily and is one of the earliest-cropping cookers. (Pollination group B; pick for cooking in August.)

✔ **Grenadier** produces medium-sized apples with green skin and white, crisp flesh that cooks well. Grenadier is a good pollinator, crops well, and is healthy. (Pollination group B; pick for cooking in August.)

✔ **Howgate Wonder** produces large, golden apples with tasty, cream-coloured flesh that cooks well and is ideal for baking. This variety blooms late and so is a good choice for colder areas. (Pollination group C; pick for cooking in November.)

✔ **Jumbo** is a vigorous variety with huge fruits. The skin is flushed red and the flesh cooks well but retains its texture and has a good, sweet flavour. These trees produce huge blossom to match the apples, are easy to grow, and compact in habit. (Triploid; pick for cooking in October).

Planting Pears

Pears come second only to apples as a home-grown tree fruit, are almost as adaptable as apples, and you can train them in all the same ways as apples (see the 'Deciding on tree types' section earlier in the chapter). Training pear trees against a warm wall – where the reflected heat works especially well – ensures good crops of perfect fruit. Pears are also beautiful in bloom, though they tend to flower a little earlier than apples and so are more prone to damage by late spring frosts. Even so, varieties exist to suit most gardens.

Pears are best for eating raw when fully ripe but you can also stew and cook them, often with apples and other fruits. Possibly the most delicious way to cook them is to poach them in red wine. Another classic combination is pears with chocolate sauce after poaching them in syrup. However you cook and eat them, though, pears are very special and delicious.

Pears have similar nutritional benefits to apples, containing potassium, iron, and vitamins B, C, E and K, biotin and folic acid.

Rooting around with rootstocks

Pears are grafted onto quince rootstocks that control the vigour of the tree. The range of rootstocks isn't as extensive as with apples and none are especially dwarfing, but the most dwarfing rootstocks do result in small trees and ensure that they crop at an early age.

The three rootstocks used for pears are:

- ✔ **Quince A,** a vigorous rootstock, suitable for all types of tree shapes and training, and a good choice for planting in rather poor soils.

- ✔ **Quince BA29,** the most vigorous rootstock, which is used to grow the weaker varieties so that they grow and crop better. Standards and half-standard trees also use this rootstock.

- ✔ **Quince C,** the most dwarfing rootstock, and trees reach about 3 metres in height if you allow them to grow naturally. This rootstock is the best choice for cordons and other neatly trimmed trees, and for average, fairly fertile garden soils.

Pear-ing up: Growing pears

Both similarities and differences exist between growing apples and pears, which I describe here.

Planting and cultivating pear trees

For the best results and for fruits that are at their maximum sweetness, pears need a sheltered and sunny location. You can plant and cultivate them in the same ways I recommend for apples in the earlier section 'Keeping the doctor away: Growing apples', although you have to wait slightly longer than with apples for the trees to start cropping. A bush tree should produce about 25 kilograms of pears, and cordons about 5 kilograms, when fully grown.

Harvesting and cultivating your pears

Unlike apples, which you can eat when unripe or store for several weeks, if not months, without them losing their taste and texture, pears are crisp, often hard, and almost inedible when unripe, which is often when they're due for picking. Pears then suddenly ripen and have a very short period when they're at their peak. Some varieties ripen on the tree but you need to pick others when they're hard and store them in a cool place to ripen – it just depends on the variety. You then need to check them every few days and eat them as soon as their flesh starts to soften and ripen.

Choosing varieties

Similarly to apples, pear varieties each belong to a pollination group (see the varieties section of 'Keeping the doctor away: Growing apples' earlier in the chapter for more about pollination groups). Conference is the nation's favourite variety of pear, but many more types exist to try that you can't buy in the shops. Here are a few of the best:

- **Beth** is an reliable, early variety with a fine texture and flavour and heavy crops. (Pollination group 3; pick for eating in September.)

- **Concorde** is a new, partly self-fertile pear and a cross between Conference and Doyenne de Comice. This variety is the perfect garden pear and crops very heavily with large, sweet, juicy fruits. (Pollination group 3; pick in October for eating in November.)

- **Conference** is a self-fertile variety, and the most popular of all pears. They store well, if you pick them early, and taste juicy and sweet. (Pollination group 2; pick in October for eating in November.)

- **Doyenne de Comice** is a large, upright tree that produces good crops of large, golden pears with exceptional flavour. Needs a warm spot to do well. (Pollination group 2; pick in October for eating in November.)

- **Durondeau** is a neat tree that crops well with golden fruits and excellent flavour, and which is a good pollinator for other pears. (Pollination group 2; pick in October for eating in November.)

- **Glou Morceau** is a green pear that changes to yellow when ripe. Reliable in a sunny spot, this variety stores well and has exceptional flavour. (Pollination group 3; pick in October for eating in December.)

- **Invincible** is an unusual pear that has two flushes of flowers and ripens over a long period. The fruits are green, crisp, and juicy at first, and then become softer and golden. (Pollination group 2; pick in September for eating in October.)

- **Jargonelle** is an old, hardy variety with greenish-brown fruits that crop very early and that you can eat straight from the tree. (Triploid (needs two pollinators); pick for eating in August.).

- **Onward** is a vigorous, fairly early pear with good crops of large, pale green fruits with creamy, delicious flesh. (Pollination group 3; pick for eating in September.)

- **Williams Bon Chrétien** is one of the most popular pears. It crops well, with golden, red-flushed, juicy fruit. (Pollination group 3; pick for eating in September.)

Sweet success: Stone Fruits

Stone fruits get their name from the single, large 'pip' in the centre of the fruit. They include some of the most delicious of our late summer fruits – plums and the closely related gages and damsons, peaches and nectarines, apricots and cherries. Delicious!

In the past, many stone fruits formed large trees, far too big for a small garden, and pollination was a problem. But the advent of new varieties and rootstocks has overcome all these disadvantages and you can now grow a few plums and cherries even in small gardens. Some people think of peaches and apricots as too tender or too exotic to be sensible crops in British gardens, but they're much more reliable and productive than you may think and a real joy to pick – fresh and ripe.

All stone fruits prefer a slightly alkaline soil and if calcium is deficient, they don't develop their stones properly. One other key factor to remember is that you prune them only in spring and summer, when in leaf, because winter pruning can lead to silver leaf disease (Chapter 7 tells you all about this serious fungal disease).

Taste of summer: Plums, gages and damsons

Plums, gages and damsons are close relations and need very similar treatment. Plums are grouped into dessert and cooking types, although cooking plums are rare, mainly because the true cooking types are unpleasant raw and you may as well grow a dual-purpose plum such as Victoria. Many people consider gages to have the finest flavour of all these three fruits, and despite their green or yellow colour, their soft, buttery flesh is melting and honeyed. The downside is that gages generally require warm, sheltered conditions to do really well and aren't as reliable as most plums. Damsons are small, dark plums that aren't really for eating raw but they do make wonderful jams and preserves. By growing your own plums, gages or damsons (or all three!), you can enjoy something really special – juicy, delicious fruits at the peak of ripeness.

You can eat plums, gages and damsons raw when fully ripe and also cook them by stewing or making them into delicious pies and jams (home-made plum or damson jam has to be one of the tastiest jams of all). Stewed plums with custard are a traditional favourite but plum crumbles and sponge-based upside-down puddings are even better!

Plums, gages and damsons are rich in sugar, calcium and potassium, and contain vitamins A, B1, B2, B6, C, E and K, biotin and folic acid.

Going pear-shaped, Asian style

Asian pears, often called nashi pears, aren't a common sight in the UK, and are quite different to the more familiar European pears. Asian pears are round, usually golden or white in colour, and their flesh is crisp, juicy, white, and has more 'gritty' particles, which people consider to be a fault in most pears. The flavour isn't as rich and complex as the best pears but Asian pears are refreshing and so expensive to buy as fruit in the shops that they are well worth growing. Easy to grow and self-fertile, you can plant and grow Asian pears in the same way as for pears and usually harvest them in September, after which they store well for several months. They look attractive and have pretty white flowers in spring.

Rootstocks

Two main rootstocks are used for grafting these three fruits:

- ✔ **Pixy** is a dwarfing rootstock that restricts the height of plums to about 2.5 metres without pruning, promotes early cropping, and is ideal for growing in containers.

- ✔ **St Julian A** is the standard rootstock, semi-dwarfing, and a better choice than Pixy for poor soils. In good conditions, fruits grow larger in size than on Pixy rootstock and trees generally reach about 3 metres high.

Planting and cultivating plums, gages and damsons

Plums, gages and damsons aren't difficult to grow. You plant them in the same ways as for apples (jump back to the earlier 'Keeping the doctor away: Growing apples' section to find out how). Finding the right spot, however, is especially important, because plums, gages and damsons (along with apricots) bloom so early in spring, and although frost doesn't usually damage flower buds, it does often damage the flowers. The trees are hardy and don't get damaged by frost, but if the flowers are open and a severe frost strikes, the cold will damage the flowers. For this reason, trees that are full of flowers in spring can sometimes produce no fruit at all.

A less severe problem is where the weather is just generally miserable and cold at flowering time. In these conditions, bees, which pollinate the flowers, can't be bothered to fly and stay in the hive, meaning that you then get no fruits. So, when planting plums, try to choose a spot that isn't likely to be too cold and frosty at flowering time. Such conditions mean that plums, gages and damsons don't always thrive in northern gardens or gardens at high altitudes. If you garden in these conditions, your best bet is to plant the trees against a sunny wall and train them as fans (see 'Deciding on Tree Types' earlier in this chapter) to protect them as much as possible against severe cold.

Make a point of mulching your tree with compost every year and giving an annual spring feed with a general fertiliser. You may need to water the tree, too, especially if the plum is growing against a wall that may keep rain off it. Water regularly rather than giving it a soak and then allowing it to suffer from drought, which causes the fruit to split.

Plums and their relatives don't need a lot of pruning if you grow them as a bush or an upright bush (or *pyramid*). When your tree is still young, you can safely limit your pruning to just shortening the main stem to about 1.2 metres in spring, when in leaf. In July of the first year, go a little further by pruning all the other shoots to 20–30 centimetres long, to an outward or downward facing leaf, bud or side shoot, to encourage a weeping appearance. In future years, you can cut the main shoot back by about half when the tree is as tall as you want it to get. At the same time, you can cut all the other young shoots back to between six and eight leaves. In this way you encourage flower buds to form, which increases the yield as well as restricting the size of the tree. Plums are also very prone to aphids on their new shoots and if you cut off the tips you remove some aphids and the unsightly, twisted leaves.

The other popular way to train a plum, gage or damson is as a fan. You have a choice here: you can either buy a ready-trained fan tree, to save you a few years' work, or start with a young *maiden* tree to save you money (they cost about a third of the price of a ready-trained fan). To start from scratch, you need to plant your young tree against a wall or sunny fence with the same arrangement of canes as for apples (see the earlier section 'Deciding on tree types'). Prune the tree in early spring by cutting it back to about 45 centimetres high, and evenly space the resulting four or five strong shoots across the framework, making sure that you tie the lowest at right and left to the lowest two canes. The following spring, remember to cut all these back by half their length and in summer spread out and tie the shoots to the 12 canes. The following spring you can cut back all these 12 shoots by half their length. Then, in summer, you just need to cut back all the new shoots (unless you need them to fill in the main framework) to four or five leaves. After that, the only pruning you need to do is to cut back the new shoots to four or five leaves every summer.

Never prune plums or cherries in winter because this increases the chance of them being infected with silver leaf disease (see Chapter 7 for more information).

Many plums and their relatives are prone to crop heavily and if all the fruits develop you may find that you have a big crop of small plums on your hands! Although having a tree full with a heavy crop can look impressive, and you may be tempted to let all the fruits develop if the tree has a good set, the strain exhausts the tree and you won't get much fruit the following year. The sheer weight of the crop can also break branches. If possible, thin the plums when they're about 1 centimetre long, leaving them evenly spaced to about 5–8 centimetres apart to moderate the crop and get the best quality, large fruits. In this way you avoid alternating years of 'boom' and 'bust', and keep your tree in a much happier, healthier condition. If you forget to thin the fruits, prop up the branches to prevent them snapping.

Wasps are always attracted to plums and they may attack fruits or just feed on fruits pecked by birds.

Harvesting and storing your plums, gages and damsons

Because these trees flower early in spring, when the weather is variable, their crops can fluctuate wildly between years; 50 kilograms isn't unusual from a moderately sized tree and a fan-trained tree can produce 10 kilograms. Pick plums and their relatives when they're fully ripe and soft unless you plan to cook them. Plums have to be eaten quickly when ripe because they don't store unless you cook them and make them into pies, jams or wine.

Choosing varieties

Many varieties, but not all, are self-fertile. If you plant just one plum, choosing a self-fertile variety means that you don't need to worry about pollination. After that you can plant any other variety and the first tree does the pollinating. If you want to grow a non-self-fertile variety you must plant two plums but remember that plums, gages and damsons are very closely related and do pollinate each other.

You have a varied selection of plums to choose from, and here are some of the best:

- ✔ **Blue Tit** produces early crops of dark purple fruits with yellow flesh; a heavy cropping, good tasting, partly self-fertile plum.

- ✔ **Coe's Golden Drop** makes a good choice if you want a really superior plum. The fruits are yellow and have a rich, sweet flavour. However, it needs a sheltered, sunny spot and another variety nearby to ensure pollination.

- ✔ **Czar** plums are dark purple with greenish flesh, and are a cooking variety that you can also use in desserts, when ripe. Czar is a hardy variety, and produces heavy crops.

- ✔ **Early Laxton** is the earliest of all plums to ripen. The trees are compact and produce yellow and red fruits with a good flavour. Early Laxtons are dessert plums but are also good for cooking.

- ✔ **Jubilee** plums are rather like Victorias, but superior. The large, yellow and red fruits have a good, sweet flavour, and the trees are easy to grow and reliable, producing heavier crops than Victoria.

- ✔ **Mirabelle** is a cherry plum that produces masses of small, round, usually orange fruits with a good, sweet taste. The trees crop heavily, are easy to grow, and are suitable for colder gardens.

- **Opal** is an early, compact variety that produces heavy crops of large, purple plums with an outstanding flavour.

- **Pershore Yellow** is an easy-to-grow, reliable golden plum. However, the flavour is only moderate and is perhaps best for cooking.

- **Victoria** is the nation's favourite plum with pale red, sweet fruits. This variety is easy to grow and reliable.

- **Violetta** produces large, violet-purple fruits with good flavour. An easy tree to grow that has a compact habit, and so needs little pruning.

If you're looking to grow gages, consider these three varieties:

- **Denniston's Superb** trees produce lots of large, green fruits that have that sweet, buttery, mild, gage flavour. This variety crops heavily and is more suitable for northern and colder gardens than most gages.

- **Early Transparent** is the best-flavoured of all gages. The trees crop well with pale yellow fruits, are self-fertile, and the tree is neat and easy to manage.

- **Oullin's Golden Gage** is a good, self-fertile dessert gage with large, golden fruits with yellow flesh that taste delicious.

If damsons are your thing, try these excellent varieties:

- **Merryweather** is the most popular damson, with large fruits, and is self fertile.

- **Shropshire Damson** is a compact, self-fertile tree with heavy crops of black fruits with green flesh.

Summer loving: Cherries

Sadly, fewer cherries grow in Britain now than in the past, not due to any great difficulty in growing them but because they're difficult to pick, which makes them expensive. But you can grow your own cherries at home that taste delicious – far nicer than those you can buy, which are probably imports from overseas.

Cherries grow well in gardens but the biggest problem with some varieties is their size. Cherry trees can grow enormous and you sometimes need a tall ladder and a fair bit of bravery to pick them (those raised platforms aren't called cherry-pickers for nothing!) Thankfully, however, you can now buy dwarf rootstocks that keep cherry trees to a more manageable size, and even enable you to grow them against a wall or fence as a fan.

If you grow sweet cherries, the best way to eat them is straight from the tree, raw. You can cook sweet cherries but they have such a delicate flavour that they won't taste of much afterwards! Cooking cherries are best for culinary purposes because of their higher acid content and because they taste less sweet – though if you like your fruit to make you pucker you could give them a try!

Cherries make great jam and ice-cream, and make great additions to sponge puddings (be sure to take the pips out first) and fruit salads.

Cherries are quite high in sugars and calories compared to most fruits. They contain minerals, antioxidants including vitamins A, C and E, and B vitamins and folic acid.

Rootstocks

Cherries are commonly available on only two rootstocks:

- ✔ **Colt** is a good rootstock that generally controls the height of trees to 3 metres but gives them enough vigour to crop well and early. This rootstock enables you to grow cherries in difficult soils.

- ✔ **Gisella 5** is even more dwarfing and limits mature trees to around 2.4 metres in height. Gisella 5 is the best general-purpose rootstock and is ideal for growing trees in containers, too. Trees on this rootstock produce crops very early in their life and crop well.

Planting and cultivating cherries

You can plant cherries in the ground and in pots in exactly the same ways as I describe for apples (refer to the section 'Keeping the doctor away: Growing apples' earlier in this chapter), but keep a few specific things in mind before you start. Cherries don't tolerate wet soils and always grow best in a deep, rich soil, although they do tolerate chalk. Also, because cherry trees flower quite early in spring and are pollinated by bees, be sure to site yours away from strong, cold winds and avoid frost pockets and high elevations, unless you can find a sheltered spot. As they grow, most people then train cherries as fans against a wall or fence, which makes them much easier to net against birds.

In general, sweet cherries do better in mild, southern areas; but cooking cherries can be successful farther north and they are generally a bit tougher.

After planting your cherry tree, you need to care for it with the same treatment and pruning as you would for plums (refer to the 'Taste of summer: Plums, gages and damsons' section earlier in this chapter). Water your tree regularly in dry weather to prevent the fruits splitting when it rains again, and treat your tree to a mulch and a feed every spring.

Birds love cherries and can eat your entire crop unless you take steps to stop them. The best way is to put a net over the trees as soon as the cherries start to ripen – obviously you can do this only if the tree is small. Cherries are also prone to black aphids that infest the young shoots and cause the foliage to twist. Chapter 7 gives you the lowdown on dealing with aphids.

Harvesting and storing your cherries

The cherries on a tree ripen over a period of several weeks, usually changing colour to red or black when ripe and ready to pick. Simply holding the cherry and pulling it from the tree causes bruising so the best way to pick cherries is to twist the stems from the branch to minimise damage. Try to eat the fruit as soon as possible after you pick it, although you can store cherries for up to a week in the fridge.

Choosing varieties

The pollination of cherries is fiendishly complicated compared to apples, pears and plums, but a few modern varieties exist that are self-fertile, which has made growing cherries much easier. To keep things easy, all the varieties bar one in the following list are self-fertile:

- ✓ **Nabella** is a cooking cherry superior to the familiar Morello because it's more compact and less prone to disease. Nabella is self-fertile and produces heavy crops of black cherries.

- ✓ **Stella** is a vigorous, self-fertile sweet cherry that ripens rather late with large, dark red fruits.

- ✓ **Summer Sun** is a popular new, self-fertile sweet cherry variety with large, black cherries, compact growth, and heavy crops.

- ✓ **Sunburst** is possibly the best garden cherry, with its heavy crops of delicious, almost black fruits. This self-fertile sweet cherry variety is quite early to ripen and forms a neat, upright tree when young.

- ✓ **Vega** is a Canadian sweet cherry that produces large, sweet, white cherries. Vega needs a pollinator and Stella is ideal. Many people (me included!) believe that white cherries have better flavour than red and black cherries.

A surprise in store: Apricots

Apricots are related to peaches, but are easier to grow because they don't suffer from peach leaf curl. However, apricots are generally larger trees than peaches and they grow vigorously. They flower very early in spring and the white flowers are attractive, if rather sparse at times.

Apricots are worth growing because when you pick them ripe from the tree they taste so very different to the 'fresh' apricots you buy in shops. Ripe apricots are sweet, soft, and as juicy as a peach. You never get them like that in supermarkets.

Although you may never have considered trying to grow something as exotic as apricots before, the commercial apricot orchards now present in the UK show that growing them is possible. Although not as foolproof as apples, I can assure you that apricots aren't difficult to grow and when you come to pick your first, sweet fruits you won't be disappointed!

Fresh, ripe apricots picked fresh from the tree are for eating raw – with a napkin! But you can also stew apricots, and use them to make jam and delicious pies.

Apricots contain high levels of carotene (vitamin A) and fibre, and are also rich in potassium, iron, calcium and vitamin C.

Planting and cultivating apricots

You can plant apricots in the same ways as apples – in the garden and in patio containers (special varieties bred to be dwarf, which are ideal for containers, are sometimes available); flip to the 'Keeping the doctor away: Growing apples' section to find out how. You can also grow apricots in cold, unheated greenhouses, although, like peaches, apricots need a cold winter period, so avoid growing them in a heated greenhouse. Remember, too, that apricots grow best in the southern counties of the UK and aren't keen on wet soils or cold, sunless sites or gardens at high altitudes that are cool in summer and subject to late frosts that can damage the flowers (see plums above).

The most popular way of growing apricots is as a fan against a sunny wall. If you use this approach, be sure to position the base of the plant at least 20 centimetres from the wall to give the roots room to grow. This method is still the best way to grow apricots in cooler northern, western or upland areas but experts have recently bred new varieties that you can successfully grow as bushes or trees in the open garden in most parts of the UK. You do need to plant them in a sheltered area to keep the early flowers free of frost, though. Frost puts off the pollinating bees who quite sensibly prefer to fly in warmer conditions. After planting your apricot tree, remember to mulch and feed it every spring.

Apricots are more vigorous than peaches and need a space at least 3 metres wide if you train one on a wall, although you can keep them to 2 metres high with careful pruning. Apricots planted in an open position in the garden (and I only recommend this if you live in a warm, mild area) will reach 3 metres high and wide.

When your tree is still young, you can encourage bushiness by pruning it back in summer, removing about half the length of the main stems. After that, you don't need to prune it as regularly. If you're training your tree as a fan against a wall, begin the pruning in the same way as for a peach (see the 'A nice pair: Peaches and nectarines' section later in the chapter). After the framework of branches is created, which takes about two years, simply shorten the side shoots to four to six leaves in midsummer to control the growth and stimulate short spurs that produce flowers. The flowers and fruits of apricots grow on older, two- or three-year-old wood, near the centre of the bush or tree, and not on young wood.

Apricots flower very early, when the weather is cold, wet and windy, and so a good idea is to protect small trees on the patio and wall-trained plants with fleece, to prevent the flowers being frosted. Bees are often lethargic at this time of year, and therefore taking on their role for yourself and pollinating the flowers by hand can really pay off (see the 'A nice pair: Peaches and nectarines' section later in this chapter for more details). With luck, lots of fruits form. Often two fruits develop next to each other, and you need to give one of them room to grow by thinning out the smaller one. Do this when they're about 1 centimetre across, and leave the remaining fruits about 10 centimetres apart.

Harvesting and storing your apricots

Apricots often develop red 'cheeks' on the sunny side as they mature but don't take this as a sign that they are ripe. The way to tell when an apricot is ripe is to gently squeeze a fruit to see if it's still hard and unripe or soft and yielding – and ripe. The fruits ripen over several weeks, starting with those on the sunny side of the tree, and you should try to pick them as they ripen if you want to eat them fresh. Alternatively, you can pick apricots unripe if you want to cook with them or make them into jam.

Apricots don't store well but you can, of course, stew and freeze them or make them into jam as a way of keeping them for later use. You can also cut them in half to remove the stone and freeze them raw for cooking later.

Choosing varieties

In the past five years a whole new generation of apricot varieties has become available in the UK. These varieties are hardy and crop reliably, enabling you to plant apricots with confidence. I can recommend any of these varieties:

- **Flavourcot** is a Canadian variety with large, succulent fruits that have a red flush. Flavourcot is a compact tree and crops well in most gardens.

- **Golden Glow** is a tough, hardy variety with good crops of large fruits that ripen in early August.

- **Isabelle** is an unusually compact variety that rarely exceeds 2 metres in height without pruning. Isabelle produces good crops of orange-red fruits with excellent flavour.

✔ **Moorpark** is the standard variety, ripening in late August.

✔ **Tomcot** is a recent improvement on older varieties and copes much better with the British climate. Tomcot produces large, sweet, tasty fruits with a red flush, and is a good variety for colder gardens.

A nice pair: Peaches and nectarines

Peaches and nectarines are basically the same plant – nectarines are simply smooth-skinned peaches – and grow in exactly the same way. Both are wonderful fruits for growing at home, as small trees and bushes, against a sunny wall or fence, in a greenhouse, or as patio container fruit trees. Peaches are hardy plants, but they do need the summer sun's warmth to mature, develop and ripen the fruits. For this reason, most gardeners grow them as a fan shape against a sunny wall, especially in areas with cool summers.

The best way to enjoy peaches, when fully ripe, is raw, fresh from the tree. However, if you have an excess crop or unripe fruits, you can poach them, or make them into mouth-watering juices, ice-creams and chutneys.

Peaches and nectarines are not only delicious but also very good for you. They contain high levels of iron, potassium and vitamins A, B1, B2 and C, as well as vitamins E and K, biotin and folic acid.

Planting and cultivating peaches and nectarines

You can plant peaches and nectarines in the same way as apples (see the earlier section 'Keeping the doctor away: Growing apples'). (You can sometimes buy special varieties bred to be dwarf, which are ideal for containers.) However, you do need to make sure that you plant them somewhere they can bask in full sun. Both are ideal fruits for a cool or cold greenhouse (where they can escape the dreaded peach leaf curl) and as potted patio trees. If you plant them against a wall, be sure to position them at least 20 centimetres away from the wall so that the roots have room to grow. They generally prefer soils that aren't too acidic, and don't like waterlogged soils. Remember to mulch the soil after planting and to water them at all times, most importantly in dry weather and as the fruits are swelling. Peaches also benefit when you apply a general fertiliser, such as fish, blood and bone, each spring.

Luckily for gardeners, peaches are self fertile and one tree is enough to give you a good crop. The pretty, pink flowers, however, open very early in spring, before many bees are about, and so hand-pollinating the flowers can increase your chances of a good crop. All you need to do is take a small, soft-haired, artist's paintbrush and, when the flowers are fully open, and on a dry day, gently push the brush into the centre of one flower after another, doing the work of a bee. Doing this several times at intervals of several days is a good idea, because not all the flowers are receptive at the same time. Hand-pollination is especially important when trees are grown in a greenhouse.

Peaches produce most of their flowers on the young shoots that the tree produced the previous year. If a good number of flowers set, the chances are that you have far more tiny fruits developing than the tree can support, and so you need to thin out the fruits. When they're about 1 centimetre in diameter, and you can be sure that they have set well and are growing, work across the tree and remove the spare and crowded fruits so that the ones you leave are no closer than 15 centimetres apart. Without thinning you get many small, often misshapen fruit, and the tree suffers and doesn't crop as well the following year.

Many people position their peaches against a wall or a fence as a support for the training wires and to protect the flowers from cold. The advantage of this approach is that you can cover your plants with a sheet of plastic or fleece in winter, or arrange some sort of wooden framework over the top of the plant, in winter and early spring, to help prevent frost damage to the flowers that open in early spring. Doing this isn't as easy on a large tree in the garden. Covering your tree also keeps water from dripping on the branches, which leads to peach leaf curl spores germinating and infecting the emerging leaves. The downside is that fleece or plastic sheets over the trees prevents bees reaching the flowers, which means that you need to pollinate the flowers by hand.

If you decide to train your peach as a fan tree, rather than buy one ready-trained, cut it back after planting to about 50 centimetres in height, just above a bud. Ideally the two buds below the cut should face in opposite directions so the top two shoots grow either side of the main stem and spread against the wall. In summer, you can remove all but the three best-placed shoots and train one of them upwards and the other two outwards across the wall. Tie them against canes (for how to place the canes when training as fans, see the earlier section 'Deciding on tree types') with the lowest two at about 45 degrees. In late summer, before the leaves drop, you then need to cut back the vertical stem hard to about two buds. Always cover cuts with a *wound paint* – a sticky paint that covers the cut surface.

The following spring, when the plant is in leaf, cut back the remaining two shoots to 40 centimetres long, and these shoots should then produce four new shoots. Tie these to the canes in midsummer, spacing them out evenly, and cut back any other shoots to a few leaves. The next year, in spring, you can just shorten all the shoots slightly, ideally pruning them back to a bud that points downwards to encourage a low, spreading fan shape. Now that you've formed the fan shape, you don't need to do much more pruning in future years other than cutting out some of the older, main stems and tying in some new ones. You can cut back to a few leaves any shoots that grow towards the wall and away from the wall, and keep the fan to about 2 metres high and 2–3 metres wide.

If you're not a fan of fans, you can also train peaches and nectarines as bushes in areas that have good summers. All you need to do is to shorten the branches by about half each spring for two years after planting to encourage a good branch network. After that, cut out badly placed branches each spring and shorten the rest. After a few years, you can just cut out some of the older stems to create room for new, more productive growth.

The biggest problem with growing peaches and nectarines in the greenhouse is red spider mite, and outside you may face peach leaf curl (you can read more about these problems in Chapter 7).

Harvesting and storing your peaches and nectarines

Fruits ripen earlier in the greenhouse than outside. Although you may think the fruits are ripe and ready to pick when they develop a red flush on the skins, that isn't a reliable guide. To check for ripeness, hold the peach carefully and see if the flesh is starting to soften. If you can feel it softening, then that is the time to pick them. Take care not to squash them, as both peaches and nectarines are vulnerable to bruising. They don't store well so try to eat them immediately – ideally as you walk back to the house, so that the dripping juice doesn't make a mess of your carpets!

Choosing varieties

Peaches usually have yellow or white flesh, often with red staining where they join the stone. Many people consider those varieties with white flesh to have the best flavour, but whatever the variety, your peaches will be superior to anything you can buy in the shops.

- ✔ **Avalon Pride** is a new British-bred variety with yellow flesh and has outstanding resistance to peach leaf curl – the scourge of all peaches and nectarines. Avalon Pride crops well and is suitable for outdoor growing, when its foliage should remain healthy.

- ✔ **Duke of York** is a popular, early-cropping peach with white flesh and deep red, large fruits that have a delicious flavour.

- ✔ **Dymond** is a very late-cropping peach with a very sweet, delicious flavour and yellow flesh.

- ✔ **Garden Lady** is one of the dwarf peaches that are ideal for growing in pots on the patio. The growth is very congested and compact, and needs some protection from extreme cold in winter. Garden Lady has yellow flesh.

- ✔ **Kestrel** is a late-ripening, white-fleshed peach with exceptional flavour.

- ✔ **Peregrine** is an easy-to-grow, mid-season, white-fleshed peach – the most popular of all – with large, firm fruits.

- ✔ **Rochester** is a reliable, heavy cropper with medium-sized fruits with yellow flesh.

- ✔ **Sanguine de Savoy** is an unusual, late variety with delicious fruits that have red flesh.

- ✔ **Saturne** is a Chinese, 'flat' peach, renowned for its superb, sweet flavour. This variety has white flesh.

Unfortunately, you have a smaller number of nectarines to choose from, but these are all worth growing:

- ✔ **Lord Napier** is the most popular nectarine, with large, richly flavoured fruits, and is fairly early to ripen.

- ✔ **Nectarella** is a dwarf patio nectarine with good crops of fruit on very small bushes.

- ✔ **Pineapple** produces large, pale yellow fruits, flushed red, with very good flavour. This tree needs a warm, sunny spot to ripen fully, and is ideal for a cold greenhouse.

- ✔ **Queen Giant** is a mid-season variety with large, red fruits with tasty white flesh.

Chapter 16

Growing Greenhouse Fruits

*D*oes your greenhouse sit in a neglected corner of your garden, doing little more than keeping your barbecue and the family's bicycles dry? If so, now's the time for a clear-out! In spring and summer you can be filling it with young plants to plant out on the allotment or the garden, and using it for growing summer crops such as tomatoes and cucumbers.

You may also want to cultivate a few permanent fruits. Although some of them do grow happily outside, as I describe in this chapter, you give yourself a wider range of varieties to choose from by planting in a greenhouse environment. You can also be more certain of getting a good crop for your efforts, safe in the knowledge that they'll ripen fully inside the greenhouse.

In addition to the fruits I talk about in this chapter, dwarf peaches, nectarines, and apricots also thrive in a greenhouse, and you can read about growing them in Chapter 15. You can grow all these fruits either in pots or in the greenhouse border but remember that although plants in pots have the advantage that you can move them around, you need to take more care with watering than with plants in the open ground, whose roots can spread wide and deep to find water and nutrients.

Cultivating Climbing Fruit

People grow climbing fruit plants in greenhouses mainly to give them the benefit of higher summer temperatures and to extend the warmth of summer into autumn, to ensure that the fruits ripen. The plants take up a fair bit of space within greenhouses, and they grow for several years before producing a crop, so growing one in your own greenhouse is something of a leap of faith. You need to put in some extra work, too, by putting up a framework of wires to support the growths (frames can get in the way if you usually put up insulation in your greenhouse). On the plus side, however, these crops don't need heat in winter, and picking a bunch of grapes that you've grown yourself is very satisfying!

Fruit of the vine: Grapes

Grapes are the most popular climbing fruit for the greenhouse and are an easy fruit to grow, although they do require a lot of work. You need to start training the plants as soon as you plant them and lavish a lot of attention on them throughout the year – especially in summer. If you neglect a grape plant it rapidly becomes a tangle of leaves and tendrils and doesn't produce a good crop. The rewards of raising a successful plant, however, are considerable because ripe grapes have a far sweeter and more complex flavour than anything you can buy in the shops.

The advantage of growing your own grapes in a greenhouse is that you can leave them on the plant to ripen fully. For some varieties this may not be until November. If you grew these varieties outside rather than in the greenhouse the frost would ruin them and the birds would eat them well before then.

If you don't have a greenhouse, don't despair – you can grow grapes outside against a sunny wall too, although they may not fully ripen or taste quite so sweet. Your choice of varieties will be a little more restricted, too – some late-ripening varieties, often those with the best taste, won't ripen at all outside, so choose wisely.

You probably eat grapes raw most often, either as they are, in fruit salads or with cheese, but you can also make jelly and, of course, wine from grapes. Some Mediterranean dishes make use of the leaves.

Grapes are rich in sugars but also contain malic acid, minerals and vitamins A, B and C. Red grapes contain antioxidants in their skins.

Planting and cultivating grapes

If you were to try to grow grapes from seed you wouldn't know for several years whether or not you were going to get a good crop. For this reason, buying a potted young grape plant from a garden centre or specialist is the best way to approach growing this fruit. Be sure to buy a named variety so that you can be sure of what you're getting. Avoid buying bare-root plants because establishing them isn't easy.

The traditional way of planting greenhouse grapes is to plant them outside the greenhouse and train the main stem into the greenhouse through a hole near the base. Although this method isn't strictly necessary, it does make watering and feeding the vine easy.

Grapes need plenty of sun, so make sure they get that in your greenhouse. They thrive on dry and chalky soils, and don't grow well in heavy, wet soils. If your soil is dry and of poor quality, you can improve it by adding lots of organic matter before planting.

Planting in the ground

Grapevines can be productive for many years, and possibly decades, so make sure you give them a good start. Here are the steps to follow when planting grapevines in the ground:

1. **Fork over the soil and add some garden compost or other organic matter and some general fertiliser (about 50 grams per square metre) before planting. Also water the plant well before planting it.**

2. **Plant your grape plants, making sure that the soil level in the pot is at the soil level in the greenhouse after planting.** You can do this at any time of year but planting in winter is best because you can prune and train them immediately.

3. **Train the grapevine as it grows from the first season.** You need a basic framework of permanent branches or *rods* from your plant, from which new shoots that carry the grapes grow each year. You can train your main rods horizontally or vertically, but you need to train the shoots that carry the grapes at 90° (in other words, at right angles) to these rods.

   The simplest way to train a grape is as a *cordon* (a single permanent stem with fruiting stems that grow from its side). To train in this way, you need to put up horizontal wires to support the plant as it grows, spacing the wires 30 centimetres apart up the side of the greenhouse, attaching them to the glazing bars. In the first year, allow a single stem to grow up a vertical cane. In January, when the vine is dormant, prune the stem so that it goes only about halfway up the side of the greenhouse. This promotes side shoots lower down on the stem, and leaving out this step would result in all the fruiting shoots appearing at the top of the resulting plant. A new shoot then grows upwards the following spring and summer and you can tie it to the cane. In summer, as the side shoots grow from the oldest, lower part of the vertical stem, tie all these to the horizontal wires. These side shoots should produce flower buds, but at this early stage of the plant's growth you need to prevent fruits from forming, so pinch out these side shoots after they've grown six leaves.

4. **In the following winter, prune the main stem back to the top of the supporting cane and cut back all the other side shoots to one or two buds.** In spring, these buds will sprout and from each cluster of one or two buds, you should only allow one shoot to grow. If more than one grows you can snap off the excess with your fingers. Train the side shoots along the wires as they grow.

Always do your pruning in the dead of winter when the plants are fully dormant, as I show in Step I of Figure 16-1. If you prune in late spring, when the sap has started to flow, the cut surfaces 'bleed' and plants l ose sap and some vigour. Plants don't bleed from the regular summer pruning you need to do to keep plants under control.

5. **Pollinate the flowers.** Clusters of small, green flowers appear in early summer, with buds that look just like tiny grapes. The flowers aren't very attractive to bees, and so pollinating the flowers yourself helps the fruit to set. You can pollinate with a fine, soft artist's brush or, more simply, by running your cupped hands over the open flowers each day while the flowers are open. This transfers the pollen from flower to flower.

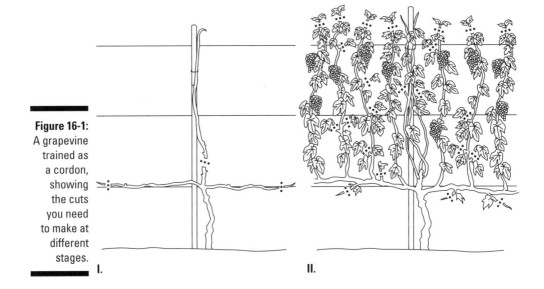

Figure 16-1:
A grapevine trained as a cordon, showing the cuts you need to make at different stages.

I.

II.

Within a short time the flowers develop into small, green berries. As they develop you may need to thin them out to give the grapes room to swell, and you can spend a great deal of time doing this! You need thin-nosed scissors to thin out effectively. If you don't thin the flowers out at all you may end up with crowded grapes that split, and rot is then likely as the grapes ripen.

6. **Make sure that the vines are well-ventilated at all times to reduce mildew and rot, and water the vines well.** If the vines are dry the grapes may shrivel (known as *shanking*). Excessively high temperatures can also damage development of the fruits.

7. **When the fruits are ripe, you can begin harvesting.** (See the later 'Harvesting and storing your grapes' section.)

After this step, you're then into regular pruning. In summer, train the side shoots out along the horizontal wires. As soon as a bunch of small flowers appears on the stems, pinch out the growing tips (as I show in Step II of Figure 16-1), counting two or three leaves beyond the flower cluster. Also remember to cut back to one or two leaves all the other side shoots that grow through summer. This cutting back allows air to get around the plant, and sun to get to the grapes and control the growth of the plant.

In the following winter, you can prune all the fruited shoots back to the main, vertical rod again, leaving just one bud. This bud grows into the next fruiting stem. A grapevine can live for a century or more so getting the pruning right from the very start is well worthwhile!

An alternative to this method is to train the main rod horizontally, 30 centimetres above the ground, and train the young, fruiting stems vertically, which I show in Step II of Figure 16-1. As you can see, you can try various different options. In my greenhouse, I have one plant trained with a horizontal rod near ground level and another trained up and then across at about 1.5 metres off the ground. I've trained the shoots from the lower rod up the side of the greenhouse and those from the top rod across the top of the roof. Just follow the basic principles and be imaginative.

Each autumn, clear up the fallen leaves and check the main rods for pests, such as scale insect (see Chapter 7 for more on pests). Many gardeners 'brush' the rods with a stiff brush to remove loose bark that can house pests.

Planting in containers

If you're short of space and want to try something to impress your friends you can train grape plants in pots as *standards* (a bare stem with a 'lollipop' head of leaves).

Growing a standard in a pot allows you to move the plant onto the patio in summer and take it back to the greenhouse in autumn, which allows late varieties to fully ripen. In the first year or two, grape plants are happy in a 30-centimetre pot but after that they need to be in at least a 45-centimetre pot. To get started, fill the pot with compost (always use John Innes No 3 compost – the plants love it!) and put in a stout stake or cane for tying the main stem to. Fix a stout cross of 25-centimetre wide timbers, about 60 centimetres long, to the top, at a height of between 1 and 1.5 metres. If space is limited, just fix a horizontal bar to the post to grow the standard in two dimensions as I show in Figure 16-2, which works just as well. As the plant grows, remove all the lower shoots on the stem, leaving only four shoots at the top of the plant to grow. Tie these shoots to the supports created by the cross of timber and prune them as usual as they grow. When you grow standards, you allow only four to six bunches to develop on each plant. If you grow the plant as a cordon, however, you can allow several bunches to develop up the main stem on the side shoots.

Figure 16-2:
A grape
plant
growing
on a stout
cross in a
container.

Harvesting and storing your grapes

Your grapes may not be ripe until the leaves start to change colour in autumn, so check for ripeness by eating one before you begin collecting them. If you want to store some of the grapes, you can do so by cutting them, with about 20 centimetres of stem below the bunch and a little beyond the bunch, and standing the stems in jars of water for a few weeks in a cool, light place. This method helps to keep them fresh.

Choosing varieties

The grapes that taste the best, and ripen latest, tend to be called Muscat grapes – these are the ones to choose for flavour. However, anyone used to supermarket grapes will discover that they all taste great! Here are some of the best:

- ✔ **Black Hamburgh** is the most famous black grape and is very popular. The good-sized bunches of large, black grapes are juicy and delicious.

- ✔ **Buckland Sweetwater** is a compact, easy-to-grow plant with reliable crops of delicious, sweet, amber grapes.

- ✔ **Flame** is a popular, seedless, bright red grape with a juicy, crunchy texture.

✔ **Lakemont Seedless** is (as the name suggests) a seedless grape that is easy to grow and suitable for growing outdoors in warm areas but crops more reliably in a greenhouse. The large bunches of pale green fruits have good flavour.

✔ **Madresfield Court** is a fine black Muscat grape with exceptional flavour.

✔ **Muscat of Alexandria** is possibly the best of all white (Muscat) grapes with large fruits with a honeyed, rich flavour. This variety does need some heat in autumn to develop its full flavour.

✔ **Phoenix** is rapidly becoming very popular because of its resistance to mildew and its heavy cropping. This variety has large, white grapes that turn golden when ripe, and have a sweet, Muscat taste and aroma. You can grow Phoenix grapes outside.

✔ **Regent** is a fine, black grape that is resistant to mildew and carries heavy crops of tasty fruit. The autumn foliage is very attractive, making this a good, dual-purpose variety. You can grow Regent grapes outside.

The Chinese gooseberry: Kiwi fruit

Growing your own kiwi fruits is perfectly possible, but be warned – doing so isn't plain sailing. Kiwi fruits are twiners and their leaves and stems are large and vigorous – this large, robust, quick-growing plant can quickly overrun your garden, let alone a greenhouse! In a single summer, this plant can grow by 3 metres, so have your secateurs at the ready! On the plus side, a kiwi fruit plant enjoying a warm summer will reward you with lots of fruit, and it's also a decorative plant, so even if you don't get a crop it will look good!

Most people eat kiwi fruits raw but you can also use them to make jam, juices and ice-cream, and add them to yoghurt and fruit salads.

Kiwi fruits are very rich in vitamin C, which they retain well in storage. They also contain vitamins A, B1, B2 and K, and nicotinic acid.

Planting and cultivating kiwi fruit

Kiwi fruit plants are hardy and in the mildest, sunniest parts of the country you can grow them in containers or outside on horizontal wires or along trellis in a similar way to raspberries or blackberries, as long as they have the protection of a sunny wall behind them. But for reliable crops, kiwi fruits are really best grown in a greenhouse – if you have the room. The extra summer heat and the extended warmth in autumn and slight protection from frost in a cold greenhouse increase your chances of getting nice, ripe fruit. But never forget that the kiwi is a rampant plant, capable of making 3 metres of growth in a year, so plant one only if you have plenty of room.

The 'kiwi' fruit: Not a kiwi at all!

In recent years the kiwi fruit has become a familiar component of fruit bowls around the world. However, until enterprising growers in New Zealand discovered that they had the perfect climate for this twining vine, and that the brown, furry fruits stored and travelled well, this odd fruit, under its former name of Chinese gooseberry, was little known in Europe. The kiwi fruit is actually a native of Asia and has nothing to do with kiwis at all – the name is just a case of clever marketing – most people have a greater affection for kiwis, whether the bird or the people, than for gooseberries!

Don't attempt to grow kiwi fruit in greenhouses that are smaller than 3 metres by 2 metres – the plants are simply too big for the space. Outside, single plants can easily cover an area 4 metres by 2 metres, and potentially much more.

To grow kiwi fruit, buy a named variety as a small, pot-grown plant. These plants prefer a deep, rich soil and so improving the soil with plenty of organic matter is always a good idea. They need plenty of water as they grow, and you need to mulch the soil around your kiwi fruit and give it a general fertiliser each spring.

So, if you like this exotic fruit and have the room to grow some, here's how to do it:

1. **Install supports for your plants.** Because kiwi fruit plants grow so rapidly, you need to do this before you start planting. The support must be very strong because of the weight of the plant and its potential crop. Horizontal wires about 30 centimetres apart, secured to the glazing bars of the greenhouse, are ideal.

2. **Water the young plant before planting, add some compost or organic matter to the soil, and plant it at the same depth as the plant was in the pot you bought it in.**

   You need a 30-centimetre pot in the first year if planting in a container, progressing to a container 60 centimetres across when the plant matures (using John Innes No 3 compost). In the greenhouse, prepare the soil well beforehand and plant in the greenhouse border. Outside, kiwi fruits are happiest growing against a sunny wall.

3. **Establish a framework of permanent branches.** Train the main branches as they grow, either horizontally (the best way) or vertically across the sides or the top of your greenhouse. Because kiwi fruit plants grow so vigorously, you can probably create this framework within a year, unless your greenhouse is huge!

4. **In winter, trim all the branches back to where you want them to be.** The plant then produces the flowers and fruits on short spurs off this main framework of branches in the second year.

5. **To be sure of a good crop you'll need to hand-pollinate the large, attractive flowers on the short spurs.** To do this, use a small paintbrush, rub it into the centre of a male flower on a male plant and then rub it in the centre of a female flower on a female plant. If you grow a variety that is both male and female (Jenny, for example) you simply need to rub the brush in the centre of each open flower at random. However, because these plants don't flower particularly early in spring, bees should be around to do the job for you. The fruits may need thinning if the flowers were pollinated well.

6. **Cut the unwanted long growths back a little throughout summer to stop the plant taking over your greenhouse, which it will do in a single season if you give it the chance!** You can leave the main prune until August.

7. **In August, after the initial earlier trim, again shorten the stems that have grown throughout summer, back to one or two leaves.** All being well, you should get fruits from these, in the third or fourth year.

8. **As the fruits grow, you may need to thin them out.**

Harvesting and storing your kiwi fruit

Kiwi fruits are usually ready to pick in October, as the leaves drop off the plant. However, you may need to store them for a while, in a cool place, for a month or so before they ripen fully and are ready to eat. Try to eat them as soon as possible or they go soft and tasteless. You can usually store them for about a month.

Choosing varieties

In the past, kiwi fruit plants were either male or female and you needed both to ensure that your fruits grew. This problem was serious for growers because the male plant, which can fertilise about six plants but doesn't produce fruit, also takes up a lot of space. Thankfully, *hermaphrodite* plants with flowers that are both male and female are now available. These varieties save space and assure a crop when the plants are mature and have reached flowering size.

Here are a couple of hermaphrodite varieties that I recommend:

- ✔ **Actinidia arguta** is a different species from the usual kiwi fruit and is more compact. This variety has small, smooth-skinned, green fruits that you eat whole, like grapes. Although new to cultivation as a fruit, this variety should be more reliable as a crop in the UK climate.

- ✔ **Jenny** is a more compact variety than most, but it's still a large plant.

Getting a Zest for Life – Growing Citrus and Other Exotic Fruits

Citrus fruits include lemons, limes, oranges, tangerines, grapefruits and many more besides, but only the first three are easy to grow in a greenhouse unless you have a lot of spare room and are prepared to provide a lot of heat in winter, which gets expensive. Citruses are all attractive plants with glossy, evergreen leaves and delightful white, fragrant flowers, and they're easy to trim and look after. You often see them for sale as houseplants but they grow less successfully in the home than in the greenhouse because conditions are usually too dark and the atmosphere too dry for them to flourish. The difference in summer and winter temperatures is also important for them to flower and fruit well, and the universally warm home doesn't provide these conditions. Citruses are, however, suitable for conservatories, where you get more light – but not if the structure is too hot to comfortably sit in during summer.

All citruses are tender plants that don't tolerate much frost. Even the more recent varieties of lemons and oranges marketed as being frost-hardy are of doubtful hardiness. Although they may survive a light frost, they're unlikely to survive in areas that frequently experience prolonged cold periods. However, you can put all these plants outside in summer and then keep them in frost-free conditions, in bright light, in winter.

Apart from oranges, lemons and limes, the other fruits that I cover in this section are less common and some can be a bit of a struggle to grow, but they make a great challenge for when you're feeling more adventurous. They aren't all always very productive but when they do produce fruits, you have an enormous and well-deserved sense of satisfaction!

Sunshine fruits: Oranges, lemons and limes

Oranges, lemons and limes are closely related to each other but vary a little in how easy they are to grow and in their requirements, mainly their tolerance of cold. Of the three, lemons are the easiest to grow and the most tolerant of poor growing conditions. Oranges are slightly more difficult and limes are the trickiest, requiring slightly higher temperatures. All are reasonably productive and you can expect a single plant in a 30-centimetre pot, about 90 centimetres high, to produce about 20 fruits a year. The plants ripen over a long period, look beautiful at all stages of growth, and produce tasty, juicy home-grown fruits to savour.

The juices of all citrus fruits are acidic and you can use them to give a fresh taste to lots of foods. The juice also prevents the oxidation of foods such as avocados and celeriac, whose flesh turns brown otherwise. Of course, you can also make drinks with them, such as your own lemonade or, if you prefer something a little stronger, limes are the perfect companion to some beers and tequila!

Citrus fruits are high in vitamin C and citric acid.

Planting and cultivating oranges, lemons and limes

When you set out to grow these fruits, I recommend buying named plants, instead of attempting to grow from seed, which results in large, spiny plants that rarely produce good fruits. You can usually buy the plants at less than 60 centimetres high, in a pot of around 12 centimetres in diameter, and you can safely leave the plant in there for a few months. Although you can grow these citrus fruits in the greenhouse border, most people usually move them to larger pots in the greenhouse. This way, you can move them onto a sunny patio in summer and put them back into the greenhouse in winter.

Here's the drill:

1. **Re-pot the specimen into a larger pot.** The best time to do this is spring or summer. Remember to choose a pot that is only about 5 centimetres bigger in diameter than the pot you bought it in. Citrus plants don't tolerate being in wet compost for long and putting small plants in pots that are too large can lead to overwatering problems.

   Citrus aren't strictly lime-haters but they are sensitive to mineral deficiencies and so the best compost to use, to be on the safe side, is lime-free John Innes. If you can't get this, use equal quantities of John Innes No 3 and standard ericaceous compost, which is acidic.

2. **After potting, give the plant a good soak to work the new compost around the roots.** Citrus, when planted in the ground, can tolerate some drought but, in a pot, you need to make sure that the plants never dry out completely. The most common problem that people experience when growing citrus is drought. If this happens, the plants drop lots of leaves and you may need to cut them back hard to reinstate their beauty. Similarly, especially when you have them outside in summer, make sure that you don't leave them standing in a saucer of water; if the roots are constantly wet (rather than just being moist), they also die and drop their leaves.

   Generally speaking, you need to ensure that citrus plants never go completely dry, though they should be drier in winter than in summer.

3. **Apply liquid feed throughout the growing season to stimulate growth.**
   You can buy specialist citrus feed that's usually available in two types:
   one for winter and one for summer. The summer food contains more
   nitrogen than the winter food, which is high in potash. Whatever food
   you use, apply it regularly, once a week in summer and once a fortnight
   in winter, and make sure that it contains trace elements as well as the
   major nutrients (see Chapter 5).

   A lack of minerals, nitrogen or trace elements such as magnesium and
   iron can cause the leaves of the plant to turn yellow. If the leaves look
   yellow, try giving a high nitrogen fertiliser boost.

   Organic liquid fertilisers may be better simply because they contain a
   wide spectrum of nutrients.

   Spraying the foliage with a weak fertiliser solution in summer is another
   way to give the growth of your plant a boost.

4. **Prune the plants routinely to keep them neat and tidy.** You can pinch
   out the soft growing tips at any time in summer – just pinch out a
   few here and there to make sure the plant is compact and a pleasing,
   rounded shape. If the plant needs more severe pruning, do so in spring
   to ensure that the plant has all summer to produce new growth. All
   citrus plants grow back well from quite hard pruning.

The white flowers that grow on citrus plants are very attractive to bees and
they usually pollinate them without any problems. The small fruits that then
develop take about a year to grow.

In summer, you can place your citrus on the patio. A sunny, sheltered patio is
best. If you're bringing plants out of the house or a shady place, into a sunny
garden, be sure to acclimatise the plant gradually to the bright sun or it may
scorch the foliage and turn it yellow. In late September, before frost starts to
arrive, put the plant in a greenhouse where the minimum temperature is 5°C
for lemons, 8°C for oranges or 10°C for limes.

Cool temperatures are important in winter to change the skin colour and
sometimes the pigment of the flesh of all citrus.

Several pests can cause trouble for citrus plants and these include mealy bug
and scale insects (see Chapter 7). You can keep both of these under control
with a systemic insecticide (be sure to check the pack to see how long after
application you should wait before picking any fruit) or by picking them off
carefully with a cocktail stick.

Harvesting and storing your oranges, lemons and limes

Most citrus fruits take at least a year from the petals dropping to the fruits being ready to pick. Most of them start green and change to their ripe colour throughout winter when the lower temperatures arrive. The fruits may not be fully ripe at that stage, though, so just make sure your fruit have been growing for at least a year and taste one first before you pick them all!

Citrus fruits remain edible, even when ripe, for months, if you leave them on the plants, so don't pick them until you're ready to use them.

Choosing varieties

Unfortunately, very few varieties of citrus fruits are available but try to buy a named plant rather than one simply called a lemon or orange. Here are some varieties to look out for:

- Lemons:

  - **Eureka** flowers almost all year and produces large lemons.

  - **Meyer, Improved Meyer or Four Seasons** is the most popular of all lemons. Meyer is easy to grow, tolerates temperatures close to freezing, and the fruits are much less acidic than the average lemon. I recommend Improved Meyer – a more vigorous, virus-free clone.

- Oranges:

  - **Sanguinelli** is a beautiful 'blood orange' with red-pigmented flesh. By keeping the tree cool in winter (in a frost-free greenhouse rather than growing it in your warm house), you can make the red colouring greater.

  - **Valencia** is a popular, edible orange with large, dark green leaves and pure white, scented flowers.

If you go for limes, look out for **Tahiti**, a dwarf plant with fragrant white flowers and small green fruits.

Another plant to consider is the dwarf Calamondin. With its small, orange-like fruits, Calamondin is a pleasant greenhouse or house plant, although its fruits aren't edible.

The taste of paradise: Figs

Figs are a wonderful fruit to grow, hardy and quite attractive, with large, lobed leaves. They seem exotic but they don't need a lot of heat. You can grow them outside in warm areas but growing them in a greenhouse, either in the ground or in pots, will ensure you get a crop of luscious figs with sweet, melting flesh. Ripe figs are so delicate they melt in the mouth – and squash in the hand – and growing your own guarantees you eat them at their peak of perfection.

The best way to eat your own, ripe figs is when they're as fresh as possible, still warm from the sun. Lovely! But you can also poach or make them into jam if you find you have too many!

Figs are rich in sugars and minerals, have some vitamins A, B and C, and are mildly laxative – so keep an eye on how many you eat!

Planting and cultivating figs

The best way to start growing figs is with a young potted plant. You can grow them outside in a sheltered spot, in full sun – against a wall or fence works best. However, figs are very vigorous and need a lot of pruning, and gardeners who grow them outside usually plant them in a pit, lined with paving slabs to create a buried container that restricts the spread of roots and thus the size of the plant. Figs also grow very well in large pots and they produce reasonable crops in this way. Alternatively, you can keep them in the greenhouse all year or just for winter and bring them onto the patio for summer.

You don't need to heat your greenhouse for growing figs. A cold greenhouse that protects the fig from the worst of the cold is sufficient, but keeping the fig free from frost improves your chances of the almost-mature figs, which start life in the spring, surviving through winter.

Figs aren't fussy about soil, though be sure not to add too much fertiliser or the plant will produce leaves instead of fruits. In pots, use a soil-based compost such as John Innes No 3.

Here's how to grow yourself some figs:

1. **Plant your fig outside, in the greenhouse border, or in a pot.** If you plant outside or go for the border option, be sure to water them well after planting. Figs aren't fussy about soil but if you decide to keep one in a pot, use John Innes No 3 compost.

2. **If growing in a pot, feed them weekly, while in leaf, with a general or high-potash liquid fertiliser. In the ground you need to water them in dry weather but you won't need to give them much extra feeding.**

3. **Water the plants regularly.** Don't let them dry out at any stage, especially in summer.

Figs produce their fruits on new growth all through spring and summer, usually producing two flushes of fruit each year – one in spring and one in late summer. This pattern of two flushes of fruits happens very year. The fruits take many months to mature from the tiny, embryo figs that you see at the tips of the shoots to the ripe fig with soft, melting flesh. You don't notice the flowers that form because figs are an odd fruit, producing their flowers *inside* the pear-shaped fruits.

Plants form a flush of figs in spring on the new growth, but these fruits don't have time to mature before the onset of winter, although they'll be almost fully grown by then. If the plants are growing outside in the soil, the frost kills them in winter and so you need to remove these wasted fruits by picking them off or pruning the stems in spring. In a greenhouse, however, or if the plants are in pots (enabling you to move the fig into the greenhouse in autumn), these figs have a chance to mature and ripen. Later growth in summer bears tiny figs which are more robust and should survive the winter cold, maturing in mid- or late summer the following year, even on plants outside. However, if you grow your figs in pots and keep them in a greenhouse you can afford to be less obsessive about taking off the figlets that form in spring.

No hard and fast set of pruning rules with figs exists. They crop even if you don't prune them, but get straggly and grow too big. My advice is to prune them little and often. Pruning your figs in spring, cutting back any straggly shoots that don't have an embryo fig on them, promotes new growth that goes on to produce tiny figs in autumn. Try to avoid pruning the plant all over because this inevitably removes some fruits (most branches have some fruits at some stage of development). However, if your plant does get too large and you have to take drastic action (though you'll lose some fruits) you can *hard-prune* (or cut back severely) in spring and the plant is rejuvenated, although you do lose some fruits by doing this.

The main pest that fig growers encounter is blackbirds, who are as keen on fresh figs as you are and start pecking at the fruits as soon as they start to ripen.

Harvesting and storing your figs

Figs are ripe and ready for harvesting when they become soft and, instead of standing sturdily on the stems, they start to droop. When they reach this stage you can pick and eat them straight away!

Choosing varieties

Here I list three varieties of figs that are popular with grow-your-own gardeners. Most garden centres only offer Brown Turkey figs so you may need to go to a fruit specialist if you want to grow a different variety.

✔ **Brown Turkey** is easy to grow and a heavy cropper; this most popular of all figs has brown fruits with a good flavour.

✔ **Brunswick** has deeper-cut leaves than Brown Turkey, and produces heavy crops of large fruits with paler flesh.

✔ **White Marseilles** produces large, delicious figs that change from green to almost white when ripe.

Growing brightly: Pomegranates

Few people grow the pomegranate as a cropping fruit tree in the UK, even though the country is only just north of the kind of areas where the fruit thrives outside and crops well. In mild areas, and in the east of the country where summer tends to be hotter, pomegranates often do surprisingly well outside against a sunny wall. However, you're safest to think of pomegranates as pot plants that you can stand outside in summer and provide with frost protection in the greenhouse through winter.

Pomegranates are twiggy, small-leaved shrubs or small trees that lose their leaves in autumn after they change from bright green to yellow. These plants are very ornamental, with their bright vermillion or scarlet ruffled petals. People are becoming more aware of the health benefits of pomegranates, so you can probably expect them to become much more popular. The chances of getting a reasonable crop, however, are questionable, but who knows – you may get lucky, and the plants are so pretty even in flower.

People usually eat pomegranates raw but you can use them for juices and syrup.

Pomegranates are relatively low in calories and high in phosphorus, potassium and antioxidants, which is why they're becoming so popular.

Planting and cultivating pomegranates

Except in the very mildest areas that are free from winter frost, which are few and far between in the UK, I recommend growing pomegranates in pots, filled with John Innes No 3 compost. You can either grow pomegranates from seed, in which case start here with step 1, or you can buy ready-grown young plants (which I recommend to save you about a year in time), in which case you can jump straight in at step 3.

1. **Sow the seeds in a propagator at a temperature of 20°C. Sow in spring so that the plants are a reasonable size to survive their first winter.** Pomegranate seeds germinate readily in a few weeks and the young plants grow well.

2. **Transplant the seedlings into 8-centimetre pots after a few weeks and keep them in these pots for the first year.**

3. **Re-pot the plants regularly until you have them in a 45-centimetre pot at maturity.** Mature plants can grow to about 4 metres high, but half that size is more likely in a pot.

4. **Throughout spring, summer and autumn, keep the plant moist and feed weekly with a general or high-potash fertiliser.**

   You can take the plant out of the greenhouse in late spring and enjoy the delicate foliage and red flowers on your patio if you like.

5. **If the plant looks untidy in spring, tidy it up a little with a light prune.** You don't need to prune pomegranates much to promote flowering and fruiting because they produce flowers on the new shoots, but you probably need to tidy up the plant a little in spring. The flowers are usually pollinated by bees.

6. **In autumn, as the leaves start to drop, move the plants into a cool greenhouse in a minimum temperature of 5°C.**

Harvesting and storing your pomegranates

You can pick the fruits at the end of autumn when they're fully ripe and then store for several months if you keep them cool.

Choosing varieties

You can get reasonable results from the seeds within pomegranates that you can buy from the shops. Named varieties, some with double or yellow flowers, do exist and are available in other countries but you see these rarely in the UK. **Nanum** is the most commonly available variety. This dwarf plant is small in all its parts and reaches only about 60 centimetres high when mature. It makes a very attractive little greenhouse or patio plant but the fruits are similarly diminutive and only about 3 centimetres across, and so are more useful for decoration than for eating.

Getting loved up: Passion fruit

Passion fruits – the fruit of passion flowers – include some of the most aromatic and delicious of all fruits. They taste better than they look – the fruits are usually wrinkled and leathery when ripe, but inside the mass of black pips is surrounded with a tangy, sweet flesh.

You can use passion fruit to transform your fruit salads and add magic to your meringues. You can also make great drinks, ice-cream, yoghurts, cakes and fools with passion fruit.

Passion fruits are rich in carotenes, phosphorus and potassium as well as vitamins A and C, niacin and riboflavin.

Planting and cultivating passion fruit

Dozens of different types of passion fruit exist and they vary in their needs; from the hardy *Passiflora coerulea*, to tropical species such as the commercial passion fruit you buy in the shops, which needs a winter minimum temperature of 10°C. All types are climbers, so need trellis or wires to grow up, but they're not difficult to grow. Growing a passion fruit in a pot is probably easier than growing one in the greenhouse border, but both are suitable.

One word of warning though – the common, hardy passion flower often produces a heavy crop of egg-shaped, bright orange fruits in summer and although you can eat them, they're insipid to say the least and have very little juice or flesh. For tasty passion fruits you need to plant an edible passion fruit and for that you need a greenhouse.

You can grow passion fruit from seed or buy plants from specialists. No named varieties of passion fruit are available in the UK, however, and you may well have to grow a plant from seed, simply by buying a passion fruit and extracting the seeds. Here are the steps to follow:

1. **Wash the flesh off, rubbing it against a sieve if necessary and rinsing well, to extract the seeds from the fruit.**

2. **Sow up to ten seeds in an 8-centimetre pot of multipurpose compost and place in a propagator in a temperature of 21°C.** The seeds should germinate in about one month.

3. **Erect a trellis or wire framework for the passion fruit to grow along.** Passion fruit is a vigorous climber, and so needs the support while growing. You can expect it to cover at least two square metres when fully grown.

4. **Transplant the seedlings into their own 8-centimetre pots when about 3 centimetres high and grow them, in warm conditions, until they reach about 45 centimetres high.** The seedlings are then ready for planting out where they are to grow and fruit.

   Although bought plants may flower in spring of the first year of being planted, seedlings won't bloom until at least two years old.

5. **You may need to pollinate the large, white and purple flowers by hand to ensure that they set fruit.** To do this, take some powdery, yellow pollen from one of the five stamens around the centre of the flower with a small, fine paintbrush, and transfer it to each of the three club-like stigmas in the centre of the bloom.

The passion fruit: Not as romantic as it sounds

Passion flowers and fruits get their name from the Passion of Christ and have nothing to do with libido! Early settlers in South America, looking for a sign of Christianity, saw the evidence of Christ's passion in the passion flower with various parts of the plant representing elements of the story. They saw the leaves as the hands of his assailants, the tendrils as the whips, and the frilly corona as the crown of thorns.

6. **Passion fruits are hungry plants, and so be sure to apply some liquid feed liberally, at least once a week during spring and summer.**

7. **After harvesting, prune the plants in late autumn or spring but avoid pruning too hard because this delays flowering the following year.**

Harvesting and storing your passion fruit

All being well, fruits should start to appear by the end of summer. These fruits are fully ripe when they start to wrinkle and will store for a few weeks in a cool place.

Choosing varieties

Here are the main options for growing from seed:

- ✔ **Passiflora edulis** is the common, edible passion fruit that you see in supermarkets. This variety isn't readily available as a plant but you can easily grow it from the many seeds in the fruits.

- ✔ **Passiflora mollissima**, or the 'banana passion fruit', has beautiful pink flowers and long yellow fruits.

- ✔ **P. caerulea** is a common, hardy passion flower that often has big crops of golden, egg-shaped fruits. These fruits are edible but they don't have much flesh and the flesh available is fairly tasteless.

The fruits of all three varieties are edible but they vary in their degree of palatability.

An acquired taste: Tree tomatoes

The tree tomato, or *tamarillo*, is a fast-growing plant with large, heart-shaped leaves, clusters of small, potato-like flowers and, often, heavy crops of plum-shaped red or gold fruits that ripen in autumn. Every now and then this South American fruit makes its way into supermarkets but it has never become very popular in Britain. Other countries take it more seriously. New Zealand, for example, grows many named varieties of tree tomatoes commercially, although they've never been as popular an export as kiwi fruits. The plants are certainly bold and attractive and make imposing patio plants for summer, but you must protect them in a greenhouse during winter and the plants will crop better if you keep them in a greenhouse all year.

People sometimes eat tree tomatoes raw, cut in half and scooped out with a spoon, but the flavour is slightly odd and acidic. You can also include them raw in fruit salads or even in savoury salads. However, people most commonly stew them, or make them into jams, sauces and chutneys.

Tree tomatoes are low in calories and rich in vitamins A, B6, C and E.

Growing and cultivating tree tomatoes

Because virtually no named varieties of tree tomato are available in the UK and plants are hard to come by, the best way of getting started is to grow your tree tomatoes (Cyphomandra betacea) from seed, which you can buy from a catalogue or extract from a bought fruit. You can then grow them outside in summer on the patio, but for a good crop you're best off growing them in a greenhouse all summer. The trees can be quite productive, but those growing in pots usually start to decline after a few years because they need more room as they grow. If you want to continue growing tree tomatoes, you can propagate more plants from seeds or cuttings.

Here's what you need to do to get that crop:

1. **Sow the seeds in 8-centimetre pots of multipurpose compost, cover lightly with compost, and keep them moist until they germinate, which should take about two weeks.** Seeds germinate readily at a temperature of 21°C.

2. **Transplant the seedlings into 8-centimetre pots when they reach about 1 centimetre high and grow them on in a similar temperature.** These young seedlings grow fast.

3. **Pot the plants into 25-centimetre-diameter pots to grow on for the first year, or plant in the greenhouse border, keeping them in a minimum winter temperature of about 5°C.** If they're warmer, they retain their leaves but at this temperature they drop most of the foliage and need to be kept almost dry. By the end of the first year, the plants should be 2 metres high.

4. **In spring, cut the top off the main stem (unless you have a very big greenhouse) and start watering and feeding a lot. Pot the plants into pots at least 40 centimetres in diameter.** New, vigorous growth should start to appear. In this second spring the plant should produce flowers. The fruits usually set quite readily without any assistance, and are ready for picking in late summer of year two.

Harvesting and storing your tree tomatoes

Tree tomatoes ripen from late summer onwards. Pick them when the tomatoes are brightly coloured and start to soften. You can usually keep them for a week or two in the fridge.

Totally tropical: Pawpaws

Pawpaws (papaya) are among the most familiar of tropical fruits, with their orange flesh and their mass of black pips. Though pawpaws are unlikely to produce a crop in the UK, even in a greenhouse, the young plants grow quickly and are attractive, so you may consider growing them as an ornamental plant.

Most people eat pawpaws raw but you can also crystallise them and make them into a tasty and unusual jam.

Pawpaws are rich in minerals and vitamins, including A and C. They also contain papain, an enzyme that 'digests' meat and thus aids digestion.

Growing and cultivating pawpaws

Seeds are sometimes available in catalogues but you can also take the risk and grow some seeds from a bought fruit. Pawpaw plants are usually male or female, so you need to grow at least three plants to give yourself a good chance of getting a female fruit-bearing plant. You can't tell the sex of these plants until they mature.

1. **Sow the seeds in a temperature of about 21°C.** If you use seeds from a fruit you've bought, remember to wash them first. The seeds germinate rapidly.

2. **As the seedlings fill their pots with roots, re-pot them in a multipurpose compost.** By the end of the first year they should be at least 1 metre high.

3. **Feed the plants once a week and give the plants lots of water in summer, as they grow rapidly.**

4. **Keep plants in a minimum temperature of 10°C over the winter, and drier than in summer.** Some of the lower, large leaves drop in winter, but the top of the stem should retain some leaves. The plants should flower the following year.

5. **Keep the plants moist and mist the leaves regularly to maintain humidity and reduce the problem of red spider mite (see Chapter 7).**

The plants grow as a single stem with large, boldly divided leaves. The creamy flowers grow directly from the main stem among the upper leaves and these flowers are followed by the large fruits.

Other fruits from seed

As well as the fruits I look at elsewhere in this chapter, you can grow others from pips found in exotic fruits available in supermarkets. Although you don't really stand much chance of actually getting a crop from these exotic fruits, they make interesting plants while young. All these plants require warm growing conditions and you can grow them in a similar way to passion fruit. Some of those you can try are:

✔ **Dragon fruit:** These spectacular cactus fruits in either yellow or vibrant pink contain jelly-like white flesh and have small black seeds. Remove the small seeds, clean them, and sow in small pots. The small seedlings grow into large, sprawling plants and may flower after about five years.

✔ **Lychee:** These aromatic, hard-shelled fruits have soft flesh and a single, large, shiny brown seed in the centre. Wash the seeds well and sow one seed per 8-centimetre pot, about 1 centimetre deep. These seeds take several months to germinate and form attractive plants with glossy green foliage. However, lychees are unlikely to survive more than a year unless you keep them in very warm and humid conditions.

✔ **Avocado:** Avocados are large trees that don't need a lot of heat to survive winter but are unlikely to crop in Britain. Clean the large seed, from the centre of a ripe pear, and sow it, pointed end uppermost, in an 8-centimetre pot with the tip of the seed above the compost. Keep the seed warm and water it sparingly until the seed splits and a shoot appears. It makes a large, but admittedly rather dull, house plant.

Harvesting and storing your pawpaws

If you're lucky enough to get a crop, you'll see your pawpaws start to change from green to orange as they ripen. As they do so they start to smell perfumed and become soft. Pick them at this stage. You can then keep your pawpaws for a few days after ripening but they're really best for eating immediately.

Choosing varieties

Few varieties of pawpaw exist; **Solo** is the only one you can buy seed for and it should have male and female flowers on the same plant. Alternatively, you can always take seeds from a fruit you buy in the supermarket.

Part V
The Part of Tens

'They may be slow but they're eco-friendly
and they also fertilise the lawn at the
same time.'

In this part . . .

Throughout this book I give you all sorts of detailed information about how to grow your favourite fruits and veg and how to deal with the pests and problems you may meet along the way. In this part of the book I had some fun thinking up ten projects to get you going and keep you busy in your garden – productive tasks that you can undertake while you're waiting for your other gardening projects to come to fruition (geddit?). I also include ten tips for growing the herbs you thought I'd forgotten in the rest of the book! Some meals just aren't complete without a sprinkling of certain herbs, and you can grow these in your own garden just as easily as the other plants in this book.

Chapter 17

Ten Tips for Planting a Herb Garden

*E*very garden has room for a few herbs, and every kitchen (and every stomach!) benefits from adding them to dishes.

Herbs are a varied lot, and with such a bewildering array of tastes available, you may wonder where on earth to start. A good idea is to think about the herbs you use regularly in your own kitchen. If you use lots of parsley and chives but never use chervil or sage, start with the herbs you know and like, and grow enough of the herbs you use daily. Only a very unusual gardener needs ten rosemary bushes and a single parsley plant!

Herbs are adaptable – many grow in a wide range of conditions – and you don't need to have a dedicated herb garden. You can grow a few herbs in pots on the patio or tuck some into your flower border where they can make attractive additions to your garden. One of my favourite combinations on my patio is red or white Busy Lizzies with deep green parsley.

Another reason for growing herbs in pots with your flowers is that you don't need to eat them to enjoy them; just brushing past them to release their aromas is a joy. You can even use a few of them to scent your home, picked and dried for pot pourri or scattered in your bath to scent the water and relax you (lavender and lemon balm are ideal for this). I advise you to be wary of using any herbs medicinally because ascertaining the correct dosage is very difficult. Culinary herbs are safe to eat, but be careful if you have a herb allergy.

The simplest way to get herbs is just to go to the garden centre and buy them, but in this chapter I show you a few ways to save money by growing your own from seed or from cuttings and I look at the best herbs to grow.

Growing Herbs from Seed

You can grow many herbs from seed. The best to grow are the annuals that last for only a year, and to keep a regular supply of tasty leaves you're often best off sowing them regularly throughout spring and summer. You can also grow some perennials from seed which you don't need to sow every year.

You can sow seeds in pots on the patio or in rows among your vegetables. Some, such as parsley, are small and neat whereas others, such as coriander and dill, reach 90 centimetres when in flower, and their small flowers attract beneficial insects such as bees and hoverflies.

Among the best herbs to grow from seed are:

- ✔ Angelica (biennial)
- ✔ Basil (annual)
- ✔ Chervil (annual)
- ✔ Chives (perennial)
- ✔ Coriander (annual)
- ✔ Dill (annual)
- ✔ Fennel (perennial)
- ✔ Garlic chives (perennial)
- ✔ Parcel (biennial)
- ✔ Parsley (biennial)
- ✔ Summer savory (annual)

The simplest way to grow herbs from seed is to fill cell trays with compost and sow a pinch of seeds (four or five) in each cell. Cover them with a little compost and water and keep them in a warm place such as in a propagator on the windowsill or in the greenhouse. Seeds germinate in as little as a week for basil and as much as two months for others such as parsley. With annuals and biennials, let all the seedlings grow but with shrubby perennials remove all but one seedling when they're about 1 centimetre high to give that one seedling room to grow.

You can harvest your herbs when they're big enough to cut from, but the flavour of most herbs is strongest after they mature, which takes several months and at least some exposure to strong sun is needed to develop the fragrant oils in most herbs.

Herbs a-plenty

Don't know your lemon balm from your lemon verbena, your bay from your basil, or your tarragon from your thyme? Here's my handy guide to the most popular grow-your-own herbs:

- **Basil:** An annual that needs sun and warmth, basil doesn't thrive in cold conditions. Although it can last a few weeks on the windowsill, basil grows best in a greenhouse or on a sunny patio, and is happy in containers. Many varieties of basil are available, for growing from seed in spring and early summer. Ideal with tomatoes and Italian dishes.

- **Bay:** A large, hardy, evergreen bush that can become a tree or an ornamental, bay is an easy-to-grow plant that's good for growing in a container. You can grow bay from cuttings or buy a young plant, and prune it into any shape to keep it small. You can use the leaves dry or fresh, and they make a great addition to stews.

- **Chives:** A popular plant with the bees! A small, herbaceous plant with grassy leaves and pretty pink flowers in late spring, chives thrive in sun and part shade, in moist soil, and are good for containers and as an ornamental plant. You can grow chives from seed or divide plants in spring. Ideal with eggs and salads.

- **Coriander:** A short-lived annual with attractive, ferny foliage and dainty white, edible flowers, coriander thrives in moist soil and light shade. This herb rapidly runs to seed so sow it frequently in spring and summer. Coriander works well in Chinese and Mexican dishes.

- **Lavender:** A small, silver-leaved shrub with attractive flowers, lavender is popular with bees, but has few culinary uses. It grows best in full sun in poor, dry soils, and grows happily in containers. Prune lavender lightly twice a year, in spring and after flowering. You can enjoy it adding it to sugar (for use in cakes) and ice cream and also eating it with lamb.

- **Lemon balm:** A hardy, herbaceous plant with lemon-scented leaves and small, white flowers that attract bees, lemon balm is a vigorous grower too big for pots that can spread by seed. Lemon balm thrives in light shade and rich soil. The variegated forms are more attractive. Rhubarb is a great companion for lemon balm, and this herb also comes in handy anywhere you need a mild lemon flavour.

- **Lemon verbena:** Slightly tender, and with small, white flowers, this small shrub is great to grow for its very aromatic, lemon-scented leaves, but lemon verbena has few culinary uses. Lemon verbena grows best in full sun.

(continued)

(continued)

- **Mint:** An invasive, herbaceous perennial with spreading, underground stems and upright stems, mint grows best in moist, rich soil, and is good for containers if you replant it each year. Some types are very ornamental. Another good plant for the bees, and ideal with lamb but also good for mint tea – just steep a handful of leaves in hot water and add sugar.

- **Oregano:** A low, semi-shrubby perennial with small, round leaves and small pink flowers in summer, oregano grows best in dry soil in full sun and is suitable for containers. Attracts bees, and is very tasty with eggs, poultry and Italian dishes.

- **Parsley:** A biennial plant that's at its best in the first year; plants flower in year two and die. Some people believe that flat-leaved parsley has the best taste but traditional, curled parsley has the looks. Best in rich, moist soil, you can grow parsley from seed, and it's happy in containers. Parsley is a universal herb that you can use in virtually anything.

- **Rosemary:** A usually upright, evergreen shrub with narrow, silvery leaves and pale blue flowers in spring, rosemary is suitable for containers and likes full sun and well-drained soil. A popular plant with the bees and a great accompaniment to roast lamb.

- **Sage:** A suitable choice for container growing, this worthwhile, small, evergreen shrub with grey leaves likes full sun and dry soils. The best forms grow from cuttings and rarely flower. Plants grown from seed flower well and are good plants for bees. Other forms with variegated and purple leaves are available. Prune sage plants every spring to keep them neat. After harvesting, sage is ideal with pork and other fatty meats such as goose, and also with cheese.

- **Tarragon:** A herbaceous perennial with upright stems of narrow leaves. French tarragon, which has the best flavour, makes a better choice than the invasive Russian tarragon. Tarragon grows best in dry soil in full sun. Ideal with chicken.

- **Thyme:** Ordinary thyme is a small, bushy plant with small, grey-green leaves and tiny pink flowers. Other thymes such as creeping, lemon thyme can also be eaten and are more attractive but aren't as flavourful. Thyme grows best in dry soil in full sun, is suitable for containers, and good for attracting bees. Thyme goes well with chicken and Italian dishes.

Growing Herbs from Cuttings

You can increase your stock of many of the shrubbier herbs from cuttings. The best time to take these is in midsummer, when sage, rosemary, thyme and lavender all take root easily. Here's how to do it:

1. **Prepare your pots and compost.** The ideal compost should be light and fluffy and a mix of equal parts multipurpose compost and perlite or vermiculite (sterile, expanded volcanic rock fragments). Fill 8-centimetre-diameter pots with this compost and firm it only by tapping the pot on

the table so some air is retained in it. You also need a propagator to maintain humidity around the cuttings but you don't need to provide artificial heat – the natural temperatures at this time of year are sufficient.

If you don't have a propagator you can cut a 2-litre plastic drink bottle, about 8 centimetres from the base, into two sections. Make a slit 8 centimetres up from the bottom of the top part so you can slide it over the bottom part and bingo – you have a mini propagator. By taking the lid off you can even allow some air to the plants as they root.

2. **Take tip cuttings from the tips of the stems.** With sage, for example, cut off a shoot tip with three pairs of leaves. Cuttings should be, on average, between 5 and 8 centimetres long. Very soft growth, often on the main stems, doesn't always root easily and the best cuttings usually come from side shoots lower down the plants.

3. **Trim the cutting carefully with a sharp knife, just below the lowest pair of leaves, and cut off the lowest pair of leaves.** The cutting is ready. With thyme, for example, having cut off a shoot about 5 centimetres long, trim it below a pair of leaves and strip the leaves off the lower half of the stem.

4. **Put the cuttings in the compost, taking care not to bury any leaves that would otherwise rot, give them a drink of clean water and put the cuttings in the propagator. Place this in a shady spot.** Cuttings take about a month to root. You may need to water the compost during that time to prevent it drying out, but take care not to make it too wet. Also remove any leaves that die or start to go mouldy. When the plants start to make new growth in the shoot tips, the cuttings have rooted. Then you can carefully pot up the little plants on their own.

What is a herb?

Herbs come in all shapes and sizes: some are fast-growing and easy to grow from seed, whereas others are long-lived shrubs. So you can't really generalise about them, except to say that you can grow at least a few in even the smallest of gardens.

Don't be fooled into thinking that herbs are related or that they need the same conditions as each other. The only thing herbs have in common is that they have fragrant or aromatic leaves. Because of this, you can find annual herbs, creeping herbs, herbaceous plants, and some that grow as bushes or trees. Many bushy herbs have silver or grey leaves and can survive tough, dry conditions – their aromatic oils may have developed to prevent grazing animals eating them.

Confusing herbs with spices is another mistake that people make. The difference between a spice and a herb is in the parts of the plant that we use: spices are aromatic but come from parts other than the leaves, such as the flower buds of cloves and the seeds of nutmeg and pepper.

Cheating with Cheap Young Plants

You can grow many herbs from seed. Some of these (usually chives, thyme, sage, parsley, basil and mint) are available from supermarkets in pots designed for keeping on the windowsill for a few weeks until you pick all the leaves and discard the pot. However, you can use pots of parsley, basil and thyme seedlings in a much more imaginative way to get plants for your garden really cheaply. The best time to buy and grow them is in spring.

Some people use parsley in larger amounts than most other herbs. Gardeners usually grow parsley from seed, but the seeds can be slow and rather difficult to germinate. Pots of seedlings, however, offer you a chance to grow at least a dozen plants much more easily. Just follow these steps:

1. **After making sure that the compost is moist, take the pot of seedlings out of the plastic sleeve and slip them out of the pot.**

2. **Push your thumbs into the side of the root ball (the compost full of roots) and pull the cluster of seedlings into two parts.** You're bound to damage a number of seedlings and pull leaves off some of them as you do this, but don't worry – plenty of others survive.

3. **Pull each part into two again and then into two once again, to give you eight clumps, and – depending on the size of the original pot – perhaps once again, to give you sixteen clumps.** Each clump should ideally have four or five seedlings, so if you have more, pull the weaker and most damaged seedlings from the clump.

4. **Put some compost in the bottom of some 8-centimetre pots, place the roots of the clump in the pot, and add more compost around it, keeping the seedlings at the right height in the pot.**

5. **Pot all the clumps and give all the pots a thorough watering.**

6. **Place the pots in a shady, cool place, out of the sun, for a couple of weeks to recover.** Most of the old leaves will wither and turn yellow – a result of the damage they've been through – but new leaves are soon produced.

7. **When the plants are growing strongly you can move them into a sunnier spot and then plant them into the garden or into larger pots.**

You can treat basil in a similar way (poor Basil!) but because it's a more delicate plant, divide the original pot into only about six clumps. Pull out the weakest plants in each clump so you have about three seedlings per pot, and keep the seedlings warm and cosy as they recover.

Thyme is a tougher plant so you should be able to divide the pot into at least a dozen plants. After potting, give the plants a haircut, trimming off about half the length of the stem. Remember to water them sparingly at first because they don't like wet compost.

Chives are about the easiest of all herbs to treat in this way – separate the clumps into a dozen or more individual clumps, trim the foliage by about half to make pulling the clumps apart easier, and get potting!

You're better off growing mint by dividing the roots of plants in the garden rather than from seed, so don't bother with pots of mint seedlings. Sage, too, grows best from cuttings of good forms, so ignore these pots as well.

Finding the Best Herbs for Shade

You may hear some gardeners say that herbs prefer a sunny spot. However, some herbs don't just tolerate shade, they actually grow better without being in the sun all day. But did you know that not all shade is the same? Shade caused by a wall or fence isn't as bad as the shade under a tree. Trees not only deprive plants of light, they also suck up lots of water from the soil, and so dry shade under trees isn't a good spot in which to grow any plants, let alone herbs. If you do have trees and want to grow plants underneath it, a good idea is to put them there in containers so you can make sure that they have nutrients and water. The shade of a building, with the sky open above the plants, isn't a big problem for many herbs, although in some cases their flavour isn't as intense as it would be if they were growing in a sunny spot.

In general, the herbs that do best in shade are those with green leaves rather than silvery leaves. A position that has sun for part of the day at least suits most of these plants. However, providing the soil is moist, most of the common annual herbs such as dill, fennel, coriander and chervil do grow well in some shade. In this sort of site, herbs are less likely to run to seed and more likely to produce lush foliage than if they grow in a sunny, dry place that suits many of the other herbs (such as those with silver or grey leaves like sage and rosemary).

Some of the best herbs for growing in the shade include the following:

- ✔ **Lemon balm** isn't the most useful herb, but it is an attractive plant, especially in its yellow-leaved form, and the fragrant leaves are a pleasure. It can, however, become a nuisance if you allow it to set seed – seedlings can spring up all over the place in future years. Lemon balm is quite happy in shade.

- ✔ **Mint** often struggles in a hot, dry soil and some get mildew or rust. This herb grows much more vigorously and productively in a semi-shady spot with moist soil, but is likely to spread where you don't want it, so be careful to control it (see 'Keeping Mint in Check', later in this chapter).

- ✔ **Sorrel** is a large, leafy perennial that looks uncannily like a dock, something between a herb and a leafy vegetable, and grows happily in shade.

Choosing Lookers

Some herbs look good enough to feature in ornamental gardens. Their coloured and variegated cream or white-splashed leaves can brighten your borders, add pizzazz to your pots, and also make your meals tastier.

Top of the list of beauties are the varied forms of sage. In its usual form, sage is an attractive, soft-leaved, grey plant that forms a mound 45 centimetres high and 60 centimetres across. However, ensure that you prune sage every spring and, perhaps, again in early summer to keep it smaller. Purple-leaved sage is a gem and in a good form, the new leaves are deep purple and age to greyish purple. As an edging to paths and in any sunny border, purple-leaved sage is a fine plant, and looks good next to all silver-leaved plants and pink flowers.

As an alternative, you can look for the variegated form of sage with purple and white leaves, which is very pretty but rather tender, and isn't a strong grower. The prettiest variety is Icterina, which is a good grower with yellow-edged leaves that always look bright. All sage varieties look good and grow well with lavenders.

The many different types of thyme and the variegated, shrubby thymes such as Silver Queen, with white-edged leaves and pink flowers, are gems for pots and for edging paths. The creeping thymes, which include lemon thyme, form low carpets and are good for planting in gravel as well as on the rock garden or in pots in the sun. They often have masses of pink or mauve flowers.

With its covering of pale blue flowers in spring, rosemary also makes a good ornamental herb. You can even use rosemary as a low hedge, trimming it now and again to keep it tidy, and a trailing, prostrate form of rosemary is good in pots and raised beds. This herb thrives in dry soils.

Some mints, too, are very pretty. The related bergamot (monarda) is an elegant, tall herbaceous plant with bright flowers in a wide range of colours, but typically bright red or pink. Bergamot, though, isn't the most useful culinary herb – tea and pot pourri are the most common uses. Chives are also good-looking plants, especially in flower and sporting a haircut after the blooms fade.

Some annual herbs also look good. You can use purple basils as contrasting foliage in patio pots, and dill and coriander look good scattered among your border plants to produce feathery foliage and airy flowers. Borage, too, is a beautiful, if large, plant with bright blue, starry flowers (which can cause itching skin) and calendulas, with their bright yellow and orange blooms, always look cheerful and flower almost all year round.

Keeping Herbs Healthy in Pots

Lots of herbs grow quite happily in pots on the patio, where they can be conveniently to hand while you're cooking, and you can even combine different herbs together to make an attractive display if the pots are big enough. Or, you can grow herbs in separate pots and put them together, as you want to create a display that's as pleasing to the eye as it is to your taste buds!

Herbs basically fall into two groups when it comes to growing them in pots: long-lived, shrubby types such as bay, rosemary, sage, thyme and lavender, chives and mint, and short-lived annuals and biennials such as basil, parsley, chervil and feverfew.

Potting herbs from the same group together in a pot isn't always a good idea. I've seen planted pots of herbs for sale containing parsley, sage, bay and fennel, mixing both groups of herbs within the same pot. They look good at an early stage but a few months later, when the fennel is 2 metres high and making the pot blow over in the slightest breeze, they look awful. Some herbs are just too tall and gawky to look good in all but the biggest pots. Bays, sages and other perennials do best in a John Innes No 3 compost and tolerate dry conditions that make annuals such as coriander run to seed in weeks. Annual and short-lived herbs grow best in multipurpose compost.

Remember to keep your herbs well watered. Many herbs have deep, questing roots that penetrate deep in the soil, enabling them to grow in dry soil, but they can't do this in pots, and so they need frequent watering and feeding. Use a general-purpose or high-potash fertiliser for the shrubby herbs and a general-purpose or high-nitrogen fertiliser for the annual herbs, applying it once a week during spring and summer.

Pruning Your Herbs to Keep Them Young

Regular pruning keeps all herb plants more compact and extends their life considerably. Pruning also encourages the production of new shoots with tender, fresh, flavour-filled leaves. In spring, when the worst frosts are over, trim them back with secateurs. This approach may seem a bit severe but the plants soon produce new leaves and a month later look neat and leafy. If they are in rich soil and growing strongly you can also give a second, lighter trim in midsummer, and perhaps dry or preserve these leaves for winter use in the kitchen.

In particular, shrubby herbs such as lavender, thyme, sage and rosemary grow very quickly and can get straggly, especially if they're in a rich soil. Ideally you prune the plants when they're young, before they start going bare in the centre and getting middle-age spread. Pruning is especially important with lavender, which doesn't grow back and produce new growth if you cut it back to old stems at the base that don't have leaves. When a plant is bare at the base you can't do anything to save it.

Always trim lavender as soon as the flowers fade to keep the plants neat.

Keeping Mint in Check

Mint is one of the most useful of all herbs, but it's a vigorous plant and a wanderer. Mint hates to be in one place for too long and wants to ramble across your garden.

The worst thing you can do is to keep cutting or digging up all the new shoots that escape from the original planting place, because the old parts gradually deteriorate and lose the will to live. So unless you can let your mint have its head and grow where it pleases, you're best off growing it in pots on the patio or in pots sunk into the border.

Mint grows well in pots of multipurpose compost but remember to replant it each spring, as follows:

1. **Simply tip the contents of the pot out and pull all the creeping stems apart.**

2. **Discard most of the stems and keep the youngest to replant.**

3. **Fill the pot with fresh compost and bury some of the stems, with some roots intact, about 2 centimetres deep, horizontally under the compost surface.**

4. **Water well.** The mint soon grows.

   At the same time you can pot some bits of the stems in small pots, bring them into the house, and put them on the windowsill to force them into early growth.

If you're putting pots of mint in your border, make sure to leave a 5-centimetre gap between the top of the compost and the top of the pot when you fill the pots with compost, to try and prevent the creeping stems from escaping over the edge into your borders.

Choosing the Best Mints for Flavour

Not all mints are born equal and you can choose from dozens of mints with varying habits, colours and flavours. If you choose yours carefully, you can use it for lots of dishes besides the obvious roast lamb. Some of the most worthwhile choices are:

✔ **Apple mint:** Universally regarded as one of the best varieties for flavour, apple mint is a robust plant that reaches 80 centimetres high and spreads widely. The stout stems have round leaves and soft, felty hairs cover the plant.

Apple mint also has a variegated form, with the leaves edged in white. This form is really pretty and slightly better behaved, and so is worth allowing into the flower garden!

✔ **Ginger mint:** A very pretty plant, low and spreading with upright stems and yellow and green leaves and lots of pink flowers; unfortunately, ginger mint doesn't taste very good!

✔ **Moroccan mint:** Perhaps the best variety of mint, Moroccan mint has a wonderful flavour and bright green leaves, and is good for all purposes from sauce to tea.

✔ **Peppermints and spearmints:** All these varieties have a strong flavour and the black-leaved versions look attractive.

Keeping Your Bay Tree in Tip-Top Condition

Bay trees are common additions to gardens, widely available in many different forms and varying in price hugely. The most expensive types are standards with round heads of foliage on stems between 80 centimetres and 2 metres high, which are often twisted to add even more drama to the plants. You can also buy small plants, 20 centimetres high, for planting in pots or in your garden. Bays grow about 60 centimetres in a season.

Although they have a reputation for being rather tender, bays are surprisingly tough and hardy. The key to keeping one in good condition is to take great care where you place it at the outset. If you plant your bay in the garden, choose a sunny site guarded against cold and with well-drained soil. Bays don't like waterlogged soils, especially in winter. They tolerate wind well and are good plants for coastal areas.

Bays tolerate full sun, part shade, and pollution (though you may not then want to eat the leaves). Bays also tolerate neglect, but don't enjoy it. They have thick, leathery leaves that don't wilt when dry. Only a month or so later, when the leaves go yellow and drop off, do you realise that you've neglected the plant. The oldest leaves, in the centre of the head, are the first to turn yellow and drop. (Don't confuse this appearance, though, with the natural dropping of some older leaves in late spring when the new growth has matured.) Your bay is evergreen and therefore needs water all year round – even in winter – and so make sure that you regularly water it. You also need to remember to give your bay liquid fertiliser once a week throughout summer.

Bays sometimes suffer damage to their foliage in winter, turning the leaves brown. You can easily remedy this problem by cutting off the affected areas in spring, as soon as the worst of the winter weather is over. Obviously this approach is only really satisfactory with fairly loosely formed plants, and isn't going to do your expensive, carefully trained, standard much good. If a bushy plant in the garden is severely damaged, you can prune it very heavily in spring, down to bare branches and even near to the soil level, and it grows back vigorously. Don't prune bays too hard after the end of May, though, because the new, soft growth doesn't have time to mature before the cold of winter.

Potted bays are usually in containers that are too small when you buy them, and so benefit from being moved into bigger pots. Choose pots with straight sides that are wider at the top than at the bottom so you can easily re-pot them later, and use John Innes No 3 compost to fill them. Make sure that the root ball is wet before you re-pot the plant by plunging it in a bucket of water for an hour. From there, re pot it into the new pot, firming the compost well, and place it in its new position.

You can trim your bay at almost any time of year but if you want to clip a large bay as little as possible, the best time to do so is in August. Fancy-shaped bays need a little more attention: the best way is to pinch out all the new growth back to one or two leaves, as soon as they're fully expanded and still light green. This technique encourages a dense covering of leaves and is far better than an occasional clip-over. Take off any shoots that grow from lower down the main stem.

A few pests are partial to bays, and all are much more common on potted plants, especially if they're suffering from drought or malnutrition. *Bay sucker* is a small insect that distorts the leaves with yellow patches. The best way to control this is to cut off badly affected areas and make sure that you water and feed the plant regularly. *Scale insect* is a small, waxy-shelled pest that sucks the sap out and drips a sticky substance on the lower leaves, which a fungus that turns the leaves black then colonises. The insect barely moves and you usually see it on the lower surface of leaves and on the stems of poorly bay trees. Scale insect is tricky to control. Systemic insecticides (see Chapter 2) are effective, but you shouldn't eat the leaves for several weeks after treatment – not that you'd eat them while they're covered in scale insect and sooty mould anyway!

Chapter 18

Ten Projects for Your Plot

. . . .

In This Chapter

▶ Starting off with some easy-to-grow crops

▶ Trying alternative cultivation methods

▶ Plotting your potting

. . . .

Gardening can take a long time to produce results. An apple tree takes several years to produce a good crop, for example. To keep you busy in the meantime, though, I've come up with ten simple projects to maintain your enthusiasm for gardening. Most of them don't take long to do and they give you a quick gardening fix, or at least reaffirm some basic principles you can find in the other chapters.

Growing a Few Salad Leaves

By far the simplest vegetables to grow are salad leaves. Perfect for beginners, salad leaves grow almost anywhere, in any soil or container, and you can harvest those sown in late spring and summer after two months. Brilliant!

But what if you have no pots, no containers, and no garden, and you have to grow your salad leaves by the back door? And what if you don't have a car and can't lug heavy bags of compost back from the garden centre? As long as you can carry home a small bag of compost, perhaps a 20 litre bag, no problem!

Salad seeds, whether lettuce, rocket or a mixture, germinate best outside throughout late spring and summer, so get going in late April for your salads to arrive in June and carry on sowing until August for crops through to October. Here's what to do next:

1. **Take the compost bag and knock and shake it to loosen the compost.**

2. **Lay the bag on its back, knock it down a bit so it sits flat and level.**

3. **Use a sharp knife to carefully make three drainage slits, about 1 centimetre long, on each side, about 1 centimetre from the base as it sits on the patio.**

4. **Cut a hole in the top to expose the compost. Carefully cut away the rectangle, leaving an edge of plastic 2 centimetres wide at the top of the bag to help contain the compost and retain some strength to the bag so the compost doesn't spill everywhere.**

5. **Water the compost thoroughly so that it's evenly moist, but not soggy and waterlogged.**

6. **Scatter your seeds thinly over the surface of the exposed compost and rough the surface to mix the seeds with the compost to bury them.** Not all the seeds are going to be completely covered, and some may be buried under more compost than others, but this usually doesn't matter.

7. **Sit back and wait!**

Depending on the variety, the seeds germinate in a week or two, and about two weeks later you can pick a few, individual leaves from some plants. After that they grow quickly and you can continue to pick individual leaves or cut off whole plants, with scissors, about 1 centimetre from their base. You should get two or three flushes of leaves over more than a month. You can then tip the contents of the bag onto the compost heap or, if you don't have a garden, someone else's compost heap!

Growing Three Different Beans in a Pot

Beans are productive, attractive and easy to grow. As patio plants, beans are ideal – runner beans and French beans are the best options – and with a little planning you can create a tower of beans with crops from the top to the bottom. Growing three different beans in one pot is perfectly possible, and because you're growing more than one kind, you benefit both from an extended cropping period and from the variety.

A good mix of beans is a short (dwarf) French bean (which tends to crop more quickly than the climbing types), a climbing French bean, and a runner bean; you can sow all these at the same time. Broad beans are best avoided here because, although delicious, they aren't quite productive enough for growing in pots, and they crop over a shorter period.

Start your three-beans-in-a-pot project between early May and July. Choose a large container with drainage holes and place it on a sunny patio or another sheltered place. A container at least 30 centimetres deep and 45 centimetres wide is ideal and a half-barrel would be excellent. When you have this ready:

1. **Fill the container with multipurpose compost.** To save money you can fill the lower half of the container with some good-quality garden compost from your heap if you have one. To save time on feeding, add a controlled-release fertiliser to the multipurpose compost, mixing it in well.

2. **Push in some 1.8–2.4-metre canes around the edge of the pot, with the bases 15 centimetres apart.** If you're using a barrel you can make this ring of canes 10 centimetres from the edge of the pot (allowing you to put flowers or other vegetables around the edge). Tie the canes together at the top to form a cone.

3. **Sow a yellow dwarf French bean such as Valdor around the edge of your container, one seed between each cane. Then sow a climbing French bean seed, such as the purple-podded Blauhilde, at the base of each cane and a runner, such as the white-flowered White Lady, on the inside of the cane, to make a ring of plants nearer the centre.** The plants grab the canes as they grow.

4. **Water the compost really well.**

Within two weeks your beans should be up and climbing around the canes. Keep the pot well watered throughout summer and you're soon rewarded with multicoloured beans and flowers among the dense foliage.

Grow Pumpkins, Beans and Sweetcorn the Native American Way

An unusual, yet traditional, way to grow these three crops is to grow them together, on the same piece of land . Sometimes called the 'three sisters', pumpkins, beans and sweetcorn all originate in the southern USA and Central America and they enjoy the same sort of conditions. All three like warmth and sun, rich soil, plenty of moisture, and coming from different families of plants, they don't compete for nutrients.

Pumpkins, beans and sweetcorn work so well together because they provide something for each other:

✔ The **sweetcorn** provides some shade for the young beans and support for them to climb.

✔ The **beans** provide some nitrogen to the soil that benefits both the other plants – especially the sweetcorn.

✔ The **pumpkins** (or other squashes) cover the ground and keep down weed growth.

Here's how to raise these three crops the way the Native Americans do – and you don't need a great big prairie of a back garden to do it!

1. **Prepare the soil well by digging in plenty of organic material.**

2. **Sow the seeds.** You can sow them directly where the plants are to grow, but because all three plants are frost-tender, you're better off sowing the sweetcorn and squashes in pots in a greenhouse first. Sow them as I describe in Chapters 3, 10 and 11, in cell trays or small pots, in late April so you can plant them out together in late May.

3. **Plant out the plants by late May.** Plant the sweetcorn first in a row, rather than in blocks (which is the usual method). Sweetcorn needs wider spacing than other plants – about 60 centimetres apart is ideal. Miss out one plant in every nine, and plant a squash in that space. They are then evenly spaced among the block of sweetcorn.

4. **Water the plants well and keep them weed-free.**

5. **After about a month, when the plants are growing strongly, sow the beans – one at the base of each sweetcorn plant.** The beans germinate and twine up the sweetcorn. Use a climbing French bean; the type you pick as dried beans and use as flageolet or haricot beans are best because you can pick them all when the sweetcorn is harvested and you don't have to wade through the mass of squash foliage to regularly pick the fresh beans!

Remember to protect your beans against the slug menace! Chapter 7 gives you some handy tips on how to do this.

By late August or September you can harvest the sweetcorn, which you can snap off without damaging the bean plants. Sweetcorn plants start to look tatty after harvesting, but still support the beans as the pods mature and dry. By early October you can harvest the beans and squashes. After all that, you can pull up and compost the old plants.

Growing Strawberries Without a Garden

Strawberries are one of the simplest and quickest of all fruits to grow. Imagine, for example, that you decide to grow your own only when the first strawberries appear in the shops and your neighbours are boasting about their wonderful crop of strawberries. Don't worry – you can have your own strawberries by the end of the summer. You don't even need a garden to produce your own crop of delicious fruits because they grow well in containers of all shapes and sizes. You can plant them in large pots, window boxes or hanging baskets. Just make sure that the container has drainage holes in the base and remember that the bigger the container, the more compost it holds, and therefore the better the plants are going to grow.

The most popular varieties of strawberry for container growing are the perpetual types that crop over many months, such as Aromel. You can buy perpetual strawberries in garden centres in individual pots or in packs of six. If you buy from a specialist by mail order (see Chapter 3 for mail-order companies) you usually have to buy ten plants – enough for three 40-centimetre diameter hanging baskets.

Here's how to succeed with growing strawberries in a container:

1. **Prepare your container.** Ready-lined baskets with a plastic inner liner are the easiest to use. Prepare them by carefully making 1 centimetre-long slits with a knife about a third of the way up from the basket base. The slits allow excess water to drain away but making them a third of the way up enables a reservoir of water to form in the base – very useful in dry weather in summer.

   Fill the container to the top with compost. The best compost is one that contains some loam, and an ideal compost is a mix of equal parts of John Innes No 3 and multipurpose compost. To this, add some controlled-release fertiliser to feed the plants through the summer and into next spring.

2. **Plant your strawberries in the container.** If you're using a hanging basket, place them in the centre of the gaps between where the chains are fixed to the basket, near the edge but leaving some compost between the root ball of the strawberry and the liner. Be sure that the 'crown' of the plant, where the base of the plant meets the compost, is at soil level and the plants aren't buried too deep.

3. **Give them a good soak and put them in a sunny spot, keeping them moist at all times.** Within a few weeks flowers should appear and you'll have some fruits about two months after planting.

Any flowers that form in October can't produce ripe fruits, so pinch these off as soon as you recognise them as flowers.

The following year, feed your plants some more, using more controlled-release fertiliser, scraped into the top of the compost, or by giving liquid fertiliser once a week. The plants will give a good crop throughout summer but then need to be replaced.

Preserving Herbs

Herbs are usually at their best in summer. Some are only available at the warmest times of the year; basil, for example, is a real sun-lover and although fairly easy to grow in high summer, growing it at other times of the year is a real struggle. Coriander is easy to grow from seed but quickly stops producing leaves and then flowers, so you can find yourself in a famine and feast situation, something that happens with many other annual herbs. Most perennial herbs also have their peak of flavour in high summer when they're just coming into flower. Wouldn't it be wonderful to be able to capture that flavour in your home-grown herbs to use all year round?

Well, you can. Fortunately you can preserve herbs in several ways:

✔ **Drying** is the simplest way to preserve herbs. You can do this in two main ways, depending on the type of herb.

- Cut and tie shrubby, woody herbs (such as sage, rosemary, lavender, thyme and bay) into small bundles and hang them up in an airy, dry, cool place, out of direct sunlight. Try to pick them on a dry day and make sure that the bundles aren't so big that too many leaves are crammed in the centre of the bundle, or they may go mouldy rather than dry.

- Lay softer herbs (such as mint, marjoram, chervil and parsley) in a thin layer on paper in trays, and place in a cool, airy dry place, such as an airing cupboard. When the herbs are completely dry you can crumble them, put them into glass jars, and store them in a cool place, out of sunlight. Not all herbs retain all their flavour after drying (basil and chives, for example) and you can find better ways to retain their flavour.

✔ **Freezing** is a very good way to preserve the more delicate taste of summer herbs such as mint, basil, chives, chervil and coriander and is very quick to do. Chop the herbs as finely as possible, pop them into ice cube trays, fill the trays with water, and freeze them. After freezing you can pop them out and store them in labelled freezer bags. If you like, you can also make mixtures of herbs in each cube.

These herby cubes are ideal for adding to stews and soups – simply pop one or more into the pot when you're cooking.

✔ **Herb butters** are the perfect way to preserve delicate herbs such as fennel, chives, parsley, and basil. Bring some butter to room temperature, soften it, add some finely chopped herbs, and blend them together. You can add some garlic too if you're partial to it. Form the mix into a sausage shape, wrap in cling film, and put in the fridge for an hour. When firm, cut into 'coins', wrap, and pop in the freezer.

When you need herb butter you simply unwrap, separate a 'coin' or two, and place in sauces, on pasta, or on fish or meat.

✔ **Flavouring oil and vinegar** (most popularly olive oil and wine vinegar) are the simplest ways to preserve herbs. Simply open a bottle and put a sprig of your favourite herbs inside and seal it for at least two weeks before using. If you use fleshy, soft herbs such as parsley remember to remove them after that time, but if you use woody herbs such as rosemary, bay or thyme you can leave them in the bottle.

✔ **Sugar** flavoured with many herbs isn't a good idea, but lavender is a firm favourite for this treatment. Simply cut some lavender flowers on a dry day and put them in a closed container with caster sugar. After a month or more simply pass the sugar through a flour sieve and you can then use it for cakes and confectionery.

Adding Colour with Edible Flowers

The idea of eating flowers may seem very alien but isn't as odd as it sounds. After all, strictly speaking, artichokes and cauliflowers are flowers. The edible flowers I mention here don't add greatly to the nutritional value of your food – they just make it look more interesting. And no – you don't have to cut a radish into a rose or a carrot into a chrysanthemum to enjoy this project!

But first, here are a few important pointers:

✔ Never eat cut flowers that you've bought. They may have been sprayed with chemicals and many are treated with silver compounds to enhance their vase life. Not good.

✔ Always give flowers a good shake before you eat them, especially if you're vegetarian! Pollen beetles often get into flowers. You can get rid of them by picking the flowers and leaving them in a dark room with the window open for an hour. These insects hate the dark and fly towards the light.

✔ Only ever eat flowers that you know for sure are edible. Never eat flowers if you only *think* that they or related flowers may be fit for human consumption.

✔ Never eat flowers that you may have sprayed with insecticide.

Here are a few flowers you can grow to add some excitement to your dinner plate. Just pick the flowers and scatter them over salads, fruit salads or other dishes. Go on – give it a try!

- ✔ **Borage:** These bright blue flowers taste of cucumber and look great in salads, in cold drinks, and as the classic garnish for Pimms. Pinch off the hard, bitter, central, black beak.

- ✔ **Calendula:** You can pick the bright yellow or orange petals off the flower head and drop them onto salads, or add them to the cooking water to colour rice. They have an aromatic, slightly bitter flavour.

- ✔ **Herb flowers (rosemary, salvia, coriander, fennel and others):** You can use the flowers of most herbs in cooking. They have a mild taste, similar to the leaves.

- ✔ **Nasturtium:** These big, bright flowers have a hot, tangy taste. You can stuff the centre of the flowers with chopped egg and mayonnaise for a bright canapé, but remember to check they are free from pollen beetles and aphids first.

- ✔ **Pansies and violas:** The edible petals don't have much taste, but are great for adding some edible decoration to your plate!

- ✔ **Rose:** Pick the petals off the flowers and cut off the white base, which is very bitter. The petals themselves have a slightly bitter taste.

Sprouting Seeds on the Windowsill

You don't need a garden of any kind, or even a patio, to grow sprouting seeds that give you a crop all year round. Sprouting seeds are among the most nutrient-rich foods you can eat. Because you eat the whole plant, you take in all the vitamins they're packed with, including all the energy reserves the adult plant laid in store in the seeds. Even better, people usually eat these plants raw, so you don't lose nutrients through cooking, and they're easy to digest too, thanks to the enzymes that have already mobilised the nutrients. Sprouting seeds may seem a rather unfamiliar food but they're really just an extension of the principle of growing mustard and cress.

Most sprouts are rich in vitamins A, C and E and many contain amino acids – the building blocks of proteins – too.

You can buy a wide range of seeds and even mixtures of seeds for sprouting. The most popular is alfalfa. You can also use shop-bought lentils, aduki beans, mung beans and chickpeas for sprouting (I always buy organic beans to be sure that they're safe to eat). You can save a fortune using shop-bought seeds rather than buying seeds specifically for sprouting.

Here are a few of the most popular sprouting seeds:

✔ **Aduki beans** are dark red and crunchy, with a fresh taste. Eat them after four days when the roots are 1 centimetre long.

✔ **Alfalfa** is a delicious and easy-to-grow choice. The sprouts have a taste similar to pea pods.

✔ **Chick peas** are surprisingly tasty – sweet and nutty. Eat them after three days when the roots are 1 centimetre long.

✔ **Fenugreek sprouts** are high in protein and have a mild, spicy and slightly bitter flavour. Eat them after five days.

✔ **Lentils** are easy to sprout and have a peppery taste. Eat them after about three days when they have a root 1 centimetre long. (Don't buy split orange lentils for sprouting because the seeds are split in half.)

✔ **Mung beans** are packed with protein, easy to sprout, and ready in five days. Home-sprouted mung beans are very short compared with the shop-bought types you may be used to, which are sprouted with weights on top, forcing them to elongate.

✔ **Radish** has a very hot, peppery taste, and is ready in five days. These seeds need constant rinsing and draining.

✔ **Red clover** is similar to alfalfa but has a mild, buttery taste. Ready in six days.

All you need to get started is a glass or plastic container and a mesh lid to drain the seeds. When you get hooked you may want to buy a *seed sprouter*, these vary from jars with plastic mesh lids to layered sprouters with mesh or slatted bases that allow you to sprout different seeds at the same time with one piece of equipment. But to start, you can use a jar, glass or bowl with a piece of net (old net curtains are ideal) or muslin, secured over the top with an elastic band.

When you've gathered your equipment, just follow these easy steps:

1. **Measure out some seeds, put them in the jar, and pour in enough water to cover them well.**

2. **You don't need to place the jar in a sunny spot but the windowsill is a good place because it allows the emerging shoots and leaves to turn green.**

3. **Leave the seeds to soak for 12 hours, and then drain off the water through the fabric covering.**

4. **Fill the container with water again to rinse them, drain them and leave them for 12 hours before you rinse again.**

5. **All you need to do then is to rinse the seeds twice a day.**

Most sprouting seeds are ready in around four days to a week in average household temperatures, although seed packets are rather more optimistic about this. You can keep your sprouted seeds in the same state, for a few days, in the fridge.

Bigger seeds such as beans and lentils are even easier to sprout because they're large and draining them is easy. You can simply use a jar and put some cling film over the top. Fill the jar with water and put your hand over the top of the open jar to drain, straining the water between your fingers. Simple as that!

Growing Carrots on the Patio

Growing carrots on the patio is easy! People are often put off growing carrots because they don't have the light soil that produces the best carrots or because carrots are so often ruined by carrot root fly. Growing on the patio eliminates these problems, though, and results in a good crop of 'clean' carrots that are easy to prepare for the kitchen.

You can sow carrots in pots, where they grow quite happily, any time between March and the end of July. Choose a 30-centimetre-deep pot for standard carrots. Large pots are best because they don't dry out as quickly as small pots, but any pot at least 15 centimetres wide and deep gives you a reasonable crop. If you use a clay or ceramic pot with a single drainage hole, place some pieces of broken pot over the drainage hole to stop the compost washing out of the base, or place a small, plastic pot, upside down, over the hole.

Choose a carrot that isn't too long, such as Bolero or Amsterdam Forcing, or Parmex, which has round roots.

Here's what to do next:

1. **Fill the pot with multipurpose compost.** Make sure that the compost is well 'fluffed up' with no lumps.

2. **Firm the compost very gently with the flat of your hand so the surface is level and about 2 centimetres below the rim of the pot. Water it well with a watering can with a rose (sprinkler) on the end.**

3. **When the water has soaked in, sow the carrot seed thinly over the surface of the compost.** Tip the seeds into the palm of your hand, take a pinch of seed with your fingers, and sprinkle it evenly so the seeds are about 1 centimetre apart. Put the spare seeds back in the packet and keep them somewhere cool for sowing later.

4. **Cover the seeds with about 5 millimetres of compost.** You can do this by taking a handful of compost and rubbing it between your hands over the seeds.

5. **Water the pot regularly to prevent the surface drying out.** The seedlings should appear in about two weeks. You can leave them if they're 1 centimetre apart. If they're closer, thin out the seedlings when they're about 10 centimetres high to give them room to grow.

6. **Make sure that the pot is always moist and, after about a month, start to feed the carrots with liquid fertiliser once a week.** As soon as the carrots are large enough to pull, start harvesting by pulling some at regular spacing across the pot so the remaining carrots have more room to grow bigger.

After harvesting all the carrots, you can plant a different crop in the pot or use the compost as a mulch in the garden.

You can also grow a good crop of carrots in a grow bag. Ideally, buy a good quality grow bag and not the cheapest. When you have your bag, just follow the steps in the 'Growing a Few Salad Leaves' section earlier in this chapter. If bags don't appeal, you can use the same method for growing carrots in garden troughs or even in window boxes.

Going Up the Wall: Wall Planters

If you don't have room to expand your vegetable plot sideways, why not do as they do in New York and 'grow up'!

Window boxes and large wall planters are big enough to grow a range of salad crops, beans, bush tomatoes and herbs. French beans are a really good choice. Choose dwarf beans and, after filling the boxes with multipurpose compost, sow the seeds 8 centimetres apart, 5 centimetres deep, any time between April and late July. If you keep the plants watered and give them liquid fertiliser every week, they're sure to produce good crops.

Lots of other vegetables and fruit are climbers, such as French beans and runner beans. The new Black Forest courgette is another sprawler that you can train upwards. Most squashes, too, are trailing plants that you can train up trellis or walls, though the heavy fruits do need support. Cucumbers are also climbers and outdoor varieties climb up trellis and give a good crop. If you don't mind getting a smaller crop, you can also sow some tall peas in pots or in the border to climb up canes or trellis.

Aiming High: Hanging Baskets

You may think that flowers have a monopoly on hanging baskets, but you can also grow a wide range of crops in them. Try to use a large basket – at least 40 centimetres in diameter – because these don't dry out as quickly as small baskets and hold more compost, and therefore support bigger plants.

The obvious crops for hanging baskets are herbs, especially parsley. Strawberries also grow very well in baskets (see the 'Growing Strawberries Without a Garden' section earlier in the chapter). Bush tomatoes are also successful in baskets, where their lax growth trails over the sides and the fruits are easy to pick. You can also grow cut-and-come-again salads, such as rocket and wrinkled cress, in a basket but, for longer-lasting results, try planting some loose-leaf lettuce such as Lollo Rosso. This crop is slow to bolt, looks lovely, and you can pick a few leaves as you need them. You can create a beautiful and useful basket by interplanting with vivid green parsley.

Index